ROCKHURST COLLEGE LIBRARY

0 0006 0075614 2

P9-DDK-663

DATE DUE

FEB 8 - 1990			
DEC 2 0 1996			
MAY 0 7 1998			
GAYLORD			PRINTED IN U.S.A.

STATISTICS AND PUBLIC POLICY

WILLIAM B. FAIRLEY
Commonwealth of Massachusetts

FREDERICK MOSTELLER
Harvard University

EDITORS

ADDISON-WESLEY PUBLISHING COMPANY

READING, MASSACHUSETTS · MENLO PARK, CALIFORNIA
LONDON · AMSTERDAM · DON MILLS, ONTARIO · SYDNEY

This book is in the
ADDISON-WESLEY SERIES IN BEHAVIORAL SCIENCE:
QUANTITATIVE METHODS

Consulting Editor
Frederick Mosteller

Copyright © 1977 by Addison-Wesley Publishing Company, Inc.
Philippines copyright 1977 by Addison-Wesley Publishing Company, Inc.

All rights reserved. No part of this publication may be reproduced, stored in a retrieval system, or transmitted, in any form or by any means, electronic, mechanical, photocopying, recording, or otherwise, without the prior written permission of the publisher. Printed in the United States of America. Published simultaneously in Canada. Library of Congress Catalog Card No. 76-10415.

ISBN 0-201-02185-4
BCDEFGHIJ-HA-7987

HA
29
57848

16.75

4/79

B&T

To

Gerard		*Gale*
and	*&*	*and*
Peter		*William*

101408

ROCKHURST COLLEGE LIBRARY

PREFACE

This collection of articles should be useful and instructive to people with a variety of interests in public policy or statistics or both. Besides people who deal with the analysis of policy as a subject in itself, practitioners and students of public service and members of such professions as law, medicine, and education will find value in the present volume.

In our own teaching we have found that it is no easy matter to assemble a collection of examples that both illustrate a wide spectrum of statistical topics and also have some important connection to public issues. We believe teachers and students of statistics and quantitative methods will find this collection particularly valuable as a source of real-life examples for many topics.

We chose articles from among those used in courses in statistical methods that we have given in the Public Policy Program of the Kennedy School of Government and in the Law School at Harvard University. These courses have principally taught basic tools of probability and statistics. At the same time we have sought to illustrate technique with examples where policy plays a major role, and to bring out themes related to statistics in the analysis of policy.

Criteria used for selecting articles were that they: illustrate frequent uses of statistics in public policy; represent the diversity of statistical tools employed in policy studies; sample the types of studies that readers interested in or engaged in the public service, the professions, or social research would want to understand; be of high quality; and not be republished elsewhere. Several appear here for the first time.

We believe this collection will be accessible to people with very different prior preparation in statistics and in the supporting mathematics. Most of the articles can be read profitably by someone without preparation in statistics and with no more than an acquaintance with high school algebra as mathematical background. Some of the articles lean on an acquaintance with statistical topics such as regression and probability.

Reading about the applications of statistics to public policy provides reasons for understanding the statistics. It also gives greater depth to that understanding by causing the reader to think about statistical ideas in actual applied contexts. This is important. We hope that the major general educational payoff of learning statistics is to increase people's ability to be critical consumers of the statistical reasoning and analyses that they will meet in diverse applied connections in their own lives.

In addition to the authors and organizations that have kindly given us permission to reproduce their work, we want to express our appreciation to Jack M. Appleman and Richard Zeckhauser, who gave us comments on our plans for this book. A generous provision for sabbatical leave to William Fairley from the Kennedy School of Government in the spring of 1976 facilitated the final preparation of this volume. Some of the work was carried out by Frederick Mosteller during his Miller Research Professorship at the University of California at Berkeley, made possible by the Miller Institute for Basic Research and Science. We thank colleagues in the Kennedy School of Government and the Law School at Harvard. Their interest in a professional curriculum of public policy and in the role of statistics in such a curriculum encouraged us to put the present collection together. The physical preparation of the manuscript was presided over first by Marion Ezell and then by Priscilla Paff.

Cambridge, Massachusetts   W.B.F.
January 1977   F.M.

CONTENTS

INTRODUCTION

The collection is organized in six parts: Part I, Introduction to Statistics and Public Policy; Part II, Exploratory Data Analysis; Part III, Statistical Analysis in Policy Issues; Part IV, Statistical Methods for Policy Analysis; Part V, Decision Making; and Part VI, Statistical Methods in Legal Settings.

Our organization is guided by the relation of the articles to their uses in policy making or policy analysis. Readers, and especially teachers of statistics, may want to consider an alternative organization using statistical topics. Part II on exploratory data analysis provides good material for descriptive statistics. Probability is the major tool in Parts V and VI—with the exception of Dawes in Part V. Statistical analyses of both qualitative and quantitative data with an emphasis on regression appear in Part III. Klitgaard and Hall in Part II and Dawes in Part V also use regression. Research design is exemplified in Part III and discussed explicitly in Part IV. We turn now to a more detailed discussion of each of the articles.

Part I introduces the collection and contains Kruskal's "Issues and Opportunities." This essay provides an overall appreciation of the use of statistics in critically examining the contributions of the federal government's statistics and statisticians. The essay first appeared in 1971 as Chapter 1 of *Federal Statistics, the Report of the President's Commission.*

Part II supplies examples of the application of exploratory data analysis, pioneered by John W. Tukey, to some policy-relevant sets of data. For a full explanation of these methods and point of view, see Tukey's *Exploratory Data Analysis*, Reading Mass.: Addison-Wesley, 1977. Fairley offers an exploratory two-way-table analysis in "Accidents on Route 2: Two-Way Structures for Data." He also illustrates how a simple descriptive model can be helpful in summarizing information and shows how the same data can be described just as well by an alternative model.

In "A Statistical Search for Unusually Effective Schools," Klitgaard and Hall present an effective illustration of the basic ideas of exploratory data analysis. To include this article we have cut it to a third of its original length, thereby omitting treatment of several data sets and additional technical material.

"The Wait to See the Doctor: An Application of Exploratory Data Analysis" is just that. Shepard shows a practical application of exploratory thinking to a problem in public administration.

Part III shows a variety of statistical tools in action. They deal with questions important to several different policy debates. "Sex Bias in Graduate Admissions" by Bickel, Hammel, and O'Connell is an observational study that seems to support an unusual conclusion. Kruskal's critique following the paper raises an important point for causal interpretations. The article is noteworthy both for carefully laying out the nature of the actual policy problem being discussed and for leading the reader through considerations involved in a choice of statistical analyses—without implying that only one analysis is useful or only one is best. Contingency tables and tests for them are the principal devices used.

We have included the Colton and Buxbaum article "Motor Vehicle Inspection and Motor Vehicle Accident Mortality" primarily because it illustrates so well the use of several methods of statistical control for extraneous variables. The article contains its own careful critique of its methods, findings, and necessary next steps.

The Lave and Seskin regression analysis of air pollution's effects on mortality, "Does Air Pollution Shorten Lives?" has been influential in the setting of national standards for allowable air pollution. Although better estimates of the effects may not be available, an observational study like this leaves unsatisfying doubts concerning what has been established about causality and the size of the causal effect, if any. Proxying (one variable masquerading as another), lack of model, no closed system of variables, and no randomized experiment are conditions that cause serious problems of interpretation. Other issues are taken up in the discussion by Fairley that follows.

Part IV discusses methods of statistical analysis that are particularly appropriate for policy work. In "Assessing Unknown Numbers: Order of Magnitude Estimation," Mosteller takes techniques from every direction to get fixes on "soft" numbers. The article illustrates the adaptation of statistical thinking to the specific needs of policy analysis.

Gilbert, Light, and Mosteller consider what gains accrue when social innovations are subjected to carefully controlled field trials. "Assessing Social Innovations: An Empirical Base for Policy" does this by reviewing a number of such studies in the social, medical, and sociomedical areas. Then the authors consider what happens when innovations are not reviewed by carefully controlled trials. Following these empirical assessments, they review some of the major difficulties with and arguments against controlled field trials, and they review costs and time taken by other techniques in major public programs.

Rivlin's "Allocating Resources for Policy Research: How Can Experiments Be More Useful?" outlines four types of policy experiments—here "experiment" is used as a name for a scientific tool, not as a synonym for an innovation. She discusses important differences between the problems that experiments treat and also the difficulties of executing them and extracting information from them.

We would take exception to two emphases here. Instead of pressing the point that experimentation is more expensive than other ways of getting data, we would emphasize how expensive and useless these other methods have often been for research or for policy purposes, especially data collected for routine management. Sample surveys, on the other hand, can be extremely useful, but they do not substitute for experiments. They too can be very expensive.

The other point deals with labeling the planned variation and performance contracting ventures as "experiments." Although expensive (largely because they pay for the direct activities of an active social program—for planned variation, a program in being), they are more like observational studies than experiments. There was no attempt to plan a well-controlled experiment. These approaches are not examples of experiments, but of their opposite: attempts to get along with something less. Repeated experience in education shows modest gains at best for new programs. To know gains have occurred requires the most careful design of measurement—well-controlled experiments.

Part V applies decision analysis to a policy choice and presents articles that bear on the usefulness of statistics as an aid in decision making. Howard, Matheson, and North, in "The Decision to Seed Hurricanes," illustrate a quantitative attack on an expensive and risky public program where information is not solid and is hard to get except through fairly expensive and possibly dangerous experiments. The expense is small, though, compared to the value of better information. A healthy exchange of a variety of views follows the article in the form of letters to the *Science Letters* column.

Dawes adds an instructive chapter to the continuing comparison of "clinical" and "statistical" methods of prediction in "A Case Study of Graduate Admissions: Application of Three Principles of Human Decision Making." See Paul E. Meehl, *Clinical versus Statistical Prediction*, University of Minnesota Press, Minneapolis, 1954, for an early statement. The article is important background for prediction in other areas of interest such as parole success.

Unaided judgments about uncertainties may involve fallacious reasoning or biases. In "Judgment Under Uncertainty: Heuristics and Biases,"

Tversky and Kahneman discuss common types of such errors, including characteristic directions of biases. While not specifically related to policy analysis, the article is provocative for thinking about the roles of judgment and of formal statistical methods in decisions. And it adds other dimensions to Mosteller's paper on guessing numbers.

Part VI raises a number of issues related to the effective and appropriate use of statistics and probability in such public arenas as the courts and in regulatory hearings. In "Evaluating the 'Small' Probability of a Catastrophic Accident from the Marine Transportation of Liquefied Natural Gas," Fairley discusses estimates of probabilities introduced in evidence at proceedings of the Federal Power Commission. Based on this experience he advances a set of guidelines for such estimates. The article is a case study in the issues of modeling, of use of data, and of judgment that estimation of small probabilities raises.

The case of *People* v. *Collins* provides a fascinating setting for thinking about the presentation of statistical work to lay audiences. We have included it here, together with its mathematical appendix (surely unique!) because of its special problems and relative inaccessibility.

Fairley and Mosteller take up statistical issues raised in the Collins case in the dialogue between a lawyer and a statistician. "A Conversation about Collins" probes deeper than the usual criticisms of this case.

A number of issues surrounding the use of mathematical models in court are debated by Finkelstein and Fairley in "A Comment on 'Trial by Mathematics'" and Tribe in "A Further Critique of Mathematical Proof." Though set in a legal context here, the issues are relevant in many other contexts as well.

PART I

INTRODUCTION TO STATISTICS
AND PUBLIC POLICY

ISSUES AND OPPORTUNITIES

WILLIAM H. KRUSKAL

INTRODUCTION

The Constitution of the United States of America provides in its first article that the federal government shall collect statistics, a decennial census. In the 181 years since the first census, designed by Thomas Jefferson, the federal statistical system has grown persistently. Its growth reflects two basic facts: a government works better if it has reliable and impartial information; and some of the information its citizens need can be provided best by their government.

The President's Commission on Federal Statistics was asked to evaluate the present performance of the federal statistical system and to suggest improvements. In the President's letter to the chairman,[1] three basic questions were posed:

1. What are the present and future requirements for quantitative information about our society?
2. How can we minimize the burden on respondents and insure that personal privacy and data received in confidence are protected?
3. How can we organize federal activities for the most effective compilation and use of statistics?

Other important questions suggested by the President included:

1. What are the appropriate dimensions of the total federal statistical program?[2]

Reprinted from *Feaeral Statistics: Report of the President's Commission*, Vol. 1, 1971, pp. 13–42.

[1] See Appendix A for the full text of the President's letter [not reproduced here].
[2] See Appendix B for expenditures since 1934 [not reproduced here].

2. Are we gathering information that is no longer needed or is of little value relative to unmet needs?
3. Are we making good *use* of the statistics we now collect?

To answer these and the other questions raised by the President, we have formulated goals for the statistical system and we have evaluated various means of achieving these goals.

Although the federal statistical system is one of the best, if not the best in the world, it is not surprising that many people have well-developed views about ways to improve it. What is perhaps surprising, though, is the lack of agreement among such critics. They disagree not only about what improvements are desirable, but also about the nature of the federal statistical system itself. They even disagree about what is meant by statistics.

Much of the disagreement arises from the fact that the word *statistics* is used in two different senses. In one sense, statistics *are* facts and figures, numerical quantities like counts, measurements, averages, ratios, and so forth. In another sense, statistics *is* a body of methods for obtaining and analyzing data in order to base decisions on them. Although we have tried to make clear which sense is intended when we use the word *statistics*, the reader of this report must have firmly in mind the distinction between statistics (plural) as numbers, and statistics (singular) as a body of methods.

Many of the shortcomings of the federal statistical system stem from a narrow view of statistics as only data. Statistical methods, we find, frequently are not applied where they should be at important stages in the marshaling of evidence for making decisions.

As a basis for our judgments on how to improve the production and use of statistics in the federal government, we have examined important characteristics of both producers and users of statistics, and we have sought to understand their satisfactions and frustrations. We present the result of our work in two parts. Part one, Chapters 1 through 5, treats the operations of the statistical system except for the issues associated with invasions of privacy and breaches of confidence. These latter issues are dealt with in Part two, Chapters 6 and 7. Chapters 1, 2, 3, 4, and 6 include our description of the federal statistical system; they outline the incentives motivating producers and factors influencing the users of data. An understanding of these underlying factors is essential for perspective on our findings and recommendations.

Chapter 1 discusses statistics in the broadest sense of the term, showing that statistics as a discipline bears on all aspects of the gathering and use of evidence in most activities that support government decision-making.

Chapter 2 reviews different methods used in generating statistical data, and describes major groups of agencies responsible for gathering and analyzing statistics used in the federal government. We describe the incentives affecting the behavior of these agencies and the important characteristics of their products.

Chapter 3 discusses the importance to users of particular qualities in statistics. The relative importance of timeliness, accuracy, frequency, detail, etc., is used to distinguish among various groups of users.

Chapter 4 discusses the need for central coordination and central action if a decentralized statistical system is to continue to serve users well. It considers alternative methods of coordinating the uses of statistics in government, distinguishing between the need for coordination and the need for central direction to move individual agencies toward action in the interest of the system.

Chapter 5 summarizes the findings and presents recommendations about the subjects treated in Part one. Findings are related to the problems generated by the conflicting incentives of producers and demands of users. Our recommendations include the assignment of new responsibilities to perform specified central functions. Also recommended are changes in budgeting practices.

Chapter 6 distinguishes between invasions of privacy and breaches of confidence and discusses the problems involved in strengthening existing safeguards of individual rights. Although these rights have not in fact been abused by the federal statistical program, its inadequacies may sooner or later weaken the statistical system.

Chapter 7 presents our findings and recommendations relating to privacy and confidentiality. Recommendations include the assignment of new responsibilities to strengthen safeguards against invasions of privacy and breaches of confidentiality.

Volume II contains materials prepared by the staff and by outside consultants. Most of the material presented in this volume documents positions taken in Volume I; the remaining materials provide background or explore new areas. This volume has not been reviewed or approved by the full Commission.

THE SCOPE OF FEDERAL STATISTICS

Statisticians construct, publish, and study the familiar graphs and tables of numbers conventionally associated with the word "statistics," but the scope of statistics as a discipline has widened considerably in the past half century. Federal statisticians, both as leaders and participants in that widening, have pursued new activities and developed new modes of analysis.

One kind of widening lies in greater understanding of the origin, meaning, and accuracy of a number. For many purposes it is not enough to say that a city has a population of 58,324. How was the count made? Does it include only citizens? What about visitors at the City Hotel on the day of the count? The cousins of the Joneses visiting from California? The Brown youngsters away at college across the state? How conscientiously did the enumerators do their job? The tabulators? Hard work on questions of that nature has given rise to a steady improvement in the analysis and control of the procedures that generate federal numerical statistics.

Another kind of widening has been a far surer handling of the efficient design, or planning, of censuses, surveys, and experiments. In estimating national unemployment, are we better off sampling 100 households in each of 50 cities, or some other arrangements at the same cost? Great strides have been made in understanding this kind of problem. The effective planning of evaluation studies for social programs is a matter of intense current interest.

A third kind of widening has been the increasingly mathematical nature of statistics, with emphasis on the theory and application of probability. Much of statistics deals with inference and prediction from incomplete, variable, and fallible data. Probability theory has become a firm intellectual foundation for most modern statistical methods as they deal with chance variation, sampling, and measurement error.

There is also another side to the applications of probability, a more directly operational side that provides analyses and guides for traffic flow, equipment maintenance schedules, information retrieval, control of floods, and other such aspects of modern national life.

Finally, the scope of the numbers themselves—the numbers whose efficient, accurate generation forms the central rationale for federal statistics—has widened enormously under constantly growing demands for more information about our society. From a relatively few economic and demographic indexes, the variety of federal statistics (in the numerical sense) is now enormous: in economics from budget studies to national income accounts; in demography from fertility studies to detailed small-area age distributions; in medicine from newly accurate and detailed mortality tables to fuller time series for epidemics. And in nearly every other area of national concern, numerical statistics are generated in new profusion and variety.

Any organization that seeks to understand itself and its surroundings, as well as to experiment with new procedures, finds its thinking pervaded with statistical questions. The federal government is such an organization, and in fact statistical activities and problems are pervasive in the government, although they may be called by other names or sometimes may not be recognized as statistical at all.

Let us turn to brief descriptions of some federal statistical activities.

Congressional redistricting

In the early 1970's there will be unusually intensive argument in many of the nation's fifty state houses. Decisions of the Supreme Court require unprecedentedly close equality of population in Congressional districts. Agonizing arithmetic and map-work is taking place. It is all based on the 1970 Census with faith, if not always with affection. Our Bureau of the Census has a well-deserved reputation for statistical competence, efficient organization, and impartiality. Without it the Supreme Court's mandates could not be carried out.

The Census has, of course, a multitude of other uses, both scholarly and administrative. For example, federal funds are distributed to the states for education, welfare, and dozens of other programs according to formulas based in part on Census totals. Similarly, the planning of highways, public utilities, sewage systems, and the like are affected by Census data.

Weather modification

On a summer day in 1965, a remarkable array of U.S. naval vessels and Air Force airplanes was deployed in the Caribbean, under the scientific command of an energetic and imaginative meteorologist, Joanne Simpson. Dr. Simpson and her colleagues had organized the complicated operation to test the effects of seeding Caribbean clouds with silver iodide. The project, which is likely to have profound effects on the theory and practice of weather modification, was a joint enterprise of the Environmental Science Services Administration (since consolidated into the National Oceanic and Atmospheric Administration) and the Navy.

Where did statistics enter? One important way was in the design of the experiment. Earlier, smaller-scale trials had been sharply criticized on the grounds that the seeding may have been applied to clouds likely to grow and precipitate anyway because of subconscious meteorological skill on the part of the scientist trying to pick clouds fairly. On the other hand, it was important to seed as many clouds as possible.

To meet this problem, the late W. J. Youden, of the Statistical Engineering Laboratory at the National Bureau of Standards, constructed a randomized design so that a cloud would first be chosen for observation, and *then* a sealed envelope would be opened to learn whether the cloud should be seeded or should be a control (an unseeded cloud). The method was arranged so that about two clouds out of three were seeded. Glenn Brier, a Weather Bureau statistician, played an important role in the analysis of the experiment's data. The apparent result was that the seeding did appreciably increase the height of cloud tops (and hence presumedly precipitation).

Continued experimentation by Dr. Simpson in Florida through 1970 provided further confirmation, both for cloud growth and precipitation. Yet, other federally-supported experimentation has not always found such clear positive results. Effects seem to depend on place, kind of cloud, and seeding method, to name some of the variables. The physics of precipitation is complicated and not yet well understood. Partly for that reason it is important to use great care, including randomization, in carrying out experiments on real clouds.

Labor–management contracts and the level of prices

In May 1948, the United Automobile Workers' (UAW) leadership faced the executives of General Motors (GM) across the bargaining table. GM wanted a union contract longer than the usual one-year term to insure minimum interruption of automobile production in the market created by the pent-up post-war demand. The UAW leadership, for its part, was under unusually strong pressure to produce a substantial increase in its members' take-home pay. A major obstacle to labor contracts lasting longer than a year was the union's fear that price increases would make wage rates negotiated two or more years earlier inadequate.

To meet this problem, the UAW and GM agreed on a wage scale that would move with the Consumer Price Index (CPI), an index of retail prices published monthly by the Bureau of Labor Statistics. The CPI is the price, compared to a base period, of a market basket (a fixed collection of commodities in fixed amounts) averaged over the country. It is an abstraction, yet highly concrete economic and political calculations turn on it.

For each rise of 1.14 points in the CPI, GM workers' hourly wage rates would increase one cent. Similarly, for each fall of 1.14 CPI points, hourly wage rates would decrease one cent, but with the proviso that the total decrease would not exceed five cents. The contract was for two years.

Other labor-management agreements had adopted similar escalator clauses, but the 1948 GM-UAW contract was by far the largest of this kind. Today more than three million workers are covered by contracts with wage rates related to the Consumer Price Index.

The CPI, then, is a monthly statistical index number that is used and trusted, illustrating well-placed faith in a statistical program carried out by reputable professionals.

Testing Salk polio vaccine

In 1954 hundreds of thousands of school children first rolled up their sleeves to receive vaccinations against poliomyelitis. This was the largest controlled public health experiment in U.S. history. It was organized by the National Foundation for Infantile Paralysis with the assistance of the U.S. Public Health Service.

Such a large sample was needed because polio, though frightening and tragic, was rare in its visible form, and because its incidence varied widely from year to year. Hence only large samples would reliably disclose the effectiveness of a vaccine.

In the essential part of the 1954 trials, about 200,000 children received the vaccine and another 200,000 a placebo control injection of salt solution. Of the control children, 138 had polio (110 paralytic); of the vaccinated children, only 56 had polio (33 paralytic). There were three deaths from polio among the control children, and no deaths among the vaccinated ones. Perhaps the most important comparison is between the rates of paralysis per 100,000 children: fifty-five for the control children and sixteen for the vaccinated children. Clearly the vaccine gave considerable protection, for it cut the paralysis rate by more than two-thirds.

Statistics entered this massive experiment in two places. First, statistics was essential in the design, where statisticians and others successfully pressed for a true controlled field study, or experiment, for a substantial fraction of the project. Second, statistical methods were required in the analysis, especially in evaluating the possible effects of chance fluctuations on the relatively small numbers of polio cases and deaths.

Food prices and welfare checks
In the spring and summer of 1969, shoppers for the Department of Agriculture went into grocery stores of low-income areas in seven cities. Each store sampled was shopped twice, once before and once after welfare checks were issued. The purpose of this large study was to test the claim that stores tended to raise prices just after welfare checks arrived.

The changes found were tiny. In the seven cities, the average price in supermarkets went up one-tenth of one percent, and the average price in neighborhood food stores hardly changed at all.

One by-product of the study was a tabulation of checkers' errors, usually in computing unit prices and sales tax. In most of the cities the net effect of these mistakes was in the customer's favor.

Randomization and the draft
On July 1, 1970, perhaps the most carefully executed lottery of all time was carried out in Washington by the Selective Service System to determine the order of induction for men born in 1951. An elaborate machinery for fairness was planned with the assistance of the Statistical Engineering Laboratory of the National Bureau of Standards and approved by an independent panel of three former presidents of the American Statistical

Association. The procedure called for several stages of operational randomization, including twenty-five random calendars and two separate drums, each containing 365 capsules, for mechanical mixing.

These procedures were in sharp contrast to those of the prior draft lottery of December 1969. In that 1969 lottery the procedure was hastily worked out, apparently without statistical aid, and the results showed a small but clear bias.

Criticisms of the draft have been made along many different lines, but, so far as we know, there has been no criticism of the utter fairness of the July 1970 lottery.

Vanishing whales

During the 1950's scientists associated with the International Whaling Commission went hunting whales—but not to kill them. In order to estimate the number of whales remaining in endangered species, small metal cylinders were fired into the thick layer of fat a whale has under its skin. The approach, sometimes called the capture-recapture method, is based on a simple but reliable measuring technique: if 500 whales are marked with metal cylinders and if 8,000 whales are later caught of which 100 are marked by a cylinder, then there must be about (500/100) times 8,000 or 40,000 whales in all. (In practice, of course, there are many complications and refinements.)

Our representatives on the International Whaling Commission include a distinguished statistician, Douglas G. Chapman, who has used extensions of the capture-recapture method, together with a variety of other statistical methods, in estimating numbers of endangered whale species. In this way we have learned that there may be as few as 5,000 blue whales left in all the southern hemisphere. The same statistical ideas have been applied to sampling and counting other species, for example, deer, wolves, and fish.

Equality of educational opportunity

Problems related to race and color in the public schools have been among the most serious the nation has recently undergone. A heavily statistical study, or, for that matter, any study, will not by itself produce solutions to such deep-rooted problems. A study may contribute towards solutions, however, by throwing quantitative light on a central area of public life.

In 1964 Congress required a survey of equality or inequality in public education with reference to pupils' race, color, and national origin. Accordingly, the U.S. Office of Education carried out the study under the general direction of an eminent statistician, Alexander M. Mood, then Assistant Commissioner for Educational Statistics. The report, published in 1966, is sometimes known as the Coleman Report, after James Coleman, the statistically-minded sociologist who had primary responsibility for the survey.

The Coleman report reached one conclusion that was hardly surprising: most American children go to schools that are mainly attended by children of the same racial background. A second major conclusion, however, was unexpected: educational achievement (with race fixed) bears a clear positive relation to the educational backgrounds and aspirations of the other students in the school. One interpretation is that characteristics of one's school-mates' homes—characteristics evidencing interest in, and encouragement of, education—are more closely related to school achievement than money spent on schools or other apparently more relevant factors. Predictably, there has been a sharp debate over this second conclusion.

These examples could readily be extended indefinitely. One need only look through annual publications such as the *Statistical Abstract*, or the *United States Government Organization Manual*, or skim the biweekly *Selected U.S. Government Publications*, to obtain a further sense of how the work of the federal government is suffused by statistical activities, questions, staff, and publications. Here, briefly, are a few other important areas where statistics enters in a significant way.

> In the Department of Defense: weapon systems evaluation, quality control, reliability analysis;
>
> In the Public Health Service: epidemiology, design of large-scale testing, special studies of the effects of smoking and the incidence of lung cancer among smokers;
>
> In the National Oceanic and Atmospheric Administration: earthquake analysis and prediction, adjustment of geodetic observations, meteorological statistics;
>
> In the Office of Business Economics, the Council of Economic Advisers, and the Federal Reserve: income-consumption relationships, the gap between actual and potential production, the income-redistribution effects of a tax change.

Our daily statistics
Statistics, then, both in the sense of numbers and the sense of methods, clearly pervade our national government. Nevertheless, some readers, while conceding that the examples above deal with interesting problems, may object that most government demographic and economic statistics are unexciting and irrelevant.

That is not so. Nearly all of the federal statistics program deals with important, interesting problems, and conscientious federal statisticians, in dealing with these problems, do battle with a host of methodological demons—ambiguity of definition (for example, unemployment), non-responsiveness in surveys, difficulties in estimating error, problems of cooperation and comparability among the states of the union—and among the countries of the world.

Statistical investigations by the Internal Revenue Service, for example, require difficult decisions about concepts and methods. Those investigations are used for basic economic analysis as well as for computations of expected yield from next year's tax proposals. They affect us all.

Vital statistics of birth and death are of great relevance to current concerns about population growth; death statistics, classified by cause, place, age, etc., can be of critical importance in discovering changes in public health. They affect us all.

Import and export statistics may sound routine, but they surely are not so to the manufacturers and traders whose goods are shipped, to the labor force, and to government officials concerned with our position in world markets. They affect us all.

Although some federal statistical work is poorly done and impenetrably presented, a great deal of this work is stirring, pertinent, and gratefully received by substantial audiences.

ACHIEVEMENTS OF THE FEDERAL STATISTICAL SYSTEM

For more than 50 years, federal statisticians have pioneered in the development of improved ways of collecting, processing, and analyzing data. The remarkable momentum developed in the 1930's carried over into the post-World War II period.

There have been many statistical achievements in the past 25 years. These achievements represent more than marginal improvements in efficiency or quality. They are, in fact, advances in the state of the statistical art, and many have had an important influence on statistical work throughout the world. These advances, to cite a few examples, include the coverage of new areas and the strengthening of our measures of complex economic and social phenomena.

The Current Population Survey

The Current Population Survey (CPS) is a monthly household sample survey of the civilian population living outside institutions. It is a multi-purpose vehicle for the collection of data on many features of our society, at specified levels of accuracy, from a nationwide sample of households. On a routine basis, it provides national and regional statistics on employment, unemployment, and other characteristics of the labor force, but the sample can be expanded to yield regional estimates as well. The CPS system is flexible, and additional panels can be added as needs develop and funds are made available. It has been used periodically to collect information on such varied subjects as education, migration, the size and composition of families, income and housing vacancies, and smoking habits.

We include mention of the CPS as an achievement, not because it uses any particular advance in methodology but because in one survey, it provides a powerful and flexible substitute for what earlier required numerous, expensive, *ad hoc* efforts. Because it is a continuing effort, enumerators can be well trained, sources of error can be identified and adjustments made to increase accuracy. Questions can be added, deleted, or changed as new public concerns arise, and results tabulated and presented in timely fashions. The CPS as a whole is thus an example of government statistical practice at its best.

The National Health Survey Program

The National Health Survey Program yields major additions to the basic health statistics of the United States.

The program has four components:

1. The Health Interview Survey—a continuing nationwide sampling of households.
2. The Health Examination Survey—a physical examination of individuals in a series of separate surveys.
3. The Health Resources Statistics—a series of sample surveys of establishments providing hospital, dental, nursing, and other types of health related care to the general population.
4. Vital Records Survey—surveys linked to mortality and natality.

All of these surveys use either a probability sample or 100 percent enumeration to provide basic data about health problems in the population. This procedure gives a much better picture of health status than can be derived from reports of doctors or institutions which may include multiple observations of the same case and do not include information about individuals who are ill but do not seek treatment.

A major contribution of this survey program is its comprehensiveness, allowing for many kinds of health data about the total population. In contrast, many previous health studies were based on a sample of a closed population, such as the recipients of a particular program or services, or the users of particular health facilities. The program thus improves our ability to link health characteristics (acute illness, injuries, chronic conditions, etc.)

with social and demographic characteristics of the population. It allows estimation of the number of "bed-disability days" which occur in the population and the loss in productivity resulting from illness. The Health Examination Survey yields information not otherwise available concerning the prevalence of specific diseases in the population. National estimates of the total availability of health facilities and manpower are derived from the Health Resources Statistics System.

Geographic coding

The lack of an efficient procedure for ordering economic and social data geographically has hampered research and operating programs that deal with local problems. Most record files concerning health, vehicle registrations, accidents, zoning permits, etc. contain information about street addresses or location but these traditionally have been ordered alphabetically or chronologically rather than spatially. It has been cumbersome and costly to regroup such record files geographically for use in planning housing, building roads, and delivering health care and social services.

The New Haven Census Use Study, undertaken jointly by the Bureau of the Census and state and local offices in the late 1960's, was designed originally to develop improved and more flexible methods of treating the small-area data forthcoming from the 1970 Census. The broader objective of the study became the development of methods for relating both census and local data on an area basis.

The assignment of codes based on locational coordinates to individual records in a file is known as geographic coding. (See Volume II, Chapter 3, for an extended discussion of geographic coding.) Manual geographic coding has been widely used for many years. An automated program for eastablishing a geographic base file for any selected geographical area is a recent advance. Such a geographic base file is a map in computer form that incorporates all the major developments in geographic coding of the last two decades. The geographic base file codes points, line segments, and enclosed plots; it contains street features and meaningful nonstreet features, such as rivers, boundaries and railroad tracks, necessary to describe the urban network.

The essential usefulness of such a computerized geographic base file is that it makes possible the use of local record files which, up to the present, have been untapped by local users. Geographic coding may well provide the means by which local communities can reduce their dependence upon the federal government as a supplier of basic information. It may also unlock valuable stores of locally generated data for creation of better national statistics.

This list of achievements only begins to suggest the variety of high quality statistical activity within the federal government. This activity

includes the excellent and widely-used statistics tables put out by the National Bureau of Standards and the Air Force Aeronautical Research
Laboratories; the application of time series analysis to problems of
economic trends; theoretical and empirical investigations into response error
by the Bureau of the Census; the National Bureau of Standards' original
work in the theory and practice of experiment design; and the advances in
both theoretical and applied statistics at the Aberdeen Proving Grounds.
Government statisticians have both produced and taken advantage of innovations, thus contributing to the development of the field of statistics.

THE FEDERAL STATISTICAL SYSTEM

The word "system," used to describe federal statistical activities, implies
purposeful interaction or even central direction of a group of agencies which
are primarily or even exclusively statistical. This may have been an accurate
term in an earlier era when the task of the federal statistical system was
largely to describe private activity. Today the system involves far more than
statistical agencies, and much of what it describes is activity of the government itself.

Producers of statistics are a heterogeneous group. Most of them are not
primarily statistical agencies but operating agencies, which view statistical
data as a by-product of their principal operations. When we add, as we
must, the private sources of data used by the federal government, the system
expands to include non-profit research affiliates of universities and private,
profit-oriented research firms.

Some formal systematization is provided by a central statistical office. It
is located within the Office of Management and Budget and it has had
various names over the years: Central Bureau of Planning and Statistics
(1918–19), Bureau of Efficiency (1919–31), Federal Statistics Board (1931–
33), Central Statistical Board (1933–39), Division of Statistical Standards
(1939–52), the Office of Statistical Standards (1952–69), the Office of
Statistical Policy (1969–70), the Statistical Policy and Management Information Systems Division (1970 to September, 1971), and currently Statistical
Policy Division. This central office reviews thoroughly and coordinates the
activities of the statistical agencies (the two largest are the Bureau of the
Census and the Bureau of Labor Statistics). The statistical activities of most
operating agencies, however, are reviewed less thoroughly—and some are
not reviewed at all.

Users and potential users of statistics are, of course, an important part
of the system. Indeed the system's usefulness can be judged only in terms of
their satisfaction. Some users—program managers, program evaluators, and
industry and trade associations—pay for the data they want, and in that
sense, are satisfied. Other users, including Congress and the public, sometimes complain that their needs are not met. This is true in large measure

because some needs are undefined, unreasonable, or unspecified in operational terms. There are, however, many valid needs that are not met, and these are discussed in Chapter 3.

The coordination of federal statistical activities was begun in an earlier day when problems were simpler and our understanding of statistical accuracy was still undeveloped. The objectives of coordination then were minimizing the burden of reporting and raising the quality of statistics. These original objectives are as appropriate today as ever. In pursuing them now, however, it is necessary to cope with program data, controlled field studies, and measurement of the effects of federal programs. Today the consequences of using inaccurate data are often far-reaching and substantial.

OPPORTUNITIES TO IMPROVE STATISTICS
AND STATISTICAL METHODS

The quest for quality
While major changes in the federal statistical system are not called for, rich opportunities abound for extending past progress.

A primary task confronts those who use and those who produce federal statistics: to improve the quality of these statistics in the decade ahead. This is the single most urgent need facing the federal statistical system.

To be sure, quantitative extension will be required, through additional series, surveys, and controlled field studies. Indeed, we offer recommendations to fill current needs, particularly in social statistics. But the enormous gaps in federal data of 40 and 50 years ago—particularly gaps in economic data—are now largely filled. Many respondents in our survey of expert users pointed to a variety of small gaps, rather than agreeing on large and glaring ones. More important, we anticipate that the statistical agencies, the Congress, and interested private groups will continue work to create specific fresh series, surveys, and controlled field studies.

The need to improve the quality of federal data cuts across nearly every field of applied statistics. It appears in economic and social areas, in research on crime and on railroad regulation, in medical studies and in the huge, historic decennial census. The U.S. already has much fuller data on its society and economy than any nation of remotely comparable size and diversity. These data are relied upon by decision-makers to shape government policies, and by citizens in evaluating the effectiveness of these policies. Hence the urgency of knowing and improving the accuracy of these statistics has become great.

Of course, no nation has statistics of complete accuracy and perfect quality. Nor do we know why anyone should. Data of complete accuracy are generally impossible, and if possible, rarely worth their cost. We know the distance to the moon with amazing accuracy—but not to the hundredth of a millimeter, because it is not worth the cost of such precision. The physician knows a patient's temperature, but not to a hundredth of a degree, because it does not matter. Most policy decisions in the real world can be made, quite sensibly, by relying on less than perfect data, provided the users understand the dimensions of accuracy in the data they use.

How much accuracy any federal statistical output should have depends on its particular uses and costs. Uses differ from person to person, and as these uses change over time, the needs for accuracy will change correspondingly. Near the beginning of this century, we knew the national level of unemployment once every ten years. In today's world we have a more precise measure of unemployment every month. A common, neutral and reliable body of evidence is needed to inform us about the success of private and public programs to meet the needs of our society. Such evidence is heavily laced with statistics. The accuracy of these statistics must be known if they are to serve such a critical function reliably and neutrally.

During the past year this Commission has conducted many inquiries, and it has benefited from suggestions made by a considerable number of expert users. We know, of course, that there are many whom we have not reached. Even more important, had we assessed precisely the needs of today, tomorrow would undoubtedly be different—and in ways that no one can now see clearly. It is not possible for any single group to stipulate required levels of accuracy for all federal statistics, even for today, much less for the future.

We consider it more urgent, therefore, to establish processes by which federal statistics can be continually improved than to propose detailed suggestions for immediate application. The basic procedure we would rely upon is the normal one by which suggestions are made to statistical agencies and Congressional committees. But that procedure will fail to improve statistics unless users regularly have access to reliable indications of the kinds and amounts of error to which the statistics are subject. Without such yardsticks, users may rely excessively on statistics, presuming an accuracy greater than exists. Moreover, without such indicators, officials in Congress and in the Executive branch are forced to judge proposals for statistical improvement with no solid basis for balancing added accuracy against added cost.

Our survey of selected federal statistical agencies indicates that it is quite feasible to provide measures of error, although it is now done only by a few of the very best statistical agencies, and then for only a few of their series. The Bureau of the Census provides monthly estimates of the sampling error in the U.S. unemployment total, and it has provided other error studies for the decennial population census. But our systematic inquiry suggests that many agencies, including some of the major statistical agencies, have only the crudest understanding of the nature and degree of error in their output. Agencies concerned with policies of great weight and moment have given us reports on the error structure of the series used every week by the Congress and the Executive branch. Some of these reports consist of little more than vacuous assurances that comparisons are made with earlier periods, or that they carefully study the returns they receive.

Both a market economy and a centrally planned economy need comprehensive, reliable data on economic performance. In our economy, such data must be widely available to individual business firms, farmers, and unions. Only through wide distribution of such data can the economy adjust to developments efficiently and with a maximum of public understanding. This can be accomplished only if the federal statistics that report on the state of the economy are comprehensive and accurate. It cannot be done well if those who rely on these data operate on incorrect and misleading assumptions as to their accuracy.

Our recommendations on error and accuracy apply to the "major statistical agencies," but we see no reason why citizens or Congressmen who use data issued by the Federal Bureau of Investigation, the Office of the Federal Courts, the Department of Defense, and other agencies should not be similarly assisted. Special studies on errors in data by the National Bureau of Standards, the Bureau of the Census, and the National Center for Health Statistics have already entered the professional literature. We look forward to the incorporation in that literature of additional extensive research, helpful to both users and producers, on the error structure of federal statistics.

The winnowing of statistics

Not all conceivable topics are appropriate for measurement by the federal statistical system. Some are inappropriate because the measurement is impossible, other because the work is impractical, and still others because the subject matter is of insufficient importance. Thus, opportunities for improvement of federal statistics may be found in improved selection procedures.

For example, the statistical study of the size of meteorite craters on the planets of distant galaxies is hardly likely to attract federal statistical resources. An experimental comparison of conscience and economic determinism in the development of the successful burglar is another example of an unlikely topic. And a third such example might be a statistical study of the supply and demand functions for childrens' lemonade stands.

Yet one could start with such topics and gradually shift to others of important, current statistical attention. Statistical studies about crater sizes on Mars and on our moon have been supported by the National Aeronautics and Space Administration because they bear on the age and development of the solar system. From a wholly impractical experiment on criminalism, one can pass to serious and feasible studies on victims and perpetrators of crime. From supply and demand for Johnny's lemonade stand, one can move to national supply and demand for automobiles, steel, or wheat.

Between clearly inappropriate and clearly appropriate topics for federal statistical attention lies a large middle region in which choice is arguable. Which of these middle topics should qualify for reasons of assisting administrative coordination, control, or the legitimate need for information of significant numbers of citizens?

We see two principles operating currently: first, the squeaky wheel— whose operator has sufficient visibility and influence—gets the grease; second, an activity once begun, for whatever reason, tends to continue.

While critical judgment must be exercised, the first principle has merit; the second is of doubtful merit. What is needed, of course, is to apply both to proposed and existing programs, objectively and impartially, a set of criteria based on uses, users, and production problems. The winnowing process must screen out the trivial, even though its proponents have influence, and it must channel resources into those areas in which federal investment in statistics will promote the general welfare. The Checklist we present in Chapter 5 has been designed with this objective in mind.

The application of statistical methods

Another area in which important opportunities for improvement are found is the application of statistical methods to the problems of federal operating agencies.

Operating agencies have progressed at very uneven rates in applying these methods. The achievements of some agencies—the Interstate Commerce Commission, for one—show that substantial improvements in operations can be made by effective use of statistics. Scientific sampling, for example, is a powerful statistical method that should be substituted for the costly, frequently pointless practice found in some agencies of examining *all* items, and for the unreliable judgment samples used in other agencies. In Chapter 5 we discuss steps that will realize the potential of statistical methods in a systematic manner. These steps include a more vigorous and careful application of statistical approaches to the evaluation of the programs of all government agencies ... economic, social, military, educational, scientific, or whatever.

The coordination of statistical activities

In addition to the many opportunities to lift the level of performance by applying modern statistical methodology and improving personnel, an important avenue of progress points to improved coordination of statistical activities. This approach, discussed in Chapter 5, calls for wider use of traditional surveys, operating program data, and controlled field studies in varying proportions.

To recapitulate some of the highlights of this chapter: federal statistics have improved steadily for more than half a century, especially in the agencies that are primarily statistical. Formerly, the bulk of federal statistics emanated from statistical agencies and the bulk of them related to private activities. The quality of the statistics from operating agencies is not, except in a few instances, adequate. The inadequacies result in part from the neglect of the modern body of methods and principles which is known as *statistics* and in part from thinking of statistics simply as numerical data. One of the most pervasive faults is failure to provide adequate measures of accuracy. Even many of the statistics from the agencies whose primary mission is statistical suffer from this defect. For the most part, opportunities for important improvements in federal statistical programs lie more in improving the quality of federal statistics than in expanding the range of statistical activity. The Commission's main effort has not been to suggest specific and immediate improvements but to propose arrangements and procedures which will continually renew and upgrade the federal statistical system for a long time, and in the face of developments and needs that cannot now be foreseen.

PART II

EXPLORATORY DATA ANALYSIS

INDEX

ACCIDENTS ON ROUTE 2: TWO-WAY STRUCTURES FOR DATA

WILLIAM B. FAIRLEY

PREFACE

The following analysis of highway accidents shows how a set of raw numbers can be organized and represented to expose fundamental information about accident frequency. The statistical tools used here are the stem-and-leaf approach to frequency distributions, pioneered by John W. Tukey, and both graphical and arithmetic approaches to the analysis of trend and seasonality in accidents. All statistical methods used are fully explained, and the exposition is primarily designed to teach the reader how some easily grasped statistical tools can help make sense out of an unanalyzed set of numbers. The reference to "two-way structures for data" in the title is to the fitting of (1) a two-way additive model for the data with year and season as the two factors, or to an alternative fitting of (2) a two-way multiplicative model using the same two factors.

The highway accident data analyzed are reported motor vehicle accidents on a suburban stretch of Route 2, a major highway entering Boston, Massachusetts from the west. The data were originally obtained from the Massachusetts Department of Public Works by Margaret C. Lewis in the course of a project on speed limits on Route 2 and their relation to accidents. This project is discussed in her paper "Lower Speed Limits and Safety," Teaching and Research Materials Number 16T, Public Policy Program, Harvard University, November 1973.

In addition to Ms. Lewis, I would also like to thank Jack M. Appleman and Frederick Mosteller for their helpful comments.

Teaching and Research Materials No. 22T, Public Policy Program, John Fitzgerald Kennedy School of Government, Harvard University, January 1975.

I. TREND AND SEASONALITY

Accidents on Route 2

Table 1 gives the numbers of reported motor vehicle accidents on a suburban stretch of Route 2 outside Boston for the four quarters of the year for 1970, 1971, and 1972. We call these numbers "counts."

TABLE 1 TOTAL REPORTED MOTOR VE-HICLE ACCIDENTS[a] ON ROUTE 2 BETWEEN ROUTE 128 AND ROUTE 27 FOR FOUR QUARTERS OF 1970, 1971, AND 1972.

Period	Total accidents
1970	
Quarter I	138
Quarter II	92
Quarter III	94
Quarter IV	152
1971	
Quarter I	74
Quarter II	84
Quarter III	108
Quarter IV	153
1972	
Quarter I	90
Quarter II	68
Quarter III	81
Quarter IV	135[b]

[a] Source of data in table: Department of Public Works, Commonwealth of Massachusetts. The entries are counts of the accidents causing bodily injury and/or over $200 damage and reported to the police.

[b] Estimated figure.

What can we learn about accident counts on Route 2 from this set of data?

First look at the data: frequency distribution

We can get an overall grasp of the data by jotting down the list of 12 counts in the table in the order of their size. To do this quickly, list the numbers by their place value for tens as in Panel A of Table 2. Thus 84 and 81 are on the same line, and 152 and 153 are on the same line, etc. Panel B of Table 2 shows the same data in Tukey's "stem-and-leaf" format. The "stems" are the place values for tens, while the "leaves" are the place values for ones.

TABLE 2 COUNTS OF ACCIDENTS FOR TWELVE QUARTERS
(LISTED BY PLACE VALUE FOR TENS).

	Panel A		Panel B Stem-and-leaf
Place value	Total accidents	Tens	Units
6	68	6	8
7	74	7	4
8	84, 81	8	4 1
9	92, 94, 90	9	2 4 0
10	108	10	8
11		11	
12		12	
13	138, 135	13	8 5
14		14	
15	152, 153	15	2 3

Table 2 shows us at a glance the large variation in the counts of reported accidents in the quarters. They range from a minimum of 68 to a maximum of 153. On a daily basis, since there are about 90 days to each quarter, the average rate ranges from over 2 to nearly 5 accidents per 3 days. The median count of accidents, 93, is the average of the middle two counts, 92 and 94 (because we have an even number of counts). Thus the median rate is about 1 accident per day. Of course we do not expect 1 accident to happen each day. The average rate of 1 per day may be composed of many days with no accidents and a few days with a large number.

Because of the orderly arrangement of the numbers in Table 2, we quickly see that the median number of accidents, 93, is much closer to the minimum, 68, than it is to the maximum, 153. The distances from the extremes are 25 (or 93 minus 68) and 60 (or 153 minus 93).

If accident totals beyond 1972 had continued to vary as much as these, we could not predict a quarterly total accurately from the information in Table 2. If we quote the median, 93, then unless there was reason to expect a change after 1972, we would expect it to be too high about half the time and too low the other half. From the observed asymmetry in Table 2, we would anticipate that our underestimates would tend to be larger than our overestimates.

Time trend and seasonal effects

What has happened to the frequency of accidents over the course of this three-year period? Do the different quarters have characteristically different counts of accidents?

In considering the first question we can compare the total accidents for the three years. These are:

Year	Total accidents
1970	476
1971	419
1972	374

We note a decline each year; between 1970 and 1971 a decline of 57, and between 1971 and 1972 a decline of 45. From 1970 to 1971 there was a 12% decline, and from 1971 to 1972 an 11% decline. Any decline in accidents is welcome, and the 12% and 11% reductions noted here seem encouragingly large. This much we can say immediately.

A subtler question is whether the declines are indicative of a time trend or readily might be explained as chance variations. The notion of a trend is that of a continuing movement over time. Certainly two declines in a row offer only weak evidence of such a continuing movement. We can go in two directions to seek further evidence: internal or external. With our present data we can look at quarterly accidents within the given three-year period of 1970 and 1972. Or we could get data for years before 1970 and after 1972. The first set of data bears only on the question of whether a trend exists within the 1970–1972 period, whereas the second would provide evidence for a trend over a larger interval as well.

Let us look at the data that we have. A graph may be helpful in detecting a trend. Figure 1 shows a plot of the number of accidents for the 12 quarters. This graph is not as helpful as we may have hoped. There is a scattershot appearance, and a trend is difficult to detect.

The four highest points on the graph give a clue to one source of this difficulty. Three out of four belong to the fourth quarter. Examining the plot further suggests that much of the variation in accident counts relates to seasonal quarterly differences. If we can adjust the data for the effects of the quarters, we might be better able to detect a trend. Thus we arrive at a question posed in the beginning of this section: What are the differences in accident counts between the quarters?

Seasonal adjustment

One measure of the effects of the quarters is the average number of accidents during each quarter over the three years. Table 3 gives the total

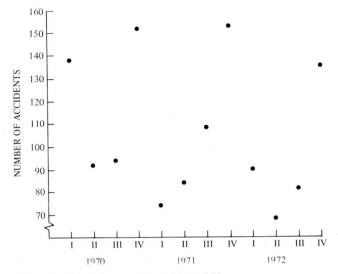

FIG. 1 *Accident frequencies, 1970–1972.*

and average numbers of accidents in the quarters. Quarter II has the lowest average annual frequency, 81.3, while Quarter IV has the highest frequency, 146.7, not quite double that of Quarter II|.

By "effects" of the quarters we mean identifiable differences in the quarterly counts that we suppose are related to accident factors that change seasonally, like weather or volume of traffic. In Table 3, effects are defined

TABLE 3 ACCIDENT COUNTS BY QUARTER.

Quarter	(1) Quarterly total (1970–1972)	(2) Quarterly average per quarter[a] (1970–1972)	(3) Quarterly effects[b] (quarterly averages minus grand average)
I	302	100.7	−5.1
II	244	81.3	−24.5
III	283	94.3	−11.5
IV	440	146.7	40.9
	1269[c]	105.8[d]	

[a] The quarterly average per quarter is the quarterly total divided by 3.

[b] Quarterly effects are the quarterly averages for each quarter (column 2) less the grand average of 105.8.

[c] 1269 is the total number of accidents in all quarters.

[d] 105.8 is the grand average of the 4 quarterly averages, and also equals 1269/12, the grand average of all quarters.

precisely as the quarterly averages minus the grand average. (There could be other precise definitions, for example employing medians, but we have chosen to use averages here.)

Clearly there are large differences between the quarters. For the moment we will put aside the question of whether these differences are indicative of seasonal effects or of haphazard variation. This is the same issue that arose in interpreting the two-year decline. The grand average of the four quarterly averages in column 2 is 105.8. This figure, the grand average for quarters, gives us an average quarterly number without seasonal effect. The differences between the four quarterly averages and 105.8 represent the quarterly effects for accidents. Column 3 of Table 3 gives these differences, or quarterly effects. For example, Quarter IV has a deviation of 40.9 accidents above the grand average of 105.8—almost 40% higher than average—while Quarter II has a deviation of 24.5 below 105.8—almost 25% below average.

The safest periods on Route 2 appear to be the spring (Quarter II) and the summer (Quarter III), with the fall (Quarter IV) by far the most dangerous, and the winter (Quarter I), surprisingly, about average. Whether these differences are attributable to differences in traffic volume, types of users, times of use, or other identifiable factors is something not considered here.

Now we are in a position to adjust the actual numbers of accidents in the twelve quarters of 1970 through 1972 for quarterly effects. To do this we subtract the quarterly effects from the observed quarterly accident counts for each year. Table 4 gives the adjusted data obtained by subtracting the respective quarterly effects from the original data in Table 1. Thus 40.9 was subtracted from each of the fourth-quarter accident frequencies and so forth.

Figure 2 shows a plot of the quarterly adjusted accident frequencies given in Table 4. This plot has less of a scattershot appearance than the plot of the unadjusted frequencies in Figure 1. Furthermore it indicates a trend over the period. Even though four of the eleven quarter-to-quarter changes are increases and the increase between Quarter I and Quarter III of 1971 is substantial, nonetheless we get an impression of a downward drift of the points.

Adjusting for quarterly effects has made it possible to check further into the presence of a time trend. The existence of a downward trend might affect decisions by highway officials responsible for vehicle safety. If the trend could be connected to a series of road improvements, for example, some evidence would be available on the success of the program. At the same time, if the improvements were costly and the accident situation more serious on other roads, then resources might need to be shifted away from Route 2. Other explanations for the decrease may be present, such as a

TABLE 4 ACCIDENT COUNTS AD-
JUSTED FOR QUARTERLY EFFECTS.

Period	Adjusted accident totals[a]
1970	
Quarter I	143.1
Quarter II	116.5
Quarter III	103.5
Quarter IV	111.1
1971	
Quarter I	79.1
Quarter II	108.5
Quarter III	119.5
Quarter IV	112.1
1972	
Quarter I	95.1
Quarter II	92.5
Quarter III	92.5
Quarter IV	94.1

[a] Data of Table 1 less respective quarterly effects given in column 3 of Table
3. For example, 143.1 for Quarter I of
1970 is $138 - (-5.1) = 143.1$.

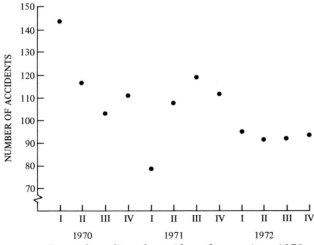

FIG. 2 *Quarterly adjusted accident frequencies, 1970–
1972.*

funneling of traffic onto other roads or a gradual decrease in overall rates of speed due to congestion. Each of these possibilities and others should be considered.

Adjustment for years

Next we ask again whether the quarterly effects represent seasonal factors influencing accidents, or whether they represent chance variations that we should not expect to continue. Again we address the question informally and carry it as far as some straightforward arithmetic and graphical devices will allow.

Figure 3 plots counts for all twelve quarters grouped by the four quarters of the year. This graph shows seasonality fairly clearly. The connecting lines drawn between points of the same year make this observation easier. What we can observe in Figure 3 is a strong tendency for quarter-to-quarter changes to be in the same direction in all three years. Thus, for example, in all three years there were increases from Quarter II to III and from III to IV. In fact, the only maverick change occurs in a change from I to II—a decrease in 1970 and 1972 and an increase in 1971.

We can use the same approach for the seasonal effects question as we did above for a time trend. Just as we adjusted observed quarterly frequencies for quarterly effects to study a time trend, so we can adjust them for yearly effects to study seasonality. Despite the relatively clear message of Figure 3, a plot of data adjusted for yearly differences reveals seasonality

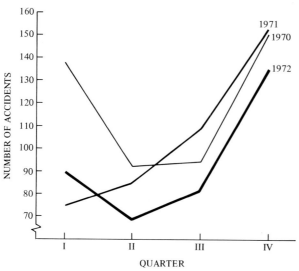

FIG. 3 *Accident frequencies by quarter.*

TABLE 5 ACCIDENT COUNTS BY YEAR.

	(1)	(2)	(3)
Year	Yearly total	Yearly average per quarter[a]	Yearly effect[b] (yearly averages minus grand average)
1970	476	119.0	13.2
1971	419	104.8	−1.0
1972	374	93.5	−12.3
	1269	105.8	

[a] Yearly average per quarter is the Yearly total divided by 4.

[b] Yearly effects are the yearly averages for each year (column 2) less the grand average of 105.8.

even more clearly. Table 5 shows a calculation for yearly effects like that made in Table 3 for quarterly effects. The differences between the averages for the years and a grand yearly average are defined as the yearly effects.

Table 6 gives the accident counts for the twelve quarters adjusted for yearly effects.

TABLE 6 ACCIDENT COUNTS ADJUSTED FOR YEARLY EFFECTS.

Period	Adjusted accident totals[a]
1970	
Quarter I	124.8
Quarter II	78.8
Quarter III	80.8
Quarter IV	138.8
1971	
Quarter I	75.0
Quarter II	85.0
Quarter III	109.0
Quarter IV	154.0
1972	
Quarter I	102.3
Quarter II	80.3
Quarter III	93.3
Quarter IV	147.3

[a] Data of Table 1 less respective yearly effects given in column 3 of Table 5. For example, 124.8 for Quarter I of 1970 is 138 − (13.2) = 124.8.

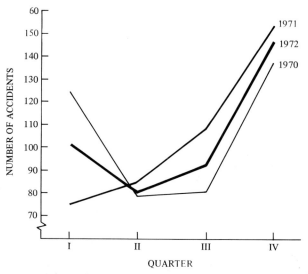

FIG. 4 *Adjusted accident frequencies by quarter.*

Finally, Figure 4 displays a plot of the adjusted data, showing the general tendency for seasonal movement and making the one exception, Quarter I to II in 1971, stand out more sharply. If the yearly effects in another set of data were more pronounced or the quarterly effects less pronounced, the advantage of plotting adjusted rather than unadjusted data would be seen more clearly, as it was in our earlier comparison of Figure 2 with Figure 1.

Recapitulation

What have we learned so far from this example that can be of general value in the analysis of data?

1. A *frequency distribution* (Table 2) of a *batch of raw data* (Table 1) can give a rapid overview of the numbers and can reveal unusual characteristics of the batch.

2. To study data along one dimension (like time) it may help to first *adjust* the data along another dimension (like seasonality) by subtracting an estimated *effect* associated with that factor. The adjusted data—shown either numerically (Table 4) or graphically (Figure 2)—may then better reveal the effect associated with the first dimension. In this example, after first adjusting for seasonality to study time, we have reversed the dimensions and adjusted for time to study seasonality.

Though we have given an example of adjustment, we have not fully explored this important idea. We shall do this in the next section.

Exercises

The data in Table 7 are the monthly accident counts on Route 2 for the same period as in the text (1970–1972).

1. Construct a frequency distribution for the data. Find the median and the range and comment on any features of the distribution that you find noteworthy.

2. Consider informally the evidence for a time trend in accidents. Use the numerical or graphical technique of the discussion above or other techniques that occur to you. Carry out an adjustment for monthly seasonal effects. Discuss the indications that the data provide about a time trend over the three years.

3. Consider informally the evidence for monthly seasonal effects in accidents. (Repeat the analysis you did in Exercise 2, but compute for monthly seasonal effects.)

4. How do your findings in Exercises 2 and 3 compare with those of the text, which were based on quarterly aggregates of these monthly data?

TABLE 7 MONTHLY ACCIDENT COUNTS
ON ROUTE 2, 1970–1972.

Month	1970	1971	1972
J	52	35	33
F	37	22	26
M	49	17	31
A	29	27	25
M	31	34	23
J	32	23	20
J	28	42	25
A	34	30	20
S	32	36	36
O	39	65	45[a]
N	50	48	45[a]
D	63	40	45[a]

[a] Estimated value.

II. ADDITIVE STRUCTURE

A two-way structure for the data: additive structure
In this section we continue with our examination of the accident data from
Route 2 during 1970–1972. Although we have studied the effects of time
and seasonality separately, we should look at them simultaneously. We have
been leading up to a discussion of "structures for data."

A "structure for data" refers to a form for representing the data. In our
example the data are simultaneously categorized by year and by quarter. In
adjusting one of these factors by the other, we have been using this two-way
feature of the data implicitly. To emphasize this two-way organization, we
array the data in a two-way matrix or cross-classification by year and season
in Table 8. Such an organization of the data is by itself a weak form of
"structure" because it imposes a way of looking at the two factors simultaneously, inviting row comparisons and column comparisons. Such organization suggests ways to summarize and display the data. Figure 3, for
example, is a graphical display of Table 8.

We can now develop a more substantial kind of two-way structure for
the data arrayed in Table 8. Suppose that we think of each of the accident
counts in Table 8 as representing the sum of a yearly effect and a quarterly
effect. Or almost. We actually start with a common base count for each of
the twelve quarters and then adjust this base count up or down for yearly
and quarterly effects.

For the common base count an easy first choice is the grand average of
quarterly accident counts, namely 105.8. For the yearly effects, we take the
deviations of averages for each year from the grand average as we did
above, and for the quarterly effects we take the deviations of the averages
for each quarter from the grand average. These effects are given respectively
in Table 5 and Table 3. A yearly effect is our estimate of the amount of
deviation associated with a particular row of Table 8 without regard to that
associated with the columns. (For quarterly effects, interchange rows and
columns.)

TABLE 8 TWO-WAY TABLE OF ACCIDENT COUNTS (BY
YEAR AND QUARTER).

		Quarter			
		I	II	III	IV
	1970	138	92	94	152
Year	1971	74	84	108	153
	1972	90	68	81	135

TABLE 9 YEARLY AND QUARTERLY EFFECTS (CALCULATED FROM A TWO-WAY TABLE OF COUNTS).

		Quarter						Yearly effect
		I	II	III	IV	Total	Mean	
Year	1970	138	92	94	152	476	119.0	13.2
	1971	74	84	108	153	419	104.8	−1.0
	1972	90	68	81	135	374	93.5	−12.3
Total		302	244	283	440	1269		
Mean		100.7	81.3	94.3	146.7		105.8	
Quarterly Effect		−5.1	−24.5	−11.5	40.9			

One of the advantages of organizing the data in the two-way array of Table 8 is to facilitate and even suggest the computations displayed earlier in Tables 5 and 3. Table 9 shows how the totals of the rows and columns of the data in Table 8 can be conveniently divided by 4 and by 3, respectively, to get average accident counts by year and by quarter and to get the grand average of 105.8 subtracted from these averages to give the effects.

Notice that the adjustments we performed earlier can now be easily made. Thus by subtracting the quarterly effects from the respective columns of accident counts in Table 9, we can generate the entries in Table 4.

We should say a word at this point about the idea of a set of numbers being "represented." There are many ways to understand a set of similar numbers. A simple way is to regard all of the numbers as fundamentally equal except for deviations owing to some uncontrolled variables. This way then represents each number in the set by one component, say the grand average of the numbers. The representation is an approximation. More generally we may introduce additional variables to help explain a number, or we may transform it—by taking its logarithm or square root, for example. Such representations may give us a simpler way of thinking about a set of numbers than thinking of each one separately or trying to think of them all at once. Representations are usually a more delicate way of thinking about sets of numbers than that suggested by a frequency distribution of the original set, because the representation ordinarily takes more things into account. As the representations get more general, we hope to go further in describing or even explaining what a process is producing. In our accident example, the process is the system of drivers and automobiles interacting with the road and weather through time. They are generating, sadly enough from our present point of view, accidents. (For other investigations they may be generating trips or speeds or numbers of passengers.)

We might try to explain these accident counts as random numbers varying about some center, or as numbers dependent to some extent on the time of year, or as numbers dependent on the year itself. Of course we understand that calendars do not themselves adjust the processes of driving and that things change with the passage of time: the quarters of the year are fair stand-ins for driving conditions in New England.

For the moment our purpose is to illustrate some ways of representing numbers by replacing them with fewer numbers. To do this we shall now approximately represent the data as a sum of a common average, yearly effect, and quarterly effect:

$$\text{quarterly accident count} \approx \left\{ \begin{array}{c} \text{common base count} \\ + \\ \text{yearly effect} \\ + \\ \text{quarterly effect} \end{array} \right\}$$

The symbol $\approx$ means "approximately." Taking Quarter I of 1970 as an example, we have:

$$138 \approx \left\{ \begin{array}{c} 105.8 \\ + \\ -5.1 \\ + \\ 13.2 \end{array} \right\} = 113.9$$

The difference of 24.1 between the count, 138, and the representational value, 113.9, measures the failure of the additive representation based on the two factors of time and season alone. We call such differences *residuals.* Quarter III in 1972 shows a much smaller difference between actual value and representation:

$$81 \approx \left\{ \begin{array}{c} 105.8 \\ + \\ -11.5 \\ + \\ -12.3 \end{array} \right\} = 82.0$$

The residual here is only -1.0.

Instead of picking and choosing, let us show the whole set of twelve representations for the twelve quarters. Table 10 gives these in a two-way array that can be easily compared with the actual counts in Table 9. We call these representations "fitted values" and the whole set of them the "fit."

How well does the "fit" fit? Displaying in a two-way array all the differences between the actual counts and the fits gives a comprehensive

TABLE 10   YEARLY   AND   QUARTERLY   FIT   TO
ACCIDENT COUNTS.

		Quarter			
		I	II	III	IV
	1970	113.9	94.5	107.5	159.9
Year	1971	99.7	80.3	93.3	145.7
	1972	88.4	69.0	82.0	134.4

view of this question. Table 11 displays these residuals in Panel C. The residuals are valuable numbers because they contain information about the size and direction of the failure of the fit.

A frequency distribution of the residuals gives us an overview of their size. Table 12 gives the stem-and-leaf display. The median of the residuals is −0.2. The median of the absolute values of the residuals (that is, the median error) is 5.5 [5.5 = (7.3 + 3.7)/2]. Exactly half are positive, corresponding to fits that underestimated the actual counts, and half are negative, corresponding to fits that overestimated the actual counts. The range equals the largest count minus the smallest count, or $24.1 - (-25.7) = 49.8$. Furthermore, the values of the residuals above and below the median are distributed approximately symmetrically.

TABLE 11 YEARLY AND QUARTERLY ACCIDENT COUNTS: DATA, FIT, AND RESIDUALS.

		Quarter			
		I	II	III	IV
Panel A:	Data				
	1970	138	92	94	152
Year	1971	74	84	108	153
	1972	90	68	81	135
Panel B:	Fit				
	1970	113.9	94.5	107.5	159.9
Year	1971	99.7	80.3	93.3	145.7
	1972	88.4	69.0	82.0	134.4
Panel C:	Residuals				
	1970	24.1	−2.5	−13.5	−7.9
Year	1971	−25.7	3.7	14.7	7.3
	1972	1.6	−1.0	−1.0	.6

TABLE 12 STEM-AND-LEAF OF THE RESIDUALS FROM YEARLY AND QUARTERLY FIT TO ACCIDENT COUNTS.

Tens	Units
2	4
1	5
0	4 7 2 1
−0	2 8 1 1
−1	4
−2	6

Figure 5 gives a plot of the fitted values in Table 10. Comparing Figure 5 to Figure 1 by eye reveals in a qualitative way how the fitted values mimic the actual values.

Figure 6 shows directly the relation of the fitted values to the actual values in a plot of the one against the other. The 45-degree line is the locus of perfect fit. The residuals are the vertical distances of the points from this line. Figure 7 shows the relation of the residuals to the fitted values.

A notion of goodness of fit can be derived by comparing the fit to a very simple competitor, namely the grand average. Table 13 gives the frequency distribution of the residuals from the grand average. These are the errors that would be made in predicting the counts from the grand average, just as

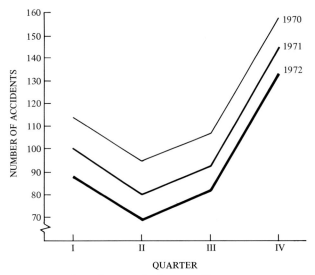

FIG. 5 *Yearly and quarterly fit to accident counts.*

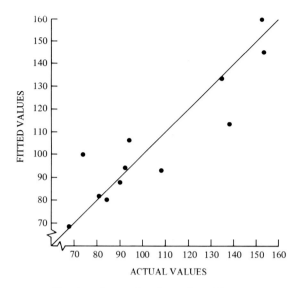

FIG. 6 *Fitted and actual values of accident counts.*

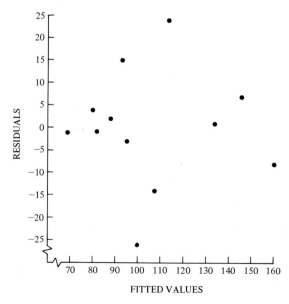

FIG. 7 *Fitted values and residuals of accident counts.*

TABLE 13 STEM-AND-LEAF OF RESIDUALS FROM FIT OF GRAND AVERAGE
TO ACCIDENT COUNTS AND FROM THE TWO-WAY FIT.

Residuals from two-way fit			Residuals from grand average
Units	Tens		Units
	4		6 7
	3		2
4	2		9
5	1		
7 4 2 1	0		2
−1 −1 −2 −8	−0		
−4	−1		−6 −4 −2
−5	−2		−5 −2
	−3		−8 −2
	−4		

the residuals in Table 12 are the errors that would be made in predicting the
counts by the full yearly and quarterly fit. The median of the residuals from
the grand average is −13. The median of the absolute values of the residuals
(that is, the median error) is 23.5 [23.5 = (25 + 22)/2], which is more than 4
times the median error, 5.5, made in using the two-way fit. The range of the
residuals is 85 [85 = 37 − (−38)], which compares with a range of 49.8 for
the residuals from the two-way fit. Showing both sets of residuals together,
as in Table 13, illustrates the dramatic improvement made by fitting the two
effects.

Usefulness of the two-way structure for data
A two-way structure for the accident data means in its weakest sense a
two-way array as shown in Table 8. The fitted values that Table 11 provides
and Figure 5 displays, however, capture the strong sense we intend for the
phrase "a structure for data." The structure here refers to the simplified
two-way representation of the accident counts by a grand average plus the
two effects. What good is such a structure? It can be useful in three ways:

1. The effects can be used to make adjustments.
2. The two-way structure of fitted effects provides a simple way to
   describe or summarize the data, and thereby helps us understand and
   discuss them.
3. The structure may help us predict future accident totals.

If, for example, we have reason to project a time trend based on the
observed trend, then we can combine a projected yearly effect with an

estimated quarterly effect to predict future totals. Such a prediction might be useful in evaluating the effects on auto accidents of a safety campaign, an experimental road, a reduction in speed limit, or highway alterations. The predicted value based on the two-way structure would be compared with the observed value during the test period.

Algebraic statement of two-way structures

To provide a convenient notation for the two-way structure we have been discussing, we need to define an algebraic statement of it. Such an algebraic statement helps us to generalize our discussion to other sets of data as well. We make the following definitions of symbols:

$$Y_{ij} = \text{the accident count in the } i\text{th year}$$
$$\text{and the } j\text{th quarter.}$$

The index letter i stands for the year. Since we have three years of data, we make i take on the values 1, 2, and 3. Similarly, the index j stands for the quarter; since there are four quarters, we make j take on the values 1, 2, 3, and 4.

Next we define the various components of the fit:

$$m = \text{the grand average of the quarterly}$$
$$\text{accident counts.}$$

In terms of the actual quarterly counts, m can be written as:

$$m = \frac{(\text{sum of all twelve } y_{ij})}{12}.$$

Using mathematical notation for sums, this is:

$$m = \frac{\sum\limits_{j=1}^{4} \sum\limits_{i=1}^{3} y_{ij}}{12}.$$

The value of m in our example is 105.8.

The yearly effects are:

$$a_i = \text{yearly effect for the } i\text{th year}$$
$$(= \text{the difference between the average}$$
$$\text{count for the } i\text{th year and } m).$$

In terms of the actual quarterly counts, a_i can be written as:

$$a_i = \left(\frac{\text{sum of all 4 counts in year } i}{4}\right) - m$$

$$= \left(\frac{\sum_{j=1}^{4} y_{ij}}{4}\right) - m.$$

The values of the a_i taken from column 3 of Table 5 are $a_1 = 13.2$, $a_2 = -1.0$, and $a_3 = -12.3$.

The quarterly effects are:

$b_j = $ quarterly effect for the jth quarter
(= the difference between the average quarterly count for the jth quarter and m).

In terms of the actual quarterly counts, b_j can be written as:

$$b_j = \left(\frac{\text{sum of all 3 counts for the } j\text{th quarter}}{3}\right) - m$$

$$= \frac{\sum_{i=1}^{3} y_{ij}}{3} - m.$$

The values of the b_j, taken from column 3 of Table 3, are $b_1 = -5.1$, $b_2 = -24.5$, $b_3 = -11.5$, and $b_4 = 40.9$.

We can now define the two-way fit algebraically. For example, the fitted value for the first quarter ($j = 1$, Quarter I) of the first year ($i = 1$, 1970) can be represented as:

$$\hat{y}_{11} = m + a_1 + b_1.$$

The caret or "hat" over y_{11} indicates that $\hat{y}_{11}$ is the fitted rather than the actual value for y_{11}. Numerically $\hat{y}_{11}$ is:

$$113.9 = 105.8 + (-5.1) + 13.2.$$

Recall that the actual count for Quarter I of 1970 was 138; that is, $y_{11} = 138$. The residual is $y_{11} - \hat{y}_{11} = 138 - 113.9 = 24.1$. In general for the ith year and jth quarter, the fitted value can be represented as:

$$\hat{y}_{ij} = m + a_i + b_j.$$

In Table 14 we show how the fitted values $\hat{y}_{ij}$ can be built up in three stages. First the counts y_{ij} can be represented solely by their grand mean, m, as shown in Panel A. Then the counts can be represented as the sum of their mean and a yearly effect, as shown in Panel B. Finally, the counts can be

TABLE 14 SUCCESSIVE FITS TO THE DATA.

		Quarter			
		I	II	III	IV
Panel A:	Grand mean				
	1970	m	m	m	m
Year	1971	m	m	m	m
	1972	m	m	m	m
Panel B:	Grand mean and year effect				
	1970	$m+a_1$	$m+a_1$	$m+a_1$	$m+a_1$
Year	1971	$m+a_2$	$m+a_2$	$m+a_2$	$m+a_2$
	1972	$m+a_3$	$m+a_3$	$m+a_3$	$m+a_3$
Panel C:	Grand mean, year effect, and quarter effect				
	1970	$m+a_1+b_1$	$m+a_1+b_2$	$m+a_1+b_3$	$m+a_1+b_4$
Year	1971	$m+a_2+b_1$	$m+a_2+b_2$	$m+a_2+b_3$	$m+a_2+b_4$
	1972	$m+a_3+b_1$	$m+a_3+b_2$	$m+a_3+b_3$	$m+a_3+b_4$

represented as the sum of their mean, a yearly effect, and a quarterly effect, as shown in Panel C.

In this representation of the counts, we have replaced the batch of twelve counts by eight statistics: m, a_1, a_2, a_3, b_1, b_2, b_3, b_4. These statistics are functions of the original data. In fact, only six of the eight statistics are independent quantities. The reader can check (see the Exercises following this discussion) that by virtue of their definition as deviations from the grand mean, the sum of the three yearly effects, a_i, is 0 and the sum of the four quarterly effects, b_j, is 0. Thus, for example, $a_1 = -(a_2 + a_3)$, and any one of the yearly effects can be obtained from the other two. Thus the twelve counts have actually been represented by only six independent quantities, since there are two constraints on the values of the eight statistics.

Recapitulation

In this part of the discussion of the accident data from Route 2, we have introduced the important idea of a *structure for data*, first simply as an arrangement of the data that emphasized their two-way character, second as a representation of the data by a particular formula, which in this case was an additive fit to the data of the *fitted effects* of the two factors. We have looked at the residuals in order to study the goodness of the fit. We have also defined an algebraic representation of the fit in order to provide a shorthand language for the counts, the fitted values, and the various components of the fit that will apply quite generally to any set of data that can be described by a two-way structure.

Exercises

1. Show that the effects add up to 0, as claimed at the end of this section. That is, show that

$$\sum_i a_i = 0 \quad \text{and} \quad \sum_j b_j = 0.$$

2. The data in Table 15 give projections for total expenditures in the city budget of New Haven, Connecticut for 1975. Each projection is made on the assumption of one of the 27 $(27 = 3 \times 3 \times 3)$ different combinations of low (L), medium (M), or high (H) levels of (1) population, (2) city services levels, and (3) salary levels. It is taken from Table 37 in *Forecasting Local Government Spending* by Claudia DeVita Scott [5].

   Discuss the extension of the two-way additive model to a three-way additive model that you propose as a structure for this data.

TABLE 15 PROJECTIONS OF CITY EXPENDITURES FOR NEW HAVEN IN 1975 UNDER ALTERNATIVE ASSUMPTIONS CONCERNING POPULATION, SERVICE, AND SALARY LEVELS IN MILLIONS OF DOLLARS[a].

	Code	Projection		Code	Projection
1.	LLL	81	15.	MMH	103
2.	LLM	86	16.	MHL	100
3.	LLH	94	17.	MHM	107
4.	LML	86	18.	MHH	117
5.	LMM	91	19.	HLL	83
6.	LMH	99	20.	HLM	88
7.	LHL	94	21.	HLH	96
8.	LHM	100	22.	HML	88
9.	LHH	109	23.	HMM	93
10.	MLL	83	24.	HMH	102
11.	MLM	88	25.	HHL	99
12.	MLH	96	26.	HHM	105
13.	MML	89	27.	HHH	115
14.	MMM	94			

[a] The original data in thousands of dollars have been rounded to millions.

Fix the level of one of the variables and consider the 3-by-3 table of data remaining when that level is fixed.

Carry out a two-way additive fit with an analysis of the residuals like that in this section or using other approaches that occur to you.

III. MULTIPLICATIVE STRUCTURE

An alternative two-way structure for the accident data: the multiplicative structure for proportions

To emphasize that there is not just one way to represent the data, we offer an alternative structure based on a multiplicative rather than an additive approach to these same data. The fitted values are almost identical. (These two ways of building the fit will not always agree so closely.)

Instead of regarding our twelve counts as counts, we can divide them by the total 1269 and regard them as proportions. Table 16 gives the proportions obtained by dividing the entries in Table 7 by 1269. Such a table is also. called a *joint frequency distribution* of the accidents by year and by quarter. Each entry in the central part of the table is the proportion of the accidents in the three-year period occurring in a given quarter and a given year.

If we add up the proportions in, say, the fourth column of Table 16, we obtain the total proportion of accidents occurring in Quarter IV. This proportion is .347, or over a third of the accidents. Similarly we find the proportions occurring in the other columns. The sums of proportions in each of the rows give the proportions occurring in the three different years of 1970–1972.

We now come to the second method of building the fit. Suppose we do not know the percentages of accidents occurring in the twelve quarters, but we do know that the proportions of accidents in the three years 1970–1972 were as given in the rightmost column of Table 16: .375 in 1970, .330 in 1971, and .295 in 1972. We also know that the proportions of accidents in

TABLE 16 PROPORTIONS OF ACCIDENTS IN 1970–1972 BY YEAR AND BY QUARTER (JOINT AND MARGINAL PROPORTIONS).

		Quarter				
		I	II	III	IV	Total
Year	1970	.1087	.0725	.0740	.1198	.375
	1971	.0583	.0662	.0851	.1206	.330
	1972	.0709	.0536	.0638	.1064	.295
	Total	.238	.192	.223	.347	1.000

the four quarters were as given in the bottom row of Table 13: .238 in Quarter I, .192 in Quarter II, .223 in Quarter III, and .347 in Quarter IV. The quarterly proportions tell the same story about seasonality that the quarterly averages did, but they use a different measure. If accident counts were the same in the four quarters, then 25% would appear in each one. We find instead about 24% in winter, 19% in spring, 22% in summer, and 35% in fall. This seasonal pattern might suggest to highway officials the value of special efforts to reduce accidents in the fall.

What would we predict for the proportions in each of the twelve quarters? The simplest assumption to make is that the quarterly pattern is the same for each of the years. Then, to find the proportion of accidents occurring in Quarter IV of 1970, for example, we multiply the 1970 proportion, .375, by the Quarter IV share, .347, to get .1301. Multiplying the 1970 proportion by the other quarterly shares for Quarters I, II, and III gives the predicted proportions for these quarters in 1970—on the assumption that the quarterly proportions in 1970 are the same as the quarterly proportions for all three years, 1970–1972. The proportions of accidents in each quarter of 1970 are shown in the following table.

Quarter	Predicted 1970 proportion	Actual 1970 proportion
I	.375 × .238 = .0893	.1087
II	.375 × .192 = .0720	.0725
III	.375 × .223 = .0836	.0740
IV	.375 × .347 = .1301	.1198

Comparing the predicted proportions for 1970 with the actual proportions for 1970, we note that the rank order of the proportions in the quarters is the same in both, but that the first quarter is underestimated by about 0.02 and the third and fourth quarters overestimated by about 0.01.

TABLE 17 PREDICTED PROPORTIONS OF ACCIDENTS IN 1970–1972 BY YEAR AND BY QUARTER (MULTIPLICATIVE STRUCTURE).

		Quarter				
		I	II	III	IV	Total
	1970	.0893	.0720	.0836	.1301	.375
Year	1971	.0785	.0634	.0736	.1145	.330
	1972	.0702	.0566	.0658	.1024	.295
	Total	.238	.192	.223	.347	1.000

TABLE 18 YEARLY AND QUARTERLY ACCIDENT COUNTS: DATA, FIT, AND RESIDUALS (MULTIPLICATIVE STRUCTURE).

		Quarter			
		I	II	III	IV
Panel A: Data					
	1970	138	92	94	152
Year	1971	74	84	108	153
	1972	90	68	81	135
Panel B: Fit					
	1970	113.26	91.37	106.12	165.13
Year	1971	99.67	80.40	93.39	145.31
	1972	89.10	71.88	83.48	129.90
Panel C: Residuals					
	1970	24.74	−.63	−12.12	−13.13
Year	1971	−25.33	3.60	14.39	7.31
	1972	−.90	−3.88	−2.48	5.10

By multiplying the proportions in 1971 and 1972 (.330 and .295) by the quarterly proportions, we generate predicted proportions for the quarters of 1971 and 1972. Table 17 gives these products for all quarters.

It is a short step from predicted proportions of accidents to predicted counts. By multiplying a predicted quarterly proportion by the total number of accidents, 1269, we get a predicted accident count for that quarter. Panel B of Table 18 gives these products.

Let us see how we have represented the accident counts. The proportions for the years and the quarters are yearly and quarterly effects. Thus we can write:

$$\text{quarterly accident count} \approx \left\{ \begin{array}{c} \text{total accident count} \\ \times \\ \text{yearly effect} \\ \times \\ \text{quarterly effect} \end{array} \right\}$$

Taking Quarter I of 1970 as an example, we have:

$$138 \approx \left\{ \begin{array}{c} 1269 \\ \times \\ .375 \\ \times \\ .238 \end{array} \right\} = 113.26$$

ROCKHURST COLLEGE LIBRARY

TABLE 19 DIFFERENCE BETWEEN TWO-WAY FITS (ADDITIVE STRUCTURE FIT MINUS MULTIPLICATIVE STRUCTURE FIT).

		Quarter			
		I	II	III	IV
	1970	.64	2.93	1.38	−5.23
Year	1971	.03	−.10	−.09	.39
	1972	−.70	−2.88	−1.48	4.50

The earlier two-way representation, which we will call the additive structure, yielded a fitted value of 113.9 for Quarter I of 1970, almost identical to the fitted value 113.26 from the present representation, which we will call the *multiplicative structure*. The differences between the earlier and the present representations are given in Table 19. They range in absolute value from .03 to 5.23, half are negative and half positive, and the difference is never as much as 5% of a fitted value. Thus the two representations, while seemingly very different, yield nearly identical fitted values.

Panel C Table 18 gives the residuals from the fit of the multiplicative structure to the data. The median residual is −.08, or nearly 0, whereas the median of the absolute values of the residuals, or median error, is 6.20. Recall that for the additive structure the median residual was −0.2, also nearly 0, and the median error 5.5, quite close to 6.20.

Algebraic statement of the multiplicative structure

We can represent the fitted values of the multiplicative structure symbolically. Let y_{ij} again stand for the accident count in the ith year and jth quarter, and $\hat{y}_{ij}$ the corresponding fitted value. Now we define:

$$N = \text{total number of accidents.}$$

N is 1249 in this example. The yearly effects we define as:

$$s_i = \text{proportion of accidents in the } i\text{th year.}$$

In terms of the actual quarterly counts, the s_i can be written as:

$$s_i = \text{proportion of all quarterly counts in year } i$$

$$= \sum_{j=1}^{4} \left(\frac{y_{ij}}{1249} \right).$$

And the quarterly effects we define as:

$$t_j = \text{proportion of accidents in the } j\text{th quarter.}$$

In terms of the actual quarterly counts, the t_j can be written as:

$$t_j = \text{proportion of all quarterly counts in quarter } j$$

$$= \sum_{i=1}^{3} \left(\frac{y_{ij}}{1249} \right).$$

Then we can give our algebraic representation of the fitted counts by:

$$\hat{\hat{y}}_{ij} = N s_i t_j.$$

We use a double-hat notation, $\hat{\hat{y}}_{ij}$, for the fitted values of the multiplicative model.

Recapitulation

We have represented the accident data in two different ways: first by an *additive structure* in which the counts were fitted as sums of effects of two factors, and second by the *multiplicative structure* in which the quarterly counts—converted to proportions of the total count—were fitted as products of effects of two factors. Both ways of representing the data were examples of two-way structures for data.

We have seen how the same data may be analyzed in different ways. The different structures may yield different insights or one may be more suitable for some uses than another, but the predicted or fitted values came out quite close. Such a coincidence in results will not always occur, but the reader should take note that a rather different approach or model may not in the end upset conclusions based on the first.

Exercises

1. Find the residuals from the multiplicative structure fit and write up a discussion of the goodness of fit of the model for the accident counts. Use numerical and graphical devices presented in the text and/or ones of your own choosing.

2. In our earlier discussion of adjustments, we made quarterly and yearly adjustments by subtracting the fitted effects of the two factors. This procedure was based implicitly on the additive structure. Study the question of a time trend in the quarterly accident counts by adjusting for quarterly effects using the multiplicative model. Discuss how the multiplicative structure is implicit in this mode of adjustment.

The two-way additive structure is discussed in *Exploratory Data Analysis*, Chapter 10, by John W. Tukey [6]. In these chapters the structure is discussed, as it is here, without reference to a true model containing true seasonal or yearly effects or to probabilistic assumptions about error terms. The additive structure is often called the two-way analysis of variance model in statistics.

The multiplicative structure is discussed in an elementary fashion in many statistics books. For example, see Chapter 17, Section 4 of *Statistics* by William L. Hays [1], or Chapter 4, Sections 1, 2, and 3 of *Probability With Statistical Applications* by Frederick Mosteller, Robert Rourke, and George Thomas [3]. Mosteller and Rourke treat the statistical analysis of counts and their probability models, including various uses of chi-square statistics, in detail in Chapters 7–11 of *Sturdy Statistics* [7].

Readers interested in discussions of statistical analyses of accident data and safety campaigns will find them in *Road Research*, Proceedings of the Symposium on the Use of Statistical Methods in the Analysis of Road Accidents, Organization for Economic Cooperation and Development [4]. Background information about the accident data analyzed in this paper may be found in a discussion by Margaret Lewis, *Lower Speed Limits and Safety* [2].

REFERENCES

[1] William L. Hays. *Statistics.* New York: Holt, 1963.

[2] Margaret Lewis. *Lower Speed Limits and Safety*, Teaching and Research Materials, Number 16T, Public Policy Program, John Fitzgerald Kennedy School of Government, Harvard University, November 1973.

[3] Frederick Mosteller, Robert Rourke, and George Thomas. *Probability With Statistical Applications.* 2d ed. Reading, Mass.: Addison-Wesley, 1970.

[4] Organization for Economic Cooperation and Development. *Road Research.* Proceedings of the Symposium on the Use of Statistical Methods in the Analysis of Road Accidents. Paris, 1970.

[5] Claudia DeVita Scott. *Forecasting Local Government Spending.* Washington, D.C.: The Urban Institute, 1972.

[6] John W. Tukey. *Exploratory Data Analysis.* Reading, Mass.: Addison-Wesley, 1977.

[7] Frederick Mosteller and Robert Rourke, *Sturdy Statistics.* Reading, Mass.: Addison-Wesley, 1973.

A STATISTICAL SEARCH FOR UNUSUALLY EFFECTIVE SCHOOLS

ROBERT E. KLITGAARD and
GEORGE R. HALL

INTRODUCTION

The search for educational effectiveness

Beginning with the path-breaking Coleman report (1966) and continuing through the most recent research efforts, scholarly analysis has eroded the belief that different school policies can increase educational achievement. Large-scale statistical studies have failed to show consistent and important relationships between what goes on in schools and variations in student learning, as measured by cognitive achievement tests (Averch *et al.*, 1972). To most people concerned with education, these are surprising and distressing results. They countermand common sense and seem to imply that belief in effective education is a delusion.

In the wake of such research, where should one look for educational effectiveness? Many educational researchers have accepted the Coleman results and concluded that effective schools do not exist, though they draw quite varied policy lessons. Some say that because no educational policy is particularly successful, less money should be spent on schools; others argue that more should be spent, in order to make up for low productivity; and still others call for a radical overhaul of the entire ineffective system. Many educators, however, have rejected the Coleman findings on the basis that the wrong outcomes are being measured. Educational effectiveness has not been found, they say, because it has not been correctly measured; achievement scores are imperfect statistics relating to only a small facet of what education is about.

Perhaps educational research has looked in the wrong places for evidence of effectiveness. Previous studies have indicated that, *on average*, school policies do not greatly affect measurable student scholastic and

Reprinted with permission from R-1210-CC/RC, The Rand Corporation, 1973.

occupational performance. Suppose this is true. Might there not remain, nevertheless, a group of schools that are different? Are there any *exceptions* to small average tendencies and insignificant regression coefficients? The mathematics of previous studies allow for such a possibility, as long as the number of exceptions is not large. In short, are there unusually effective schools?

Considering the enormous diversity among the nation's public schools, it seems obvious that some should be much better than others. Furthermore, parents and children, administrators and teachers, journalists, and taxpayers seem to *act* as if some schools were unusually effective. And, clearly, schools do differ in their performances. Some consistently have higher achievement scores, lower drop-out rates, more college-bound graduates, wealthier alumni, and so forth.

These differences, however, cannot be attributed entirely to the schools themselves. Pupils bring different amounts of intellectual capital to their educational experiences, due to varying social, economic, and personal characteristics. Schools with privileged students will tend to achieve superior results. Furthermore, even when socioeconomic and personal background factors are identical among students in different schools, random variation will ensure that some schools will perform better than others. The question of unusually effective schools must therefore be carefully phrased: *Do some schools consistently produce outstanding students even after allowance is made for the different initial endowments of their students and for chance variation?*[1]

This is an important policy question. Even if unusually effective schools are rare, so long as some exist and can be identified, there is hope that their superior performance might be replicated throughout the educational system.[2] But if no exceptional schools exist, we have to consider alternatives radically different from present attempts to discover and diffuse "best practice." We may need to make substantial changes in educational expenditures, or even overhaul the entire educational system. Thus, investigating the existence of unusually effective schools is not merely a matter of

---

[1] Note that unusual effectiveness is a relative concept here. An unusually effective school achieves educational results for its students that are superior to the average results achieved by schools with student bodies with similar characteristics. This concept, sometimes called the "value-added" or "gain" approach to school effectiveness, is set out in a paper by Dyer in Mosteller and Moynihan (1972). See also Barro (1970).

[2] Hilgard (1972) succinctly expressed this view when he told the House Committee on Education and Labor, "We can make immediate advances in the schools by doing more widely what we already know how to do, and what more successful schools are already doing" (p. 56).

On the negative side, replication might not occur for several reasons. Educational "production functions" may differ from school to school and area to area, hampering technology transfer. Educational objectives may also vary, especially in a system emphasizing local control. Also, the oft-cited (if still imperfectly understood) institutional barriers to change in schools may hamper the diffusion of superior techniques. Our empirical efforts ignore these questions and ask, "Do any schools exist that because of unusual success merit replication?"

scientific curiosity, but a necessary foundation for a rational public policy toward educational improvement.

The scope of our empirical investigation of this question is limited in two ways. First, in this exercise we used only achievement scores to measure effectiveness. After initial experimentation, we chose not to use other measures of student achievement or alternative methodological approaches, because of their insufficient conceptual development and lack of appropriate data. Our studies are thus exploratory and conditional: If one takes as the measure of success achievement scores controlled for nonschool background factors, does one find any evidence that some schools are exceptionally successful?

Second, we do not answer a multitude of interesting and policy-relevant questions that can be asked about unusually effective schools. As Sherlock Holmes properly reminded Henry Baskerville, the prior question is, "Does the beast exist?" The null hypothesis asserts that there are no exemplary schools. If we can discover evidence that there are, we shall leave to future researchers the detailed and important work of discovering why they exist and how (if at all) their success can be copied.

We feel that test results can reflect progress toward valid educational objectives. Our investigations can thus be viewed as an assessment of the value of using achievement data to locate unusually effective schools. In this research, we examined six data sets:

1. Michigan schools, 1969–1970 and 1970–1971, grades 4 and 7.
2. New York City elementary schools, 1967–1971, grades 2 through 6.
3. Project Talent data, 1960, grades 9 and 12.
4. New York state school districts, 1969–1970 and 1970–1971, grades 3 and 6.
5. New York state schools, 1966, grade 1; 1968, grade 3; and 1971, grade 6.
6. Project Yardstick data, many years and grades.

The rest of the report is divided into three parts. Section II outlines the methodology we used to locate outliers[3] and reviews and assesses the relevance of previous studies of achievement scores to the search for unusually effective schools. Section III presents the results of our data analyses and discusses their implications.

---

[3] "Outliers" are unusual data points. John W. Tukey has divided "outliers" into two categories—"outside values" and "detached observations"—and has given them more or less quantitative definitions (1970, Ch. 5, p. 17. In this report, the term will be used qualitatively to indicate observations that are exceptional compared with the data's central tendency and overall distribution.

STATISTICAL ANALYSIS

Methodology

Like many previous studies that used achievement scores as a proximate measure of school results, our basic statistical tool is regression analysis. Unlike past studies, however, we are not looking for global relationships, so we care less about characteristics of all schools and more about features of some of them. Consequently, we use a different approach to the regressions.

1. Instead of concentrating on the properties of the regression line, the percentage of variation explained (R^2), and the coefficients of the regressor variables, we pay special attention to the *residuals* from the regression line.

2. Instead of explicitly including school variables in the regression equation, we control for only socioeconomic and other nonschool background factors that affect achievement, and assume that the variation remaining after such a fit represents school effectiveness (and random variation). School effectiveness in most past studies has been measured by the size and significance of the regression coefficients of the school variables.

3. Instead of including an abundance of regressor variables to explain as much variation as possible, we try to avoid overcontrolling.

Three reasons dictate these departures from previous practice. First, previous studies have shown that educational achievement is determined largely by nonschool factors. That is, both school effects and purely random fluctuation have been small. Residual variation could arise from many causes besides school differences: imperfections in measurement, misspecification of background factors, omitted variables, poor choice of fitting technique, incomplete data, and the combined random fluctuations involved in all the regressor variables. Previous studies, however, by dint of their high R^2s, imply that such errors are not likely to be large. Such findings do not mean, as we shall see, that we can attribute residual effects solely to schools; but from past experience we can take comfort in the expectation that systematic errors will be small.

Second, statistical problems hinder the identification of a school's unique effect. If school and nonschool variables suffer from multicollinearity (Bowles and Levin, 1968) or somehow have a joint effect not attributable to school or background alone (Mayeske *et al.*, 1969), judging the true impact of schools becomes nearly impossible. One might reason that, since we are seeking outstanding schools that are replicable, we should perhaps run two-stage least-squares regressions or specifically include an interaction term in the regression. That way, we would not classify as a school effect any variable that was inextricably bound up with socioeconomic and other background factors. But this argument is inappropriate here. We do not want to prejudge the question of replicability nor eliminate school effects that are intercorrelated with background effects. Most important, *there is no convincing model showing the school variables that should be included explicitly to capture the entire school effect.* Thus, we shall use ordinary least squares and be wary of controlling for too many background factors, which might drown out the school effects.

Third, our null hypothesis posits that no unusually effective schools exist; if true, this hypothesis has serious consequences for educational policy. The significance of affirming the null hypothesis requires us to be very sure we do not accept it if it is false (we want to avoid a Type II error). Controlling for too many background variables increases the chance that, because of statistical interactions, real outliers will not show up. Controlling for too *few* variables risks the identification of "outliers" that could be explained by some missing regressor. However, the absence of outliers under such circumstances would be a strong result indeed. The best strategy is thus to avoid the risks of overcontrolling and to give exceptional schools every opportunity to exhibit themselves by regarding the entire residual as the school's effect, even though this practice imparts an upward bias to the estimate.

The outliers displayed by our method may not be due to unusually effective schools. They may be merely the product of chance perturbations or various statistical errors. But our task may be likened to that of a detective, in contrast to that of a judge. The detective searches for clues, the judge evaluates them. Our task is to find *prima facie* evidence for unusually effective schools, not to prove their existence absolutely. Only after candidates for exceptional schools are studied thoroughly can the verdict come in.[4]

Basically, the task is to find school outliers on achievement scores that are not explained by nonschool factors or random variation. Histograms of the residuals on socioeconomic factors from a regression of school achievement scores, as in Figure 1, provide a good starting point. Histograms allow easy visual inspection for "lumpiness" in the distribution or unusual right tails, both of which may signal the presence of exceptional schools. Lumps would show that groups of schools are massed together in a discontinuous fashion, which may indicate several schools using different educational technologies or procedures. The right tail of the histogram is of keen interest. If it is very thick, it may imply that more schools than one would expect are performing

---

[4] We adopt here the philosophy of John W. Tukey. For his use of the judge–detective metaphor, see Tukey (1970), Vol. 1, pp. 1–2.

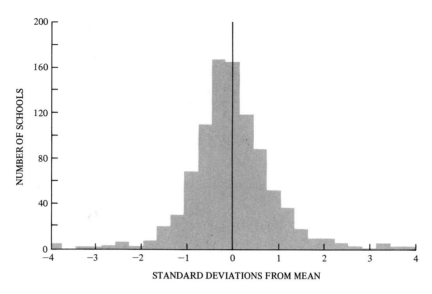

FIG. 1 *Example of a histogram of residuals.*

far above average. A long tail, stretching out to four, five, and six standard deviations above the mean, is evidence that some schools are extremely high achievers.

However, we are not attempting to prove absolutely that the tails are unusual; we are only exploring for evidence that warrants further investigation. Neither lumpiness nor unusual right tails would constitute conclusive evidence of anything; but they would provide interesting clues of where to concentrate our attention.

The second tool involves looking at *series* of distributions of residuals. Each individual distribution (for schools in a particular year, for example) will show the effects of random variation. A series of distributions (over many years) showing the same schools with scores consistently some distance above the mean provides fairly strong evidence that those schools are unusual and deserve further study.

The null hypothesis says that all schools are equally effective and that all the variation in a particular distribution of residuals results from chance. To test this hypothesis, we would like a cumulative measure of school performance over many distributions, after controlling for background factors, to see whether the distribution of cumulative measures differs significantly from a theoretical distribution obtained by treating all the individual distributions of residuals as statistically independent.

To create this cumulative measure, each school in a given distribution (for a particular year, say) was assigned a score of one if it was more than one standard deviation above the mean and a zero otherwise. Then each school's totals were added over all years considered, and we searched for schools consistently above one standard deviation.

For example, assume a set of data for schools for a certain grade during four successive years. The calculations of the cumulative measure are indicated in steps 1 and 2 of Figure 2. Step 3 computes the theoretical distribution, using the binomial theorem and, in this case, a (constant) probability of 0.16 that a school would be more than one standard deviation above the mean in any one distribution. Step 4 compares the actual and expected distributions, using the Chi-square test for goodness of fit. In this hypothetical case, the null hypothesis could not be rejected at the 0.05 level.

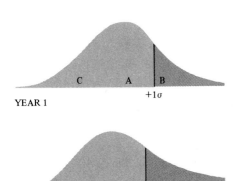

YEAR 1

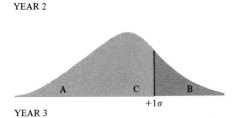

YEAR 2

YEAR 3

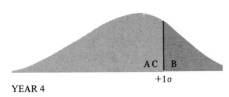

YEAR 4

Procedure

1) Add totals for each school.

School	Number of Times $> 1\sigma$
A	2
B	4
C	0
.	.
.	.
.	.

2) Display frequency distribution of number of times > 1.

Number of Schoois	Number of Times $> 1\sigma$
400	0
301	1
95	2
10	3
2	4

3) Using binomial theorem and assuming independence, compute theoretical frequency distribution of number of times $> 1\sigma$.

$$P(x \text{ successes}) = \binom{4}{x}(0.16)^x (0.84)^{4-x}$$

4) Compare the theoretical and actual distributions using a Chi-square test.

Number	Theoretical		Observed
0	$P = 0.50$	404	400
1	$P = 0.38$	307	301
2	$P = 0.11$	89	95
3	$P = 0.014$	11	10
4	$P = 0.0007$	1	2

Note: $\chi^2 = 4.370$ (not significant)
Degrees of freedom $= 4$

FIG. 2 *Hypothetical illustration of analysis of sets of residuals.*

If some schools appear to be outliers, it is important to see how they differ from the average school. Since in this report we are trying to discover only *if* such schools exist and not *why*, the point of the comparison is not to uncover causal mechanisms, although we may find some clues. Our goal is to separate nonrandom outliers from random variations. If many school-related characteristics of the top performers differ from those of the average school, they will provide strong evidence that we have indeed located schools worthy of detailed study, and not mere statistical quirks. On the other hand, if the only differences are in socioeconomic factors, the outliers may be the result of an omitted variable or heteroskedasticity in the regression.[5]

Michigan school data

The largest of the six data sets examined in this study is the school file compiled by the state of Michigan for 1969–1970 and 1970–1971. More than 2400 schools reported fourth-grade test results for both years, and some 900 schools had seventh-grade results for both years. Most of the schools with seventh-grade results also provided fourth-grade scores. In addition to large sample size, the data have other desirable properties—timeliness, relative novelty,[6] and a large range of variables.

Schools' average scores for five basic achievement tests and a composite were reported, as well as information on policy-related variables, such as staff size, pupil/staff ratios, and teacher characteristics, though these differed somewhat between the 1969–1970 and 1970–1971 data sets. Socioeconomic data came from questionnaires filled out by students when taking the achievement tests; three separate SES indicators and one composite SES index were computed by the state of Michigan for each school. In addition, other questions measured student "friendliness" and attitudes toward achievement, self, and school. Approximately 12% of the schools reported no achievement score data at all, so the results do not reflect a complete sample of Michigan schools.

Preliminary explorations. We examined both mathematics and reading achievement as separate indicators of school effectiveness, and we computed

---

[5] Heteroskedasticity refers to nonconstant variance of residuals around the regression line. If, for example, schools in wealthy areas show greater variability in their achievement scores than those in low- and middle-income areas, most of the high (and low) outliers will be the wealthier schools. The problem is distinguishing "real" socioeconomic differences in residual variation from those occasioned by some property of the socioeconomic measure. This difficulty arose with respect to rural schools in the Michigan data.

[6] Another analysis of the Michigan fourth-grade data has recently appeared (Brown, 1972).

TABLE 1 REGRESSIONS ON MICHIGAN DATA, 1969–1970 AND 1970–1971, FOURTH AND SEVENTH GRADES, READING AND MATHEMATICS TESTS.

Test	Equation	F-ratio	R^2	Control
R769–70	Reading = 32.3 + 0.37(SES)	238	0.20	SES769–70
M769–70	Math = 32.0 + 0.38(SES)	187	0.17	SES769–70
R469–70	Reading = 28.3 + 0.44(SES)	750	0.23	SES469–70
M469–70	Math = 27.4 + 0.46(SES)	802	0.24	SES469–70
R770–71	Reading = 20.5 + 0.60(SES)	739	0.46	SES770–71
M770–71	Math = 16.1 + 0.69(SES)	723	0.45	SES770–71
R470–71	Reading = 20.7 + 0.60(SES)	1949	0.44	SES470–71
M470–71	Math = 18.5 + 0.64(SES)	2107	0.46	SES470–71

Note: R769–70 stands for the regression on reading scores for the seventh grades in 1969–1970. The other symbols are interpreted similarly.

sets of eight regressions on both tests for both grades for both years. To give outliers every opportunity to display themselves, in our first runs we controlled only for socioeconomic status, using the composite SES index for each grade and year. The results appear in Table 1.

Both the reading and mathematics achievement scores are standardized nationwide to have a mean of 50 and an interstudent standard deviation of 10. The range of school mean scores uncontrolled for background factors is large. Between the highest and lowest schools, the range is about 35 points; the difference between the mean scores for the top and bottom 100 schools is around 13 points; and the standard deviation among schools is about 4 points.[7]

The histograms of the residuals are instructive primarily for what they do not show. The overwhelming impression is how normal everything is. Two typical histograms are displayed in Figures 3 and 4.[8] The residuals all display unimodal massing around the mean with little skewness. The small amount of skewness in evidence is inconsistent: skewness statistics range from −0.94 to 0.35; five are negative, three positive. Some tails wander out to four standard deviations, but, given the large sample size, such extensions are not surprising. No lumps or discontinuities appear in the distributions. In short, the histograms reveal a most well-behaved set of residuals—especially since only SES was used as a control. There is no hint that some schools are extraordinarily far above the mean nor that there is discontinuity in educational effectiveness among schools.

---

[7] All these figures were computed from the 1970–1971 fourth-grade reading data.

[8] We plotted nearly 40 additional histograms, all very much like Figures 3 and 4.

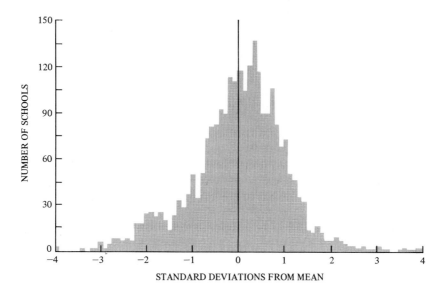

FIG. 3 *Histogram of residuals for 1970–1971 Michigan fourth-grade mathematics test, after controlling for socioeconomic status.*

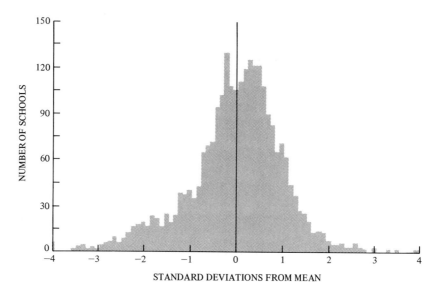

FIG. 4 *Histogram of residuals for 1970–1971 Michigan fourth-grade reading test, after controlling for socioeconomic status.*

However, some schools may remain in the right tails of the distributions of residuals over time, even if each distribution appears to be normal. We checked to see if some schools consistently had residuals more than one standard deviation above the mean, using the cumulative measure outlined earlier. There were three complications to this analysis. First, not every school had a score for each test in each year and grade. (For example, less than 10% of the schools appeared in all eight regressions.) Schools were therefore grouped by how many times out of eight "chances" they reported scores. Different theoretical distributions were computed for schools with eight, six, four, and two chances to be more than one standard deviation out.

A second problem involved the correlation of the mathematics and reading residuals. The correlation between the raw scores for mathematics and reading in the same grade and year was very high, 0.9; and the residuals were correlated about 0.78. This high correlation is not surprising, since the same children were taking the tests, but we had to modify our assumptions that the different residuals were strictly independent.

The following tree shows the eight residuals. There are two years, two grades per year, and two tests per grade. Only the last four pairs of forks are not assumed to be independent by the null hypothesis that no consistently exceptional schools exist. Since the reading and mathematics residuals were correlated about 0.78 for each year, the null hypothesis mi ht be reworded: the four *pairs* of test scores are independent, and each pair is bivariate normally distributed with $\rho = 0.78$. A theoretical distribution could then be computed and compared with the actual distribution using a Chi-square test for goodness of fit.

However, a third problem arises. The empirical distributions of the pairs of scores taken individually did not look bivariate normal. Let X_i be the number of scores in the reading–mathematics pair (R_i, M_i) that exceeds one standard deviation above the mean. X_i has the possible values 0, 1, or 2. If a pair of scores is distributed bivariate normally with $\rho = 0.78$, then $P(X = 0) = 0.777$, $P(X = 1) = 0.128$, and $P(X = 2) = 0.095$. But the average pair of Michigan reading and mathematics scores actually displayed

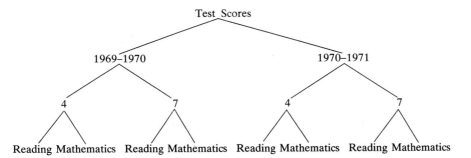

a different distribution: $P(X = 0) \cong 0.846$, $P(X = 1) \cong 0.088$, and $P(X = 2) \cong 0.066$.[9]

The actual distribution is "tighter" than the bivariate normal; that is, schools are less likely to be one standard deviation above the mean at least once in two chances. Also, $P(X=2)$ is larger compared to $P(X=1)$ than in the bivariate normal case, indicating that schools have a greater tendency to be outside both times, given that they are outside at least once.

A score T was computed for each school, where T was the sum of the X_i's for each of the school's n pairs of scores. That is,

$$T = \sum_{i=1}^{n} X_i.$$

(In the case of a school reporting all four pairs of scores, $T = X_1 + X_2 + X_3 + X_4$.) Assuming the X_i's were independent, null distributions were computed using the actual probabilities of 0, 1, and 2 successes per pair, instead of a bivariate normal with $\rho = 0.78$. Then the actual distributions were compared to the null distributions using a Chi-square test.[10]

Table 2 presents the results of our search for schools that consistently had residuals more than one standard deviation above the mean. Here is strong evidence that some schools are persistent outliers. In every case, there are more schools with residuals greater than one standard deviation above the mean than would have been expected on the basis of chance alone. For example, among schools with reported scores for each test/grade/year regression, chance would predict that only five would have four or more residuals (out of eight chances) greater than one standard deviation above the mean, whereas in fact thirty-four did.[11]

---

[9] The actual probabilities for each pair of tests were:

Grade/year	N	$P(X = 0)$	$P(X = 1)$	$P(X = 2)$
469–70	2485	0.841	0.091	0.068
769–70	942	0.868	0.076	0.055
470–71	2469	0.833	0.097	0.070
770–71	876	0.871	0.064	0.065

[10] If a school had eight chances to be outside, the null hypothesis worked from a basis of four pairs of tests; if only six chances, then three pairs of tests; if four chances, two pairs. The chances occurred only in reading–mathematics pairs (any school that reported a reading score for a given grade and year also reported a mathematics score for that grade and year). For simplicity in calculation, we computed the probability for an average Michigan pair from all grades and years and based our null distributions on it. This procedure assumed that it did not matter which particular test pairs made up a school's set of chances, which seemed reasonable in light of the relatively constant sizes of the probabilities across different grades and years.

[11] In order that the Chi-square approximation be accurate in contingency tables with more than one degree of freedom, one must pool cells with small expectations. Throughout this report, we follow a pooling rule proposed by Yarnold (1970, p. 865): "If the number of classes s is three or more, and if r denotes the number of expectations less than five, then the minimum expectation may be as small as 5r/s."

TABLE 2 RESULTS OF CHI-SQUARE TESTS OF DIFFERENCES BETWEEN OBSERVED AND EXPECTED DISTRIBUTIONS OF RESIDUALS FOR MICHIGAN SCHOOLS.

Schools reporting 8 times			Schools reporting 6 times			Schools reporting 4 times		
No. >1	Observed	Expected	No. >1	Observed	Expected	No. >1	Observed	Expected
0	69	84	0	90	102	0	1995	1893
1	31	34	1	37	31	1	309	383
2	18	30	2	22	27	2	197	307
3	9	8	3	6	5	3	69	32
4	10 ⎫		4	8 ⎫		4	56	11
5	6 ⎪		5	4 ⎬ 12	2			
6	8 ⎬ 34	5	6	0 ⎭				
7	3 ⎪							
8	7 ⎭							

$\chi^2 = 200.9$, Degrees of Freedom $= 4$	$\chi^2 = 46.7$, Degrees of Freedom $= 4$	$\chi^2 = 301.1$, Degrees of Freedom $= 4$

Note: All residuals are derived from a fit of achievement to SES alone. All Chi-square statistics are significant at the 0.005 level.

However, significant Chi-square statistics alone must not be taken as evidence of consistent positive outliers, since the Chi-square statistic reflects differences between the actual and the estimated distributions throughout the entire distribution. A larger number of underachievers than expected can therefore affect the Chi-square as much as a larger number of over-achievers. The Chi-square statistics in Table 2 are therefore less important than the visual evidence that consistent overachievers may exist.[12]

Since we controlled only for socioecomonic status in determining these residuals, the outliers could reflect some other, uncontrolled background variables and not the existence of overachieving schools. To examine this possibility, we first ranked schools on the basis of one of the regressions (the size of their fourth-grade reading residuals for 1970–1971) and then compared 19 school and background variables among the top 100, middle 100, and bottom 100 schools. The results appear in Table 3. Our goal was to determine whether the top schools differed significantly from the others in terms of some omitted nonschool factor.

Controlling for additional variables. As a result of Table 3, we ran new regressions that included controls for racial composition and community

---

[12] Of course, if the Chi-square statistic is not significant, it provides strong evidence that consistent outliers do not exist.

TABLE 3 COMPARISONS AMONG THE TOP 100, MIDDLE 100, AND BOTTOM 100 MICHIGAN SCHOOLS RANKED BY RESIDUALS ON THE FOURTH-GRADE READING TEST, 1970–1971.

Variable	Bottom 100		Middle 100	
	Mean	Std. dev.	Mean	Std. dev.
Teacher characteristics				
Pupil/teacher ratio	25.1	0.4	25.6	0.4
% Teachers with over 5 years' experience	57	17	55	13
% Teachers with Master's degrees	27	15	26	16
% Teachers earning over $11,000	41	20	38	22
Test scores				
Vocabulary	43.3	3.8	51.1	3.4
Reading	41.3	3.3	51.5	2.5
Mechanical engineering	42.4	3.9	51.3	2.9
Mathematics	42.6	4.3	51.5	3.2
Composite	42.2	3.6	51.5	2.7
Attitude scores				
Toward achievement	51.6	3.5	50.1	2.3
Toward self	50.3	2.4	49.9	2.6
Toward school	49.3	3.3	49.9	2.3
"Friendliness"	49.3	5.1	50.5	2.6
Background factors				
% White enrollment	38	38	89	15
Composite SES (regressor)	46.6	5.0	51.3	4.2
SES factor 1	45.2	5.3	51.3	3.1
SES factor 2	50.2	3.6	50.4	4.3
SES factor 4	47.4	3.0	50.1	2.8
Urban/rural (urban core = 1, rural = 5)	2.1	1.6	3.3	1.4

type.[13] Two other studies of the Michigan data also use community and regional differences as regressor variables. Brown (1972) found achievement differences that appeared to be related to rural–urban location. Arthur Alexander, in an unpublished investigation, compared 22 high-scoring

---

[13] The Michigan data set classifies schools according to their location in one of five "community types":
    1. Metropolitan core
    2. City (population from 10,000–50,000)
    3. Town (2,500–10,000)
    4. Urban fringe
    5. Rural (less than 2,500)

TABLE 3 Continued

Variable	Top 100		t-Statistics		
	Mean	Std. dev.	B − M	M − T	B − T
Teacher characteristics					
Pupil/teacher ratio	24.4	0.4	−0.8	3.0*	1.2
% Teachers with over 5 years' experience	65	21	0.8	−7.5*	−4.8*
% Teachers with Master's degrees	20	18	0.2	3.6*	4.2*
% Teachers earning over $11,000	27	26	1.0	5.2*	7.3*
Test scores					
Vocabulary	54.4	4.4	−15.4*	−9.8*	−29.3*
Reading	55.8	2.4	−24.5*	−16.7*	−43.5*
Mechanical engineering	54.5	3.9	−18.2*	−11.4*	−30.8*
Mathematics	55.0	4.0	−16.7*	−10.9*	−29.0*
Composite	55.1	3.0	−20.5*	−13.3*	−35.5*
Attitude scores					
Toward achievement	49.9	4.6	1.2	5.3*	4.9*
Toward self	48.8	4.4	0.9	4.5*	6.1*
Toward school	50.8	3.8	−1.6	−4.1*	−4.8*
"Friendliness"	50.8	5.0	−7.2*	−1.3	−8.8*
Background factors					
% White enrollment	90	12	−12.5*	−0.6	−13.7*
Composite SES (regressor)	47.2	4.1	−7.3*	9.6	−1.3
SES factor 1	50.1	5.2	−10.0*	3.8*	−9.3*
SES factor 2	46.5	4.1	−0.4	9.0*	10.0*
SES factor 4	49.2	4.9	−6.7*	3.5*	−5.9*
Urban/rural (urban core = 1, *rural* = 5)	3.8	1.4	−5.6*	−3.5*	−10.6*

Note: An asterisk (*) indicates difference not equal to zero at the 0.005 significance level.

schools with 32 low-scoring schools. Both sets of schools were also compared with the total group of 2400 schools. After selecting his samples, Alexander compared pupil/teacher ratios, class size, SES variables, community type, and differences in the characteristics of school principals. He found that the only major difference between the two groups was geographical. The high-scoring schools were concentrated in small towns and rural areas, whereas the others tended to be in large cities and industrial suburbs.

TABLE 4 MICHIGAN SCHOOL REGRESSIONS, CONTROLLING FOR RACIAL COMPOSITION, COMMUNITY TYPE, AND SOCIOECONOMIC STATUS.

Test	Equation	R^2	Standard error	Number of schools
R469–70	$Y = 32.17 - \underset{\substack{(\% \text{ minority}) \\ 904.3}}{0.08} + \underset{\substack{(\text{SES 4}) \\ 829.9}}{0.40} \underset{\substack{(\text{C1}) \\ 25.0}}{-1.09} + \underset{\substack{(\text{C2}) \\ 0.1}}{0.08} \underset{\substack{(\text{C4}) \\ 27.8}}{-0.97} + \underset{\substack{(\text{C5}) \\ 0.1}}{0.07}$	0.53	2.86	2485
M469–70	$Y = 31.39 - \underset{\substack{(\% \text{ minority}) \\ 867.8}}{0.08} + \underset{\substack{(\text{SES 4}) \\ 844.6}}{0.41} \underset{\substack{(\text{C1}) \\ 13.7}}{-0.83} + \underset{\substack{(\text{C2}) \\ 0.4}}{0.16} \underset{\substack{(\text{C4}) \\ 19.0}}{-0.82} + \underset{\substack{(\text{C5}) \\ 0.1}}{0.06}$	0.52	2.94	2485
R769–70	$Y = 34.07 - \underset{\substack{(\% \text{ minority}) \\ 261.0}}{0.08} + \underset{\substack{(\text{SES 7}) \\ 246.4}}{0.35} \underset{\substack{(\text{C1}) \\ 1.4}}{-0.43} + \underset{\substack{(\text{C2}) \\ 5.1}}{0.94} \underset{\substack{(\text{C4}) \\ 10.2}}{-1.00} + \underset{\substack{(\text{C5}) \\ 1.4}}{0.35}$	0.48	2.74	942
M769–70	$Y = 33.79 - \underset{\substack{(\% \text{ minority}) \\ 275.5}}{0.09} + \underset{\substack{(\text{SES 7}) \\ 215.7}}{0.37} \underset{\substack{(\text{C1}) \\ 8.5}}{-1.19} + \underset{\substack{(\text{C2}) \\ 0.2}}{0.21} \underset{\substack{(\text{C4}) \\ 14.1}}{-1.30} + \underset{\substack{(\text{C5}) \\ 2.0}}{0.46}$	0.50	3.04	942
R470–71	$Y = 28.98 - \underset{\substack{(\% \text{ minority}) \\ 429.7}}{0.06} + \underset{\substack{(\text{SES 4}) \\ 1097.9}}{0.46} \underset{\substack{(\text{C1}) \\ 33.9}}{-1.17} + \underset{\substack{(\text{C2}) \\ 0.6}}{0.17} \underset{\substack{(\text{C4}) \\ 30.5}}{-0.92} + \underset{\substack{(\text{C5}) \\ 2.3}}{0.27}$	0.58	2.64	2469
M470–71	$Y = 26.99 - \underset{\substack{(\% \text{ minority}) \\ 417.4}}{0.06} + \underset{\substack{(\text{SES 4}) \\ 1181.1}}{0.49} \underset{\substack{(\text{C1}) \\ 11.7}}{-1.00} + \underset{\substack{(\text{C2}) \\ 1.2}}{0.26} \underset{\substack{(\text{C4}) \\ 15.6}}{-0.69} + \underset{\substack{(\text{C5}) \\ 1.1}}{0.19}$	0.58	2.78	2469
R770–71	$Y = 29.06 - \underset{\substack{(\% \text{ minority}) \\ 134.5}}{0.06} + \underset{\substack{(\text{SES 7}) \\ 346.2}}{0.45} \underset{\substack{(\text{C1}) \\ 0.9}}{-0.31} + \underset{\substack{(\text{C2}) \\ 0.3}}{0.21} \underset{\substack{(\text{C4}) \\ 1.1}}{-0.29} + \underset{\substack{(\text{C5}) \\ 2.0}}{0.45}$	0.55	2.38	876
M770–71	$Y = 27.96 - \underset{\substack{(\% \text{ minority}) \\ 165.0}}{0.07} + \underset{\substack{(\text{SES 7}) \\ 222.6}}{0.48} \underset{\substack{(\text{C1}) \\ 17.8}}{-1.53} + \underset{\substack{(\text{C2}) \\ 0.1}}{0.10} \underset{\substack{(\text{C4}) \\ 4.4}}{-0.70} + \underset{\substack{(\text{C5}) \\ 1.4}}{0.34}$	0.60	2.59	876

Note: C1, C2, C4, and C5 are dummies for community types: 1 = metropolitan core; 2 = city (10,000–50,000); 4 = urban fringe; 5 = rural (<2500). R469–70 stands for the regression on reading scores for the fourth grades in 1969–1970. The other symbols are interpreted similarly. Figures below the regression coefficients are the F-ratios $(= t^2)$.

Editors' Note: In the table the following convention has been adopted. The variable given in parentheses under each regression coefficient is to be multiplied by that coefficient. Thus, the top equation is to be read Y equals 32.17 less 0.08 times (% minority) plus 0.40 times (SES 4), etc.

We investigated the changes in the relationship between achievement and background variables when dummy variables for community type are added to the estimating equations, and when the racial composition of the school is controlled. Table 4 shows some of the results. The addition of these variables increases the explanatory power of the regression. A comparison of Table 4 with Table 1 shows that the R^2's are now about 10 to 30 percentage points higher. Moreover, the explanatory power of the 1969–1970 regressions now matches that of the 1970–1971 regressions. The inclusion of racial composition and community type apparently compensates for the imperfections in the 1969–1970 SES questionnaire.

If a regional variable is not included, some of the community types enter with significant coefficients. If both community type and region are included in our equations, the regional coefficients are significant but the community-type coefficients have low F-values.

Interestingly, the histograms of residuals from these more complicated regressions show some evidence of unusual right tails. Figures 5 and 6 give two examples. Compared with the histograms from the simpler fit, these show far more schools three and four standard deviations above the mean. Apparently, these outliers were masked earlier by the variability due to racial composition and community type. The two additional background controls reduced overall variability, allowing unusually effective schools to stand out more in the right end of the distribution. Table 5 compares the actual number of outliers to the number expected if the residuals were distributed normally. The mathematics scores in particular show many schools on the right tail.

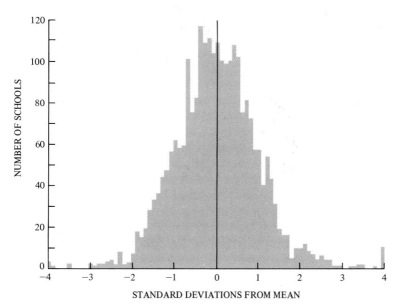

FIG. 5 *Histogram of residuals for 1969–1970 Michigan fourth-grade mathematics test, from a regression controlling for racial composition, community type, and socioeconomic status.*

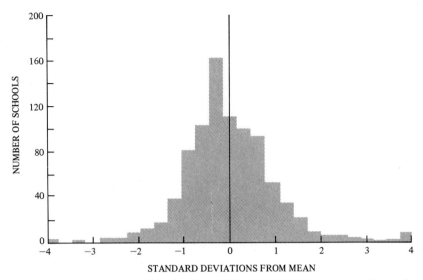

FIG. 6 *Histogram of residuals for 1970–1971 Michigan seventh-grade mathematics test, from a regression controlling for racial composition, community type, and socioeconomic status.*

These deviations from normality are, however, not astoundingly large. We cited earlier a number of reasons to expect deviations from a normal distribution even if all schools had the same effectiveness. A more powerful test is available. As before, we can examine the distribution of residuals over tests and over time. When controlling the SES alone, we found that more schools than chance would allow consistently exhibited residuals greater than one standard deviation above the mean. If these outliers disappear after we control for racial composition and community type, it would seem that our previous results were a function not of unusually effective schools but of previously uncontrolled background factors.

However, Table 6 indicates that, even after controlling for race and community type, there are still more outliers than chance would predict.[14] In

---

[14] The reading and mathematics residuals were again correlated for each grade and year, in the following fashion:

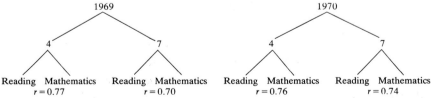

TABLE 5 NUMBER OF EXPECTED AND OBSERVED MICHIGAN SCHOOLS WITH LARGE RESIDUAL TEST SCORES AFTER CONTROLLING FOR RACIAL COMPOSITION, COMMUNITY TYPE, AND SOCIOECONOMIC STATUS.

Residuals	Number observed	Number expected in normal distribution	Total number of schools
R469–70 ≥ 2 std. dev.	50	56.7	2486
≥ 3 std. dev.	8	3.2	
≥ 4 std. dev.	3	0.1	
M469–70 ≥ 2 std. dev.	75	56.7	2485
≥ 3 std. dev.	18	3.2	
≥ 4 std. dev.	10	0.1	
R769–70 ≥ 2 std. dev.	24	21.5	943
≥ 3 std. dev.	8	1.2	
≥ 4 std. dev.	2	0.05	
M769–70 ≥ 2 std. dev.	32	21.5	942
≥ 3 std. dev.	12	1.2	
≥ 4 std. dev.	1	0.05	
R470–71 ≥ 2 std. dev.	57	56.2	2469
≥ 3 std. dev.	16	3.2	
≥ 4 std. dev.	5	0.1	
M470–71 ≥ 2 std. dev.	79	56.2	2469
≥ 3 std. dev.	22	3.2	
≥ 4 std. dev.	7	0.1	
R770–71 ≥ 2 std. dev.	21	20.0	876
≥ 3 std. dev.	8	1.1	
≥ 4 std. dev.	3	0.05	
M770–71 ≥ 2 std. dev.	30	20.0	876
≥ 3 std. dev.	14	1.1	
≥ 4 std. dev.	4	0.05	

Note: R469–70 stands for fourth-grade reading scores in 1969–1970. Other symbols are interpreted similarly.

The empirical probabilities for each pair are:

Grade/year	N	$P(X=0)$	$P(X=1)$	$P(X=2)$
469–70	2485	0.826	0.099	0.076
769–70	942	0.860	0.084	0.056
470–71	2469	0.830	0.097	0.073
770–71	876	0.858	0.079	0.063

For simplicity in calculating the theoretical distributions, we assumed each pair had $P(X=0)=0.84$, $P(X=1)=0.09$, and $P(X=2)=0.07$.

fact, there are nearly as many schools above one standard deviation with the complicated controls as with SES alone. The interschool standard deviation is now slightly smaller: the standard errors for the regressions using SES, racial composition, and community type range between 2.38 and 3.04, as opposed to a spread of 2.61 to 3.92 with SES alone. The new results therefore suggest that the earlier findings were not mere statistical artifacts resulting from undercontrolling.

To verify this interpretation, we examined the characteristics of the top 15 schools of those reporting scores for all 8 test/grade/year combinations ($N = 161$). These are the 15 schools that are "outside" at least 6 times out of 8. They average 2 standard deviations above the mean per test; the top 2 average 2.8 standard deviations above the mean. Since the standard errors of the regressions are approximately 3 points, the top 15 schools average about 6 points above the mean even after controlling for SES, racial composition, and community type.

Are 6 points a lot? Recalling that the tests are constructed with an interstudent standard deviation of 10 points, the 15 top schools raise their children about three-fifths of a standard deviation. Put differently, about 9% of the schools are unusually effective in the sense that they seem to raise students on average from the fiftieth to the seventy-second percentile, holding SES, racial composition, and community type constant. In grade-equivalent terms, three-fifths of a standard deviation on the fourth-grade

TABLE 6 RESULTS OF CHI-SQUARE TESTS OF DIFFERENCES BETWEEN OBSERVED AND EXPECTED DISTRIBUTIONS OF RESIDUALS FOR MICHIGAN SCHOOLS, REVISED REGRESSIONS.

Schools reporting 8 times			Schools reporting 6 times			Schools reporting 4 times		
No. >1	Observed	Expected	No. >1	Observed	Expected	No. >1	Observed	Expected
0	65	80	0	96	99	0	1946	1856
1	29	35	1	32	32	1	328	400
2	24	32	2	22	28	2	230	331
3	12	9	3	7	5	3	62	32
4	7⎫		4	6⎫		4	63	13
5	9⎪		5	4⎬10	3			
6	5⎬31	5	6	0⎭				
7	3⎪							
8	7⎭							
$\chi^2 = 133.9$, Degrees of freedom = 4			$\chi^2 = 22.7$, Degrees of freedom = 4			$\chi^2 = 266.6$, Degrees of freedom = 4		

Note: All residuals are derived from a fit of achievement to SES, racial composition, and community type. All Chi-square statistics are significant at the 0.005 level.

TABLE 7 CHARACTERISTICS OF FIFTEEN OVERACHIEVING MICHIGAN SCHOOLS.

School	Mean SES	Community type	Percent minority
1	44.6	Rural	0
2	44.1	Rural	0
3	44:6	City	4.9
4	45.9	Rural	0
5	53.2	Rural	0
6	47.1	City	0
7	48.1	Rural	0
8	47.8	Rural	9.1
9	46.1	City	0
10	43.1	Rural	1.8
11	44.2	Rural	0
12	47.1	City	0
13	42.4	Rural	0
14	41.7	Rural	4.3
15	46.3	Rural	0
State averages	49.9	Metropolitan core = 808 City = 331 Town = 659 Urban fringe = 1257 Rural = 1062	11.0

Note: Top 15 schools computed from among 161 schools that reported scores for all 8 test/grade/year combinations. Regressors were mean school SES, percent minority enrollment, and community-type dummy variables.

Iowa reading test is about four-fifths of a year. On the seventh-grade test, it is equivalent to about one full grade.[15]

The differences between these exceptional schools and schools that are below average are, of course, even larger.

Do the top schools have any features in common? Table 7 characterizes them along the three control variables. Even after controlling for SES, racial composition, and community type, the top fifteen schools are predominantly below the state averages on both SES and minority enrollment and tend to be located in rural communities. Only one was above the state SES average; only four had any nonwhite students, and the highest percentage of minority students (9.1) was still below the state average. Only four schools were not located in community type 5, but even these four were in the predominantly

---

[15] The grade equivalents are slightly lower for the Iowa mathematics tests: about three-fifths of a year for the fourth-grade test and nine-tenths of a year for the seventh-grade test (Lindquist and Hieronymus, 1964). Three-fifths of an interstudent standard deviation on most IQ tests is nine points.

rural Michigan peninsula region. How could these results occur after controlling for all three of these variables in the regressions?

There are a number of possible explanations. Suppose the rural schools are simply not as large as the others. If many fewer students were tested in such schools, we would expect the variation of rural school means to be higher. If so, both the underachieving and overachieving schools might be rural, merely because of their smaller sample size.[16]

To test this explanation, we ran a new regression that controlled for number of students tested as well as SES, racial composition, and community type. The variable for number tested was barely significant, and added only 0.005 to the percentage of variation explained (its regression coefficient was −0.008). Similar results occurred when the natural logarithm of the number tested was used in the multiple regression.

We also plotted achievement scores against the number tested for a random sample of 400 schools for the fourth-grade reading data from 1970–1971. The result appears in Figure 7. The variation of school means is nearly constant to about 100 tested; then it appears to drop slightly. But it is really the average school score that diminishes, not the variability of the data. The schools with larger numbers of students tested also turn out to be those with lower SES, so they also have lower mean achievement scores. Comparing the vertical spread of the data around two hypothetical group averages, one sees that the number of children tested does not seem to correlate with differences in the variability of school means. Most importantly, the highest- and lowest-achieving schools do not have the smallest number tested. Thus, some variable besides sample size must be adduced to explain the results of Table 7.

Heteroskedasticity problems. Perhaps some aspect of the fitting procedure accounts for these results. One might expect an equal number of outstanding schools with both low and high SES, with low and high minority enrollment, and from all five community types—but only if achievement has a linear relationship with these independent variables and the residuals have a constant variance. Thus, two characteristics of the data might have caused the exceptional schools to be mostly low SES, white, and rural. First, the dependence of achievement on these variables might not be linear. Second, the residuals from a linear fit might not display a constant variance for all levels of SES, percent minority, and community types.

---

[16] Suppose all children had an expected score of 50 and a standard deviation of 10 and were randomly distributed throughout the state. The large schools might average 100 children tested; the small schools only 10. The standard deviation of the estimate of a school's true score is a function of the number tested: std. dev. $(\bar{x}) = \sigma/\sqrt{n}$. Thus, the standard deviation of $(\bar{x})$ for schools of size 100 would be $10/\sqrt{100} = 1$; whereas for schools with 10 students tested it would be $10/\sqrt{10}$—more than three times as large. One would therefore expect the smaller schools to have more outliers than larger schools, even though by hypothesis they have "identical" students.

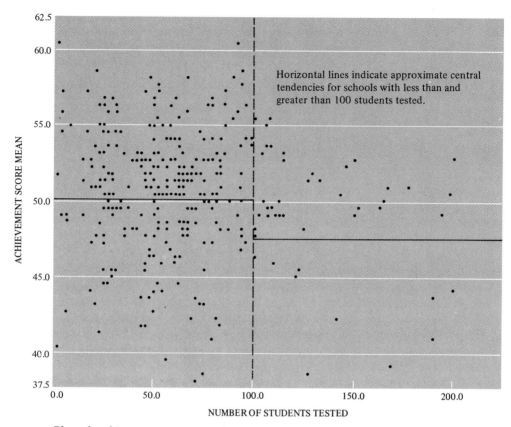

FIG. 7 *Plot of achievement scores and number of students tested, random sample of 400 Michigan schools (R470-71).*

To find out, we checked the plotted residuals for evidence of curvilinearity and heteroskedasticity. Figure 8 displays the plot of achievement scores against percent minority enrollment. It exhibits curvilinearity—note the U-shape of the plot—but more important, it shows unequal residual variance as well. The variability of school means among schools with low percentages of minority students is much larger than among those with greater percentages. The set of schools with very low minority enrollment therefore contains both overachieving and underachieving schools to a greater extent than the set with more minority students.

Heteroskedasticity also occurs with respect to community types. For each of the five types, we regressed fourth-grade reading scores for 1970–1971 against SES and racial composition. The results appear in Table 8. The fit is best for the metropolitan core schools ($R^2 = 0.74$); it is by far the worst for the rural schools ($R^2 = 0.07$). Such a fit means, of course, that rural schools exhibit far more variability than other schools, which could account for their disproportional presence among the top 15 schools.

The results of Table 8, then, reflect heteroskedasticity. The greater variance of rural schools may reflect some important characteristics unique to those schools, but the danger is that it instead reflects imperfections in the SES measures. It is notoriously difficult to compare the economic well-being of rural and urban communities. If the heteroskedasticity is a result of imperfect SES controls, our efforts to locate unusually effective schools may succumb to all manner of misidentification.

Therefore, we tried new regressions to avoid the heteroskedasticity problem. All rural schools were excluded. Instead of treating minority enrollment as a continuous variable, we dichotomized it: all schools with less

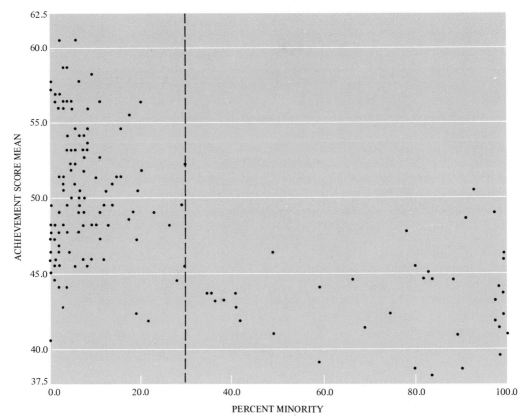

FIG. 8 *Plot of achievement scores and percent minority, random sample of 400 Michigan schools (R470-71).*

TABLE 8 MICHIGAN SCHOOL REGRESSIONS STRATIFIED BY COMMUNITY TYPE, FOURTH-GRADE READING TEST, 1970–1971.

Community type	Equation	R^2	Mean R470	Mean SES	Mean % minority	Standard error	Number of schools
1. Metropolitan core	R470 = 24.01 + 0.54 (SES) − 0.06 (% minority)	0.74	47.5	47.5	34.3	2.56	424
2. City	R470 = 28.63 + 0.47 (SES) − 0.06 (% minority)	0.57	51.3	49.9	10.6	2.59	224
3. Town	R470 = 31.70 + 0.40 (SES) − 0.09 (% minority)	0.27	51.6	50.0	3.4	2.44	374
4. Urban fringe	R470 = 27.55 + 0.46 (SES) − 0.05 (% minority)	0.51	51.5	51.9	3.4	2.24	824
5. Rural	R470 = 37.45 + 0.28 (SES) − 0.02 (% minority)	0.07	50.9	49.1	3.2	3.23	547

than one-third minority students were assigned a dummy value of one, all others a zero.[17] SES and community type for the remaining schools were controlled as before, except that the more valid 1970–1971 SES rating was used for the 1969–1970 data as well.[18] The results of these regressions appear in Table 9.

A few details about these regressions are noteworthy, although not central to the task of discovering whether consistent outliers still exist. First, they have greater explanatory power. Second, the SES variable has a relatively stable coefficient in all the equations, hovering around 0.5. Third, the new regressions explain seventh-grade scores much better than fourth-grade scores. The R^2's for the former range from 0.72 to 0.78, whereas those for the latter vary between 0.59 and 0.66. Perhaps this result is due to the

---

[17] We experimented with various nonlinear transformations of the minority enrollment variable on a sample of the data, but they neither significantly raised the percentage of variation explained nor solved the heteroskedasticity problem. Looking again at Figure 8, one might imagine two sets of data divided by the dotted line. Both sets appear to be randomly distributed around two lines with zero slopes but different intercepts. The data provide a classic case where the use of a dummy variable is warranted: identical slopes but different intercepts.

[18] The 1970–1971 SES data refer, of course, to the particular fourth- and seventh-graders who provided them. Thus, they do not correspond to the exact data that would have been obtained from the 1969–1970 students. However, we judged that the correspondence would be close enough to warrant the use of the vastly superior 1970–1971 ratings.

TABLE 9 MICHIGAN SCHOOL REGRESSIONS. OMITTING RURAL SCHOOLS.

Test	Equation						R^2	Standard error	Number of schools
R469–70	$Y = 22.18 +$	4.12 (MIN) 325.1	$+$ 0.50 (SES 4) 1200.0	$-$ 0.78 (C1) 16.1	$+$ 0.27 (C2) 1.6	$-$ 0.78 (C4) 21.9	0.62	2.56	1836
M469–70	$Y = 22.32 +$	4.14 (MIN) 299.1	$+$ 0.50 (SES 4) 1077.9	$-$ 0.53 (C1) 6.7	$+$ 0.02 (C2) 0.0	$-$ 0.65 (C4) 13.9	0.59	2.68	1836
R769–70	$Y = 21.00 +$	2.73 (MIN) 86.7	$+$ 0.54 (SES 7) 647.3	$+$ 0.02 (C1) 0.0	$-$ 0.46 (C2) 2.2	$-$ 0.44 (C4) 4.5	0.75	1.72	480
M769–70	$Y = 20.40 +$	3.61 (MIN) 99.1	$+$ 0.54 (SES 7) 422.2	$-$ 0.56 (C1) 3.4	$+$ 0.71 (C2) 3.5	$-$ 0.44 (C4) 2.9	0.72	2.13	480
R470–71	$Y = 22.65 +$	4.13 (MIN) 373.6	$+$ 0.50 (SES 4) 1346.8	$-$ 1.45 (C1) 62.9	$+$ 0.06 (C2) 0.1	$-$ 1.01 (C4) 42.3	0.66	2.44	1891
M470–71	$Y = 20.33 +$	4.39 (MIN) 385.1	$+$ 0.54 (SES 4) 1433.5	$-$ 1.26 (C1) 43.2	$+$ 0.16 (C2) 0.5	$-$ 0.79 (C4) 23.9	0.66	2.55	1891
R770–71	$Y = 20.88 +$	3.89 (MIN) 184.5	$+$ 0.53 (SES 7) 661.5	$-$ 0.40 (C1) 2.6	$+$ 0.23 (C2) 0.6	$-$ 0.44 (C4) 4.6	0.78	1.78	530
M770–71	$Y = 20.80 +$	4.65 (MIN) 200.8	$+$ 0.53 (SES 7) 491.7	$-$ 1.84 (C1) 42.9	$+$ 0.11 (C2) 0.1	$-$ 0.79 (C4) 11.1	0.78	2.04	530

Note: SES is based only on the school's 1970–1971 fourth- and seventh-grade scores. The minority enrollment dummy variable (MIN) has a value of 1 if percent minority < 33.3, 0 otherwise. C1, C2, and C4 are dummies for community types with those numbers. Figures below the regression coefficients are the F-ratios ($= t^2$) R469–70 stands for the regression on reading scores for the fourth grades in 1969–1970. The other symbols are interpreted similarly.

Editors' Note: See Editors' Note below Table 4 for reading the regression equations in this table.

larger number of students tested in the average seventh grade (about 220) compared to that in the average fourth grade (about 65). The larger the sample size, the smaller the sampling error—and, consequently, the larger the percentage of variation explained by the regression line.

Our main concern, however, is the presence of consistent overachievers.

Table 10 gives the results of the new Chi-square analysis.[19] The results are encouraging. Of the 87 schools reporting eight scores, five have seven or eight scores above one standard deviation, when less than one was expected by chance alone. These schools average 2.0 interschool standard deviations above the mean on each test. Since the standard errors of the regressions averaged 2.24, these five schools score four to five points higher than the average school, even after controlling for SES, percent minority enrollment, and community type. Fourteen schools are outside at least four times, compared to only four predicted by the null distribution.

Among schools reporting four scores, 72 are outside each time, compared to 13 predicted by chance. These 72 schools average 1.65 standard deviations above the mean each time, or about 3.7 points higher than the average school's test score. Restating these results in more intuitive terms:

- Of the schools reporting eight scores, about 6% move their students from the fiftieth to the sixty-seventh percentile, after allowing for chance variation and controlling for SES, percent minority enrollment, and community type.

- Of the schools reporting four scores, about 2.5 percent move their students from the fiftieth to the sixty-fifth percentile, after allowing for chance variation and controlling for SES, percent minority enrollment, and community type.

---

[19] The residuals were correlated as follows:

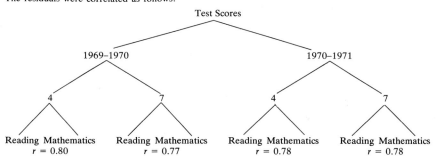

The empirical probabilities for each pair are:

Grade/year	N	P(X = 0)	P(X = 1)	P(X = 2)
469–70	1836	0.808	0.104	0.088
769–70	480	0.831	0.092	0.077
470–71	1891	0.806	0.112	0.082
770–71	530	0.832	0.083	0.085

For simplicity in calculating the theoretical distributions, we assumed each pair had $P(X = 0) = 0.82$, $P(X = 1) = 0.10$, and $P(X = 2) = 0.08$.

TABLE 10 RESULTS OF CHI-SQUARE TESTS OF DIFFERENCES BETWEEN OBSERVED AND EXPECTED DISTRIBUTIONS OF RESIDUALS FOR MICHIGAN SCHOOLS, OMITTING RURAL SCHOOLS.

Schools reporting 8 times			Schools reporting 4 times		
No. >1	Observed	Expected	No. >1	Observed	Expected
0	36	39	0	1493	1432
1	18	19	1	282	349
2	11	19	2	203	303
3	8	6	3	81	34
4	7 ⎫		4	72	13
5	1 ⎪				
6	1 ⎬ 14	4			
7	2 ⎪				
8	3 ⎭				
$\chi^2 = 32.6$, Degrees of Freedom = 4			$\chi^2 = 387.2$, Degrees of Freedom = 4		

Note: The Chi-square statistics are significant at the 0.005 level.

We can also make a strong negative statement. No schools in this sample of Michigan schools raise children's scores more than two-thirds of an interstudent standard deviation above the mean.[20] Thus, after giving schools credit for all residual variation and all possible errors resulting from undercontrolling, no school seems able to raise children, on average, more than about six or seven test points (on tests with mean 50, standard deviation 10).

Characteristics of exceptional schools. Our next task was a preliminary investigation of differences between the overachieving schools and the average ones. We did not attempt to locate causal relationships, although of course the existence of regular differences would suggest such relationships. The primary purpose was to see if the schools that seemed to be unusually effective represented truly nonrandom phenomena or merely statistical artifacts.

For both the top 72 schools[21] and all the Michigan nonrural schools, we tabulated the means and standard deviations for eleven variables, which fell into three groups:

---

[20] The highest average for any school is 2.96 interschool standard deviations.

[21] We used the 72 schools that reported four out of four scores at least one standard deviation above the mean. These schools composed about 2.5 percent of the total number of nonrural schools that reported four scores. See Table 10.

1. *School variables.* These included percentage of teachers with more than five years' teaching experience, master's degrees, and salaries exceeding $11,000 annually, as well as the school's pupil/teacher ratio. We hypothesized that, if several of these variables showed significant differences between top schools and the state average, it would provide strong corroborating evidence that these top schools were not mere random deviations.

2. *Background variables.* We examined differences in racial composition and SES for both fourth and seventh grades. Differences along these variables might indicate that the fit was not linear or that heteroskedasticity still existed. Differences here might therefore imply that the outliers were a product of imperfect statistical controls, especially if no differences existed in school variables.

3. *Number of students tested.* Although earlier regressions showed that adding the number of students tested as an independent variable did not appreciably help the fit, this variable might still have a significant effect on the outliers. As indicated earlier, we would expect schools with fewer students tested to exhibit greater variation in their mean scores. If the 72 outstanding schools all had very low numbers of students tested, they might rightly be called statistical artifacts instead of unusually effective schools.

In addition, we compared the top and average schools along geographical (both community type and region) and other variables. The results appear in Tables 11 and 12.

Clear and important differences appear in the school-related variables between the top and average schools. Three of the four differences are statistically significant. The unusually effective nonrural schools tend to have lower pupil/teacher ratios, more experienced teachers, and more teachers earning annual salaries over $11,000. They also tend to have more teachers holding Master's degrees, but the difference is not significant.

None of the background variables shows significant differences. The percentage of minority enrollment is close, with $z = 1.61$ ($z_{0.05} = 1.645$). The average nonrural school has 17% minority students, whereas the 72 top schools average only about 13%. Interestingly, the unusually effective schools are slightly below average on SES, although not significantly so. Given our control variables, the richer schools do not tend to excel. Both the percent minority and SES results are reassuring: errors in the control variables probably did not account for the 72 schools at the top.

The differences between the top and average schools in number of students tested show up as highly significant for fourth grades, but not at all for seventh grades (in fact, in one case the sign is the opposite). The top 72 schools tend to have fewer fourth-graders tested than the average school. However, this difference is only about 10 to 13 students; both sets of schools have enough children tested (50 to 60) to make differences in variability due to sample size extremely small. Thus, the variation in outcomes between the top 72 and average schools does not seem attributable to differences in the numbers of students they had tested.

The results for community type are also encouraging. The outstanding schools tend to be distributed among the four nonrural types randomly, so the dummies for community type are not responsible for the 72 outliers. The regional results do show significant differences between the top and average schools: a disproportional number of the top schools are located in the

TABLE 11 COMPARISONS BETWEEN THE TOP 72 AND ALL NONRURAL SCHOOLS, MICHIGAN DATA.

Variables	Top 72 schools[a]			All nonrural Michigan schools			z-Statistic[b]
	Mean	Std. dev.	Number tested	Mean	Std. dev.	Number tested	
School variables							
% Teachers with >5 years' experience	67.5	16.6	72	59.1	18.6	2951	*4.23†*
% Teachers with Master's degrees	29.2	15.1	72	28.7	15.2	2704	*0.28*
% Teachers earning >\$11,000	51.1	21.5	72	46.2	20.4	2828	*1.91**
Pupil/teacher ratio	24.5	3.5	72	25.3	3.8	2910	*−1.91**
Background variables							
% Minority enrollment	12.9	21.1	72	17.0	31.3	3056	*−1.61*
SES470	49.4	4.4	57	50.1	4.9	1923	*−1.18*
SES770	46.9	7.8	15	49.8	4.8	555	*−1.43*
Number tested							
469–70	53	24	57	66	34	1986	*−3.98†*
769–70	208	146	17	214	133	610	*−0.17*
470–71	56	25	57	66	34	1984	*−2.94†*
770–71	237	155	15	228	137	579	*0.22*

Note: 469–70 stands for the regressions on both reading and arithmetic tests for the fourth grades in 1969–1970. The other symbols are interpreted similarly.
[a] The "top 72" schools are those that were at least one standard deviation above the mean four out of four times. (See Table 10.)
[b] An asterisk (*) indicates significance at the 0.05 level. A dagger (†) indicates significance at the 0.001 level. All other z-statistics are insignificant.

TABLE 12 GEOGRAPHICAL COMPARISONS BETWEEN TOP 72 AND ALL NONRURAL SCHOOLS, MICHIGAN DATA.

Community type and location	Top 72 schools[a]				All nonrural Michigan schools				χ^{2b}
	1	2	3	4	1	2	3	4	
Community type									
Number	21	9	19	24	808	331	659	1257	
Percentage	29.1	11.1	26.3	33.3	26.4	10.8	21.6	41.1	2.04
Region									
Number	21	33	5	13	1271	1413	116	121	
Percentage	29.1	45.8	6.9	18.0	41.6	46.2	3.8	4.0	40.11*

[a] The "top 72" schools are those that were at least one standard deviation above the mean four out of four times. (See Table 10.)

[b] An asterisk (*) indicates significance at the 0.005 level.

northern peninsula region (18% compared to 4%). Although rural schools are specifically excluded from this analysis, the northern peninsula of Michigan has a decidedly rural flavor, even in its towns and suburbs. The relatively large number of top schools from this region may be another sign that there is a rural component contributing to unusual educational effectiveness. Whether this factor reflects a statistical property of the SES measures or a real difference in the ability or interest of rural schools to raise achievement scores is an important question for further research.

Despite the disproportionate number of northern peninsula schools among the top 72, in absolute terms they still represent only a small minority of the overachievers. Most of the 72 are located in southern and central Michigan, and most are in central city or suburban areas. Unusually effective schools—or at least these candidates for that title—are not wholly or even largely a rural or regional phenomenon.

Tables 11 and 12 are extremely important. On balance, they indicate that the outliers we located were indeed nonrandom, and the outstanding schools seem to share certain policy-related attributes. The consistently superior scores of the top 72 schools apparently represent real differences between them and the average school—differences that deserve detailed study at the local level.

CONCLUSIONS

This report comprises a series of exploratory investigations into the existence of unusually effective schools. We assumed that school effectiveness could be gauged by mean performance on standardized achievement tests.

5

82 EXPLORATORY DATA ANALYSIS

Because nonschool factors significantly affect achievement scores, we did not define "effectiveness" in absolute terms. Rather, we examined school performance after controlling for a variety of background variables. We assumed a simple model of the form:

Achievement score = f(background, school).

Then, using multiple regression techniques, we experimented with various controls for the background influences, using such measures as previous test scores, SES, minority enrollment, community type, and others, in varying combinations.

Instead of concentrating on the properties of the regression lines obtained, we studied the *residuals* from those lines. Although we recognized that residual variation would stem from sources other than different school effects, we decided on the basis of previous studies and the nature of our problem to proceed as if all variation after the fit resulted from the schools (and some random factors). Then, by examining series of residuals from the same schools both cross-sectionally and longitudinally, we tried to eliminate random effects and locate true outliers that would be candidates for further, more detailed study. Although the existence of such outliers would not necessarily be due to unusually effective schools, to discover no outliers under such circumstances would be a very strong negative result. Finally, where possible, we investigated the apparent overachievers for shared characteristics, in a further attempt to separate random from nonrandom outliers.

Jencks and others (1972) have shown how tight the distribution of school achievement scores is after controlling for nonschool background factors. Our various regressions support that finding. Even in regressions where the percentage of variation explained is not high, the standard errors are small compared with the interstudent standard deviation of the achievement test. Figure 9 contrasts the interstudent distribution of test scores with a typical interschool distribution controlled for background factors. There is more variation within schools than between them. This general result is true whether our primary control is previous test scores or an explicit socioeconomic measure.

The second unanimous finding from all our disparate explorations involves the normality of the distribution of residuals. The overwhelming impression is one of smooth, well-behaved, random variation. There is no evidence of extreme outliers nor of discontinuity in educational effectiveness among schools.

The results of analyzing school performance over many grades and years are more suggestive, but quite mixed. They can be summarized as follows:

The Michigan data provide evidence of unusually effective schools.

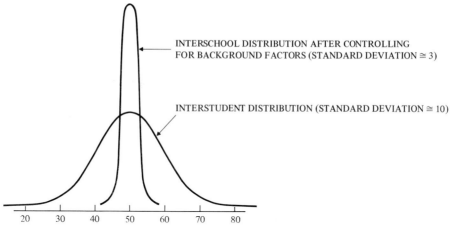

FIG. 9 *Schematic representation of interschool and interstudent variation of achievement scores.*

1. Including rural schools, the Chi-square tests showed a greater number of consistently overachieving schools than chance alone would allow. For example, among the 161 schools that reported scores for all eight test/grade/year combinations, 15 were at least one standard deviation above the mean six out of eight times (less than one was expected by chance). That is, about 9% of the schools seemed able to raise their students, on average, by an amount equal to an increase from the fiftieth to the seventy-second percentile, given equal background factors. However, most of these outstanding schools were rural and all white, even after controlling for community type and percent minority, which reflects heteroskedasticity in the control variables. By running regressions stratified by community type, we found that our regressor variables could explain only 7% of the variation among rural schools, compared with 50–60% for the other four community types combined. These results may reflect unique characteristics of rural schools, or they may proceed from imperfect measures for SES.

2. Not including the rural schools, we found evidence of consistent overachievers in two of the four Chi-square tests. For example, among the 2131 schools that reported scores for four test/grade/year combinations, 72 were at least one standard deviation above the mean all four times (13 were expected by chance). In other words, about 2.5 percent of these schools seemed able to improve their students an amount equivalent to an increase from the fiftieth to the sixty-fifth percentile, given equal background factors.

Furthermore, these 72 schools differed significantly from the average nonrural school on three out of four school-related factors. The top 72 schools tended to have smaller classes, more teachers with five or more years of experience, and more teachers earning $11,000 or more annually. Despite some significant differences in the number of children tested in the fourth grade, different sample sizes could not account for the position of the top 72 schools. Neither could differences in nonschool factors, although the overachieving schools were slightly lower than average in SES. The overachievers tended to be located more in northern Michigan than the average; once again, despite eliminating rural schools, this grouping may be evidence of some regional/rural factor contributing to unusual effectiveness.

For the New York City data, the results were equivocal. Although in one year for all grades and for one grade over time we found some evidence of consistent overachievers, random variation could account for almost all the outliers observed in the other year and grade. Furthermore, the consistent overachievers that were identified averaged only 1.5 interschool standard deviations above the mean, not so much as in the Michigan schools. Very few schools indeed were above one standard deviation every time.

The Project Talent data showed no evidence of consistently overachieving schools apart from that predicted by chance alone. This negative finding seems even stronger when one considers that only SES was used as a regressor.

Thus, the policy relevance of this exercise comes down to a question of valuation. We located some schools that were statistically "unusual," but whether they can be considered unusually *effective* depends on one's subjective scale of magnitude. Is half an interstudent standard deviation a lot? How much better would a school have to be before it would be worth studying in detail for purposes of replication? And can present educational research and development policy, with its emphasis on diffusing and imitating best practice, base itself on interschool differences of these magnitudes? Such normative questions clearly transcend statistics.

Nonetheless, moving away from average effects in educational research and policy making does seem worthwhile. We have located schools and districts that consistently perform better than their peers. It is probably worthwhile to continue such research and to begin looking for unusually effective classrooms and programs. The methodology developed in this report should prove useful in such efforts. As educational researchers continue to devise new measures of school outcomes, and as they begin to focus on types of students rather than school means, they should remember that most statistical techniques concentrate on the *average* effects of all schools. For both policy and research purposes, however, exceptions to the rule may be more important.

BIBLIOGRAPHY

Acland, Henry D. "School Effects: An Analysis of New York Elementary Schools." Unpublished.

Averch, Harvey A., *et al. How Effective is Schooling?* The Rand Corporation, R-956-PCSF/RD, 1972.

Barro, Stephen M. "An Approach to Developing Accountability Measures for the Public Schools." *Phi Delta Kappan*, Vol. 52, No. 4 (December 1970), pp. 196–205.

Bowles, Samuel, and Herbert Gintis. "IQ and the U.S. Class Structure." *Social Policy*, Vol. 3, No. 4 and 5 (Nov./Dec. 1972 and Jan./Feb. 1973.)

Bowles, Samuel, and Henry M. Levin. "The Determinants of Scholastic Achievement—An Appraisal of Some Recent Evidence." *Journal of Human Resources*, Vol. 3, No. 1 (Winter 1968), pp. 2–24.

Brown, Byron W. "Achievement, Costs and the Demand for Public Education." *Western Economic Journal*, Vol. 10, No. 2 (June 1972), pp. 198–219.

Coleman, James S., *et al. Equality of Educational Opportunity*, U.S. Department of Health, Education, and Welfare, Office of Education, OE-38001 (U.S. Government Printing Office, Washington, D.C., 1966).

Cronbach, Lee J., and Lita Furby. "How We Should Measure 'Change'—Or Should We?" *Psychological Bulletin*, Vol. 74, No. 1 (July 1970), pp. 68–80.

Dyer, Henry S. "The Measurement of Educational Opportunity." In Frederick Mosteller and Daniel P. Moynihan, eds. *On Equality of Educational Opportunity*. New York: Random House, Vintage Books, 1972, pp. 513–527.

Guthrie, James W. "What the Coleman Reanalysis Didn't Tell Us." *Saturday Review*, July 22, 1972.

Hanushek, Eric A. *The Value of Teachers in Teaching*, The Rand Corporation, RM-6362-CC/RC, December 1970.

Harris, C. W., ed. *Problems in Measuring Change*. University of Wisconsin Press, Madison, 1963.

Harsh, J. R. "Problems of Measuring Student Gain." In S. A. Haggart, G. C. Sumner, and J. R. Harsh, *A Guide to Performance Contracting: Technical Appendix*, The Rand Corporation, R-955/2-HEW, 1972.

Hilgard, Ernest R. "The Translation of Educational Research and Development into Action." In United States Congress, House of Representatives, Committee on Education and Labor, *Educational Research: Prospects and Priorities*, 92d Congress, 2d session, January 1972. Appendix 1 to hearings before the Select Subcommittee on Education on H. R. 3606, to create a National Institute of Education, United States Government Printing Office, Washington, D.C., pp. 51–57.

Jencks, Christopher S. "The Coleman Report and the Conventional Wisdom." In Frederick Mosteller and Daniel P. Moynihan, eds., *On Equality of Educational Opportunity*. New York: Random House, Vintage Books, 1972, pp. 69–115.

Jencks, Christopher S., *et al. Inequality*. New York: Basic Books, 1972.

Kiesling, Herbert J. *The Relationship of School Inputs to Public School Performance in New York State*, The Rand Corporation, P-4211, October 1969.

Lindquist, E. F., and A. N. Hieronymus. *Iowa Tests of Basic Skills: Manual for Administrators, Supervisors, and Counselors.* Boston: Houghton Mifflin, 1964.

Mayeske, George W., *et al. A Study of Our Nation's Schools,* United States Department of Health, Education, and Welfare, Office of Education, United States Government Printing Office, Washington, D.C., 1969.

Shaycoft, Marion F. *The High School Years: Growth in Cognitive Skills.* Interim Report 3, Project 3051, Contract OE-6-10-065, American Institutes for Research, Palo Alto, California, 1967.

Smith, Marshall S. *"Equality of Educational Opportunity: The Basic Findings Reconsidered."* In Frederick Mosteller and Daniel P. Moynihan, eds., *On Equality of Educational Opportunity,* New York: Random House, Vintage Books, 1972, pp. 230–342.

Stevens, William K. "Test Expert Calls I.Q. and Grade Equivalency Scores 'Monstrosities,'" *New York Times,* March 23, 1971.

Tukey, John W. *Exploratory Data Analysis* (limited preliminary edition, 3 vols.). Reading, Mass.: Addison-Wesley Publishing Company, 1970.

United States Department of Health, Education, and Welfare, Office of Education, National Center for Educational Statistics (Division of Data Analysis and Dissemination). "Characteristics Differentiating Under- and Over-achieving Schools," Washington, D.C., March 1968 (unpublished).

University of the State of New York, State Education Department, Bureau of School Programs Evaluation. *New York State Performance Indicators in Education, 1972 Report,* Albany, New York, September 1972.

Yarnold, James K. "The Minimum Expectation in χ^2 Goodness of Fit Tests and the Accuracy of Approximations for the Null Distribution." *Journal of the American Statistical Association,* Vol. 65, No. 330 (June 1970), pp. 864–886.

THE WAIT TO SEE THE DOCTOR: AN APPLICATION OF EXPLORATORY DATA ANALYSIS

DONALD SHEPARD

THE PROBLEM: INTRODUCTION AND BACKGROUND

At 5 minutes to 10 o'clock one morning, Mrs. Smith and her son Tommy checked in at an out-patient clinic of a children's hospital. Tommy had been seen a month prior to that time about a minor ailment and had been told to return at 10 : 00 that morning so the doctor could assure that Tommy's ailment had been cured. The Smiths were told to take a seat and wait; Tommy would be called. At 10 : 30, Mrs. Smith asked the nurse whether the doctor had forgotten about Tommy. The doctor had not forgotten him, the nurse explained, looking somewhat embarrassed, but the clinic was behind schedule that morning. The nurse did not call Tommy until 11 : 30, an hour and a half late. The examination took 15 minutes; the Smiths left. The delay had irritated both the Smiths and the nurse—and most of the morning had passed while they waited.

This example is not an isolated one. In fact, a survey of users of out-patient facilities at another hospital indicates that excessive waiting time is the patients' most frequently mentioned complaint.[1]

With the nation's increasing interest in improving the quality of medical care,[2] we may wish to monitor determinants of patient satisfaction such as waiting time as well as measures of health outcomes. Whereas the latter are often quite difficult to measure, indices such as waiting times are relatively easily obtained. Doctors and administrators acknowledge that patients do

Teaching and Research Materials No. 17T, Public Policy Program, John Fitzgerald Kennedy School of Government, Harvard University, January 1974. This paper was written while the author was supported by a National Science Foundation Graduate Fellowship.

[1] Paul B. Hoffmann and John F. Rockart, "Implications of the No-Show Rate for Scheduling OPD Appointments," *Hospital Progress*, August 1969, pp. 35–40.

[2] See, for example, Eli Ginzberg, "Notes on Evaluating the Quality of Medical Care," *New England Journal of Medicine*, 292 (1975), 366–368.

wait, but they generally add that long delays are rare, or that delays are unavoidable if clinics are scheduled so that doctors' time is used efficiently. Techniques of exploratory data analysis from Tukey's *Exploratory Data Analysis*[3] will be applied here to this specific problem area in health services administration, namely, to delays in an out-patient clinic. We will argue that at least in the clinic studied, long waits are not unusual and that those longer than 15 minutes are *not* a necessary component of clinic operations. Exploratory data analysis seems appropriate because of our desire to find out what factors probably contribute to waiting in clinics, and whether or not (and how) they should be changed.

Long and recurrent delays are annoying not only to patients but also to ancillary hospital staff such as nurses and administrative assistants, who must continually apologize for appointments that run behind schedule. This analysis was begun, in fact, in response to just such a situation. Parents and their children, who frequently were kept waiting over an hour past the appointment time, blamed the nurses and secretaries. Children became restless and difficult to examine. Nurses were embarrassed to have to apologize constantly for delays. In order to document the delays and present the evidence to the doctors in charge of the clinic, some members of the nursing and secretarial staffs began the data-collection exercise forming the basis of this paper. The data were gathered for three weeks in December 1972 (December 4 to 22) and for five weeks in the spring of 1973 (March 5 to April 6). There were three morning and one afternoon clinic sessions each week. The results of this survey for March 14 are given in Table 1; for March 15, see Table 2.

For this survey clinic secretaries were asked to record three times: the time of the patient's appointment, the time of the patient's arrival, and the approximate time that the clinic (doctor's) service began.[4] In addition, certain summary measures for each day were recorded: the number of doctors on duty, their arrival time, and the total number of patients seen. For March 14, 35 patients kept their appointments and all 4 doctors arrived on time at 1:00 p.m. On the following day, 24 patients were seen by 4 doctors who arrived in the morning at 7:55, 9:15, 10:00, and 10:20. Recording these data was, of course, of secondary importance to caring for patients. As a result, some data were omitted.

We shall use the data from the samples of December 1972 and spring 1973 with the techniques of exploratory data analysis to examine delays in

---

[3] John W. Tukey, *Exploratory Data Analysis*, Reading, Mass.: Addison-Wesley, 1977.

[4] The approximate time service began specifically means the time the patient was called from the main waiting room to a seat by the door of the examining room. Although the exact time at which the examination began could not be recorded, patients were generally called into the examining room within a few minutes after taking a seat just outside it.

TABLE 1 SAMPLE DATA: APPOINTMENT LOG FOR MARCH 14, 1973.

No.	Medical record number	Appoint-ment time	Arrival time	Start of service	Left clinic	Early/Late E/L (hour:min)	Waiting time (hour:min)
1	72–40–73	2:30	1:25	2:05	2:45	1:05E	40
2	59–36–76	2:00	12:55	1:25	2:30	1:05E	30
3	76–70–43	2:30	2:10	2:50	3:45	20E	40
4	57–26–85	1:30	1:35	2:30	3:30	5L	55
5	61–78–51	3:00	3:00	3:30	4:35	0E	30
6	70–89–19	1:00	1:00	2:00	2:45	0E	1:00
7	56–91–50	3:00	2:05	2:40	?	55E	35
8	69–45–95	1:00	12:30	1:25	2:05	30E	55
9	77–03–50	2:30	2:15	2:55	3:45	15E	40
10	60–89–30	2:00	2:00	2:35	?	0E	35
11	72–99–48	3:30	3:45	3:50	4:05	15L	5
12	65–92–13	3:00	2:50	3:00	4:10	10E	10
13	69–23–63	2:00	1:00	2:05	2:45	1:00E	1:05
14	77–97–72	2:30	2:40	3:15	4:15	10L	35
15	70–80–43	2:30	2:40	3:15	4:15	10L	35
16	77–44–63	3:00	2:25	2:55	?	35E	30
17	70–61–59	1:30	1:00	1:30	2:35	30E	30
18	69–36–83	1:30	1:15	2:15	2:50	15E	1:00
19	73–01–60	1:30	12:50	1:25	?	40E	35
20	59–07–98	2:00	3:00	3:25	3:45	1:00L	25
21	73–43–58	2:00	1:30	2:35	3:45	30E	1:05
22	64–14–10	1:30	2:00	2:30	3:20	30L	30
23	59–95–18	3:30	3:25	3:55	5:00	5E	30
24	77–97–55	1:30	1:20	2:05	2:55	10E	45
25	57–42–66	none	?	?	?	N.A.	?
26	58–72–94	none	12:00	1:25	?	N.A.	1:25
27	76–54–92	1:00	12:35	1:00	1:25	25E	25
28	78–12–43	1:00	12:35	1:00	1:25	25E	25
29	78–20–65	1:00	1:00	1:10	1:35	0E	10
30	77–44–79	1:00	1:10	1:20	1:35	10L	10
31	76–90–99	2:00	1:50	2:35	3:05	10E	45
32	64–06–56	3:00	2:35	3:10	4:30	25E	35
33	68–49–21	2:30	2:50	3:25	5:00	20L	35
34	59–52–33	3:30	3:10	3:45	4:30	20E	35
35	42–38–40	?	4:00	4:05	4:25	?	5

TABLE 2 SAMPLE DATA: APPOINTMENT LOG FOR MARCH 15, 1973.

No.	Medical record number	Appoint-ment time	Arrival time	Start of service	Left clinic	Early/Late E/L (hour:min)	Waiting time (hour:min)
1	77–29–52	8:30	8:15	8:40	?	15E	25
2	77–83–34	10:00	9:30	10:25	11:15	30E	55
3	78–13–55	8:30	8:45	9:00	9:15	15L	15
4	69–57–98	9:00	9:00	9:45	10:20	0E	45
5	77–83–64	9:30	9:20	10:05	10:40	10E	45
6	65–88–10	10:00	10:00	10:55	12:30	0E	55
7	62–73–21	9:30	9:00	9:15	10:00	30E	15
8	54–97–19	9:30	10:00	10:40	?	30L	40
9	71–25–84	8:30	8:45	9:15	9:45	15L	30
10	64–97–51	9:00	9:00	10:00	10:20	0E	1:00
11	67–37–20	9:00	9:00	10:00	10:20	0E	1:00
12	67–34–42	10:30	10:20	10:55	11:45	10E	35
13	52–40–91	9:00	9:00	9:45	10:50	0E	45
14	54–83–86	10:00	9:50	10:40	11:10	10E	50
15	61–54–75	9:30	9:50	10:30	11:15	20L	40
16	69–06–33	9:30	?	10:25	11:00	?	?
17	76–91–33	8:00	8:00	8:05	?	0E	5
18	72–08–30	8:00	8:15	8:20	8:30	15L	5
19	62–73–21	?	?	?	?	?	?
20	62–98–34	9:00	9:10	9:25	9:35	10L	15
21	75–62–68	9:30	9:20	9:25	9:40	10E	5
22	53–06–21	9:30	9:30	10:10	10:35	0E	40
23	75–22–87	10:00	9:30	9:30	9:50	30E	0
24	37–42–66	None	11:45	11:50	12:05	N.A.	5

this clinic. First, the analysis is presented by answering three specific questions. Next, conclusions are drawn and recommendations made; finally, a brief epilogue is given.

ANALYSIS
Three specific questions are important in this analysis. First, how long is the delay; that is, how long do patients wait? Second, what factors explain the variation in these delays? And third, what changes in clinic procedures would reduce the delays? Let us explore each of these questions separately.

How long do patients wait?
Operationally, we define waiting time as the difference between a patient's time of arrival and the time he or she is called to the door of the examining

room. Our computations show that the average (tri-mean)^5 initial waiting time is 46 minutes. A meaningful description of waiting time cannot be given as a single number, but rather must be given as a distribution of numbers. To compute such a distribution, Tukey's "stem-and-leaf" proved a very adaptable technique.

Question 1.^{6} Using the data in Tables 1 or 2, analyze the distribution of waiting time for March 14 or 15 with a stem-and-leaf. Calculate hinges, median, and tri-mean. For March 14 you can compare your results with those in Table 3.

TABLE 3 DISTRIBUTION OF WAITING TIME FOR MARCH 14, 1973.

Stem and leaf

Cumulative count (Total : 34)	Count	Waiting, Hour : minute^a	Time, minutes
2	2	0:0	55
5	3	0:1	000
8	3	0:2	555
√	14	0:3	00555500500555
12	5	0:4	00055
7	2	0:5	55
5	4	1:0	0505
1	0	1:1	
1	1	1:2	5

Summary of Distribution

	Statistic	Time, hour : minute	
Minimum	*	0:05	(Observation 1)
Hinge	H	0:25	(Observation 9)
Median	M	0:35	(Average of Observations 17 and 18)
Hinge	H	0:45	(Observation 9 from End)
Maximum	*	1:25	(Observation 1 from End)
Tri-mean		1:35	

^{a} Minutes by tens.

---

^{5} The tri-mean is the average of (1) the median and (2) the average of the "hinges." The hinges are the first and third quartiles of the sample. See Tukey for these definitions and further discussion.

^{6} These questions are provided for the reader who wants to become more familiar with exploratory data analysis. This and other odd-number questions raise points in anticipation of subsequent discussion. Even-numbered questions extend the analysis beyond that presented here.

Table 3 gives a stem-and-leaf of waiting time for March 14, 1973, the day for which the data are recorded in Table 1. Notice that this particular afternoon clinic had especially short delays. The "stem," or the numbers to the left of the vertical line, represents hours and the tens digit of minutes, and each number to the right (each "leaf") represents the units digit of minutes. On the third line of the stem-and-leaf, for example, the stem is "0:2," indicating 0 hours and 20 minutes. To the right of the vertical line are the three leaves, three 5's for five minutes. Thus there were three patients on March 14 who waited 0 hours, 20 + 5 minutes, or 0 hours, 25 minutes. Since all times were recorded only to the nearest five minutes, waiting times were always a multiple of that interval. Below the stem-and-leaf we have written the extrema (denoted by *), the hinges, for first and third quartiles (denoted by H), and the median (denoted by M). As a summary measure of the day's waiting times, we have the "tri-mean." Another way to summarize this stem-and-leaf is by the frequency counts for each 10-minute interval. To the left of the stem in Table 3 are the frequency counts and the cumulative counts from both extrema to the center.

Since a statement about waiting time should not be based on a single day, in Table 4 we show the frequency counts for 7 days in late March and 1 in early April representing a mixture of morning and afternoon clinics. We see that waiting time ranges from 5 minutes to at least 190 minutes (3 hours, 10 minutes). Adding the daily frequency counts, we obtain the combined, 8-day distribution in the "Total Count" column, from which we calculate the summary statistics such as the median, the hinges, etc. The counts by 10-minute intervals show four local modes, at 0:10 (really 0:10 to 0:19), 0:30, 1:20, and 2:00 hours. Since some of these peaks might be due to the random error of a small sample, we have attempted to smooth the distribution by aggregating to larger intervals as shown in the column labeled "Count by Half-hour Interval." The final column in Table 4 standardizes the distribution by converting it into percentages.

After smoothing, the frequency distribution is still multimodal with local peaks in two intervals: 30 to 50 minutes; and 2 hours to 2 hours, 29 minutes. The percentage frequencies are 40 and 8, respectively. Often multimodality arises because several distinct populations have been combined. In this case the probable explanation is that some of the patients must wait twice. First they are checked or given such medications as eye drops by a doctor or nurse; after the medication has had time to act and the doctor is available, these patients are seen. Other patients see the doctor only. The local mode in the interval after 2 hours represents patients who are seen twice, while the 30-minute mode represents patients seen only once by the doctor. Figure 1 is a histogram of the percentage distribution of waiting times based on half-hour intervals (the last column in Table 4). Like the stem-and-leaf in Table 3, the frequency distribution in Figure 1 also has a

TABLE 4 WAITING TIME DISTRIBUTION SUMMARY BETWEEN MARCH 14 AND APRIL 4, 1973.

| Wait hr:min | \multicolumn{8}{c}{Frequencies by date} | Total count by 10-minute interval | Count by half-hour interval | Percent |
| | \multicolumn{7}{c}{For March} | For April | | | |
	14[a]	15	22	26	28[a]	29	30	4			
0:00	2	5		2	3				12		
0:10	3	3		2	19	1			28		
0:20	3	1	2	4	1			2	13	50	25
0:30	14	2	6	1	4	2	1	3	33		
0:40	5	6	5	2	1	3	3	2	27		
0:50	2	3	6		2	2	1	4	20	80	40
1:00	4	2	2				3	3	14		
1:10			4	1				4	9		
1:20	1		2	1	1	1	2	6	14	37	19
1:30			1	1					2		
1:40			3	1		1			5		
1:50			1			3			4	11	6
2:00			2	4		4			10		
2:10			3				1		4		
2:20				1					1	15	8
2:30				1					1		
2:40											
2:50										1	1
3:00				1					1		
3:10				1					1		
3:20										2	1
Totals	34	22	36	24	31	17	11	24	199	199	100

[a] Afternoon clinic session

	Hr:Min
*	05
H	25
M	45
H	1:10
*	3:10
tri-mean	0:46

long right-hand tail. We have cut the distribution at 1 hour, 30 minutes into components 1 and 2, which may characterize the patients by the number of times they are seen by the doctor or nurse in their visit. In summary we find that the tri-mean waiting time is 46 minutes, but 35% of the patients wait longer than 1 hour, and 9% must wait more than 2 hours.

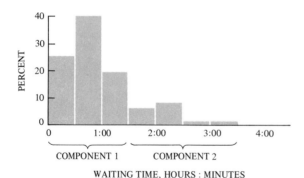

FIG. 1 *Frequency distribution of patients' waiting time.*

Question 2. Although it is obvious that the clinic secretaries rounded times to multiples of 5 minutes, it is possible that there was further rounding. Is there any evidence in the data in Tables 1 and 2 that whole hours, half hours, quarter hours, or 10-minute multiples were preferred? If so, how would this affect our analysis using these times?

What factors explain the variation in waiting time?

Waiting time may be analyzed along a number of dimensions. Some of these are whether the patient is early or late for an appointment, the time of day, the date, backlog, and doctors' arrival time. We shall now look at each of these dimensions in order to determine whether or not they can explain a variation in waiting time.

Lateness. it has been observed that patients often arrive either early or late for appointments. Of those patients with morning appointments, we found for a 3-day sample that 24% of them arrived a half hour or more late; and 9% a half hour or more early. The two distributions of patient lateness in both morning and afternoon clinics are shown in Figure 2. The distribution for morning clinics is based on three days in the December 1972 sample (December 4th, 7th, and 8th). The distribution for the afternoon clinics is based on December 6 and 13, 1972. In Figure 2, patients who arrived at the border of two intervals are counted in the earlier (left-hand) interval. For example, a patient who arrived exactly one hour late is counted in the interval 0:30 to 1:00.

It was the general opinion of the clinic staff that patients' erratic arrivals were the cause of waiting in out-patient clinics. For this reason appointments were deliberately set well in advance of the time the patient was

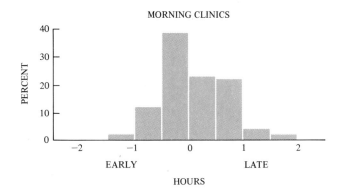

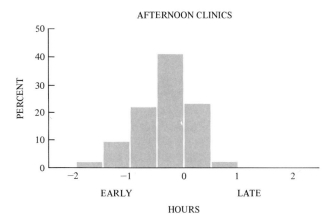

FIG. 2 *Arrival time of patients in relation to their scheduled appointment.*

expected, according to conventional wisdom, because patients are tradition-ally late. An unfortunate by-product of this kind of thinking and the procedure it fosters is that patients who arrive on time are forced to wait.[7]

> *Question 3.* Using the data in Tables 1 and 2, see how waiting time varies with lateness. You might plot patients' arrivals on a graph of early/late versus time spent waiting. Compare with Figure 3.

Figure 3 was drawn to examine the relation between lateness and time spent waiting. Although the relation is weak, there is a suggestion of

---

[7] If the expectation that patients will arrive late is not to become self-fulfilling, then the clinic should operate so that patients who arrive on time are rewarded by a shorter wait than latecomers.

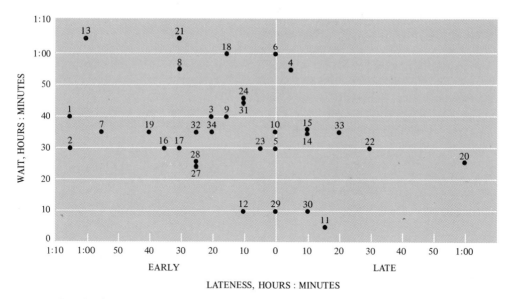

FIG. 3 *Graph of waiting time by lateness, based on data from Table 1. Numbers beside the plotted points are the patient sequence numbers from the lefthand column of Table 1.*

convoluted incentives; that is, patients who arrive late for their appointments wait for less time than those who arrive slightly early. Other days show the same pattern, that late arrivals wait for less time than early arrivals do.

After reviewing clinic procedures, we found that the pattern is entirely understandable. Appointment times serve mainly to distribute arrivals over the clinic session. The actual order of service is on a first-come, first-served basis, with actual appointment times almost irrelevant. If the appointment schedule were strictly adhered to, then we should have measured waiting time as the time a patient waits after he or she could have expected to be seen: the listed appointment time.

> *Question 4.* If waiting time is measured from the appointment for those patients who arrive early, and from the arrival time for latecomers, does the first group still "wait" less than latecomers? Use the data in Figure 3.

Time of day. Another important variable related to tardiness is the time of arrival relative to the time at which the clinic formally opens. The clinic from which these data come meets three mornings (formally opening at 8:30 a.m.) and one afternoon (formally opening at 12:30 p.m.) each week.

We arbitrarily chose two dates with afternoon clinics, (March 14 and April 4) and two with morning clinics (March 15 and 16) for which we had already calculated waiting time. Hourly stems and leaves were made for each day; they are reproduced in Table 5, showing the distribution of the duration of clinic visits.[8] Hour 0 denotes the interval containing the clinic session starting time: 8:00 to 8:59 in morning clinics, and 12:00 noon to 12:59 p.m. in afternoon clinics.

> *Question 5.* How does waiting time vary as the clinic proceeds? Analyze the stems and leaves in Table 5 and compare them with Figure 4.

For each stem and leaf in Table 5 the median duration was calculated. An average median for each hour was obtained as the average of the two corresponding daily medians. For example, the median durations for hour 0 of the morning clinics are 0:30 and 1:10. The average median for hour 0 of morning clinics is thus 0:50. To understand how delay varied during the course of the clinic, these sets of average medians are drawn in Figure 4. For comparison, the tri-mean duration for all visits in Table 5 is 1 hour, 21 minutes. The change during the clinic session is very marked, showing that patients who arrived during the middle hours of the session experienced long delays (up to 2 hours for the total visit), whereas those who arrived at the beginning and end needed as little as 20 minutes for the entire visit. This pattern, which some patients may have learned through experience, shows that patients with appointments in the middle of the clinic session were wise if they came very early or late.

Backlog. Since arrivals are handled on a first-come, first-served basis, the pattern of waiting time suggests that waiting time increases with the backlog in the clinic. Backlog is defined as the number of patients who have arrived at the clinic and checked in and are waiting to be seen; presumably small it is at the beginning of the clinic, increases as arrivals exceed departures, and finally decreases as the rate of arrivals falls and doctors attend to waiting patients. At the end of the clinic, by definition, the backlog is zero.

To test the backlog hypothesis, we selected three other clinic sessions (March 19, 22, and 23) and made frequency distributions of the time patients arrived at the clinic, the time they "started service" (were called to the doctor's examining room), and the time they left. Patients for whom any one of these times was not recorded were deleted from the tabulations. For arrivals and start-of-service there were only two omissions for each day (out of 35 patients). The counts were aggregated into half-hour intervals and converted to percentages. The resulting distributions, shown in Figure 5, show that the distribution of starting time is about $1\frac{1}{2}$ hours to the right of arrival times, supporting our hypothesis that backlog is highest at the middle hour of the clinic.

---

[8] Duration was used instead of waiting time because the cases of missing data were fewer. On the average, duration exceeds wait by 41 minutes (the time for preparation and examination).

TABLE 5 DURATION OF CLINIC VISIT BY TIME OF ARRIVAL.

Hours after clinic start	Hour of arrival	Duration of visits			
		Hour	Minutes (by 10s)	Hour	Minutes (by 10s)
	Morning clinic	March 15		March 16	
0[a]	8:00–8:59	0	31[b]	0	
		1	0	1	301
		2		2	
1	9:00–9:59	0	222	0	5
		1	4220225220	1	20215
		2		2	
2	10:00–10:59	0		0	
		1	2	1	04
		2	3	2	1021
3	11:00–11:59	0	2	0	
		1		1	
		2		2	
	Afternoon clinic	March 14		April 4	
0[c]	12:00–12:59	0	55	0	53
		1	33	1	2
		2		2	5
1	1:00–1:59	0	32	0	4
		1	354433331	1	3445
		2		2	22251
2	2:00–2:59	0		0	
		1	3323325	1	35
		2	1	2	11
3	3:00–3:59	0	24	0	
		1	332	1	
		2		2	
4	4:00–4:59	0	2	0	
		1		1	
		2		2	

[a] Difference between midpoint of interval and nominal starting time of 8:30 a.m.

[b] Interpretation: In a stem-and-leaf the stem (the hours digit in this table) applies to each subsequent digit, or leaf, in that row. Thus the first row represents the durations of two patients' visits, which took (to within 10 minutes) 0 hours, 30 minutes and 0 hours, 10 minutes. In this table all leaves represent minutes by tens; the units digit has been dropped for simplicity.

[c] Difference between midpoint of interval and nominal starting time of 12:30 p.m.

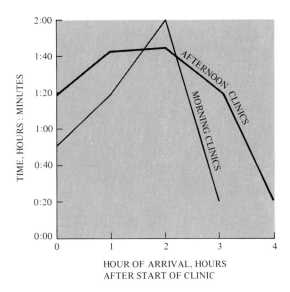

FIG. 4 *Total time in clinic by hour of arrival.*

We observed that backlog begins to accumulate when the clinic opens. Although patients begin arriving at 8:00, for all practical purposes examinations do not begin until 9:00 o'clock; although these morning clinics should have ended at 12:30, the backlog extended the sessions until 2:00 p.m. (see Figure 5). Furthermore, the maximum number of patients whose examination can be started in any half-hour interval (the mode in Figure 5 "Starting Time with Doctor") is 20% of the daily clinic attendance of 28 patients. If more than this number arrives in any half hour, a backlog is created. Thus the clinic starts with a small backlog: those patients who arrive before 9:00 a.m. Those patients who arrive between 9:00 and 9:30 add considerably to the backlog, and those who arrive between 9:30 and 10:30 increase it slightly. Finally, after 10:30 the rate of arrivals drops below the rate at which examinations can be started, and doctors begin to "catch up." Although the observed pattern in delays could have been caused by corresponding variations in the complexity of examinations, this explanation does not apply here. The mixture of examination types between new (generally long) and return was the same for each half hour.

The third graph in Figure 5 shows the frequency distribution of completion times and gives the best measure of clinic throughput. For the peak half-hour intervals between 10:00 a.m. and 12:00 noon, an average of 4.2 patients or 15% of the daily clinic attendance finish their visits in each half-hour interval. Thus, on the average, each of the three doctors completes

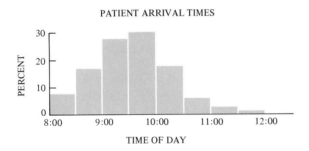

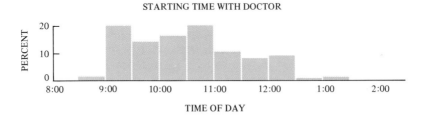

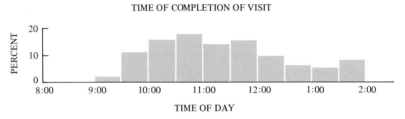

FIG. 5 *Frequency distributions of arrival, starting, and completion time of day based on three morning clinics (March 19, 22, and 23, 1973).*

an examination every 21 minutes.[9] We found that delay and the duration of clinic visit show a trend according to the time in the clinic session at which a patient arrives. Patients are seen quickly at the beginning and end, but they experience long delays in the middle.

> *Question 6.* Duration of clinic visit is the sum of two components: waiting time and service time. Using the data from either Table 1 or Table 2, see how these two components vary with time of arrival. Is there any systematic variation? Does the fact that some patients must see the doctor twice (discussed in connection with Table 4) give any insight into the variation in service times? Do there seem to be other factors that might explain the variations?

---

[9] We shall make more use of this maximum throughput later, in the section on recommendations.

Date. We have seen that the time spent waiting depends on when the patient arrives relative to when the clinic begins service. How does waiting time vary from one date to another? We can summarize waiting time on any day by finding the tri-mean, a measure which is easy to calculate and not too sensitive to a few extreme observations. The daily tri-means of waiting time for the December 1972 and spring 1973 clinic sessions varied by a factor of 3, from 18 to 72 minutes.

Data are not available on a number of factors, such as the mood of the doctors or the complexity of the patients' complaints on any day, but we do have a few basic items of data which might help explain the differences in waiting time. These are the number of patients attending the clinic session (both by appointment and on a walk-in basis), the number of doctors on duty in the clinic, and the actual starting time of the clinic (the time the first examination begins). From the first two numbers we can calculate the workload (patients per doctor). From the third, we can determine whether the clinic started late or on time.

We also recorded whether the clinics met in the morning or afternoon. It was expected that clinic sessions with heavy workloads and those that started late (because doctors were delayed by other commitments) would have longer waits. Table 6 lists recorded characteristics and waiting time for 14 days.

> *Question 7.* How does waiting time depend on workload (patients per doctor) and prompt starting of clinic sessions? Define discrete categories for these variables for the data in Table 6 and see how much your categories explain the variations in waiting time. Compare your results with those in Table 7.

Since the relation between the independent variables and mean waiting time may be nonlinear, and since we did not want to impose a particular functional form, the independent variables were classified into two categories. To do this the days have been separated into two categories by workload with equal numbers of cases—those clinic sessions in which each doctor had to see more than 7 patients, and those in which each doctor had to see 7 patients or fewer. To investigate the association between late starting and delay, we have cross-tabulated 14 clinic sessions for which waiting time was known with those that started early or on time (there were 5) and those that started late (the remaining 9). For clinic sessions in each of the four combinations of workload and clinic starting time, we calculated the median waiting time (see Table 7). We can separate the effects of the two factors using the procedures outlined in a chapter on two-way tables of Tukey's *Exploratory Data Analysis.* First we calculate the column means (36.5 for 7 or fewer patients per doctor and 53 for more than 7) and subtract them from the elements in the corresponding columns to obtain the

TABLE 6 SUMMARY OF WAITING TIME AND SELECTED CHARACTERISTICS
FOR FOURTEEN DAYS.

Date	Morning or afternoon clinic	Workload (patients per doctor)	Arrival time	Mean wait, minutes
December 1972				
4	AM	7.0	Late	46
6	PM	6.2	On time	24
7	AM	6.2	Late	43
8	AM	5.0	Late	36
13	PM	7.8	Early	50
14	AM	8.2	Late	62
15	AM	5.8	Late	56
March 1973				
14	PM	8.8	Early	36
15	AM	6.0	Early	30
22	AM	10.0	Late	70
26	AM	8.3	Late	72
28	PM	8.0	On time	18
29	AM	7.3	Late	70
30	AM	7.0	Late	61
Sample tri-mean		7.2		49

TABLE 7 DAILY WAITING TIME TABULATED BY PROMPT-
NESS AND WORKLOAD (IN MINUTES).

Clinic starting time	Workload (patients per doctor)	
	7 or fewer	More than 7
Early or on time	27	36
	$(n = 2)^a$	$(n = 3)$
Late	46	70
	$(n = 5)$	$(n = 4)$
Column mean	36.5	53

[a] The number of observations (clinic sessions) in each
cell is denoted by n.

TABLE 8 RESIDUALS DERIVED FROM TABLE 6.[a]

| Clinic starting time | Workload (patients per doctor) | | Row mean of residuals |
	7 or fewer	More than 7	
Early or on time	−9.5	−17	−13.25
Late	9.5	17	13.25
Column mean[b]	36.5	53	

[a] Since these calculations of effects make no use of the number of observations in each cell, they form an unweighted estimate of effects. In confirmatory data analysis, the preferred technique for analyzing two-way classifications with unequal cell sizes is to weight each cell mean in inverse proportion to the number of observations. (See George W. Snedecor and William G. Cochran. *Statistical Methods.* 6th ed. Ames, Iowa: Iowa State University Press, 1967, pp. 483–484.) In this example weighting would increase the effects, yielding 21.1 for the minimum, plus 18.7 for the workload effect, plus 27.2 for the lateness effect.

[b] Column mean is derived from original elements in Table 6.

residuals. Taking the mean of the residuals in each row gives −13.25 and 13.25, respectively, as shown in Table 8. We obtain the predicted value for any cell by adding the mean for its column and the residual for its row. For example, the predicted value in the upper left cell is $36.5 + (−13.25) = 23.25$ or about 23. The difference between the column means (16.5, or about 17) measures the column effect, the increase in waiting time attributable to a heavy workload; similarly the difference in the row means, 27 after rounding, measures the row effect, the effect of a late start. We can summarize our two-way analysis as:

Predicted waiting time in minutes = 23
+ 17 if workload exceeds 7 patients per doctor
+ 27 if clinic started late.

This additive, linear model is depicted graphically in Figure 6. The vertical axis represents waiting time. The horizontal axis has no meaning by itself, except that the points are spaced along the horizontal axis such that the four vertices predicted by the linear model form a rectangle. The most important thing to note about the rectangle is that the distance between the sides corresponding to lateness is much greater than that corresponding to work-load. Thus starting time explains much more of the variability than workload. (Recall from the foregoing equation that late starting adds 27 minutes to expected waiting time, whereas heavy workload adds only 17 minutes.)

Careful examination of Figure 6 reveals the interaction between the two factors. The arrows represent residuals between predicted and actual waiting times for each combination. They show that increasing the workload adds little (only 3 minutes) to waiting time if the clinic starts on time, but adds 24 minutes if the clinic starts late. Viewed differently, late starting is much more serious in a clinic with a heavy workload than in one with a light load.

It is possible that the apparent effects of late starting or heavy workload are due to their association with some other variable. Clinic sessions meeting in the afternoon instead of in the morning, for example, is a characteristic closely associated with prompt starting. There are no systematic differences, however, in the starting times or types of patient seen between morning and afternoon clinics. Thus it seems most reasonable that differences in the promptness of clinic starting are responsible for differences in average delays. With the small sample of only 14 days for which all data were available, our findings are tentative. A large sample would permit the investigator to control for more variables, reducing the problem of spurious associations.

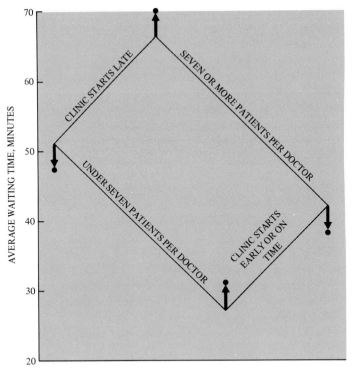

FIG. 6 *Effect of doctors' lateness and heavy patient load on patients' waiting time.*

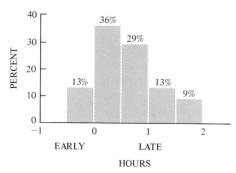

FIG. 7 *Distribution of doctors' lateness.*

Doctors' arrival time.   Figure 7 is a histogram of the lateness of doctors, based on doctor arrivals over 14 days. From this figure we can see, roughly, why late starting adds some 26 minutes to expected wait: doctors arrived late (after 8:30 a.m.) 87 percent of the time for morning clinics, and the average lateness of these arrivals was 43 minutes. Assuming that patients' arrivals and doctors' rate of work are unaffected by the physicians' lateness, each minute that a doctor is late adds one minute to the waiting time of each patient he or she sees. Thus, we might have expected doctors' lateness to contribute 37 minutes (87 percent of 43) to average waiting time. Since the actual contribution was only 27 minutes, there must have been some compensating factors. Perhaps the later the doctors arrived, the faster they worked or the fewer stops they made. Or on the days doctors were late, the patients were later than usual. Or random errors, such as differences in case mix, happened to be correlated with lateness.

It is well known that doctor lateness is not confined to the clinic studied here. In part the lateness must be caused by doctors having busy schedules containing unpredictable components (some examinations may take longer than expected due to complications). Probably a more important reason is in the historical tradition of hospital out-patient clinics. Medical historians write that out-patient facilities were established as an obligatory community service, or as a necessary duty to patients previously treated in the hospital, or, in teaching hospitals, as a vehicle for discovering interesting cases for admission. According to this tradition, clinics should be scheduled for the doctors' convenience, and doctors should not be expected to make special efforts to be prompt.

What changes in clinic procedures would reduce waiting time?
We have observed three factors that apparently contribute to waiting time: (1) doctors arrive late, (2) more patients are scheduled at the beginning of

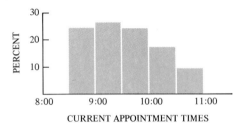

FIG. 8 *Present distribution of appointment times (morning clinics).*

clinic sessions than can be accommodated at that time, and (3) the patient/doctor ratio exceeds seven to one for some sessions.

Organizationally, the third factor would seem easiest to alter: lower the patient/doctor ratio by reducing the number of patients per clinic session or by increasing the number of staff hours. A broader study might indicate how the hospital could reduce the number of patient visits, or increase the effective staffing of the clinic, but for purposes of the present study these factors were considered inflexible, being dictated by the hospital's budget and community obligations. Our remaining alternative, then, is to find improvements in clinic scheduling within these constraints. We have two good leads: reducing the lateness of doctors and re-allocating the appointment "slots" over the clinic session.

To combat the problem of recurrent lateness by doctors the director of the clinic could encourage doctors to arrive more promptly or postpone the first morning appointment slot to an hour more convenient for physicians, say around 9:00 a.m. Second, appointment slots should be reallocated to schedule patient arrivals at the approximate time they can be seen. In Figure 5, we saw that during the peak period of the morning (9:00 to 11:00 a.m.) the three doctors completed an average of 4.2 patient visits every half hour. Since this is the maximum rate at which patients can be seen, they should not be scheduled to arrive at any substantially faster rate to avoid congestion in the clinic.[10] Nevertheless, as shown in Figure 8, under the present distribution of appointment slots, more patients are scheduled than can be accommodated in all of the appointment periods except the last (by which time there is already a 90-minute backlog).

Although it might be argued that early appointments are necessary because patients will be late, the first graph in Figure 5 shows that actual arrivals were just as concentrated as appointment schedules. (The only difference is that there were fewer actual arrivals than scheduled in the 8:30-to-8:59 a.m. interval because some patients started arriving before 8:30.) If the present morning clinic hours of 8:30 to 12:30 can be made

---

[10] Arrivals might still be slightly overscheduled to assure that physicians are not kept waiting.

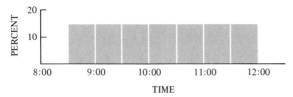

FIG. 9 *Proposed distribution of appointment times* (*morning clinics*).

workable by reducing the problem of doctor lateness, then the most sensible allocation of appointment slots is to spread them evenly over the six half-hour intervals between 8:30 and 1:30 inclusive. As shown in Figure 9, this allocation means that 16.7 percent of the clinic workload, or 4.7 patients, should arrive in each half-hour interval. While this rate is still one patient per hour above the number that can be seen, the excess provides a cushion against doctors being idle if patients are unusually late or the fraction of missed appointments is higher than expected. Under the proposed distribution of slots, the last morning appointment would be for 11:30.

It has been argued that appointments cannot be scheduled too near to the clinic closing time (12:30), because patients may arrive late. Allowing a half hour for the examination, the distribution of lateness in Figure 2 shows that there would be no problem for the 74% of the patients who arrive not more than one-half hour late. Patients arriving excessively late would have to be re-scheduled to return another day. While some exceptions might have to be made during the transition period, the combination of explaining revised clinic procedures and showing patients how waiting has been reduced should reduce the frequency of patient lateness and make the revised schedule successful.

We have argued that the optimal number of patients to arrive each half hour is 4.7, so that 28 patients could be seen in the course of a clinic session. It would be misleading to leave the impression that there should be 4.7 *appointment slots* every half hour. In most out-patient clinics at the hospital in this study, as in most other out-patient facilities, the rate of appointments not kept (and not canceled by the patient ahead of time) is 30%. For an expected clinic attendance of 28 patients, it is necessary to schedule 40 patients. Since Figure 9 is expressed in percentage terms, we can apply it equally to appointment slots. We should schedule 16.7% of the patients, or an average of 6.7 patients, in each half-hour interval. Since we cannot in practice have a fraction of an appointment slot, we should arrange 7 slots in 4 of the intervals, and 6 slots in the remaining 2 intervals. The unpredictability of missed appointments[11] precludes any attempts to schedule appoint-

---

[11] A related study showed that reminders could reduce missed appointments significantly. See Donald S. Shepard and T. A. E. Moseley, "Mailed Versus Telephone Reminders to Reduce the Rate of Broken Appointments in an Outpatient Clinic," *Medical Care*, March 1976.

ments more precisely than by half-hour blocks and means that waiting times in a clinic cannot be reduced below about 15 minutes.

The two simple changes described above—assuring that doctors begin the clinic promptly and spacing out appointments throughout the clinic session—should reduce the average waiting time from 47 minutes to about 15 minutes. We obtained this estimate by noting from the formula for predicted waiting time that prompt starting alone should reduce average wait by about 17 minutes, or from 47 to 30 minutes.[12] Spacing out appointments should cut about 39 minutes from the average clinic wait. This estimated reduction is the difference between the overall tri-mean time for a clinic visit of 1 hour, 21 minutes and the mean time of 42 minutes for a visit during uncongested hours—the first and last hours of the clinic session. If the two changes were entirely additive in effect, the net wait would be zero. There is undoubtedly interaction between the improvement effects of better appointment spacing, because improvements are easiest when the clinic is most congested. Although it would be optimistic to assume that the delay could be reduced to zero minutes, a reduction to about 15 minutes, or half the interval between successive block appointments, is quite reasonable.

CONCLUSIONS AND RECOMMENDATIONS

Given a problem and a set of data, the techniques of exploratory data analysis have led us through a series of steps: summarizing the extent of the problem (that is, the distribution of waiting time and total visit time), finding some factors that partly explain waiting time, and examining whether the clinic could be improved given staff constraints. We have found that the average (actually, tri-mean) of waiting time is 46 minutes and of total duration is 1 hour, 21 minutes. But the total visit time varied from 20 minutes, when there is little backlog, to 2 hours in the middle of the clinic session, when the backlog is substantial. Appointments are clustered in the beginning of the clinic session, so that patients arrive faster than they can be seen and queuing is inevitable. We propose re-allocating appointment slots evenly over the clinic session, so that patients arrive at about the same rate as they can be seen.

We have also found that doctors' lateness is a major cause of long clinic delays. Our data indicate that doctors arrived late 87% of the time. In those clinic sessions that started on time, the average wait was 27 minutes less than in comparable sessions starting late. Thus it is recommended that appointment slots be rearranged and clinic sessions be started promptly, on

---

[12] Compared to late starting, prompt starting would reduce waiting time by 26 minutes. But assuming the days in Table 6 are representative, at present 9/14ths or 64% of the clinics start late. Thus the benefit from expected reductions in waiting from prompt starting compared to current conditions is 64% of 26 minutes, or 17 minutes.

schedule. These changes could be expected to reduce the average clinic wait to about 15 minutes.

EPILOGUE

In the period since these data were gathered, there have been two changes in the clinic. Most important, a "fellow" has joined the clinic staff, increasing the average number of doctors available for every clinic session to four. Second, some appointments (though not as many as recommended above) have been switched from 8:30 and 9:00 a.m. to a later time. As a result, waiting time has been reduced noticeably, and both patients and staff are more satisfied.

PART III

STATISTICAL ANALYSIS
IN POLICY ISSUES

SEX BIAS IN GRADUATE ADMISSIONS: DATA FROM BERKELEY

PETER J. BICKEL, EUGENE A. HAMMEL, and J. WILLIAM O'CONNELL

Determining whether discrimination because of sex or ethnic identity is being practiced against persons seeking passage from one social status or locus to another is an important problem in our society today. It is legally important and morally important. It is also often quite difficult. This article is an exploration of some of the issues of measurement and assessment involved in one example of the general problem, by means of which we hope to shed some light on the difficulties. We will proceed in a straightforward and indeed naive way, even though we know how misleading an unsophisticated approach to the problem is. We do this because we think it quite likely that other persons interested in questions of bias might proceed in just the same way, and careful exposure of the mistakes in our discovery procedure may be instructive.

DATA AND ASSUMPTIONS

The particular body of data chosen for examination here consists of applications for admission to graduate study at the University of California, Berkeley, for the fall 1973 quarter. In the admissions cycle for that quarter, the Graduate Division at Berkeley received approximately 15,000 applications, some of which were later withdrawn or transferred to a different proposed entry quarter by the applicants. Of the applications finally remaining for the fall 1973 cycle 12,763 were sufficiently complete to permit a decision to admit or to deny admission. The question we wish to pursue is whether the decision to admit or to deny was influenced by the sex of the applicant. We cannot know with any certainty the influences on the evaluators in the Graduate Admissions Office, or on the faculty reviewing

Reprinted with permission from *Science*, Vol. 187 (February 7, 1975), pp. 398–404. Copyright © 1975 by the American Association for the Advancement of Science.

committees, or on any other administrative personnel participating in the chain of actions that led to a decision on an individual application. We can, however, say that if the admissions decision and the sex of the applicant are statistically associated in the results of a series of applications, we may judge that *bias* existed, and we may then seek to find whether *discrimination* existed. By "bias" we mean here a pattern of association between a particular decision and a particular sex of applicant, of sufficient strength to make us confident that it is unlikely to be the result of chance alone. By "discrimination" we mean the exercise of decision influenced by the sex of the applicant when that is immaterial to the qualifications for entry.

The simplest approach (which we shall call approach A) is to examine the aggregate data for the campus. This approach would surely be taken by many persons interested in whether bias in admissions exists on any campus. Table 1 gives the data for all 12,763 applications to the 101 graduate departments and interdeparmental graduate majors to which application was made for fall 1973 (we shall refer to them all as departments). There were 8442 male applicants and 4321 female applicants. About 44 percent of the males and about 35 percent of the females were admitted. Just this kind of simple calculation of proportions impels us to examine the data further. We will pursue the question by using a familiar statistic, chi-square. As already noted, we are aware of the pitfalls ahead in this naive approach, but we intend to stumble into every one of them for didactic reasons.

We must first make clear two assumptions that underlie consideration of the data in this contingency table approach. Assumption 1 is that in any given discipline male and female applicants do not differ in respect of their intelligence, skill, qualifications, promise, or other attribute deemed legitimately pertinent to their acceptance as students. It is precisely this assumption that makes the study of "sex bias" meaningful, for if we did not hold it any differences in acceptance of applicants by sex could be attributed to differences in their qualifications, promise as scholars, and so on. Theoretically one could test the assumption, for example, by examining presumably

TABLE 1 DECISIONS ON APPLICATIONS TO GRADUATE DIVISION FOR FALL 1973, BY SEX OF APPLICANT—NAIVE AGGREGATION. EXPECTED FREQUENCIES ARE CALCULATED FROM THE MARGINAL TOTALS OF THE OBSERVED FREQUENCIES UNDER THE ASSUMPTIONS (1 AND 2) GIVEN IN THE TEXT. $N = 12{,}763$, $\chi^2 = 110.8$, d.f. $= 1$, $P = 0$ (*18*).

| | Outcome | | | | | |
| | Observed | | Expected | | Difference | |
Applicants	Admit	Deny	Admit	Deny	Admit	Deny
Men	3738	4704	3460.7	4981.3	277.3	−277.3
Women	1494	2827	1771.3	2549.7	−277.3	277.3

unbiased estimators of academic qualification such as Graduate Record Examination scores, undergraduate grade point averages, and so on. There are, however, enormous practical difficulties in this. We therefore predicate our discussion on the validity of assumption 1.

Assumption 2 is that the sex ratios of applicants to the various fields of graduate study are not importantly associated with any other factors in admission. We shall have reason to challenge this assumption later, but it is crucial in the first step of our exploration, which is the investigation of bias in the aggregate data.

TESTS OF AGGREGATE DATA

We pursue this investigation by computing the expected frequencies of male and female applicants admitted and denied, from the marginal totals of Table 1, on the assumption that men and women applicants have equal chances of admission to the university (that is, on the basis of assumptions 1 and 2). This computation, also given in Table 1, shows that 277 fewer women and 277 more men were admitted than we would have expected under the assumptions noted. That is a large number, and it is unlikely that so large a bias to the disadvantage of women would occur by chance alone. The chi-square value for this table is 110.8, and the probability of a chi-square that large (or larger) under the assumptions noted is vanishingly small.

We should on this evidence judge that bias existed in the fall 1973 admissions. On that account, we should look for the responsible parties to see whether they give evidence of discrimination. Now, the outcome of an application for admission to graduate study is determined mainly by the faculty of the department to which the prospective student applies. Let us then examine each of the departments for indications of bias. Among the 101 departments we find 16 that either had no women applicants or denied admission to no applicants of either sex. Our computations, therefore, except where otherwise noted, will be based on the remaining 85. For a start let us identify those of the 85 with bias sufficiently large to occur by chance less than five times in a hundred. There prove to be four such departments. The deficit in the number of women admitted to these four (under the assumptions for calculating expected frequencies as given above) is 26. Looking further, we find six departments biased in the opposite direction, at the same probability levels; these account for a deficit of 64 men.

These results are confusing. After all if the campus had a shortfall of 277 women in graduate admissions, and we look to see who is responsible, we ought to find somebody. So large a deficit ought not simply to disappear. There is even a suggestion of a surplus of women. Our method of examination must be faulty.

SOME UNDERLYING DEPENDENCIES

We have stumbled onto a paradox, sometimes referred to as Simpson's in this context (*1*) or "spurious correlation" in others (*2*). It is rooted in the falsity of assumption 2 above. We have assumed that if there is bias in the proportion of women applicants admitted it will be because of a link between sex of applicant and decision to admit. We have given much less attention to a prior linkage, that between sex of applicant and department to which admission is sought. The tendency of men and women to seek entry to different departments is marked. For example, in our data almost two-thirds of the applicants to English but only 2 percent of the applicants to mechanical engineering are women. If we cast the application data into a 2×101 contingency table, distinguishing department and sex of applicants, we find this table has a chi-square of 3091 and that the probability of obtaining a chi-square value that large or larger by chance is about zero. For the 2×85 table on the departments used in most of the analysis, chi-square is 3027 and the probability about zero. Thus the sex distribution of applicants is anything but random among the departments. In examining the data in the aggregate as we did in our initial approach, we pooled data from these very different, independent decision-making units. Of course, such pooling would not nullify assumption 2 if the different departments were equally difficult to enter. We will address ourselves to that question in a moment.

Let us first examine an alternative to aggregating the data across the 85 departments and then computing a statistic—namely, computing a statistic on each department first and aggregating those. Fisher gives a method for aggregating the results of such independent experiments (*3*). If we apply his method to the chi-square statistics of the 85 individual contingency tables, we obtain a value that has a probability of occurrence by chance alone, that is, if sex and admission are unlinked for any major, of about 29 times in 1000 (*4*). Another common aggregation procedure, proposed to us in this context by E. Scott, yields a result having a probability of 6 times in 10,000 (*5*). This is consistent with the evidence of bias in some direction purportedly shown by Table 1. However, when we examine the *direction* of bias, the picture changes. For instance, if we apply Fisher's method to the *one-sided* statistics, testing the hypothesis of no bias or of bias in favor of women, we find that we could have obtained a value as large as or larger than the one observed, by chance alone, about 85 times in 100 (*6*).

Our first, naive approach of examining the aggregate data, computing expected frequencies under certain asssumptions, computing a statistic, and deciding therefrom that bias existed in favor of men has now been cast into doubt on at least two grounds. First, we could not find many biased decision-making units by examining them individually. Second, when we take account of the differences among departments in the proportions of men and women applying to them and avoid this problem by computing a statistic on each department separately, and aggregating those statistics, the evidence for campus-wide bias in favor of men is extremely weak; on the contrary, there is evidence of bias in favor of women.

The missing piece of the puzzle is yet another fact: not all departments are equally easy to enter. If we cast the data into a 2×101 table, distinguishing department and decision to admit or deny, we find that this table has a chi-square value of 2195, with an associated probability of occurrence by chance (under assumptions 1 and 2) of about zero, showing that the odds of gaining admission to different departments are widely divergent. (For the 2×85 table chi-square is 2121 and the probability about zero.) Now, these odds of getting into a graduate program are in fact strongly associated with the tendency of men and women to apply to different departments in different degree. *The proportion of women applicants tends to be high in departments that are hard to get into and low in those that are easy to get into.* Moreover this phenomenon is more pronounced in departments with large numbers of applicants. Figure 1 is a scattergram of proportion of applicants that are women plotted against proportion of applicants that are admitted. The association is obvious on inspection although the relationship is certainly not linear (7). If we use a weighted correlation (8) as a measure of the relationship for all 85 departments in the plot we obtain $\hat{p} = .56$. If we apply the same measure to the 17 departments with the largest numbers of applicants (accounting for two-thirds of the total population of applicants) we obtain $\hat{p} = .65$, while the remaining 68 departments have a corresponding $\hat{p} = .39$. The significance of $\hat{p}$ under the hypothesis of no association can be calculated. All three values obtained are highly significant.

The effect may be clarified by means of an analogy. Picture a fishnet with two different mesh sizes. A school of fish, all of identical size (assumption 1), swim toward the net and seek to pass. The female fish all try to get through the small mesh, while the male fish all try to get through the large mesh. On the other side of the net all the fish are male. Assumption 2 said that the sex of the fish had no relation to the size of the mesh they tried to get through. It is false. To take another example that illustrates the danger of incautious pooling of data, consider two departments of a hypothetical university—machismatics and social warfare. To machismatics there apply 400 men and 200 women; these are admitted in exactly equal proportions, 200 men and 100 women. To social warfare there apply 150 men and 450 women; these are admitted in exactly equal proportions, 50 men and 150 women. Machismatics admitted half the applicants of each sex, social warfare admitted a third of the applicants of each sex. But about 73 percent of the men applied to machismatics and 27 percent to social warfare, while about 69 percent of the women applied to social warfare and 31 percent to machismatics. When these two departments are pooled and expected frequencies are computed in the usual way (with assumption 2), there is a

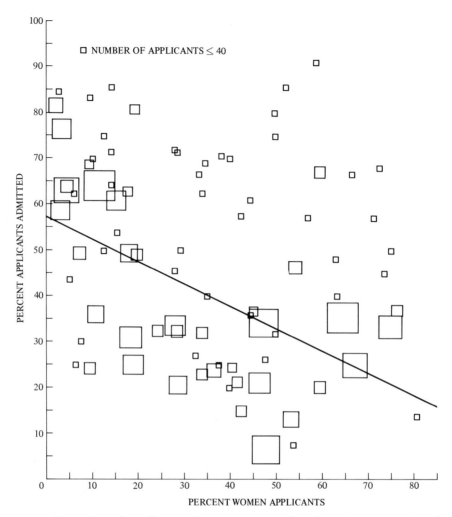

FIG. 1 *Proportion of applicants that are women plotted against proportion of applicants admitted, in 85 departments. Size of box indicates relative number of applicants to the department.*

deficit of about 21 women (Table 2). A discrepancy in that direction that large or larger would be expectable less than 2 percent of the time by chance; yet both departments were seen to have been absolutely fair in dealing with their applicants.

The creation of bias in our original situation is, of course, much more complex, since we are aggregating many tables. It results from an interaction of the three factors, choice of department, sex, and admission status, whose

TABLE 2 ADMISSIONS DATA BY SEX OF APPLICANT FOR TWO HYPOTHETICAL DEPART-
MENTS. FOR TOTAL, $\chi^2 = 5.71$, d.f. = 1, $P = 0.19$ (ONE-TAILED).

	Outcome					
	Observed		Expected		Difference	
Applicants	Admit	Deny	Admit	Deny	Admit	Deny
	Department of machismatics					
Men	200	200	200	200	0	0
Women	100	100	100	100	0	0
	Department of social warfare					
Men	50	100	50	100	0	0
Women	150	300	150	300	0	0
	Totals					
Men	250	300	229.2	320.8	20.8	−20.8
Women	250	400	270.8	379.2	−20.8	20.8

broad outlines are suggested by our plot but which cannot be described in any simple way.

In any case, aggregation in a simple and straightforward way (approach A) is misleading. More sophisticated methods of aggregation that do not rely on assumption 2 are legitimate but have their difficulties. We shall have more to say on this later.

DISAGGREGATION

The most radical alternative to approach A is to consider the individual graduate departments, one by one. However, this approach (which we may call approach B) also poses difficulties. Either we must sample randomly from the different departments, or we must take account of the probability of obtaining unusual sex ratios of admittees by chance in a number of simultaneously conducted independent experiments. That is, in examining 85 separate departments at the same time for evidence of bias we are conducting 85 simultaneous experiments, and in that many experiments the probability of finding some marked departures from expected frequencies "just by chance" is not insubstantial. The department with the strongest bias against admitting women in the fall 1973 cycle had a bias of sufficient magnitude to be expectable by chance alone only 69 times in 100,000. If we had selected that department for examination on a random basis, we would have been convinced that it was biased. But we did not so select it; we looked at 85 departments at once. The probability of finding a department that biased against women (or more biased) by chance alone in 85 simultaneous trials is about 57 times in 1000. Thus that particular department is not quite so certainly biased as we might have first believed, .057 being a very much larger number than .00069, although still a small enough probability to warrant a closer look. This department was the worst one in respect of bias against women in admissions; the probability of finding departments less biased by chance alone is of course greater than .057. We can also examine events in the other direction. The department most biased against men had a bias sufficiently large to be expectable by chance alone about 20 times in a million, and the chance of finding a department that biased (or more biased) in that direction by chance alone in 85 simultaneous trials (9) is about .002.

There is a further difficulty in approach B. Although it makes a great deal of sense to examine the individual departments that are in fact the independent decision-making entities in the graduate admissions process, some of them are quite small, and even in some that are of ordinary size the number of women applying is very small. Calculation of the probability of observed deviations from expected frequencies can be carried out for such units, but when the numbers involved are very small the evidence for deciding whether there is no bias or gross bias is really worthless (10). This defect is evident not only in approach B but also if we use some reasonable method of aggregation of test statistics to avoid the pitfalls of approach A such as that of Fisher, or even the approach we suggest below. That is, large biases in small departments or in departments with small numbers of women applicants will not influence a reasonable aggregate measure appreciably.

POOLING

The difficulty we face is not only technical and statistical but also administrative. In some sense the campus is a unit. It operates under general regulations concerning eligibility for admission and procedures for admission. It is a social community that shares certain values and is subject to certain general influences and pressures. It is identifiable as a bureaucratic unit by its own members and also by external agencies and groups. It is, as a social and cultural unit, accountable to its various publics. For all these reasons it makes sense to ask the question, Is there a campus bias by sex in graduate admissions? But this question raises serious conceptual difficulties. Is campus bias to be measured by the net bias across all its constituent subunits? How does one define such a bias? For any definition, it is easy to imagine a situation in which some departments are biased in one direction and other departments in another, so that the net bias of the campus may be zero even though very strong biases are apparent in the subunits. Does one look instead at the outliers, those departments that have divergences so extreme

TABLE 3 SUM OF EXPECTED DEPARTMENTAL OUTCOMES OF WOMEN'S APPLICATIONS COMPARED WITH SUM OF OBSERVED OUTCOMES, GRADUATE DIVISION, BERKELEY, FALL 1973. $\chi^2 = 8.55$, d.f. $= 1$, $P = .003$ (TWO-TAILED).

Expected female admittees	1432.9
Observed female admittees	1493.0
Difference $(O - E)$	60.1

as to call their particular practices into question? How extreme is extreme in such a procedure, and what does one do about units so small as to make such assessment meaningless?

We believe that there are no easy answers to these questions, but we are prepared to offer some suggestions. We propose that examination of campus bias must rest on a method of estimation of expected frequencies that takes into account the falsity of assumption 2 and the apparent propensity of women to apply to departments that are more difficult to enter.

We reanalyze Table 1, using all the data leading to it, by computing the expected frequencies differently than in approach A, since we now know the assumptions underlying that earlier computation to be false. We estimate the number of women expected to be admitted to a department by multiplying the estimated probability of admission of any applicant (regardless of sex) to that department by the number of women applying to it. Thus, if the chances of getting into a department were one-half for all applicants to it, and 100 women applied, we would expect 50 women to be admitted if they were being treated just like the men. We do this computation for each department separately, since each is likely to have a different probability of admission and a different number of women applying, and we sum the results to obtain the number of women expected to be admitted for the campus as a whole (11). This estimate proves to be smaller by 60 than the number of women observed to have been admitted (Table 3).

The computation of Table 3 is as follows: For a four-cell contingency table of the following format:

	Admit	Deny
Men	a_i	b_i
Women	c_i	d_i

the particular cell of interest is c_i, containing the number of women admitted. The expected frequency under the hypothesis of no bias is $E = w_i p_i = (c_i + d_i)(a_i + c_i)/N_i$, where N_i is the total of applicants to department i. The observed number, O, is the number in c_i. The difference between these two quantities, $O - E$, summed over n departments is

$$\sum_{i=1}^{n} (O - E) = DIFF$$

Then, $$\chi^2 = \frac{(DIFF)^2}{\sum_{i=1}^{n} (a_i + b_i)(a_i + c_i)(c_i + d_i)(b_i + d_i)/N_i^2(N_i - 1)}$$

with d.f. = 1. Ninety-six departments were included in the computation, since 5 of the total 101 each had only 1 applicant. If $N_i - 1$ is replaced by N_i in the denominator, all 101 departments can be included, yielding $\chi^2 = 8.61$: $O - E$ remains 60.1 and the expected and observed female admittees are each increased by 1. (This statistic makes it possible to include contingency tables having an empty cell, so that no information is lost; there is thus an advantage over methods that pool the chi-square values from a set of contingency tables.)

The probability that an observed bias this large or larger in *favor* of women might occur by chance alone (under these new assumptions) is .0016; the probability of its occurring if there were actual discrimination against women is, of course, even smaller. This is consistent with what we found using Fisher's approach and aggregating the test statistics: there is evidence of bias in favor of women. [The test used here was proposed in another context by Cochran (12) and Mantel and Haenszel (13).]

We would be remiss if we did not point out yet another pitfall of approach A. Whereas the highly significant values of the Mantel-Haenszel or Fisher statistics just mentioned for 1973 are evidence that there is bias in favor of women, the low values obtained in other years (see below) do not indicate that every department was operating more or less without bias. Such low values could equally well arise as a consequence of cancellation. We illustrate with the hypothetical departments of machismatics and social warfare. If machismatics admitted 250 men and 50 women, creating a short-fall of 50 women, while social warfare admitted 200 women and no men, creating an excess of 50 women, the aggregate measure of bias we have introduced would be zero. We only argue that if an aggregate measure of bias is wanted the one we propose is reasonable. Of course, if we combine two-sided statistics by the Fisher method this phenomenon does not occur.

We would conclude from this examination that the campus as a whole did not engage in discrimination against women applicants. This conclusion is strengthened by similarly examining the data for the entire campus for the years 1969 through 1973. In 1969 the number of women admitted exceeded the expected frequency by 24; the probability of a deviation of this size or larger in *either* direction by chance alone is .196. In 1970 there were four fewer women admitted than expected, the probability of chance occurrence being .833. In 1971 there were 25 more women than expected, with a probability of .249. In 1972 there were seven more women than expected, the probability being .709. For 1973 as shown above the deviation was an excess of 60 women over the expected number: the probability of a chance deviation that large or larger in either direction is .003. These data suggest that there is little evidence of bias of any kind until 1973, when it would seem significant evidence of bias appears, in favor of women. This conclusion is supported by all the other measures we have examined. For instance, pooling the chi-square statistics by Fisher's method yields a probability of .99 in 1969, 1970, and 1971, a probability of .55 in 1972, and a probability of .029 in 1973 (*14*).

We may also take approach B and look for individual department outliers. Because the numbers of women students applying to some of them in any one year are often small, we aggregated the data for each department over the 5-year span, using the method just explained. (This procedure of course hides the kind of change that the aggregating approach reveals when pursued through time, but it enables us to focus on possible "offenders" in either direction in a campus that is on the average behaving itself.) During the 5-year period there were 94 units that had at least one applicant of each sex and admitted at least one applicant and denied admission to at least one in at least one year. Two of the 94 units, one in the humanities and one in the professions, show a divergence from chance expectations sufficient to arouse interest. One of these admitted 16 fewer women than expected over 5 years, a shortfall of 29 percent; the probability of such a result by chance alone in 94 trials is about .004. The other unit admitted 40 fewer women than expected over the 5-year period, a shortfall of 7 percent, with a probability in 94 trials of about .019. The next most likely result by chance was at a level of .094 and the next after that at .188. Conversely there were two units significantly biased in the opposite direction, with chance probabilities of occurrence of .033 and .047, accounting for a combined shortfall of 50 men, 13 and 24 percent respectively of the expected frequencies in the individual units.

The kinds of statistics we may wish to use in examination of individual departments may differ from those employed in these general screening processes. For example, in one of the cases of a shortfall of women cited above it seems likely that an intensified drive to recruit minority group members caused a temporary drop in the proportion of women admitted, since most of the minority group admittees were males. In most of the cases involving favored status for women it appears that the admissions committees were seeking to overcome long-established shortages of women in their fields. Overall, however, it seems that the admissions procedure has been quite evenhanded. Where there are divergences from the expected frequencies they are usually small in magnitude (although they may constitute a substantial proportion of the expected frequency), and they more frequently favor women than discriminate against them.

MORE GENERAL ISSUES

We have already explained why assumption 1—the equivalence of academic qualifications of men and women applicants—is necessary to the statistical examination of bias in admissions. But the assumption is clearly false in its most extensive sense; there are areas of graduate study that men and women simply have not hitherto been equally prepared to enter. One of the principal differentiators is preparation in mathematics, which is prerequisite in an elaborate stepwise fashion to a number of fields of graduate endeavor (15).

This differentiation would have little effect on women's chances to enter graduate school if it were unrelated to difficulty of entry. But it is not. Although it would appear in a logical sense that the departments requiring more mathematics would be more difficult to enter, in fact it appears to be those requiring less mathematics that are the more difficult. (For the 83 graduate programs with matching undergraduate majors, the Pearson r between proportion of applicants admitted and number of recommended or required undergraduate units in mathematics or statistics is .38.) In part this may be because departments requiring less mathematics receive applications from persons who might have preferred to enter others but cannot for lack of mathematical (or similar) background, as well as from persons intrinsically inclined toward nonmathematical subjects. In part it is because in the nonmathematical subjects (that is, the humanities and social sciences) students take longer to get through their programs; in consequence, those departments have lower throughput and thus less room, annually, to accept new students. Just why this is so is a matter of debate and of great complexity. Some of the problem may lie in the very lack of a chain of prerequisities such as that characterizing graduate work in, let us say, the physical sciences. Some may lie in the nature of the subject matter and the intractability of its data and the questions asked of the data. Some may lie in the less favorable career opportunities of these fields and in consequence a lower pull from the professional employment market. Some may lie just in the higher proportion of women enrolled and the possibility that women are under less pressure to complete their studies (having alternative options of social roles not open generally to men) and have less favorable employment possibilities if they do complete, so that the pull of the market is less for them. Whatever the reasons, the lower productivity of these fields is a fact, and it crowds the departments in them and makes them more difficult to enter.

The absence of a demonstrable bias in the graduate admissions system does not give grounds for concluding that there must be no bias anywhere else in the educational process or in its culmination in professional activity. Our intention has been to investigate the general case for bias against women in a specific matter—admission to graduate school—not only because we had the data base to do so but also because allegations of bias in the admissions process had been aired. Our approach in the beginning was naive, as befits an initial investigation. We found that even the naive question could not be answered adequately without recourse to sophisticated methodology and careful examination of underlying processes. We take this opportunity to warn all those who are concerned with problems of bias about these methodological complexities (*16*).

We also find, beyond this immediate area of concern in graduate admissions, that the questions of bias and discrimination are more subtle than one might have imagined, and we mean this in more than just the methodological sense. If prejudicial treatment is to be minimized, it must first be located accurately. We have shown that it is not characteristic of the graduate admissions process here examined (although this judgment does not eliminate the possibility of individual cases of prejudicial treatment, and it does not deal with politically or morally defined null hypotheses). The fairness of the faculty in admissions is an important foundation for further effort. That effort can be made directly by universities in seeking to equalize the progress of men and women toward their degrees (*17*). A university can use its powers of suasion to equalize the preparation of girls and boys in the primary and secondary schools for entry into all academic fields. By its own objective research it may be able to determine where and how much bias and discrimination exist and what the suitable corrective measures may be.

SUMMARY

Examination of aggregate data on graduate admissions to the University of California, Berkeley, for fall 1973 shows a clear but misleading pattern of bias against female applicants. Examination of the disaggregated data reveals few decision-making units that show statistically significant departures from expected frequencies of female admissions, and about as many units appear to favor women as to favor men. If the data are properly pooled, taking into account the autonomy of departmental decision making, thus correcting for the tendency of women to apply to graduate departments that are more difficult for applicants of either sex to enter, there is a small but statistically significant bias in favor of women. The graduate departments that are easier to enter tend to be those that require more mathematics in the undergraduate preparatory curriculum. The bias in the aggregated data stems not from any pattern of discrimination on the part of admissions committees, which seem quite fair on the whole, but apparently from prior screening at earlier levels of the educational system. Women are shunted by their socialization and education toward fields of graduate study that are generally more crowded, less productive of completed degrees, and less well funded, and that frequently offer poorer professional employment prospects.

REFERENCES AND NOTES

1. C. R. Blyth, *J. Am. Stat. Assoc.* **67**, 364 (1972).

2. J. Neyman, *Lectures and Conferences on Mathematical Statistics and Probability* (U.S. Department of Agriculture Graduate School, Washington, D.C., ed. 2, 1952), p. 147.

3. R. A. Fisher, *Statistical Methods for Research Workers* (Oliver and Boyd, London, ed. 4, 1932).

4. Fisher's statistic is

$$F = -2 \sum_{i=1}^{n} \ln p(T_i)$$

where $p(T_i)$ is the P value of the test statistic calculated for the ith experiment (department). F is referred to the upper tail of a chi-square distribution with $2n$ degrees of freedom where $n =$ number of experimental results to be aggregated, here 85. In our application here, T_i is the usual contingency table chi-square statistic, with P value obtained from a table of the chi-square distribution with 1 degree of freedom.

5. This method uses as a statistic

$$\sum_{i=1}^{n} \chi_i^2$$

having a chi-square distribution with d.f. $= n(=85$ here). χ_i^2 is the usual χ^2 statistic in the ith 2×2 table.

6. In this application of Fisher's statistic (*4*), T_i is $\pm$ the square root of the chi-square statistic with sign plus if there is an excess of men admitted and sign minus otherwise; the P value is the probability of a standard normal deviate exceeding T_i.

7. Transformation to linearity by simple changes of variable, for example to log (odds), is also not successful.

8. If π_i, p_i, and p_i' represent, respectively, the probability of applying to department i, the probability of being admitted given that application is to department i, and the probability of being a male given that application is to department i, then a reasonable measure of the association of the numbers p_i, p_i' is the correlation (weighted according to the share of each major in the applicant pool)

$$\rho = \Sigma \pi_i (p_i - p.)(p_i' - p_.')/[\Sigma \pi_i (p_i - p.)^2 \Sigma \pi_i (p_i' - p_.')^2]^{1/2}$$

where $p.$, $p'.$ are defined by $\Sigma \pi_i p_i$, $\Sigma \pi_i p_i'$, respectively. As usual, $|\rho| = 1$ indicates linear dependence between the p_i, p_i' while $\rho = 0$ suggests "no relation." Positive values indicate "positive association" and so on.

This correlation can be estimated by substituting the observed proportions of applicants to department i, admitted applicants to department i among applicants to department i, and male applicants to department i among applicants to department i for π_i, p_i and p_i', respectively. This is the statistic we call $\hat{\rho}$.

We can use $\hat{\rho}$ as a test statistic for the hypothesis that $\rho = 0$. To do so we need the distribution of $\hat{\rho}$ under that hypothesis. It turns out that $\hat{\rho}/(\text{Var } \hat{\rho})^{1/2}$ has approximately a standard normal distribution. The expression Var $\hat{\rho}$ is complicated because of the statistical dependence between p_i and p_i'. Editorial considerations have prompted its deletion. It is obtainable from the authors.

9. The probability that an observation as extreme as (or more extreme than) the most extreme one would occur by chance alone, where $n =$ number of simultaneous independent experiments or observations, and $p =$ probability of occurrence by chance of the most extreme observation if it had been selected at random for a single observation, is $1 - (1 - p)^n$, and thus for p close to zero is approximately np.

10. Smallness of numbers of women applicants also invalidates the normal approximation used in the significance probabilities of approach B, but this can be remedied.

11. This may be expressed as

$$\sum_{i=1}^{85} (w_i)(p_i)$$

where w_i is the number of women applying to the ith major and p_i is the probability of entry of any applicant into the ith major, the latter being estimated from the number of admittees divided by the number of applicants.

12. W. G. Cochran, *Biometrics* **10,** 417 (1954).

13. N. Mantel, *J. Am. Stat. Assoc.* **58,** 690 (1963).

14. Further analysis of these data, in particular examination of individual units through time, is in progress.

15. Research currently being conducted by L. Sells at Berkeley shows how drastic this screening process is, particularly with respect to mathematics.

16. There is a real danger in naive determination of bias when the action following positive determination is punitive. On the basis of Table 1, which we have now shown to be misleading, regulatory agencies of the federal government would have felt themselves justified in withholding substantial amounts of research funding from the university. A further danger in punitive action of this kind is that, being concentrated in the research area, which provides an important source of support for graduate students, it punishes not only male but also female students—women in areas in which women have traditionally been enrolled, such as the social sciences, and also pioneering women in the physical and biological sciences, where federal support has been more concentrated.

17. In fact, data in hand at Berkeley suggest a dramatic decrease in the early dropout rates of women and the disappearance of the differential in dropout rates of men and women. It will be several years before we will be able to judge whether this phenomenon is one of decreased or simply of delayed attrition.

18. If the same naive aggregation is carried out for the 85 departments used in most of the analysis, $N = 12{,}654$, $\chi^2 = 105.6$, d.f. $= 1$, $P = 0$.

19. The investigation was initiated by E.A.H., using data retrievable from a computerized system developed by V. Aldrich. Advice on statistical procedures in the later stages of the investigation was provided by P.J.B., and programming and other computation was done by J.W.O'C.

NOTES[1]

Dear Peter,

I write to praise your article on sex bias in graduate admissions. Your article stands out in the literature that attempts to apply statistical methods to detect and measure discrimination; its publication is highly praiseworthy.

Yet it does not fully come to grips with the central, perhaps insoluble, problem of any study dealing with survey information alone... that is, of any study without the randomized assignment of a proper experiment or at least without a well understood underlying theoretical structure. That central problem is the inevitable arbitrariness of stratifications used in the analysis.

Your paper begins with a simple two-by-two table for Berkeley graduate admissions: Male–Female vs. Admit–Deny. The classical hypothesis test applied to those data (under assumptions of independence and homogeneity) comes out with apparent discrimination against women at very high levels of statistical significance. By more refined analysis, however, department by department, followed by recombination of the individual departmental results, a different picture emerges: now there is apparent discrimination in favor of women and at a less extreme level of statistical significance.

---

[1] The following correspondence has been slightly edited with the approval of the authors for this collection.

Yet suppose that another stratification had been used—for example, California residency vs. nonresidency, ethnic background, or age. Such a stratification might have been proposed in place of the departmental one, or in addition to it. There is no a priori reason to think that the apparent results on discrimination would remain the same under a different stratification, either by itself or intersecting the department stratification.

To illustrate the general point, your paper gives a hypothetical example with two departments for which proportions of acceptance for men and women are the same within each department, but where pooling the two departments gives a very different picture of apparent discrimination. (This is a standard sort of statistical example that resembles models used in factor analysis, latent structure analysis, and elsewhere...mixtures with stochastic independence in the separate components.)

Yet it is not clear what our conclusions would be if another dichotomy—say California residency vs. nonresidency—were considered. Suppose, to take an extreme case, that there were sharp discrimination *against* California women residents and *in favor* of nonCalifornia women. Then we might have the following frequencies (where M = Men, W = Women, A = Admit, D = Deny):

Dept. A.

	Resident A	Resident D		Nonresident A	Nonresident D		Total over residency A	Total over residency D
M	200	0	M	0	200	M	200	200
W	0	100	W	100	0	W	100	200

Dept. B.

	Resident A	Resident D		Nonresident A	Nonresident D		Total over residency A	Total over residency D
M	50	0	M	0	100	M	50	100
W	0	300	W	150	0	W	150	300

(The two tables on the right are those given in your paper.) If now we add over the two departments, we obtain

	Resident A	Resident D		Nonresident A	Nonresident D		Total over residency A	Total over residency D
M	250	0	M	0	300	M	250	300
W	0	400	W	250	0	W	250	400

and we see plainly the sharp discriminations in opposite directions for the two residency categories.

In practice one would hardly expect anything so extreme, and in fact one can manufacture cases in which the apparent picture oscillates as fresh stratifications are brought in.

This problem is a general one of inference and of practice; it arises, for example, if one thinks about what criteria to use in setting insurance premiums.

You and your colleagues would presumably argue for the primacy of the departmental stratification because the departments are the primary decision-making units. If so, that would seem to me a non sequitur, for the central difficulty is the possible presence of unsuspected or not-allowed-for causal variables.

Quite aside from the problem of stratification one might well be concerned about treating student admissions data of this sort as if they came from a probability sample of any kind. Surely heavy selective pressures and complex dependencies must exist at the stage of application making by potential students.

For the important social problem of discrimination, it seems to me too crude to use statistical data of the kind your paper discusses. Rather, the more appropriate techniques seem to me those of careful opinion elicitation and of social psychological experimentation. Both of these rely on statistical method, but they also rely on long-studied disciplines of human behavior and of psychological experimentation.

Sincerely yours,
William H. Kruskal

Dear Bill:

(1) You are of course right to raise the fundamental point of choice of stratification. I see a nonstatistical question here. What do we mean by bias? Does discrimination by a decision-making unit based on arbitrary criteria coupled with sex constitute bias if averaging on these other criteria leaves us with independence? Somehow I feel that averaging over things like residency, which are criteria considered by a decision maker, is different from averaging over departments which are the decision-making units.

(2) Your point on the nature of the data is incontrovertible. We certainly thought only vaguely of populations of putative applicants and the P values really represent only subjective measures of the strength of the evidence.

(3) Largely through ignorance and prejudice, I wonder how effective careful opinion solicitation and the techniques of social psychology would be here. I have a high regard for the powers of deception of my colleagues if they wish to deceive. Also establishing the connection between differential attitudes to the sexes and actions on admission would still rest with data such as ours.

Having said all this, I agree wholeheartedly with your main point as expressed in your second paragraph. Data of this kind cannot settle the main questions unless we make uncheckable and possibly unwarranted assumptions. What do you think of the following semifrivolous proposal for getting a more satisfactory assessment? Let's treat the applicants to each department each year as separate populations. Suppose (for large departments) before any applications are processed we select substantial subsamples of males and females and switch sexes carefully throughout the dossier before sending them on to the departments. Significant differences between the admission pattern for the sex change group and the rest of the population would be evidence of bias (in our sense). Aggregate measures of bias could then be computed in the usual way. Of course, things like your residence-sex interaction could still not be spotted.

All the best,
Peter J. Bickel

Dear Peter:

Proper experiments of the kind you describe have indeed been done, although I do not have citations at my fingertips. One article I've read describes such an experiment for college admission, and Betty Scott has told me of a similar experiment in connection with hiring young faculty. As you suggest, the ethical and practical difficulties are large, but the latter at least are not insurmountable.

That the decisions about graduate admissions lie primarily with the departments does not seem to me a compelling reason to stratify by department and then stop. First, some important decisions are not made by the department and are highly diffuse ... decisions about where to live, whether or not to apply, where to apply, in what field, etc. Second, the node of immediate decision need not be related to the relevant causal mechanism. For example, if I take the wrong turn on an auto trip at an intersection because a sign post is twisted, the decision was mine but the cause wholly separate.

Cordially,
William H. Kruskal

MOTOR VEHICLE INSPECTION AND MOTOR VEHICLE ACCIDENT MORTALITY

THEODORE COLTON and
ROBERT C. BUXBAUM

The toll measured in lives lost, injury sustained, and property damage from motor vehicle accidents needs no emphasis. It is a medical, social, and economic problem of national importance. Attention has recently been focused on the vehicle, its design deficiencies and its propensity toward mechanical failure. Thus, the vehicle is viewed as an etiologic agent that, along with other factors such as the driver, the environment, and others, contributes to serious injury and death. We are concerned in this report with the role of mechanical failure in motor vehicle accident mortality.

The underlying rationale of this investigation is as follows: If mechanical failure contributes to mortality, then an attempt at identifying and correcting mechanical failure should decrease mortality. Compulsory motor vehicle inspection is one attempt to identify and correct mechanical failure. Some states have statewide inspection programs, others do not. Hence, the question we pose is, do states with compulsory motor vehicle inspection exhibit lower motor vehicle accident mortality rates?

We have previously reported on this and showed that among males age 45–54 in 1960 the mortality was lower in inspection than in noninspection states. Furthermore, this difference was larger for nonwhites compared to whites and was maintained over a variety of other disturbing type variables which included population density, per capita income, and mortality from other accidents. The purpose of this report is to consider all age groups, and both sexes as well.

MATERIAL AND METHODS
Our sources of information are publicly available in vital statistics (2) and census (3) reports.

Reprinted with permission from *American Journal of Public Health*, Vol. 58, No. 6, pp. 1090–1099.

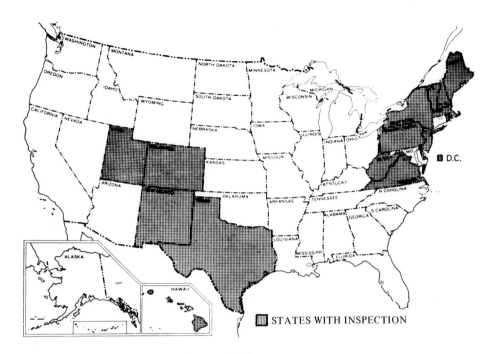

FIG. 1 *Motor vehicle inspection states, 1960.*

The year 1960 was chosen because calculation of mortality requires data on motor vehicle accident deaths and population at risk classified by state, race, sex, and age. The detailed population information is available only in census years.

The states with compulsory motor vehicle inspection (4) in 1960 are shown in Figure 1. In this report we have grouped inspection states regardless of their varying inspection procedures. Furthermore, some states inspect only once a year, some twice. Some use state-owned and state-run inspection sites: others use private garages and filling stations franchised by the state. With the data at hand, we felt it was not possible to analyze adequately any subgrouping of inspection states.

New York, which inspects only those automobiles four or more years old, was classified as an inspection state. Connecticut, which requires inspection of used cars purchased out of state and instate cars ten or more years old when ownership changes, was classified as a noninspection state. Several states have inspection programs only in isolated municipalities. These states were classified as noninspection states.

In 1960 there were 17 inspection (including the District of Columbia) and 34 noninspection states.

The analysis utilizes age-specific and age-adjusted mortality rates. The age-adjusted mortality rates have been calculated by the direct method using the total population by age of the United States in 1960 (*3*). The elimination of the disturbing or concomitant variables and the significance testing is achieved by weighted covariance analysis.

RESULTS

Sex-race-age-specific mortality

The age-specific motor vehicle accident mortality rates in the aggregate of the inspection and noninspection states are shown in Figure 2 separately for white males, nonwhite males, white females, and nonwhite females. The striking feature of Figure 2 is that for all four sex-race groups the motor

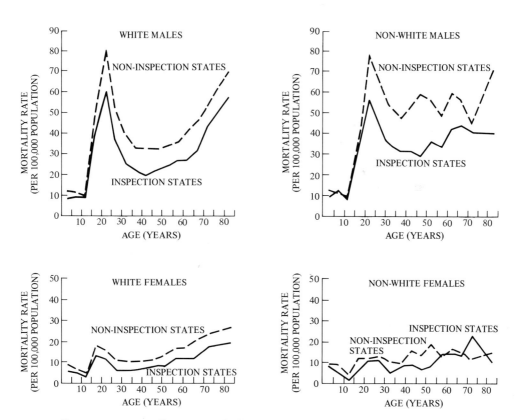

FIG. 2 *Sex-race-age-specific motor vehicle accident mortality rates in inspection and noninspection states, 1960 (rate per 100,000 population).*

vehicle accident mortality rate is higher in the noninspection compared with the inspection states at almost every age.

Figure 2 also indicates some previously well-known information regarding motor vehicle accident mortality by age, race, and sex. First, the rates at each age are higher in males than in females. For females there is little difference in the age-specific rates of whites and non-whites. For males, both whites and nonwhites have their highest mortality at age 20–25 with a sharp decrease after age 25. For white males there is a fairly steep rise beginning at about age 50, while for nonwhite males there is a moderate rise beginning at this age. It is at the older ages that pedestrian deaths become increasingly important and the rise in over-all motor vehicle mortality beyond age 50 is mainly this pedestrian effect. In the middle years, age 25 to 65, the nonwhite males have appreciably higher mortality rates than their white counterparts. The largest differential in white and nonwhite male mortality is at age 45–54, the subject of our previous report.

The age-adjusted mortality rates by sex and race are shown in Table 1. These age-adjusted rates are for all ages and for ages 15–64, the age group which encompasses almost all of the driving population at risk. For each sex-race category the age-adjusted rates are higher in noninspection than in inspection states. The 15–64 age-adjusted rates exhibit a remarkably consistent pattern of a 50 percent higher rate in the noninspection states. Table 1 also shows male higher than female mortality, nonwhite male higher than white male mortality, and white female approximately equivalent to nonwhite female mortality.

Table 2 gives age-specific rates, regardless of sex and race. Again, at each age there are higher rates in noninspection states. On a percentage basis, the largest discrepancy occurs between ages 25–54.

TABLE 1 AGE-ADJUSTED* MORTALITY RATES FROM MOTOR VEHICLE ACCIDENTS BY SEX AND COLOR IN INSPECTION VS. NONINSPECTION STATES, 1960 (RATE PER 100,000 POPULATION).

		All ages			Age 15–64		
		Non-inspection states	Inspection states	Ratio†	Non-inspection states	Inspection states	Ratio†
Males:	White	35.0	25.4	1.38	44.0	30.0	1.47
	Nonwhite	41.4	28.5	1.45	54.6	36.1	1.51
Females:	White	12.4	8.4	1.48	13.5	9.1	1.49
	Nonwhite	11.4	8.4	1.36	13.1	9.0	1.45
Total population		23.8	16.8	1.42	29.1	20.0	1.45

* Adjusted to total US population by age in 1960.

† Rate in noninspection states/rate in inspections states.

TABLE 2 MORTALITY RATE FROM MOTOR VEHICLE ACCIDENTS BY AGE IN INSPECTION AND NONINSPECTION STATES, 1960 (RATE PER 100,000 POPULATION).

Age (years)	Nonin-spection states	Inspection states	Ratio*
Under 15	9.3	7.0	1.34
15–24	41.6	31.0	1.34
25–34	27.7	18.2	1.52
35–44	22.2	14.0	1.59
45–54	24.4	16.1	1.52
55–64	28.2	20.1	1.41
65 and older	38.1	28.6	1.33
Total population	23.8	16.8	1.42

* Rate in noninspection states/rate in inspection states.

Age-adjusted mortality by state

For each state the age-adjusted mortality rate among white and nonwhite males age 15–64 appears in Table 3. The rank of the state in its male age-adjusted motor vehicle accident mortality is also indicated (1 means lowest mortality). It is clear from Table 3 that (a) there are large differences in motor vehicle accident mortality among the states, and (b) there is overlap in the mortality rates of inspection and noninspection states.

The age-adjusted motor vehicle accident mortality among white males 15–64 is lowest in Rhode Island with a rate of 13.4 per 100,000 and highest in Wyoming with a rate of 96.0 per 100,000, more than a sevenfold range in rates. Among inspection states, Colorado, Vermont, New Mexico, and Texas rank high in mortality and illustrate one aspect of overlap. Among noninspection states, Connecticut, Illinois, Maryland, and Washington rank low in mortality, and illustrate the other aspect of overlap.

The age-adjusted motor vehicle accident mortality among nonwhite males 15–64 is ranked only in those 24 states where there is a population base of at least 50,000. Rates range from a low of 20.6 in the District of Columbia to a high of 76.0 in Oklahoma. Among the five inspection states, none has an appreciably high rate. Among the 19 ranked noninspection states Illinois, Indiana, Maryland, Michigan, and Ohio have low rates.

Comparing white and nonwhite rates within states, some states have appreciably higher white than nonwhite rates (Mississippi and Michigan), some have about the same white and nonwhite rates (Indiana, Texas, and the District of Columbia) and others have appreciably lower white than nonwhite rates (Florida, Oklahoma, New Jersey, North Carolina, Maryland).

TABLE 3 AGE-ADJUSTED* MOTOR VEHICLE ACCIDENT MORTALITY RATES BY STATE FOR WHITE AND NONWHITE MALES 15–64 YEARS OLD, 1960, AND CHANGE IN RATE FROM 1950 TO 1960 (RATE PER 100,000 POPULATION).

State	White males					Nonwhite males				
	1960 pop'n 15–64 (000)	1960 rate	Rank	Change from '50 to '60	Rank	1960 pop'n 15–64 (000)	1960 rate	Rank	Change from '50 to '60	Rank
Inspection states										
Colo.	495	49.9	31	−1.3	22	16	(27.6)		(−9.9)	
Del.	114	37.5	14	−3.9	17	18	(54.4)		(−32.0)	
D.C.	113	20.6	2	−6.6	11	121	20.6	1	−14.6	2
Maine	276	29.6	8	3.5	34	2	(204.6)		(70.7)	
Mass.	1,455	21.0	5	3.0	33	37	(20.1)		(−7.8)	
N.H.	174	37.4	13	3.5	35	1	(0.0)		(0.0)	
N.J.	1,683	20.9	3	0.4	28	152	41.5	8	−3.8	12
N.M.	253	79.1	47	11.1	43	19	(177.3)		(32.7)	
N.Y.	4,583	23.2	6	1.4	30	438	27.7	4	1.7	15
Pa.	3,081	28.1	7	0.9	29	245	26.1	2	−2.7	13
R.I.	254	13.4	1	−3.6	18	6	(21.5)		(−80.6)	
Tex.	2,477	47.7	27	−12.9	4	321	47.5	11	−7.8	7
Utah	241	42.4	21	−5.7	13	5	(196.6)		(161.5)	
Vt.	110	51.4	35	4.9	36	0	(0.0)		(0.0)	
Va.	980	35.7	12	−13.3	3	228	40.9	7	−17.7	1
W.Va.	504	42.1	20	0.1	26	23	(83.0)		(45.9)	
Total	16,791	30.8		−1.8		1,632	37.3		−4.7	

Table 3 also lists, for each state, the change in the age-adjusted motor vehicle accident rate between 1950 and 1960 and the state's rank in change. In some states the rate has risen, in others it has declined. Furthermore, declining rates are not necessarily associated with inspection. For white males, Idaho, a noninspection state, had the largest decline, while Wyoming experienced the largest increase. For the nonwhite males the largest 1950 to 1960 decrease occurred in Virginia while the largest increase occurred in Oklahoma.

Table 4 shows the aggregate changes in rates from 1950 to 1960 for those states inspecting throughout the decade, those initiating inspection between 1951 and 1959 (New Mexico, New York, Rhode Island, Texas, and West Virginia), and those that did not inspect at all during the decade. The results for white males do not provide any evidence that continual inspection or the initiation of inspection are associated with an appreciable change in mortality. For nonwhite males there is some indication of a slight trend. On

TABLE 3 Continued

State	White males					Nonwhite males				
	1960 pop'n 15–64 (000)	1960 rate	Rank	Change from '50 to '60	Rank	1960 pop'n 15–64 (000)	1960 rate	Rank	Change from '50 to '60	Rank
Noninspection states										
Ala.	677	57.5	42	−7.1	8	236	66.7	19	13.0	21
Ariz.	352	57.7	43	−15.5	2	34	(108.2)		(15.9)	
Ark.	406	56.2	41	12.8	45	89	53.8	14	17.7	22
Calif.	4,416	47.7	24	−4.2	16	392	47.8	12	−7.4	8
Conn.	724	21.0	4	−2.0	19	32	(42.6)		(−3.4)	
Fla.	1,177	40.9	18	−10.6	6	246	73.9	23	6.6	17
Ga.	854	51.1	34	0.3	27	279	59.2	17	−3.9	11
Idaho	188	52.6	36	−20.8	1	3	(100.3)		(17.1)	
Ill.	2,692	31.3	10	−7.1	9	297	26.3	3	−13.7	3
Ind.	1,269	47.7	28	1.9	32	74	46.8	9	−9.3	6
Iowa	764	43.0	22	1.6	31	8	(10.7)		(−17.6)	
Kans.	601	44.6	23	−4.8	14	28	(24.6)		(−17.5)	
Ky.	815	53.8	38	6.1	38	59	68.4	20	8.5	20
La.	649	49.0	30	8.9	42	254	60.4	18	17.9	23
Md.	784	30.3	9	−6.7	10	149	47.4	10	−5.3	9
Mich.	2,054	40.7	17	−4.4	15	209	31.2	5	−12.7	4
Minn.	941	41.2	19	7.0	39	12	(74.8)		(27.1)	
Miss.	376	66.5	46	14.2	46	208	55.5	16	4.2	16
Mo.	1,135	47.9	29	−11.0	5	104	52.5	13	−5.2	10
Mont.	189	62.4	44	5.7	37	6	(155.6)		(26.5)	
Neb.	392	39.8	16	−1.5	21	10	(44.5)		(−5.8)	
Nev.	87	95.3	48	14.5	47	7	(107.1)		(−66.9)	
N.C.	1,042	53.0	37	−0.6	23	295	71.7	22	7.9	18
N.D.	179	55.5	40	19.1	48	3	(0.0)		(−39.7)	
Ohio	2,570	38.0	15	−2.0	20	224	34.3	6	−11.7	5
Okla.	624	49.9	32	8.1	41	55	76.0	24	33.6	24
Ore.	504	50.3	33	−6.1	12	11	(89.3)		(−32.3)	
S.C.	472	55.4	39	−8.3	7	199	69.6	21	1.3	14
S.D.	185	62.4	45	12.7	44	7	(282.9)		(95.2)	
Tenn.	880	45.0	25	−0.3	24	149	55.1	15	8.1	19
Wash.	816	35.5	11	0.0	25	32	(84.1)		(24.4)	
Wisc.	1,103	47.6	26	8.0	40	25	(36.5)		(−58.0)	
Wyo.	97	96.0	49	25.7	49	2	(88.4)		(73.7)	
Total	30,011	44.6		−1.8		3,738	55.2		0.4	

Note: Figures in parentheses indicate the rate has a population base less than 50,000.
* All rates adjusted to total United States population by age in 1960.

TABLE 4 CHANGE IN AGE-ADJUSTED MOTOR VEHICLE ACCIDENT MORTALITY RATE FROM 1950 TO 1960 FOR WHITE AND NONWHITE MALES 15–64 YEARS OLD BY INSPECTION STATUS (RATE PER 100,000 POPULATION).

Inspection status of states	1950–1960 change in rate (per 100,000 population)	
	White males 15–64	Nonwhite males 15–64
Began inspection before 1950	−0.7	−8.6
Began inspection between 1951 and 1959	−2.9	−0.7
Did not inspect during 1950 to 1960	11.8	+0.4

the average, states maintaining inspection throughout the decade exhibited a decrease in mortality (−8.6 per 100,000), those beginning inspection exhibited a very slight decrease (−0.7 per 100,000), while those not inspecting during the decade show a slight increase (+0.4 per 100,000).

Influence of other variables

In examining the role of inspection in motor vehicle accident mortality it is important to recognize that the inspection states are a self-selected group. Hence, the comparison of mortality in inspection and noninspection states should account for the possibility that the inspection and noninspection states may be very different in several ways other than inspection and that perhaps these other variables explain the observed mortality difference. For example, population density is inversely related to motor vehicle accident mortality; the denser the population, the lower the rate. If inspection states tend to be the more densely populated (which, from Figure 1, seems to be the case), then some or perhaps all of the difference between the inspection and noninspection mortality rates is explainable by differences in population density. The question is how much of this difference is attributable to population density? Does any residual difference not explainable by population density provide evidence for a separate effect of motor vehicle inspection?

The same argument applies to other variables such as per capita income and mortality from other accidents. (The argument with the latter is that inspection states are more cautious and safety-conscious, and hence tend to be states with lower mortality rates for other accidents as well. In other words, the difference in motor vehicle accident mortality is not specific but is related to or explainable by mortality from other accidents.) Finally, the argument applies to all three of these variables simultaneously.

Removal of the influence of these disturbing variables is handled by a weighted covariance analysis and the results are shown in Table 5. The significance tests of Table 5 examine whether the difference in mortality between the aggregate of inspection and noninspection states is above and beyond what might be expected by chance considering the state-to-state mortality variation. For this purpose we consider the age-adjusted mortality rate in each state as an observation from a random sample, with the state as the sampling unit. The units are unequal in size (size is the population 15–64) and the subsequent analysis takes this into account (5), weighting according to the size of the state.

The results indicate that the difference in white male age-adjusted motor vehicle accident mortality between inspection and noninspection states is highly significant (P < 0.001). Furthermore, after accounting for

TABLE 5 STATISTICAL COMPARISON OF MOTOR VEHICLE ACCIDENT MORTALITY* IN INSPECTION AND NONINSPECTION STATES, UNITED STATES 1960.

Statistical comparison	Rate* per 100,000 population				
	Noninspection States	Inspection states	Difference	SE of difference	P-value
	White males				
No adjustments	44.6	30.8	13.8	3.70	<0.001
Covariance adjustment for:					
Other accident mortality rate	43.3	33.5	9.8	2.72	<0.001
Log population density	42.3	35.6	6.7	2.07	<0.001
Per capita income	43.9	32.2	11.7	3.17	<0.001
All three variates simultaneously	42.3	35.5	6.8	2.10	<0.001
	Nonwhite males				
No adjustments	55.2	37.3	17.9	6.53	<0.01
Covariance adjustment for:					
Other accident mortality rate	54.9	37.8	17.1	4.64	<0.001
Log population density	52.6	42.9	9.7	5.57	N.S.
Per capita income	52.6	43.0	9.6	4.80	<0.05
All three variates simultaneously	53.0	42.0	11.0	3.90	<0.01

* Rates used are the age-adjusted rates for the population 15–64 years old (see Table 3).

disturbing variables with covariance analysis (we have examined population density, per capita income and other accident mortality rate, both individually and simultaneously) this difference persists in being statistically significant (P < 0.001).

Note that as covariance analysis is applied the magnitude of the difference decreases. For example, with white males from a difference of 13.8 per 100,000 with no covariance adjustment, after adjustment for log population density the difference is only 6.7 per 100,000—about a 50 per cent reduction from the unadjusted difference. But log population density also accounts for a sizable portion of the state-to-state variation. Hence, removing the variation attributable to log population density the residual state-to-state variation yields a standard error of 2.07 to accompany the adjusted 6.7 per 100,000 difference. Thus, with covariance adjustment the difference remains statistically significant (P < 0.001).

A similar although not as pronounced pattern exists for nonwhites. For nonwhite males the level of statistical significance is not as pronounced as that for white males. The magnitude of the difference is larger than that for white males, but this is accompanied by a larger standard error. This is due to the substantially higher state-to-state variation in mortality for nonwhites. With covariance adjustment for log population density alone, the difference fails to reach statistical significance (P < 0.05). However, all other covariance adjustments yield statistically significant differences. In particular, adjustment for the three covariates simultaneously results in a highly significant difference (P < 0.1).

DISCUSSION

The results of this investigation of all ages confirm the previous observation in males 45–54 that motor vehicle inspection is associated with lower motor vehicle accident mortality rates. This difference is statistically significant and persists in being so after making adjustments for differences in population density, per capita income and other accident mortality rate.

These results are consistent with those reported by Recht (6). Recht performed many multiple regression analyses to identify factors which would explain the state-to-state variation in motor vehicle accident mortality. Motor vehicle inspection is one of the several factors he found to be significantly related. These results are also compatible with a similar report by Fuchs and Leveson (7). They performed a multiple regression study in which the 1960 age-adjusted motor vehicle accident mortality rates by state were regressed on inspection, on the three variables included in the covariance analysis in Table 5, and on other variables including motor fuel consumption per capita, per cent of the state's population 18–24 years old, alcohol consumption per capita, per cent of motor vehicles more than nine years old, the median number of school years completed by the state's population 25 years old and over, and whether or not the state requires vision inspection with license renewals. Their results indicated that population density and gasoline consumption are the only variables with regression coefficients which differ significantly from zero. When all variables are accounted for simultaneously, the effect of vehicle inspection did not achieve statistical significance although the data showed a trend in that direction. The authors concluded that their results support the hypothesis of an effect of inspection on motor accident mortality, but its magnitude is considerably smaller than that suggested by our previous report (1).

One might expect that inception of inspection would affect motor vehicle accident mortality. The results of our investigation are crude in that we could only compare mortality from 1950 to 1960. Those states beginning inspection during this decade do not show any pronounced decrease in their motor vehicle accident mortality rate. In view of the large state-to-state variation in mortality, the changes in mortality exhibited in Table 4 can hardly be classified as clear-cut. They do suggest, however, that at least for nonwhite males the observed changes are consistent with the claim that inspection has some effect on mortality.

An immediate question with motor vehicle inspection is to estimate how many of the present 50,000 deaths on the highway could be prevented if a nationwide program of motor vehicle inspection were adopted. We feel that the data presently available are insufficient to warrant any such firm estimate. We note that if the noninspection states had the same age-sex-race-specific mortality rates as inspection states, there would be 7,977 lives saved. However, it is not evident that a nationwide program of inspection would achieve this lowering of mortality rates. Furthermore, as the covariance analysis of Table 5 indicated, not all the difference in mortality between inspection and noninspection states is attributable to inspection. Some of the difference is attributable to differences in other factors such as population density per capita income, and mortality from other accidents. At best, if all states could achieve mortality rates as low as Rhode Island's (the state with the lowest age-adjusted 1960 rate), the number of lives saved would be enormous. Unfortunately, we do not know, nor are we likely to know, just what to do to reduce each state's mortality to this level.

The Arthur D. Little (8) report surveying the current state of information on traffic safety concluded, "There is no single factor identified in the literature which can be labeled a principal 'cause' of highway hazard, and which could be remedied to reduce traffic accident losses markedly."

Fuchs and Leveson (7) using the results of their multiple regression analysis, speculated with a cost-benefit analysis of a nationwide motor vehicle inspection program. Their calculations suggested "... that the expected value of the total economic benefits might well exceed the estimated costs, but the margin may not be extraordinarily large." Solid data underlying these results are lacking and some fairly gross assumptions had to be made. For example, it is assumed that the morbidity differential between the inspection and noninspection states is the same on a percentage basis as the observed mortality differential. Also, it is assumed that a national program would bring the noninspection states to the level of the inspection states. Since inspection states differ in the thoroughness of inspection, it is conceivable that a national uniform program of high standards might reap additional benefits in those states that are now inspecting. Clearly no data are available concerning the response, if any, of motor vehicle accident morbidity and mortality to increasing doses of more stringent inspection procedures.

The evidence on the role of inspection in motor vehicle accident mortality in this report is retrospective and circumstantial. Further investigation is needed to clarify this association. Perhaps the next step is to obtain evidence on a prospective basis with studies in defined populations using tried and tested epidemiological methods. Furthermore, for inspection as well as for many other control measures that have been suggested, it would seem that an analogue of the controlled clinical trial as used for evaluating new drugs, medical and surgical procedures could be adopted for evaluating effects on traffic safety.

Editors' Note: Edward Tufte discusses the comparison of death rates between inspection and noninspection states in *Data Analysis for Politics and Policy*, Englewood Cliffs, N.J.: Prentice-Hall, 1974, pp. 5–30. He discusses controlling for the additional variable of total miles driven.

REFERENCES

1. Buxbaum, R. C., and Colton, T. Relationship of Motor Vehicle Inspection to Accident Mortality. J.A.M.A. 197:. 31–36, 1966.

2. Vital Statistics of the United States: 1960, National Center for Health Statistics. Washington, D.C.: Gov. Ptg. Office, 1963, vol. 2, pt. 13.

3. U.S. Census of Population: 1960. U.S. Bureau of the Census. Washington, D.C.: Gov. Ptg. Office, 1963. vol. 1, pt. 1–51.

4. Digest of Motor Laws. American Automobile Association, 1960.

5. Cochran, W. G. Sampling Techniques (2nd ed.). New York, N.Y.: Wiley, 1963, pp. 64–67.

6. Recht, J. L. Multiple Regression Study of the Effects of Safety Activities on the Traffic Accident Problem. Chicago, Ill.: National Safety Council, 1965.

7. Fuchs, V. R., and Leveson, I. Motor Accident Mortality and Compulsory Inspection of Vehicles. J.A.M.A. 201: 657–661, 1967.

8. The State of the Art of Traffic Safety. Arthur D. Little, Co., 1966, Cambridge, Mass.

DOES AIR POLLUTION SHORTEN LIVES?

LESTER B. LAVE and EUGENE P. SESKIN

1. INTRODUCTION

The cause of a disease is often difficult to establish. For chronic diseases, establishing a cause and effect relationship is especially difficult. Many studies show that populations exposed to urban air pollution have a shorter life expectancy and higher incidence of lung cancer, emphysema, and other chronic respiratory diseases [1–3]. Yet it is a long step to assert that this observed association between air pollution and ill health is proof that air pollution causes ill health and that steps ought to be taken to abate air pollution for public health reasons. There is disagreement among physicians as to whether air pollution causes lung cancer, bronchitis, or emphysema, or generally reduces life expectancy [1, 4–6]. A related argument is that the effect of air pollution is so slight that it is not a matter of public concern [6].

The situation is similar to the controversy as to whether cigarette smoking causes lung cancer. Both the cigarette smoking and air pollution controversies stem from the fact that many other possible causal factors are present. Urban dwellers live in more crowded conditions, get less exercise, and tend to live more tense lives. Since each of these factors is known to increase the morbidity and mortality rates, care must be taken to control or account for each factor before drawing inferences from the association between air pollution or cigarette smoking and ill health. Some confidence stems from the fact that numerous independent studies with various controls have found an association, thereby endowing it with a level of confidence that no single study warrants [1–3].

Reprinted from John W. Pratt (ed.), *Statistical and Mathematical Aspects of Pollution Problems*, Marcel Dekker, Inc., New York, 1974, pp. 223–247 by courtesy of Marcel Dekker, Inc.

2. METHOD

Laboratory methods are of limited use in settling these controversies. Instead, the methods required are those of epidemiology. The basic problem is one of controlling all causal variables. Accounting for confounding factors in observed data is one of the purposes of multivariate statistical analysis. Since we have some notion of the model and desire estimates of the partial contribution of each factor, an appropriate technique is multiple regression.

The mortality data for our analysis come from two sources. Mortality data are tabulated in Ref. 7 with more detailed mortality rates reported in Ref. 8. The first source reports total (and total nonwhite) mortality rates, with an additional breakdown for infants under 1 year and under 28 days. The second source disaggregates the rates by race, sex, and age. We have analyzed four age groups: 0–14, 15–44, 45–64, and 65 and older.

Data were collected on 117 Standard Metropolitan Statistical Areas (SMSAs) for 1960.* Air pollution data were gathered by the National Air Sampling Network [9]. Data for 1960 were collected on suspended particulates and total sulfates. Biweekly measurements were taken; we used the smallest and largest readings, as well as the arithmetic mean of the 26 readings. Socioeconomic data were taken from the 1960 Census [10].

Multiple regression attempts to explain the variation in a dependent variable (the mortality rate) in terms of the variation in each of a set of independent or explanatory variables (measured air pollution, and socioeconomic variables). Since we had little a priori knowledge as to which measures of air pollution or which socioeconomic variables would be important, all were initially tried using the 1960 data. Some variables contributed little to the statistical significance of the regression. For example, there were three measures of suspended particulates and three measures of sulfates, some of which were certain to be redundant. Variables whose coefficients were greater than their standard error were retained and the others eliminated, subject to two qualifications. Since interest centered on the air pollution variables, at least one was retained from each set. In reestimating the relation, we often found that the refined air pollution variable was now significant (which is not surprising, given that we eliminated two air pollution measures which were highly correlated with the included one). Sometimes the retained air pollution variable still contributed little to the statistical significance of the regression. Such variables were eliminated, subject to the restriction that at least one air pollution variable was retained in the final equation. We note again that our criterion for retention of a variable was that its estimated coefficient exceed its estimated standard error. Since these estimated relations are ad hoc, they must be reviewed with care.

---

* These SMSAs were selected because of the availability of pollution data.

3. RESULTS

3.1 Statement of results

The first estimated relation is shown in Eq. (1), where the total mortality rate in 1960 is "explained" by: Mean P (the arithmetic mean of the biweekly suspended particulate readings in $\mu g/m^3$), Min S (the smallest of the biweekly sulfate readings in $\mu g/m^3 \times 10$), P/M^2 (the population density in the SMSA in people per square mile), % NW (the percentage of the SMSA population who are nonwhite $\times 10$, i.e., the number per thousand), % ≥ 65 (the percentage of the SMSA population 65 and older $\times 10$), and e (an error term):*

$$MR = 19.607 + 0.041 \text{ Mean P} + 0.071 \text{ Min S} + 0.001 \text{ P/M}^2 \qquad (1)$$
$$(2.53) \qquad\qquad (3.18) \qquad\qquad (1.67)$$

$$+ 0.041 \text{ (% NW)} + 0.687 \text{ (% } \geq 65) + e.$$
$$(5.81) \qquad\qquad (18.94)$$

These independent variables explain the total mortality rate across 117 SMSAs extremely well, since 82.7% of the variation is explained ($R^2 = 0.827$). The effect of each variable on mortality is estimated by the coefficient; each is statistically significant (as shown by the t statistics below the coefficients). Note that both measures of air pollution are significant explanatory factors of the mortality rate across cities. Thus, the data fit the model quite well and the estimated effect of air pollution on mortality is quite substantial. This regression is also reported as the first row in Table 1.

Another way of illustrating the regression results is to focus on one of the cities we studied. In 1960, the total mortality rate for Pittsburgh was 103 per 10,000 population, the mean biweekly level of suspended particulates was 166.0 $\mu g/m^3$, the smallest biweekly sulfate reading was 6.0 $\mu g/m^3$, the population density was 788.0 people per square mile, 6.8% of the population was nonwhite, and 9.5% was 65 and older. Fitting these values into the equation leads to a prediction that the mortality rate would be 100 per 10,000 population; this estimate is in error by 3 per 10,000 population.

The percentage of older people is the most important variable. A one point increase (in percentage multiplied by ten) of people 65 and older is associated with a rise in the total death rate of 6.87 per 10,000. Increasing nonwhites in the population ($\times 10$) by one percentage point is estimated to raise the total death rate by 0.41 per 10,000. An increase of 1 $\mu g/m^3$ in the

---

* The specification of this relation, and of each of the relations shown in Table 1, comes from Ref. 11. As described above, ad hoc techniques were used to derive a good specification for the aggregate mortality rates in 1960. The specification continued to provide a good fit for 1961 mortality rates [11] and seems to fit the age-, race-, and sex-specific mortality rates quite well.

TABLE 1 MORTALITY REGRESSIONS: AGE-, RACE-, AND SEX-SPECIFIC DEATH RATES.[a]

Row no.	Age group	Race	Sex	R^{2b}	Const.	Regression coefficients of explanatory variables[c,d,e]						
						Min P	Mean P	Min S	P/M^2	% NW	% ≥65	% Poor
1	All ages	W+ NW	M+ F	0.827	19.607	0.041 (2.53)	0.071 (3.18)	0.001 (1.67)		0.041 (5.81)	0.687 (18.94)	
2		NW	M+ F	0.339	9.181	0.186 (3.53)	0.106 (1.49)	−0.003 (−2.16)		0.148 (6.52)	0.547 (4.70)	
3		W	M	0.198	102.405	0.033 (1.81)	0.044 (1.77)	0.001 (1.83)		0.028 (3.51)	0.034 (0.85)	
4		NW	M	0.208	103.813	0.074 (1.55)	0.071 (1.09)	0.001 (0.41)		0.101 (4.87)	0.149 (1.40)	
5		W	F	0.389	61.899	0.035 (2.79)	0.070 (4.02)	0.001 (2.54)		−0.007 (−1.24)	0.023 (0.82)	
6		NW	F	0.340	67.412	0.107 (2.82)	0.191 (3.72)	−0.001 (−0.80)		0.088 (5.41)	0.054 (0.64)	
7	<28 days	W+ NW	M+ F	0.271	149.428	0.083 (1.62)	0.120 (1.82)			0.098 (4.04)		0.056 (1.45)
8		W	M	0.276	175.240	0.036 (0.75)	0.026 (0.42)			−0.011 (−0.48)		0.097 (2.67)
9		NW	M	0.080	314.580	0.147 (0.73)	−0.145 (−0.56)			0.278 (2.85)		−0.368 (−2.39)
10		W	F	0.115	125.836	0.053 (1.34)	0.068 (1.34)			−0.033 (−1.78)		0.098 (3.31)
11		NW	F	0.130	206.087	0.270 (1.61)	0.344 (1.61)			0.254 (3.13)		−0.293 (−2.29)
12	<1 year	W+ NW	M+ F	0.537	185.802	0.365 (2.82)				0.186 (6.52)		0.157 (3.38)
13		W	M	0.070	231.196	0.129 (0.93)				−0.069 (−2.25)		0.140 (2.82)
14		NW	M	0.126	379.376	0.578 (1.02)				0.447 (3.49)		−0.206 (−0.99)
15		W	F	0.174	162.805	0.293 (2.76)				−0.086 (−3.67)		0.162 (4.27)
16		NW	F	0.119	251.032	1.125 (2.45)				0.205 (1.98)		0.118 (0.70)
17	0–14 years	W	M	0.185	66.994	0.058 (1.46)				−0.045 (−4.44)	−0.107 (−2.67)	0.063 (4.39)
18		NW	M	0.096	100.558	0.220 (1.51)				0.070 (1.84)	−0.042 (−0.29)	0.016 (0.29)
19		W	F	0.313	51.000	0.068 (2.59)				−0.041 (−6.06)	−0.111 (−4.16)	0.058 (6.08)
20		NW	F	0.163	53.138	0.293 (2.72)				0.044 (1.58)	0.094 (0.87)	0.078 (1.95)

TABLE 1 Continued

Row no.	Age group	Race	Sex	R^{2b}	Const.	Min P	Mean P	Min S	P/M^2	% NW	% ≥65	% Poor
						Regression coefficients of explanatory variables[c,d,e]						
21	15–44 years	W	M	0.236	52.921	0.036 (2.05)	−0.021 (−0.87)	0.000 (0.59)	−0.023 (−2.35)	−0.062 (−1.52)	0.069 (5.06)	
22		NW	M	0.321	49.719	0.150 (1.73)	0.028 (0.23)	0.003 (0.96)	0.140 (2.92)	0.033 (0.17)	0.180 (2.67)	
23		W	F	0.164	28.626	0.026 (2.74)	−0.005 (−0.37)	0.001 (1.89)	−0.013 (−2.53)	−0.025 (−1.14)	0.023 (3.13)	
24		NW	F	0.345	30.009	0.111 (1.99)	0.068 (0.89)	0.001 (0.89)	0.104 (3.37)	0.054 (0.43)	0.110 (2.52)	
25	45–64 years	W	M	0.336	245.138	0.127 (1.91)	0.069 (0.75)	0.006 (3.01)	0.107 (2.87)	0.202 (1.31)	0.154 (2.96)	
26		NW	M	0.311	237.856	0.252 (1.00)	0.099 (0.29)	0.006 (0.78)	0.326 (2.33)	0.406 (0.71)	0.667 (3.39)	
27		W	F	0.395	131.695	0.086 (2.33)	0.185 (3.61)	0.003 (2.84)	−0.028 (−1.36)	0.065 (0.77)	−0.009 (−0.33)	
28		NW	F	0.477	141.855	0.373 (1.99)	0.980 (3.85)	−0.004 (−0.68)	0.472 (4.56)	−0.109 (−0.26)	0.333 (2.29)	
29	≥65 years	W	M	0.385	698.367		0.637 (4.15)			0.103 (2.24)		
30		NW	M	0.051	679.310		0.927 (2.29)			−0.066 (−0.54)		
31		W	F	0.295	470.984		0.806 (6.36)			−0.064 (−1.67)		
32		NW	F	0.108	499.750		0.904 (3.42)			−0.066 (−0.84)		

[a] For means and standard deviations of the relevant variables, see Tables 1a and 1b.

[b] The coefficient of determination. In row 1, the entry 0.827 indicates that 82.7% of the variation in the total mortality rate across 117 cities is explained by the regression.

[c] The entries in each row under the general heading "Regression coefficients of explanatory variables" give the equation for the mortality rate of that segment of the population described by the age, race, and sex entries in that row. Thus row 1 gives the total mortality rate, row 2 gives the rate for all nonwhites, etc.

[d] For example, the entry 0.041 in row 1 under "Mean P" indicates that an increase of 0.1 $\mu g/m^3$ is estimated to increase the total death rate by 0.041 per 10,000 population.

[e] Figures in parentheses are the t statistics for the coefficients (the ratio of the coefficient to its standard error). A value of 1.66 is significant using a one-tailed test.

TABLE 1a MORTALITY RATES.

					Mortality[a]				
Race	Sex	All ages	<28 days	<1 year	≤14 years	15–44 years	45–64 years	≥65 years	Total
W+	M+		187.3	254.0					91.3
NW	F		(24.5)	(36.4)					(15.3)
W	M	115.4	196.9	253.8	66.4	60.9	326.2	741.4	
		(7.9)	(20.5)	(27.5)	(8.3)	(7.9)	(32.2)	(54.9)	
	F	71.1	148.8	194.7	50.2	32.3	153.2	501.1	
		(6.3)	(17.1)	(22.3)	(6.0)	(4.1)	(18.7)	(49.8)	
NW	M+								97.9
	F								(24.8)
	M	141.5	294.5	425.8	118.8	123.6	472.7	714.1	
		(20.6)	(84.0)	(113.5)	(28.7)	(40.1)	(116.6)	(134.5)	
	F	104.1	233.5	349.7	93.9	85.0	340.1	533.4	
		(17.9)	(71.7)	(91.7)	(22.0)	(26.3)	(98.8)	(90.6)	

[a] Mean mortality per 10,000 population or per 10,000 live births. Standard deviations are given in parentheses.

minimum biweekly sulfate level or mean biweekly particulate level is associated with a rise in the total death rate of 0.71 or 0.041, respectively. This regression is presented in Table 1 along with regressions explaining the mortality rate for all nonwhites (row 2), for white males (row 3), nonwhite males (row 4), white females (row 5), and nonwhite females (row 6).

Also presented in Table 1 are regressions for the under-28-day death rate (rows 7 to 11), for the under-one-year death rate (rows 12 to 16), for

TABLE 1b MEANS AND STANDARD DEVIATIONS OF EXPLANATORY VARIABLES IN THE REGRESSION ANALYSIS OF MORTALITY.

Variable	Mean	Standard deviation
Min Particulates (μg/m^3)	45.5	18.6
Mean Particulates (μg/m^3)	118.1	40.9
Min Sulfates (μg/m$^3 \times 10$)	47.2	31.3
Population per square mile	756.2	1370.6
Percentage nonwhite ($\times 10$)	125.1	104.0
Percentage 65 and over ($\times 10$)	83.9	21.2
Percentage poor ($\times 10$)	180.9	65.5

children 14 and younger (rows 17 to 20), for young adults 15–44 (rows 21 to 24), for middle-aged adults 45–64 (rows 25 to 28), and for people 65 and older (rows 29 to 32).

The general model and estimation techniques seem to be appropriate for this analysis. A high proportion of each mortality rate is explained by the independent variables. In almost every case, air pollution is a significant factor in explaining the mortality rate.

3.2 Qualifications

The results of the analysis cannot be accepted at face value. A great deal of care must be taken in interpreting them in view of certain omissions and approximations. For example, the mortality rate is known to depend on characteristics of the individuals at risk, including their habits and exposures, and on the environment [12–14]. Using socioeconomic variables from the Census, some of these characteristics have been controlled. However, no measures are available for occupational exposure, personal habits, and smoking, to name a few important variables. If these effects are not included in measured socioeconomic variables and are related to the level of air pollution, then our pollution estimates will be biased as indicators of causality. Since we have explained much of the variation in the mortality rates, we would argue that the omitted variables would not substantially alter the results. More important, the results seem to be reasonably consistent across the various mortality rates.

It must be noted that measurement errors can be important in these data. For example, generally only a single location in an SMSA was used for sampling air pollution; since there are different pollution sources and varying terrain, a single source is not likely to be representative of the entire area. The mortality data also have a number of problems. For some age-, race-, and sex-specific deaths, the number of reported deaths sometimes exceeded the population at risk; three SMSAs were deleted in analyzing the nonwhite death rates for this reason. Another problem is the mobility of the population. Many of the people injured by pollution migrate to less polluted places while many people who grew up in rural areas, with little previous exposure, migrate to industrial areas. This migration will lead the estimated coefficients of air pollution to be biased downward as indicators of causality. Perhaps the only pure data, from the viewpoint of measured exposure, are for infant death rates where the exposure is known with reasonable accuracy. This and other problems are discussed in Ref. 15.

4. DISCUSSION

Multiple regression appears to be a good tool for explaining variations in mortality rates. Between the air pollution and socioeconomic variables, most

of the variation in the mortality rates is explained.* Air pollution is
implicated in almost every mortality rate as a significant factor, even after
accounting for race, sex, age, and the important socioeconomic variables.
This result is evidence that the previously observed "urban factor" is not the
only cause of higher morbidity and mortality; air pollution is a significant
contributor even after accounting for most of the factors associated with
urban living.

4.1 A decision framework

Is this evidence sufficient to justify government action to abate air pollution
as a public health menace? Epidemiologists have been critical of simple
cross tabulations or univariate regressions which attempt to show the effect
of air pollution on mortality [16]. The questions are: (1) did a particular
association occur merely by chance, and (2) given that the observed association is more than a chance occurrence, is this a basis for action? More
precisely, the concern is whether the association observed between A and B
is a basis for attempting to influence B by manipulating A. Children who get
little to eat, especially a diet low in vitamins, have a higher incidence of
rickets. To eliminate rickets, we must find a variable (both easy and
inexpensive to manipulate) which will prevent it. Classically, we attempt to
find what "causes" rickets and then to intercede in the sequence of events.
Thus, one "cause" of rickets is malnutrition and the crucial dietary variable
to manipulate is the ingestion of Vitamin D. Note that this is not the same as
concluding that children must be given a balanced diet, must eat only
healthy foods, or must eat regularly. There are many ways of achieving the
goal of ingesting the proper amount of Vitamin D.

There has been a rather unfortunate tendency for physicians to fix on
the word "proof" and attack various associations as not having been proved
to be causal [17]. This is given as a reason why no attempt should be made
at manipulation in order to deal with a health problem. However, as soon as
the problem is stated in a decision context, the emphasis on the word
"proof" can be seen to be out of proportion. While it certainly is correct
that interference in a known, deterministic, causal chain is certain to lead to
results, it is not generally in the public interest to hold off action until
causality is established to everyone's satisfaction. In public health situations
where the potential gain is high (as in stopping an epidemic) and the cost is

---

* In disaggregating the mortality rates by age, sex, and race, there is a large decline in the explanatory
power of the regression, R^2. This decline stems from the fact that the principal factors which are known
to affect the mortality rate have been used to define more specific mortality classes. This decline in
explanatory power is expected and is not important as long as estimated coefficients continue to display
magnitudes and signs which are consistent with what is expected from the aggregate mortality rates. It is
this consistency that we find most important and reassuring.

low (as in adding more chlorine to the water), no one would advocate waiting until everyone is sure that the drinking water was really the cause of the epidemic.

The point is that the level of confidence required for general acceptance of proven causality is not required in order to warrant action. For most health situations with relatively high benefits and low costs, a much lower level of confidence is called for. Thus, a prudent man would have thought seriously about giving up cigarettes long before it was generally accepted that cigarettes cause ill health. (We have no confidence that widespread agreement would be obtained today among scientists that it has been proved that cigarette smoking causes lung cancer, emphysema, and heart disease [18–21].*)

4.2 A comparison across mortality rates

The estimated coefficients presented in Table 1 depend on the way dependent and independent variables are scaled. Another way of presenting these results is to show the estimated effect of a 100% increase in the explanatory variables. For example, doubling the mean level of particulates would increase the total mortality rate by 5.29%, and doubling the smallest sulfate reading would increase the total mortality rate by 3.68%. These percentage effects are presented in Table 2. (Coefficients which were quite insignificant are shown in parentheses.)

The first block of percentage effects are for the smallest biweekly sulfate reading. Sulfates have more effect on the very young and the very old, more effect on nonwhites than on whites, and more effect on females than on males. The same pattern of effects holds for the two measures of particulate pollution.†

Interpreting the relative size of the estimated percentage effects in this way is somewhat dubious in that the exact estimate may be more an artifact of the particular variables and data than a true expression of the relation.

---

* Another way of viewing the problem stems from observing that A is associated with B. Thus, either A causes B, B causes A, or C causes both A and B and the association between them is spurious because we haven't thought to measure C [22]. However, the human body is so complex that medicine is of very limited help in providing such a theory [4, 23–25]. While we have not heard anyone suggest seriously that lung cancer leads to cigarette smoking, the set of possible causal factors, C, is very large. In general, the only way that evidence can be compiled is by sampling a great many groups with differing characteristics. The convincing evidence is that a factor such as smoking is associated with lung cancer under a wide variety of conditions, in a wide variety of groups. It is the weight of a number of studies which rules out the possibility that the association is a sampling phenomenon; it is the weight of many studies in many settings which dismisses the possibility that some uncontrolled factor is the true cause of lung cancer.

† These effects may be due, in part, to the relationship between air pollution exposure and the socioeconomic distribution within an SMSA. For example, it has been shown that nonwhites reside in areas subject to higher pollution than are areas where whites reside [28]. Thus, the patterns for the different groups may result from doubling different base levels of pollution affecting the groups.

TABLE 2 ELASTICITIES FOR EACH EXPLANATORY VARIABLE.

Variable	Sex	Race	Elasticity (×100)[a]						
			All ages	<28 days	<1 year	≤14 years	15–44 years	45–64 years	≥65 years
Minimum	M+	W+	3.68	3.04					
sulfates	F	NW							
	M	W	1.80	(0.63)			(−1.65)	(1.00)	4.06
		NW	2.34	(−2.29)			1.04	(0.98)	6.06
	F	W	4.62	2.16			(0.71)	5.69	7.59
		NW	8.58	6.87			(3.72)	13.44	7.91
	M+	NW	5.06						
	F								
Mean	M+	W+	5.29	5.22					
particulates	F	NW							
	M	W	3.33	(2.16)			7.01	4.61	
		NW	6.15	(5.89)			14.24	6.29	
	F	W	5.80	4.17			9.52	6.63	
		NW	12.09	13.61			15.41	12.92	
	M+	NW	22.32						
	F								
Minimum	M+	W+			6.53				
particulates	F	NW							
	M	W			(2.32)	3.95			
		NW			6.16	8.42			
	F	W			6.84	6.19			
		NW			14.60	14.16			
Percentage	M+	W+		5.39	11.17				
poor	F	NW							
	M	W		8.90	9.98	17.18	20.60	8.52	
		NW		−22.52	−8.71	(2.37)	26.22	25.47	
				11.91	15.07	20.96	12.91	(−1.12)	
				−22.66	(6.10)	14.91	23.24	17.64	

However, since some of the interpretations tend to shed light on the nature of the relationship, we will present them and caution the reader about putting much confidence in them.

The percentage effects of the variable "percentage of families who are poor" display an interesting pattern. Females tend to be more sensitive than males to poverty in childhood, the reverse later on. Poverty seems to lower the death rate for nonwhite children under 28 days. It is difficult to know

TABLE 2 Continued

Variable	Sex	Race	All ages	<28 days	<1 year	≤14 years	15–44 years	45–64 years	≥65 years
			Elasticity (×100)[a]						
Population per sq. mi.	M+	W+	0.66						
	F	NW							
	M	W	0.64				(0.40)	1.44	
		NW	(0.30)				(1.53)	(0.95)	
	F	W	0.99				1.30	1.59	
		NW	(−0.64)				(1.32)	(−0.85)	
	M+	NW	−2.53						
	F								
Percentage over 65	M+	W+	63.21						
	F	NW							
	M	W	(2.49)			−13.54	−8.47	5.19	
		NW	8.73			(−2.93)	(2.21)	(7.14)	
	F	W	(2.71)			−4.16	−6.46	3.56	
		NW	(4.32)			(8.29)	(5.28)	(−2.67)	
	M+	NW	46.42						
	F								
Percentage nonwhite	M+	W+	5.68	6.57	9.15				
	F	NW							
	M	W	3.03	(−0.69)	−3.38	−8.50	−4.76	4.10	1.74
		NW	9.11	12.10	13.46	7.51	14.52	8.85	(−1.19)
	F	W	−1.20	−2.80	−5.50	−10.22	−5.20	−2.29	−1.59
		NW	10.88	13.93	7.53	6.01	15.71	17.81	(−1.60)
	M+F	NW	19.36						

[a] Percentage change in the mortality rate that is estimated to occur if the particular explanatory variable were to double in intensity. For example, if the minimum sulfate level doubled, other factors held constant, the total mortality rate is estimated to increase by 3.68% and the mortality rate for nonwhite females, 65 and older, is estimated to increase 7.91%. Where the regression coefficient was less than its standard error, the elasticity is in parentheses. These elasticities are derived from the regression coefficients listed in Table 1.

whether this result is simply an artifact of the estimation procedure, but it is consistent with the notion that areas with concentrations of the poor have good welfare facilities.

The percentage effects of "proportion of nonwhites in the population" also display an interesting pattern. Concentrations of nonwhites are associated with much higher death rates. Concentrations of nonwhites always lower the female white death rate. For white males, concentrations of nonwhites tend to lower the death rate through age 44. The simplest hypothesis for these effects is one of economic exploitation of nonwhites where there is a sizeable proportion of them, i.e., concentrations of non-whites lower the white death rate and raise the nonwhite death rate. The results are consistent with a mechanism wherein nonwhite women assume many of the household chores and increase the leisure of white women. For males, nonwhites might assume the jobs requiring particularly difficult labor or involving health risks. There is a striking difference between races for the three categories of death rates among children. White children have a lower death rate when there are many nonwhites (presumably because nonwhites tend them); nonwhite children have a higher death rate (presumably because they are unwatched).

Abating air pollution is one way to reduce the death rate. Other ways are to raise the income of the poor, lessen population density, and deal with some of the ills of urban areas with a high proportion of nonwhites. Some of these other effects can be estimated and are shown in Table 2. For example, doubling air pollution (both sulfates and particulates) is estimated to in-crease the total death rate by 8.97% (3.68% + 5.29%). Doubling the proportion of poor families in the city, the population density, or the proportion of the population which is nonwhite would be estimated to increase the total death rate by 5.39%, 0.66%, or 5.68%, respectively. Thus, air pollution is the most important of the three factors affecting the total death rate (and by inference morbidity and longevity).

5. CONCLUSION

The effect of air pollution on mortality is examined in 32 regressions, in which mortality rates are characterized by age (under 28 days, under 1 year, 14 years and younger, 15–44, 45–64, and 65 and older), by race (white and nonwhite), and by sex (male and female). Air pollution has more effect on women than on men, and more effect on nonwhites than on whites. The very young and the very old are most sensitive to air pollution.

In addition to the relations shown here, air pollution continues to be a significant factor when meteorological and heating variables are added [26] or when occupation variables are added [27]. Consistent effects are also obtained in explaining variations in disease-specific mortality rates across the same SMSAs. Finally, a subset of the mortality rates has been gathered for 1961, the results essentially replicating the 1960 ones [11].

Another way to view the effect of air pollution (or of any factor causing ill health) is in terms of its effect on the economy. When people are sick they lose time from work and must spend money on medical care; if illness could be reduced, there would be a savings in these categories. As estimated elsewhere, a 50% abatement in air pollution would reduce the "economic cost" of morbidity and mortality by 4.5% [2]. The importance of this improvement in health might be assessed by noting that the economic cost of all cancers is 5.7% of the total economic cost of ill health in the U.S. Thus, abating air pollution by 50% is estimated to have almost the same effect on economic cost as eradicating all cancer. Such an abatement is probably the most effective way of improving the health of middle-class families. Note that the middle-class family can do something about smoking, but is powerless to lower its exposure to air pollution (except by leaving the city).

These studies show a rather consistent relation between air pollution and mortality across a number of different specifications. All show that mortality rates could be lowered substantially by abating air pollution. For example, lowering the measured levels of minimum sulfate pollution and the mean particulate pollution by 10% would result in a 0.90% decrease in the total death rate.

Even so, there are many reasons to believe that these estimates are gross understatements of the health cost of air pollution. Chronic diseases generally involve long periods of illness. The economic costs, calculated as the sum of lost work and medical expenditures, grossly understate the amount that would be paid to achieve good health for such a chronically ill period. In addition, death may not result from the chronic illness itself, but rather from one or another complication. For example, chronic bronchitis or emphysema is likely to result in death due to heart disease or pneumonia, rather than from the chronic disease.

Perhaps the only good way to estimate the health costs of air pollution would be to analyze morbidity rather than mortality data. It seems certain that such an investigation would give a higher health cost, since no one can die of emphysema or other chronic illnesses who has not suffered them, while some of the people with chronic illnesses die from other causes. In addition, such an investigation would detect increases in morbidity rates, such as those of simple respiratory diseases, which may occur long before death is a consideration. Other much less severe illnesses known to be associated with air pollution are unrelated to mortality. For example, eye irritation is a common reaction to acute pollution; costs from this malady will never be reflected in mortality statistics (except possibly for accidents).

We have concentrated on the health effects of air pollution, without alluding to costs associated with cleaning and deterioration of inert materials, with vegetation and animal damage, and with the aesthetic effects of living in a dirty, uncomfortable, overcast world. These costs can be substantial [15].

In view of the resources devoted to attaining better health, it seems clear that social welfare would rise substantially with the spending of resources to abate air pollution. It is time that we pressed forward with a program of abatement.

ACKNOWLEDGMENTS
This research was supported by a grant from Resources for the Future, Inc. We thank Myrick Freeman, Martin Geisel, Edwin Mills, and Robert Strotz for helpful comments. Any errors and opinions are those of the authors.

REFERENCES
1. D. Anderson, *Can. Med. Assoc. J.*, *97*, 528, 585, 802 (1967).
2. L. Lave and E. Seskin, *Science*, *169*, 723 (1970).
3. U.S. Public Health Service, *Air Quality Criteria for Sulfur Oxides*, Pub. No. AP-50, Nat. Air Poll. Control Admin., U.S. Gov. Printing Office, Washington, D.C., 1970.
4. M. Battigeni, *J. Occup. Med.*, *10*, 500 (1968).
5. I. Greenwald, *Arch. Ind. Hygiene Occup. Med.*, *10*, 455 (1954).
6. W. H. O., Seminar report, *Bull. W.H.O.*, *23*, 264 (1969).
7. U.S. Dept. of Health, Education, and Welfare, *Vital Statistics of the United States*, *1960*, U.S. Gov. Printing Office, 1961, Washington, D.C.
8. E. Duffy and R. Carroll, *United States Metropolitan Mortality*, *1959–1961*. Pub. No. 999-AP-39, U.S. Public Health Service, Nat. Center for Air Poll. Control, 1967, Cincinnati, Ohio, 1967.
9. U.S. Public Health Service, *Analysis of Suspended Particulates*, *1957–1961*, U.S. Gov. Printing Office, Washington, D.C., 1962, Pub. No. 978.
10. U.S. Dept. of Commerce, *County and City Data Book*, U.S. Gov. Printing Office, Washington, D.C., 1962.
11. L. Lave and E. Seskin, *J. Amer. Stat. Assoc.*, *68*, 284 (1973).
12. B. Ferris, Jr., *Arch. Environ. Health*, *16*, 511 (1968).
13. J. Kosa, A. Antonovsky and I. Zola, Eds., *Poverty and Health*, Harvard Univ. Press, Cambridge, Mass., 1969.
14. J. Lave and L. Lave, *Law Contemp. Prob.*, *35*, 252 (1970).
15. L. Lave in *Environmental Quality Analysis* (A. Kneese and B. Bower, Eds.), Johns Hopkins Press, Baltimore, Maryland, 1972, p. 213.
16. P. Lawther, *J. Inst. Fuel*, *36*, 341 (1963).
17. B. MacMahon, T. Pugh, and J. Ipsen, *Epidemiological Methods*, Little, Brown and Co., Boston, Mass., 1960.
18. K. Brownlee, *J. Amer. Stat. Assoc.*, *60*, 722 (1965).
19. S. Cutler, *J. Amer. Stat. Assoc.*, *50*, 267 (1955).
20. R. Fisher, *Brit. Med. J.*, *2*, 297 (1957).
21. U.S. Public Health Service, *Smoking and Health*, Pub. No. 1103, U.S. Gov. Printing Office, Washington, D.C., 1964.
22. H. Simon, *J. Amer. Stat. Assoc.*, *49*, 467 (1954).

23. M. Amdur and D. Underhill, *Arch. Environ. Health*, *16*, 460 (1968).

24. A. Goetz, *Int. J. Air Water Poll.*, *4*, 168 (1961).

25. A. Goetz, in *Inhaled Particles and Vapours*, (C. Davies, Ed.), Pergamon Press, New York, 1961, p. 295.

26. L. Lave and E. Seskin, *Amer. J. Pub. Health*, *62*, 909 (1972).

27. L. Lave and E. Seskin, *Swed. J. Econ.*, *73*, 76 (1971).

28. A. M. Freeman, III, in *Environmental Quality Analysis* (A. Kneese and B. Bower, Eds.), Johns Hopkins Press, Baltimore, Maryland, 1972, p. 243.

Note: The mortality rate analyzed in Eq. (1) was defined as the total number of deaths divided by the total population of an SMSA. It was not adjusted for age, sex, or race. Similarly, the mortality rates analyzed in Table 1 for all ages, 0–14, 15–44, and 45–64 were not adjusted for age. These rates were computed without taking account of the differences in the population at risk of the individual age categories which were aggregated. These adjustments in the mortality rates have now been made and are reported in Chapter 4 of L. Lave and E. Seskin, *Air Pollution and Human Health*, in press for Resources for the Future, Inc., Johns Hopkins University Press. The results indicate that while the estimated parameters change, the qualitative conclusions described here remain unchanged. For example, lowering the levels of minimum sulfate pollution and mean particulate pollution by 10 percent would be associated with a 0.63 percent decrease in the adjusted total mortality rate instead of the 0.90 percent decrease in the unadjusted total mortality rate documented in this paper.

DISCUSSION BY WILLIAM B. FAIRLEY

The authors have in my view wisely separated the scientific question of the existence of a link between air pollution and ill health from the decision problem of whether or not to abate air pollution. A decision to abate pollution might rest on a likelihood or even only a suspicion of the important health effects suggested by their analysis and by those of others. And of course a decision to abate air pollution may be based on other undesirable effects, such as reduced visibility, eye irritation, effects on materials, local or worldwide climatological effects, etc.

In this paper Lester Lave and Eugene Seskin discuss the implications of their research on the effects of air pollution on age-, sex-, and race-specific mortality. I will direct my discussion to the strategy adopted for establishing a causal link between pollution and mortality. The investigations reported here use published data on air pollutant levels and on mortality in 1960 in 117 urban areas of the United States (specifically, in 117 Standard Metropolitan Statistical Areas or SMSAs). The statistical method employs multiple regression to study the relation of mortality to air pollutant levels in urban areas while controlling for a variety of other variables which might affect the relationship. It should be noted that this is a study of mortality only, not morbidity or ill health generally, and that it is a study of the effect on mortality of two selected air pollutants—particulates and sulfates—not of air pollution generally.

This regression study supports the existence of a causal link between levels of particulates and sulfates on the one hand and mortality rates on the other. I will organize my comments around two questions. First, are the regression coefficients for levels of particulates and sulfates statistically significant? Second, are there other plausible factors which might account for the observed association between mortality and the pollutant levels? The two principal issues, then, are significance and control.

Taking up the question of significance first, I find the statistical analysis presented convincing as far as it goes, but I would suggest three extensions. I would note that further analysis is not just gilding the lily in this case, because in the regression of total mortality on pollutant levels and other variables the quoted t values of 2.53 for mean particulates (Mean P) and 3.18 for minimum sulfates (Min S), while large, are not so large as to defy reversal after reanalysis. Direct evidence for this position comes from the range of numbers quoted in the paper for these t values as different mortality rates and different sets of independent variables are examined. For the particulates coefficient this range is 0.73 to 3.53 and for the sulfates coefficient it is −0.87 to 4.02.

First, the interpretation of the quoted t statistics rests on assumptions about the statistical model underlying the least squares fitting procedure. The authors rely on the robust nature of least squares analysis, but it is possible to make some checks on the adequacy of the assumptions that make a least squares fit of a multiple regression equation reasonable. There are no references in this paper to examinations of the data and/or formal statistical tests for heteroscedasticity, correlation of error terms (for example, geographic), nonlinearities, or gross departures from normality.

Second, alternative techniques for assessing the variation in the coefficients could be tried. One of these is the jackknife, in which in essence successive blocks of data are left out, the coefficients computed on the remaining data, and the resulting coefficients compared. In the same spirit would be a comparison of the coefficients for different subgroups of the 117 SMSAs, e.g., between regional groupings of the SMSAs.

A third comment on significance levels is that they are in this case computed from variations in essentially one replicate of the data. The data is almost entirely for a single year and is for a single country. Analysis for additional years and within different countries is called for.

Turning now to the issue of control for other variables that might either mask or spuriously suggest a causal link, I find the paper to be very clear on the requirements for good control. Control is sought in this and other papers through a combination of (1) entering additional explanatory variables such as climate and occupation into the models, and (2) studying the models within narrower population subgroups, that is through age-, sex-, race-, and disease-specific equations. One device for control that was not used is blocking of the SMSAs (e.g., regionally), as suggested earlier in the discussion on significance.

The questions that remain with control can be grouped in two parts: (1) questions about variables left out and (2) questions about variables included. As to variables which might help to explain mortality differences between SMSAs it is not hard to think of additional candidates for study, such as absolute city size, extent of migration, indices of health care, to name three, but, of course, trying other variables is a never ending game. At the same time, the subject of explaining mortality differences between SMSAs is apparently sufficiently young that there will no doubt be surprises ahead. And, again, the significance levels of the pollutant levels are not so large that one can suppose they will be unaffected by better models of SMSA mortality differences.

To be more confident that the relation of mortality and pollutant levels is not spurious it would be very helpful to better understand the relation of air pollution itself to other variables. That is, it would be helpful to understand why SMSAs differ in levels of particulates and sulfates, and then to check whether the causes of pollutant levels were or were not independent causes of mortality.

Turning now to a discussion of the variables included in the equations for mortality, I will make one or two comments.

The age variable "percentage over 65" is the most important variable for explaining differences in total mortality. If this variable is significantly associated with pollutant levels, inclusion of the entire age distribution by appropriate variables instead of the single variable "percentage over 65" might both improve the mortality model and make substantial changes in the coefficients for the pollutant levels.

The same point can be made about the partial measurements of income distribution in the SMSAs by a "percentage poor" variable, although this variable did not appear nearly as important as age.

PART IV

STATISTICAL METHODS FOR POLICY ANALYSIS

ASSESSING UNKNOWN NUMBERS: ORDER OF MAGNITUDE ESTIMATION

FREDERICK MOSTELLER

THE PROBLEM OF UNKNOWN NUMBERS

Norman Dalkey (1969) says:

> One of the thorniest problems facing the policy analyst is posed by the situation where, for a significant segment of his study, there is unsatisfactory information. The deficiency can be with respect to data—incomplete or faulty—or more seriously with respect to the model or theory—again either incomplete or insufficiently verified. This situation is probably the norm rather than a rare occurrence.

In this chapter we discuss methods of estimating numbers that are unknown to us, but necessary for the analysis of policy problems. Max Singer (1971) treats an example in his instructive article "The vitality of mythical numbers." He wishes to estimate the amount of money per year taken in muggings, robberies, and burglaries by the heroin addicts of New York City. This figure offers one measure of the severity of the side effects of the drug problem. In this question as in many others, some facts are approximately known, such as the population of New York City, the number and amounts of reported robberies (of all kinds, not just by heroin addicts), and the number of addicts in jails or prison. By shrewd guesses and various devices, some of which we illustrate later, Singer comes out with a figure of $250 million per year, which is considerably smaller than amounts that had previously been suggested.

The main methods for estimating such unknown numbers are as follows:

1. Look up the number in a *reference source.*

This work was facilitated by National Science Foundation Grant SOC72-05257. Jack M. Appleman, Norman Dalkey, Persi Diaconis, William Fairley, William H. Kruskal, and Carl Overhage have contributed helpful advice, and Judith Selvidge kindly allowed us to present Table 3.

2. Collect the number through a *systematic survey* or other investigation.

3. Guess the number.

4. Get experts to help you guess the number.

Often orders of magnitude are what are needed. Physical scientists and others refer to powers of 10 as orders of magnitude: $10^1 = 10$, $10^2 = 100$, $10^3 = 1000$, $10^6 = 1,000,000$, and so on.

Example. *Vanity plates.* Someone suggests that vanity license plates with up to 5 letters would not offer enough variety so that everyone who ordered could get one. What is the order of magnitude of the number of vanity plates possible using only up to 5 letters of the alphabet? Exactly, it is $26 + 26^2 + 26^3 + 26^4 + 26^5$. Since 26^5 is bigger than the rest put together, let's estimate it. It is about 11,000,000 and should handle the demand in most states.

For the policy analyst, a first consideration must be whether policy is sensitive to the size of the number under consideration. In some problems, the policy response will be a smooth function of the number. Or perhaps once a number like the thefts from heroin exceeds a minimum amount, say $10,000,000 per year, the policy is the same until it reaches, say, $5 billion per year. When the amount is small enough, no action beyond regular police action is required, but when it gets large, then substantial new action may be necessary. We shall not pursue this aspect further in this paper, but shall concentrate instead on ways of gathering information.

We use the expression "order of magnitude estimation" to suggest situations where the actual figure may not be possible to get, or where very rough figures may be adequate for the purposes at hand.

REFERENCE SOURCES

Obviously, the amount stolen by heroin addicts is unlikely to be in a reference source, but much information is readily available in standard works such as almanacs, *Statistical Abstracts of the United States*, encyclopedias, census publications, handbooks, and other materials. (World almanacs for different years carry some different information, not just the same information for different years.) First-class libraries are excellent resources for information, and reference librarians are often ingenious at figuring out where such numbers may be found.

Naturally the found numbers have to be examined with care. A good source for a number will usually have some footnotes so that you know just what the number is supposed to be. And when the authorities go into detail, it probably means that they know that slight changes in the definition can make substantial differences. We should think kindly of the footnotes because they are trying to tell us whether the number given is the one we want, and if it is not, perhaps how to get our number. Almanacs and abstracts sometimes omit the footnotes provided in their primary sources. When we look up a number in more than one place, we may get several different answers, and then we have to exercise care. The moral is not that several answers are worse than one, but that whatever answer we get from one source might be different if we got it from another source. Thus we should consider both the definition of the number and its possible unreliability.

Example. *Number of speakers of a language.* Wallis and Roberts (1956) report a study that compares the estimates taken from two different almanacs of the number of people in the world speaking various languages. The most spectacular percentage difference was for Arabic, where one almanac gave the figure 29 million, the other 58 million.

In 1972, the same two almanacs reporting on speakers of Great Russian gave 206 million and 135 million, respectively. Part of the explanation is that one almanac estimates total speakers and the other estimates the number of native speakers, so much of this difference would be cleared up by understanding the distinction between the populations being described.

Wars and politics provoke great debates over unknown numbers partly because the size of the number may be important, partly because the protagonists are trying to prove points for their own side, and partly because of differing definitions and inability to document one's case.

Example. *American exiles.* How many Americans left the United States to go to other countries because of their unwillingness to serve in the armed forces in Vietnam? Patrick J. Buchanan, a Special Consultant to the President of the United States, writes of this in the *New York Times*, February 20, 1973. He quotes Senator Robert Taft on December 14, 1971 as estimating the number in exile to be "as high as 70,000." A journalist then reported that "over 70,000" were in prison or in exile. Others announced on January 1, 1972 there were "at least 70,000 and some say as many as 100,000 young American men in Canada who have quit the military or refused the draft." (Note that the original total for *all* countries—not just Canada—was "as high as 70,000." Buchanan then cites others giving estimates in this general range, some assigning about 15,000 to Canada.

Buchanan then considers some data from official sources. He reports that the Pentagon estimates the number of deserters and draft avoiders in Canada as just under 4000 and those outside Canada and the United States as about 1200. The Pentagon had a bad record for statistical accuracy during this period.

Canadian statistics say that between 1960 and 1964, there were 1300 United States males annually who became "landed immigrants" in Canada. The total American males between 14 and 30 years of age becoming "landed immigrants" between January 1965 and January 1972 is reported (a little backhandedly) as 17,000. Buchanan then goes on to give information from the second most popular haven for these young men, Sweden. Sweden reports that 585 entered the country from 1967 to 1970.

On the basis of all this information, estimate the number of young men in exile over the Vietnam war as of January 1, 1972. Your answer should take some account of the various biases of the reporting institutions and biases created by the method of gathering data.

COLLECTING THE NUMBER

If a number is not available through reference agencies, there may be time and resources to collect the number, perhaps in a sample survey or inventory that would be made in any case. Many private, university, and even government survey organizations can assist in such a job, not only in doing the interviewing and collecting the data, but in helping formulate the questions and definitions. For example, the Survey Research Center at the University of Michigan has gathered data on plans to purchase automobiles. These have been used with other data to estimate future purchases. On a regular basis the Current Population Survey of the Bureau of the Census carries out a sample study of employment and unemployment.

It should be mentioned too that the Bureau of the Census has special data tapes giving a sample of 1 individual per 1000 in the census. From these tapes additional analyses can be made.

Some ways of collecting numbers that do not call for troubling people directly are given in Webb et al., 1966. For example, to find out which articles in an encyclopedia were used most, an investigator looked at a copy in a library and found where the edges were particularly dirty. This device was used in several libraries in different parts of the country to find out which articles people had found especially useful.

GUESSING THE NUMBER

In the problem of the amount stolen by heroin addicts in New York City, we can see that none of the above methods is going to be completely successful, and we are going to have to do some guessing, perhaps based on other numbers that we can get. The most extensive discussion we have seen of methods designed to help with guessing was developed by James Vaupel and Howard Raiffa and appears in *Decision Analysis.*

Some specific ideas that one may lean on to get estimates arise from thinking about quantities that do not vary much from one occasion to

TABLE 1 VOTING REGISTRATION RATE AND POPULATION IN THOUSANDS IN 1960 IN NEW ENGLAND CITIES OVER 100,000.

	Registration percent	Population in thousands
New Haven, Conn.	79.2	152
Springfield, Mass.	77.1	174
Boston, Mass.	74.0	697
Cambridge, Mass.	73.8	107
Hartford, Conn.	70.7	162
Bridgeport, Conn.	70.6	157

Sources: Edward R. Tufte, "Registration and voting," in Judith Tanur *et al.*, eds., *Statistics: A Guide to the Unknown*, Holden-Day, San Francisco, 1972, pp. 153–161, and *Boston Herald Traveler, 1972 World Almanac*, 1971.

another—for example, "A pint's a pound the world around" applies fairly well to liquids and fats. Ordinarily, rates of things of the same sort do not change as fast as the things themselves.

For example, suppose that one wants to know the number of registered voters in cities in New England. The total number of people in cities in the states of New England changes substantially from city to city, but the percentage of the population that is registered to vote does not change drastically within this region.

Table 1 shows that for large New England cities, the registration rate varies less than 5% each way from 75%, but the populations vary by a factor of more than 6. We can think of the number of registered voters as roughly proportional to the population. The adult population would be an even better set of numbers to provide such proportionality, and it is readily available from census figures.

Similarly, death rates change relatively slowly but birth rates are a bit jumpier, as Table 2 shows. Percentages are a form of rate—so many per hundred—and so are many physical constants.

Rules of thumb and lore

Each discipline has a certain amount of lore of its own for making rough estimates. This lore is usually based on what numbers have been especially useful in the past. When involved in a problem related to a specific discipline, it would be well to talk to experts in that discipline to find out what sorts of rules of thumb they have. It is well to distinguish between the

TABLE 2 ESTIMATED DEATH RATES
AND BIRTH RATES IN THE UNITED
STATES.

	Death rates	Birth rates
1945	10.6	19.5
1950	9.6	23.6
1955	9.3	24.6
1960	9.5	23.7
1965	9.4	19.4
1970	9.4	18.2

Source: *Boston Herald Traveler, 1972
World Almanac*, 1971.

rules that have a sound basis and those that are casual empirical observations that may change from time to time.

Example. *Building trades.* The building trades have manuals that give unit costs for a vast array of items. In estimating the price of a building from the square feet of floor area, the rule of thumb is that the areas for the basement and attic floors are multiplied by the factors 0.5 and 0.3, respectively, before the unit costs are applied. Similarly, as a rule of thumb, a contingency factor of about 10% is included for unexpected events such as delays due to weather, strikes, and breakdowns.

Two other rules of thumb from the building trades differ: authorities differ as to how close the bids of the low bidder and the next lowest bidder should be, some saying 5 to 7%, others, within 15%. When a low bidder is very low, say 25%, then contract awarders are likely to worry about the reliability of the bidder unless they see special advantages, such as equipment and plant in the area.

Regression
Of course, we have already available the whole method of regression. Consequently, if we have measured a number of entities on several predictor variables as well as on the outcome variable, and if we have predictor variables but not the outcome variable for the new entity, then regression offers one way of getting an estimate.

Regression methods offer one way to relate outside available measures to the measure of interest. There is a considerable literature in the area of "clinical prediction versus statistical prediction." The ingredients of this discussion are: (1) some well-trained experts are called upon to make clinical predictions on the basis of the observations given to them but without extra statistical methods. These forecasts might deal with future performance in school or on a job, or with diagnosis or prognosis of a disease. (2) The statistical predictors used in these discussions have available the theory and the variables that are used by the person making the clinical forecast. The statistical prediction is based on some method of combining all the observations into a forecast, usually a formula or a table. (In principle, the statistical prediction might even throw the clinician's forecast into the formula, though this is not often done when the two methods are being evaluated. Similarly, the clinician could, again in principle, use the statistical forecast in helping make his or her own prediction.)

Although this comparison of performance has led to much controversy, especially in the fields of education and psychology, particularly clinical psychology, the findings seem to be rather firm. Statistical prediction seems to win (Meehl, 1954), though there is no reason to suppose this must always happen. For example, if the clinician hasn't communicated the right variables, the statistical prediction will not work. Before rushing to defend the artist and the clinician, the sensitive reader should realize that there is no victory here implied for statisticians. The latter are taking the tools provided by the clinician and adding to them the systematic forecasting methods developed by their profession. They take the clinician's judgements and devices and use them a little more systematically. Thus they seem to be able to accept the intent of the clinician and carry it out a little more reliably than the clinician unaided by statistical equipment. The general lesson is that systematic effort often pays off, provided useful measures have already been found by the subject-matter expert.

Putting the emphasis on the relative strengths of the clinician and statistical methods rather misses the point of the whole finding. The important point is that specialists can often bring their strength to a problem, setting it up so that variables can be routinely (or even nonroutinely) measured and combined in a standard way. This leaves them free to pursue the next important problem.

On a number of occasions researchers have worked out very simple scoring schemes to estimate how our Supreme Court will decide certain kinds of cases. Such a routine scheme might be useful to a lawyer with a standard sort of case and no new point of law to offer. She or he gets an estimate of the chances in advance. Some legal experts observing such schemes may well say that they can make better forecasts than the scoring scheme. It may be true. But if the scoring scheme has a high rate of being correct (indeed, it may carry with it information about *when* it is likely to be correct—very high or very low scores), then such a mechanical device may often be adequate. There are still plenty of problems left for the specialist, who may be needed especially when the device is uncertain. The thing to emphasize is that the dimensions on which the scoring is done will ordinarily have been developed by the specialist. The matter is not one of glory, but of practicality and expeditiousness. By taking advantage of experts' previous developmental work, the policy analysts can often develop an inexpensive method valuable in their own work.

Beyond these techniques, we can consider various ways to break the problem up into chunks.

Linear relations

When we have one independent variable, x, and rates of change in y with x, we may wish to predict y from x by one of the linear functions: $y = rx$, $y = b + x$, and $y = b + mx$. Thus to estimate the number of registered voters in a northeastern town we might, on the basis of our previous information, set $r = 0.75$ and $x =$ adult population at last census and apply $y = 0.75x$ as the estimate.

Example. *Marijuana and hashish smuggling.* The *New York Times*, January 7, 1974, reports a formula used by the Senate Internal Security subcommittee to estimate amounts of marijuana and hashish being brought into the United States. If $x =$ pounds seized during a year, then $y = 10x$ is estimated as the amount brought in during the year. On this basis, Senator James D. Eastland of Mississippi said that 17 million pounds of marijuana and 500,000 pounds of hashish were consumed in the United States in 1973.

Example. *Updating town population.* To estimate the number of people in a town at a given moment we might apply $y = b + mx$ by taking b as the latest census figure; m as the proportion of increase, r, in that part of the country per year times the number of years, n, since the last census; and x as b itself. Thus the equation would have the form $y = b + rnb$. If the rate r were a decrease, -0.01, and it had been 3 years since the last census, for a town of 10,000 at last census we estimate

$$y = 10{,}000 - 0.01(3)(10{,}000) = 9{,}700.$$

Factoring

This last example sows the seeds of a general method of factoring. Sometimes, if we break things up enough, we can estimate each of several rates reasonably well when we cannot seem to estimate the total by itself. Suppose, for example, we wanted to know how much a certain service in a welfare program would be likely to cost, all told, at prices of a given year.

The general idea is to try to break the total cost up into the product of a number or rates:

$$y = r_1 r_2 \cdots r_n x.$$

For example, r_1 might be the price per delivery of the service on the average, r_2 the number of services per person per month, r_3 the number of months per year, r_4 the number of persons per family, and x the number of families to be served. In this example, r_2 might be the only quantity that would have to be guessed outright.

Example. *Probability of a catastrophic incident.* The United States Coast Guard exercises regulatory authority over the operations of vessels carrying hazardous cargoes in United States waters, such as a tanker carrying liquefied natural gas (LNG). A spill in port might result in a fire covering many city blocks. The Coast Guard has commissioned studies of the risk of a significant spill of hazardous cargoes. A study done by William A. Dunn *et al.* (1974) estimated the probability of a significant spill, $P(S)$, by factoring this probability into a probability of a vessel casualty, $P(C)$, and the probability of a spill given a casualty, $P(S \mid C)$. It was thought that analyses of casualties lead to an estimated rate of significant spills, $P(S \mid C)$, and that an estimate of the rate of casualties, $P(C)$, could be derived from available Coast Guard data. This approach to estimating the probability of a catastrophic accident from an LNG tanker has been used in materials presented to the Federal Power Commission to support applications to bring LNG tankers into United States ports. (For references and a fuller discussion of these estimates of LNG tanker accident probabilities, see the first article in Part VI of this book.)

Bounds, subgroups, and supergroups
Mathematicians make special efforts to set bounds on their estimates. In estimation of the type we are discussing, we may not be able to set very useful bounds, but we may find it especially convenient to work from upper or lower bounds and estimate discount or expansion factors.

For example, we may try to think of a group related to the one we are working on and use it not only as a bound but also as a base for a rate. We have already illustrated this: the adult population is the upper bound in an honest registration of voters. The factor 0.75 is the reducing fraction.

Mathematical models
Frequently very complicated mathematical models are developed on simulations of processes carried out. Whole books are written about such endeavors. Suppose that we want to know how many heroin addicts there are in New York City. We have information about how many are in jail or prison. We also may be able to estimate from their records how much of their time they spend in jail. Suppose they spend a fourth of their time in jail. Then a lower bound for the number of addicts might be 4 times the number in

prison and jail. We say it is a lower bound because the ones in jail are the ones more likely to be caught, on the average, and the ones out of jail are less likely to be caught. We might consider for individuals what the distribution of the probability of being detained in jail or prison at a given moment would be and use this distribution as a basis for further mathematical analysis. It would probably serve to shake our confidence in our guess of the factor of 4 and to make us recognize our uncertainty about it.

Example. *Illustrative mathematical model for imprisoned addicts.* To illustrate, let p be the probability that an addict is in prison or jail at any given instant, and f the probability density function of p (see Figure 1) over addicts. Then the proportion of those having p's between a given p and $p + dp$ (where dp is regarded as a small interval in the usual physics manner) and who are imprisoned at a given moment is $pf(p)\,dp$. The proportion who have values of p in the interval is given exactly by the shaded area in the figure, or approximately by $f(p)\,dp$. The proportion of those who are in jail is p, so $pf(p)\,dp$ approximates the contribution of this group to the jailed population. The total of those who are imprisoned is therefore the integral over p

$$\mu = \int_0^1 pf(p)\,dp.$$

We use μ for this quantity because the right hand side happens to be the definition of the average value of p. The conditional distribution of p for addicts who are prisoners, from the above discussion, has ordinates proportional to $pf(p)$. And $\int_0^1 pf(p)\,dp = \mu$, so the proportionality constant is $1/\mu$. Therefore, we have

$$f(p \mid \text{imprisoned}) = pf(p)/\mu.$$

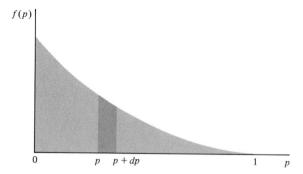

FIG. 1 *Probability density function f of p, the probability of being in jail at a given instant.*

The mean of this conditional distribution is:

$$E(p \mid \text{imprisoned}) = \int_0^1 pf(p \mid \text{imprisoned})\, dp$$

$$= \int_0^1 p\left[\frac{pf(p)}{\mu}\right] dp$$

$$= \frac{1}{\mu}\int_0^1 p^2 f(p)\, dp$$

$$= \frac{E(p^2)}{\mu},$$

where $E(p^2)$ is the second raw moment of p for the original density $f(p)$. What we have shown is that this value is about 1/4 in our example—that is, jailed addicts are spending one-fourth of their time in jail.

We might take as a specialized model for the distribution of p

$$f(p) = (r + 1)(1 - p)^r$$

The general idea for positive values of r is that most addicts have little chance of being in prison at a given moment, and as p increases, the fraction goes down. That is, there are relatively few addicts who are almost certain to be in jail at any given moment. The parameter r is left open. If it were 0, the distribution would be uniform. If it were large, the probability would be concentrated at the left—hardly any addicts would be in prison.

Then to get $E(p)$ and $E(p^2)$, we compute

$$E(p^t) = (r + 1)\int_0^1 p^t(1 - p)^r\, dp$$

$$= \frac{(r + 1)t!r!}{(t + r + 1)!}.$$

This gives

$$E(p) = \frac{1}{r + 2},$$

$$E(p^2) = \frac{2}{(r + 3)(r + 2)},$$

$$\frac{E(p^2)}{E(p)} = \frac{2}{r + 3}.$$

Substituting the value of 1/4 for $E(p^2)/E(p)$ gives

$$\frac{2}{r + 3} = \frac{1}{4}.$$

Solving for r, we get the value

$$r = 5.$$

When $r = 5$, the proportion of all addicts in prison is

$$E(p) = \frac{1}{r + 2} = \frac{1}{7},$$

and consequently, instead of multiplying the number observed in prison by 4, we should multiply by 7 according to this model. We note that the multiplier has increased, as we expected it to.

Similarity

How shall we find our rates? We may have good rates already available on the same kinds of quantities that we want to make estimates about. But sometimes we may have to think about "similarity."

Example. *Hernias*. When Duncan Neuhauser (in press) wanted to know, for a cost-benefit analysis of hernia operations in the elderly, the strangulation or incarceration rate, he had no data for the United States in modern times. He discovered data from a Parisian physician, Paul Berger, who ran a truss clinic in 1880–1884 when elective operations for hernias were not done. These complications are called "accidents," and Berger asked 10,000 patients when the hernia first appeared and whether an accident had occurred. Among those asked, 1.43% recalled accidents. Those who died would not have appeared. Berger had data suggesting an 8.5% mortality rate from accidents. Neuhauser increased the 1.43% to 1.5% to allow for this. Neuhauser noted that among 8633 patients over the age of 10, the mean age of onset is 43.1 years and the mean age of arrival at the clinic is 51.3 years. Including the 10% factor, these patients had 242 accidents, yielding a probability of accident per hernia year of 0.0037.

Then Neuhauser found another source of data from modern times in Cali, Colombia, where few elective operations for hernias are performed. Here, from hospital records and census data, physicians Ray Neutra and Adolfo Velez were able to compute an estimate of 0.0029 accidents per hernia year.

Thus Neuhauser was able to get two sets of data on populations similar but not identical to the one that interested him. His whole paper has to deal with numbers that cannot surely be assigned to hernias in the United States population over 65. His article offers several instructive exercises in assessing unknown numbers, and the book in which it appears has many illustrations of calculations of the sort being discussed here.

Decomposing

We might stratify the population under consideration and make estimates based on each part. In the service delivery example, for instance, we might break the population into men and women and age groups, perhaps under 6, 6–20, 21–65, and 66 and over. Then we might estimate rates for each sex and age group and compute the total costs from the pooling of the several pieces, $y = \Sigma\ r_i x_i$.

Triangulation

Frequently, there may be more than one approach to estimating the same quantity. When this happens we have the opportunity to make comparisons based on the several methods. This approach is sometimes called triangulation, since it gives more than one fix on a quantity. Triangulation has many merits: it may show us what our method is especially sensitive to; it may tell something about the uncertainty overall; and it may call our attention to some unreasonable numbers we have been using in one or another of the analyses.

Example. *Total driving miles.* How far did the American motorist drive in 1972? How one manipulates numbers may be rather personal, so the discussion is given in the first person singular to emphasize that others might work differently.

   Approach 1. There are 93,000,000 cars registered in the United States (*1972 World Almanac*). They probably average between 6,000 and 20,000 miles per year apiece. I get these bounds because I average 6,000 in my car and all my friends tell me this is very little, and I get the 20,000 because those who drive this much are said to be driving a lot. As a compromise, let us use 11,000, the geometric mean between these limits. Then the total mileage for cars is $9.3 \times 10^7 \times 1.1 \times 10^4 \approx 10 \times 10^{11} = 10^{12}$, which is about a trillion miles.

   Approach 2. The United States gasoline use for 1970 was 2.2×10^6 thousand 42-gallon barrels (*1972 World Almanac*). If it were all used by cars and cars averaged 12 miles per gallon (perhaps an overestimate, as people tend to exaggerate their mileage), we would have 92×10^9 gallons all told. Since $92 \times 12 \approx 1100$, this gives us about 1.1 trillion miles.

Although the agreement between 1 and 1.1 is close, we cannot be satisfied because perhaps a quarter of this fuel is used for trucks and other equipment. This would cut our estimate to about 825 billion miles. Modest changes in miles per gallon in Approach 2 and of miles per year in Approach 1 would put these numbers into agreement. The range based on these two approaches seems to be 800 to 1100 billion miles.

Approach 3. Try to use the fact that there are 3.2×10^6 miles of rural road, 0.5×10^6 miles of urban streets, and 2.9×10^6 miles of surfaced roads to estimate the passenger car mileage. Perhaps you can make some guesses about how many cars per day cover an average point.

Approach 4. Look the number up in the *1972 World Almanac*, remembering that the number is only an order-of-magnitude estimate.

Convolutions

Consider a sum or convolution of several components. Some authors recommend getting probability limits on the component estimates and then figuring out what the distribution of the sum would be in the light of the stated uncertainties of the components. Usually this combining would be done as if the components were independent. Although the method has its attractions, it is likely to be a time-consuming job, unless there are, say, only two components. Furthermore, the results may be rather misleading because the estimates for the components are likely to have highly correlated errors. For example, if we underestimate the usage to be made of a service by one group of people, we are likely to underestimate it for several of the groups. Admittedly a sophisticated effort is possible here, but it is not always clear whether combining components is worth the effort.

We do not want to give the wrong impression in saying this. To indicate some subjective probabilistic bounds for the distribution of the total may be a useful procedure, and if the only way to do this is through hanky-panky with the components, we do not try to avoid this approach. But we are suspicious of the result for reasons that the next section makes clear.

EMPIRICAL RESULTS ON GUESSING BEHAVIOR

Marc Alpert and Howard Raiffa (1969) have performed a number of experiments on guessing behavior. Individuals were asked to estimate quantities they might have been expected to have some information about, such as the fraction of students in their class preferring bourbon to scotch, the number of physicians and surgeons listed in the Boston telephone directory, the egg production of the United States, and so on. The participants were

graduate students at the Harvard School of Business Administration and
students in the Faculty of Arts and Sciences at Harvard.

In addition to the basic estimate, the students were asked to provide
fractiles; that is, numbers below which various subjective probabilities would
lie. To quantify his subjective distribution for the true value, the reporter
gives the median $x_{0.50}$, a number that he thinks the true value has an equal
chance of being above or below. In general, x_p is a number that he thinks
the true value has probability p of being below, and probability $1 - p$ of
being above. Some groups were asked to give $x_{0.01}$, $x_{0.25}$, $x_{0.50}$, $x_{0.75}$, and
$x_{0.99}$. The interval from $x_{0.25}$ to $x_{0.75}$ should contain 50% of the subjective
probability. An important question that we would like to answer is this:
What is the relation between these subjective probabilities and the frequency with which the true answers lie in the subjectively chosen intervals?

Though tentative, the results of Alpert and Raiffa's investigations are
most informative. The intervals formed by the successive fractiles were used
to assess 100 responders on the same 10 questions each. Here are the
results. Overall, the true values fell (see Figure 2)

15.8% in the first (leftmost) interval, where 1% should have been

12.0% in the second interval, where 24% should have been

16.4% in the third interval, where 25% should have been

17.0% in the fourth interval, where 25% should have been

12.0% in the fifth interval, where 24% should have been

26.8% in the sixth (rightmost) interval, where 1% should have been.

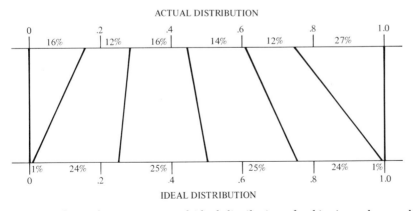

FIG. 2 *Relation between requested ideal distribution of subjective values and
actual frequencies of true values.*

If we think of the upper and lower 1% intervals as ones where a responder should be seriously surprised, then these responders were seriously surprised in 42.6% (15.8% + 26.8%) of the guesses, or about 21 times as often as they should have been if estimates matched true uncertainty. This makes us strongly suspect the frequency interpretation of the subjective estimates of the far tails of the distribution.

What doesn't seem quite so bad is that the middle two intervals, which should have contained 50% of the responses, did contain 33.4%. This is rather encouraging because it suggests that, perhaps by expanding estimates of the middle a little, one could get a fairly reliable interval. The 33.4% is only an average, however. Instead of 50%, the specific ten questions got the following 10 percentages correct in the "interquartile range" $x_{0.25}$ to $x_{0.75}$: 60, 54, 57, 7, 41, 25, 20, 23, 27, and 20. The very bad item which gave only 7% was a question about the opinion expressed by the nation in a Gallup Poll having to do with a possible war in the Middle East. The last 5 questions were all almanac sorts of questions. The first three items were estimates of the fraction of their classmates holding certain views. All told, then, the responders did better on items dealing with the opinions and preferences of people they were familiar with—and poorer on the almanac questions.

Alpert and Raiffa have gone much further with their experimentation and analysis than we describe in this short discussion. But we have gone far enough to see that brainy, experienced adults are very likely to overestimate the degree of certainty of their estimates. This overestimation holds especially when they try to predict the rarity of extremely large or extremely small numbers.

People are too sure of their information. Whether this is a fault of the reporting methods or a universal human failing has yet to be discovered.

An alternative attitude suggested to me by Persi Diaconis is that these mistakes represent an opportunity for training people to make better guesses by giving them practice and experience and a knowledge of the type of mistakes that are commonly made.

THE DELPHI METHOD

The Delphi method has been developed by Olaf Helmer, Norman Dalkey, Bernice Brown, and others—largely at the Rand Corporation and later elsewhere. The general method is similar to that described in connection with the experiments of Alpert and Raiffa. The purpose is to use a set of experts to get better estimates for numbers or guesses about unknown events than one could get by oneself. Experts are asked to make estimates, predict the future, or what have you, and they are asked to estimate

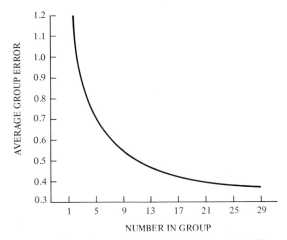

FIG. 3 *Effect of group size (after Dalkey, 1969).*

fractiles, typically the 25%, 50%, and 75% points of their distributions. Then some observer assembles the data and feeds it back to the experts, and they have an opportunity to revise their opinions in the light of the information their fellow experts have given. This process may, of course, be iterated.

The general idea, as Dalkey says, is not only that two heads are better than one, but that *n* heads may be better than one. Indeed, he points out that this is almost a tautology, for if the several experts are equally knowledgeable from the point of view of the user, then some estimate of the center of their distribution, such as the median, would be better than an estimate from one randomly chosen expert. Of course, weights could be used if the experts did not appear to the user to be equally knowledgeable.

Using almanac types of questions, Dalkey and others performed experiments with individuals in groups of varying sizes.

Figure 3 shows the effect of group size on the accuracy of the answers. The error was measured on a logarithmic scale, and the average group error was computed for groups of various sizes. The curve shows the improvement in average error with increasing group size.

Figure 4 shows the increasing reliability obtained by increasing the size of the group. To construct this graph, groups of identical size were randomly paired. For each, the median response on each of the twenty questions was obtained, and the correlation between the two sets of medians was computed. The average of such correlations for a given group size was graphed, and the result appears in Figure 4. As the group size increased, the results became more reliable.

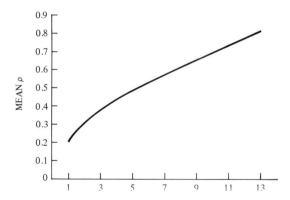

FIG. 4 *Reliability in relation to group size (after Dalkey, 1969).*

Discussion or controlled feedback?

A major issue is how the information from the initial round of questions should be fed back to the respondents. Should they get together and thrash it out? Or should some more bland and standard procedure be used?

The result of a series of experiments trying both methods is not clear-cut, but it is suggestive. Let A stand for face-to-face discussion and B for questionnaire feedback. Then twenty questions were studied in four blocks of five by groups following an ABBA design. The discussion groups chose a discussion leader at random, tried to reach a consensus, and did in 19 out of 20 cases. The questionnaire procedure involved four rounds of estimates, fed back medians and quartiles ($x_{0.25}$, $x_{0.50}$, $x_{0.75}$) from the previous rounds, and got re-estimates. Subjects rated their own competence to answer each question. The median response of the questionnaire group was more accurate in 13 out of the 20 cases, that of the discussion group in 7. A variety of other experiments suggest that discussion as now constituted does not seem to be as good as controlled feedback. It is easy to give reasons why discussion is not good (dominant individuals, noise in the communication system, pressure for conformity). The experimenters' observations of the groups did confirm these particular shortcomings of the discussion method. But had the results come out in the opposite way, we would also have had good explanations for the contrary result.

In another experiment, changes made in the estimates between the first and second round using the controlled feedback method improved 8, degraded 4, and left 8 estimates unchanged.

It has also been found that people who rated themselves as especially competent on a task *did* perform better on it, so it is worth eliminating those who claim no skill or at least giving their guessing less weight.

In discussing the problem of the tightness of the distribution of estimates by experts—the too certain reports—Dalkey points out that one does not automatically know what the remedy should be, even if it could be implemented. Is it that the distributions should be spread more broadly, or is it that the spread is all right but the location poor, as when a marksman puts his bullets in a very tight cluster, but off the mark. He reports (private communication) that when positive numbers are being estimated his experts tended to underestimate, and that the 65th percentile gave better estimates than the median short-range prediction and almanac questions.

JUDITH SELVIDGE'S FINDINGS FOR QUANTIFYING PROPORTIONS

Judith Selvidge got individuals to estimate the percentages implied by various vague words and phrases such as "considerably," "often," "possibility," "slim," "virtually every," and "rare," as shown in Table 3.

TABLE 3 MEDIANS AND QUARTILES OF PERCENTAGES ASSOCIATED WITH SEMI-QUANTITATIVE TERMS OBTAINED BY JUDITH SELVIDGE.

Semi-quantitative terms	Without context $f_{.50}$	With context $f_{.50}$	Without context $f_{.25}$	Without context $f_{.75}$
rare[a]	1		1	3
tiny sliver	2	2	1	5
seldom, if ever	3	5.1	1	5
pitifully small minority	4	5	2	5
handful	5	10	10	20
slim	10	10	5	10
small minority	10	10	5	10
unlikely	10	10	5	20
possibility	20	20	10	50
appreciably	25	10	15	35
might	25	30	15	40
some	30	15,20,30	25	30
often	60	50	50	75
largely	65	75	60	75
probably predominantly	65	70	60	80
considerable	75	70	60	80
most	75	75,80,80,80,80	60	80
probable maximum loss	80	80	70	98
very high probability	90	91	80	90
practically certain	90	90	90	99
beyond reasonable doubt	95	85	90	99
overwhelming probability	95	99	90	99
virtually every	98	95	95	99

[a] "Rare" occurred only in the without-context version.

In one questionnaire she asked that the estimate be made on the basis of a statement without context; in another a context or contexts were provided. In Table 3 the words have been ordered according to their *median* percentages. The subjects were Harvard Business School students in the Master in Business Administration program—59 in the without-context study, 127 in the with-context study.

One use for this list might be to choose among vague terms those that best quantitatively express one's meaning. Also, one may have an empirical ordering of the sizes of these vague terms when used as percentages.

The list might also be used to make a rough estimate of the percentage implied by an author who used a vague term. And thus one may be able to take some advantage of these values in estimating quantities that have been appraised only qualitatively. And one gets some notion of the variability in meaning from the final two columns of Table 3. There is, of course, considerable uncertainty in the numbers.

The notations $f_{.25}$, $f_{.50}$, $f_{.75}$ refer to the 25%, 50% (median), and 75% point of the distributions of the estimates made by the subjects in the investigation.

We see that "very high probability" and "practically certain" have about the same median quantitative meaning—90%. In addition, from the $f_{.25}$ and $f_{.75}$ information we see that "practically certain" is generally a higher number than "very high probability."

SUMMARY

Getting reasonable estimates for unknown numbers, especially when they are nowhere available, will always be a problem for the policy analyst. The main methods in developing such an estimate are looking in a reference work, collecting it through a survey or other investigation, guessing it based on one's own information, or getting experts to help with the guessing.

Reference sources may disagree, perhaps because of definitions or because they too are leaning on guesses. Sample surveys may be effective for gathering some kinds of numbers, and many survey organizations are equipped to help the policy analyst.

If one must guess based on material one has in hand or can gather quickly, using rates or proportions may help if they are fairly stable. Some industries and disciplines have rules of thumb that can be useful—or can fail miserably. One rule of thumb is that a barrel hoop should be three times the diameter of the barrel, plus a generous thumb's length. This is not a bad rule for small barrels. But look out for large barrels.

We can sometimes use past experience together with regression methods to estimate new numbers. Or we may find simple linear functions helpful, whether from regression equations or from casual estimates. We may find it helpful to break an estimate into multiplicative (factoring) or additive (decomposing) components. And we may even try to build mathematical models appropriate to the occasion.

Sometimes similarity helps—other populations suffering from the same problem or from seemingly similar problems may produce data of value. When we can estimate the same quantity by several different methods (triangulation), we get some feeling for the uncertainty of the estimates.

Sometimes others, especially experts, can help us guess, as in the Delphi method. Research suggests that people may report themselves as too sure of their answers. In one experiment the numerical intervals subjects guessed to be 98% sure to include the true value of a number were so short or so misplaced that they included the true value only 57% of the time.

We may be able to improve our communication about quantitative matters expressed qualitatively by reviewing Selvidge's findings (Table 3). For example, a "small minority" is estimated in percentage terms as about 10%.

REFERENCES

Alpert, Marc, and Howard Raiffa. "A Progress Report on the Training of Probability Assessors." Unpublished paper, August 28, 1969.

Buchanan, Patrick J. *New York Times*, February 20, 1973.

Dalkey, Norman. "An experimental study of group opinion, The Delphi Method," *Futures*, Vol. 1, No. 5 (September 1969), pp. 408–426.

DeArmond, Fred. "Letter to the Editor." *New York Times Book Review*, September 19, 1971.

Dunn, William A. "Spill Risk Analysis Program. Phase II. Methodology Development and Demonstration." Operations Research, Inc. Prepared for the Coast Guard, August 1974. Distributed by National Technical Information Service.

Helmer, Olaf. *Social Technology*, New York: Basic Books, 1966.

Golenpaul, Dan, ed. "Languages of the World," *Information Please Almanac for 1972*. New York: Simon and Schuster, 1971, p. 487.

Linstone, Harold A., and Murray Turoff, eds. *The Delphi Method: Techniques and Applications*. Reading, Mass.: Addison-Wesley, 1975.

Long, Luman H., ed. "Automobile Registration," *The 1972 World Almanac*. New York: Newspaper Enterprise Association, 1971, p. 120.

Long, Luman H., ed. "The Principal Languages of the World." *The 1972 World Almanac*. New York: Newspaper Enterprise Association, 1971, p. 334.

———. "U.S. Motor Fuel Supply and Demand." *The 1972 World Almanac*. New York: Newspaper Enterprise Association, 1971, p. 417.

Meehl, Paul E. *Clinical versus Statistical Prediction*. Minneapolis: University of Minnesota Press, 1954.

Neuhauser, Duncan. "Elective inguinal herniorrhaphy versus truss in the elderly." In J. Bunker, B. Barnes, and F. Mosteller, eds., *Costs, Benefits, and Risks of Surgery*. Oxford University Press (in press).

Pill, J. "The Delphi Method: Substance, content, a critique and an annotated bibliography." *Socioecon. Plann. Sci.*, 5 (1971), pp. 57–71.

Raiffa, Howard. "The Art and Science of Probability Assessment." In *Decision Analysis. A Self-Instructional, Self-Paced Course*, Module 10. 1972.

Selvidge, Judith. *Assigning Probabilities to Rare Events*. Doctoral dissertation, Graduate School of Business Administration, George F. Baker Foundation, Harvard University, 1972.

Singer, Max. "The vitality of mythical numbers." *The Public Interest*, Spring 1971, pp. 3–9.

Statistical Abstracts of the United States, United States Government Printing Office, Washington, D.C.

Wallis, W. Allen, and Harry D. Roberts. *Statistics: A New Approach*. Glencoe, Ill.: Free Press, 1956.

Webb, E. J., D. T. Campbell, R. D. Schwartz, and L. Sechrest, *Unobtrusive Measures: Nonreactive Research in the Social Sciences*. Chicago: Rand McNally and Company, 1966.

ASSESSING SOCIAL INNOVATIONS: AN EMPIRICAL BASE FOR POLICY

JOHN P. GILBERT, RICHARD J. LIGHT, and FREDERICK MOSTELLER

I. THE GENERAL IDEA

How effective are modern large-scale social action programs? To see how well such programs accomplish their primary mission, we have reviewed the performance of a large number. At the same time, we have also examined methods of evaluation and their possible contribution toward social improvements. We particularly focus on evaluations that identify causal effects because they provide the most direct means for learning how to increase program effectiveness.

Reviewing these programs and their evaluations has led us to some fresh insights. We invite the reader to join us in looking at the data and considering some of their implications for choosing methods of evaluation. Our examples are drawn from public and private social action programs, from applied social research, and from studies in medicine and mental illness. Thus, though our writing is oriented especially to policy-makers in government, the findings should also be informative to investigators in the fields of applied social research and to those who fund them.

In our collection of well-evaluated innovations, we find few with marked positive effects. Even innovations that turned out to be especially valuable often had relatively small positive effects—gains of a few percent, for example, or larger gains for a small subgroup of the population treated. Because even small gains accumulated over time can sum to a considerable total, they may have valuable consequences for society. In addition, understanding the causes of even small specific gains may form a basis for evolutionary improvements in the programs. The empirical findings for the programs described here emphasize the frequent importance of detecting small effects and, since these are difficult to measure, the need for well-designed and well-executed evaluations. Many would agree that, where

Reprinted with permission from Carl A. Bennett and Arthur A. Lumsdaine (eds.), *Evaluation and Experiment*: *Some Critical Issues in Assessing Social Programs*, Academic Press, Inc., New York, 1975, pp. 39–193. That version is much longer.

practical and feasible, randomized field trials are currently the technique of choice for evaluating the results of complex social innovations. Our data suggest that such careful evaluations may be needed much more often in the future if society is to reap the full benefits of its expenditures for new programs.

While realizing the theoretical effectiveness of randomized trials, investigators often use nonrandomized trials for a variety of practical reasons, including apparently lower costs and easier execution. When we examine the findings of well-executed nonrandomized studies, we often find conflicting interpretations even after a large, expensive, time-consuming evaluation. Frequently the question is, "Were the differences found the result of how the samples were chosen or were they due to program effects?" In several large sets of parallel studies, the results of nonrandomized and randomized evaluations of the same programs conflict. These difficulties with nonrandomized trials lead us to re-examine some of the common objections to randomized trials.

Although we consider the force of these objections in some detail, we are not striving for completeness. The length of this paper arises from the discussions of numerous programs—almost two score—and their evaluations, rather than from an attempt to provide a manual to aid in carrying out field trials or from a systematic treatment of political and organizational programs. We understand only too well that such problems exist. Insofar as we do discuss them, our stimulus comes primarily from the empirical studies presented here, and secondarily from occasional considerations of constraints on evaluations where more freedom of action may be available than is often supposed. What we offer are data suggesting that a decision maker has more reason for carrying out a randomized field trial than he may suspect.

Despite the difficulties of organizing and implementing randomized field trials, our examples show that such trials have been done successfully in education, welfare, criminal justice, medical care, manpower training, surgery, and preventive medicine. The fact that these randomized trials were actually carried out and that valuable social and medical findings emerged, documents the importance and feasibility of randomized trials even in sensitive areas. Beyond this, we re-examine such issues as costs, timeliness, and flexibility, and suggest some steps that could improve the availability and effectiveness of the randomized controlled field trial as a method of evaluation.

II. INTRODUCTION

A. The plan of the paper

Section I gives the general ideas of this paper, and Section II briefly describes methods of gathering information about social programs with emphasis on randomized controlled field trials and their merits. To give the reader a flavor of the innovations to be discussed and to exemplify randomized and nonrandomized field trials, in Section III we describe three instructive studies which are prototypes of material treated in Sections IV and V. Section IV explains the idea of ratings for innovations and why we want to make them. Our main empirical study of 29 innovations in Section IV reviews the frequency with which innovations offer clearly beneficial effects as evaluated by randomized controlled field trials, the innovations being drawn from social, socio-medical, and medical areas. Having looked at how often innovations turn out well, we provide case studies in Section V of what happens when innovations are evaluated by nonrandomized field trials, including comments on such issues as costs, timeliness, reliability, and validity of findings. Section VI deals at more length with special topics related to randomization, and with developmental needs. Three short sections deal with feasibility of making evaluations (Section VII), costs and timeliness (Section VIII), and the implementations of innovations (Section IX). Section X sums up our findings and recommendations.

For the reader who wishes a highly streamlined look at the main findings of this paper, we suggest the following path:

- Section III to get an idea of the studies being rated in Sections IV and V.
- Sections IV-A, B, C, and one or two further innovations, especially one that received a low rating; for example, Section IV-D-3 (Delinquent Girls), or IV-F-4 (Probation for Drunk Arrests), or IV-H-8 (Large Bowel Surgery). The reader will already have seen innovations with high ratings in Section III.
- Section IV-J, the summary of the ratings for the randomized studies.
- Section V-A-3 to get a feeling for nonrandomized studies, and Section V-C, the summary of Section V.
- Sections VIII–A and VIII-E to tune in on some facts about dollar costs and time in evaluations.
- Section X, the grand summary and recommendations.

B. Evaluating social programs

Extensive public spending on many innovative social programs makes it essential to document their benefits and evaluate their impact. We trace here the results of a number of social, medical, and socio-medical programs, and present an empirical view of their effectiveness.

The review of these studies leads us to the conclusion that randomization, together with careful control and implementation, gives an evaluation a strength and persuasiveness that cannot ordinarily be obtained by other means. We are particularly struck by the troublesome record that our

examples of nonrandomized studies piled up. Although some nonrandomized studies gave suggestive information that seems reliable, we find it
hard to tell which were likely to be the misleading ones, even with the power
of hindsight to guide us.

It is also true that not all randomized trials are successful in their quest
for an accurate appraisal, and one of our chief concerns is that enough of
these randomized studies be done so that both decision makers and the
public may learn their strengths and weaknesses, just as they have learned to
appreciate the strengths and weaknesses of sample surveys. In the course of
such a development we would hope to see the emergence of the organizational and technical skills necessary for applying randomization effectively in
field studies of program effectiveness, just as we have seen the development
of both practical and theoretical aspects of sample surveys over the past few
decades and their effect on decision making.

We recognize that the word "evaluation" has for some years had
different meanings for different people. One form of evaluation involves
examining managerial records, such as when one wants to find out who
received what treatment. A second form focuses upon measuring inputs to a
program, such as how much money per pupil is being spent in different
school districts. We concentrate throughout this paper on a third type of
policy-oriented evaluation. Such investigations usually ask the question,
"What are the effects of a program on its intended beneficiaries?" Thus, our
focus is upon the output, or result of the program, and the evaluative
question generally before us is how to improve the program so that it may
better serve its clients.

We are aware that the effectiveness of any program must be related to
its costs by policy makers; nevertheless, we largely confine our discussion to
the prior problem of rating program effects. If an effect is a slam-bang
success and does not cost much, then it is almost certainly cost effective. If it
is a slight success, its costs may put it near the borderline. For innovations
that have no effect or even a harmful effect, obviously the net value is
negative, and many of the innovations examined have these properties.
Beyond this simple-minded thinking about cost effectiveness, we also discuss
some aspects of the costs and cost effectiveness of different methods of
conducting program evaluations in Section VIII.

C. Initial ignorance
A knifelike truth that the policy maker, the economist, the social scientist,
the journalist, and the layman—indeed, all of us—need to learn to handle is
that we often do not know which is the best of several possible policies and,
worse yet, that we may not know if any of them betters what we are now
doing. Economic reasoning, sophisticated analysis, sample surveys, and

observational studies will give us some good ideas, suggestions—let's be plain, guesses—but we still will not know how things will work in practice until we try them *in practice*. This is a hard lesson and often an unwelcome one. We want medical and social helpers to know for sure what ails us and how to cure us. If there is some sort of dilemma, we want to know the comparative chances of success under each available regimen. Ironically, neither request can be answered unless the regimens have been studied in a controlled way, a way we call the randomized controlled field trial—a practical tryout under field conditions.

The theme of the policy man must always be that evaluative studies should provide information required for policy decisions and not necessarily that required, let us say, for progress in science. This position helps avoid policies that are obviously expensive and have but little yield, and often helps to choose a good way for carrying out a program. But the key question in many programs comes when we ask how much benefit will be derived from the program—How many points will IQ be raised? How many accidents prevented? How many fish will be saved? How many additional happy, disease-free days will be provided? How much will the air be cleansed? We can think and dream and compute and theorize and observe and temporize, but the answers to such questions, even approximate and uncertain answers, must finally be found in the field. We *all* know this; even our language knows it: "The proof of the pudding is in the eating." George Box (1966) put it well in addressing statisticians and the social science community in general when he said, "To find out what happens to a system when you interfere with it you have to interfere with it (not just passively observe it)" (p. 629). The social policy maker will find this advice particularly valuable when the system being investigated is complicated, and when there is no large body of experience available to predict reliably what happens when the sytem is actually changed. In contrast to more predictable effects in simpler laboratory investigations in the physical sciences, where considerable experience and proven theory offer guides, we focus here primarily on social and medical settings that are much more unpredictable. For example, it is difficult to foresee how effective a job training program will be before instituting it and systematically investigating its effects on trainees.

D.   Methods of investigation

Let us review the main ways of gathering information to assist us in policy decisions and in other forms of evaluation.

1.   *Introspection, theory, analysis, and simulation* today form an important group of parallel methods for finding out how a policy might work. Although these methods can all have substantial inputs from empirical

information, we put them first to emphasize that they often do not have a strong empirical base; indeed, sometimes they have none, except for casual observation and analogy.

2.   *Anecdotes, casual observation, and case studies* are very commonly used in medicine, anthropology, law, sociology, business, and education. Like the first set of methods, they are likely to suggest theories and discover difficulties that we might not otherwise detect. They provide a firm record of a special event. They are especially weak, however, in giving us a bridge from the case at hand to the wider realm of situations that we wish to influence in the future. The inference from a case study to the more general practical policy may be a very long step.

3.   *Quantitative observational studies,* including sample surveys and censuses, and very widely used now. They are especially good at telling us the current state of the world. Our own Section IV is an observational study to indicate how often innovations give clear benefits. This kind of study is ordinarily not designed to include the administration of new treatments. Usually sample surveys involve a stage of random sampling, but this randomness is designed to reduce certain kinds of bias in collecting information; it is not ordinarily connected with the administration of treatments, but rather is used for deciding which items should be observed. We may, for example, observe how people with various characteristics respond to different treatments. But in sample surveys we ordinarily do not initiate the treatments. The response observed in the survey may well not be to the treatment that we have in mind as the potential causal agent.

Censuses are a form of observational study. Again, they are ordinarily designed to aid our appreciation of matters as they stand, rather than to administer treatments and see what their effect might be.

Among quantitative observational studies we include searches of records and studies to see how various people fare under various treatments that have been imposed through the natural processes of society, without the investigator's interfering with those processes. From the evaluation point of view, the general feature of an observational study is that some individuals, groups, or institutions have in the course of events experienced one regimen, and others have experienced other regimens, and these regimens have led to outcomes on variables of interest. We hope to find out from a thoughtful examination of the outcomes following each regimen what the approximate effect of the regimen was. This hope has often been frustrated by a variety of difficulties.

Innovations and experiments.   When we have an innovation in society, such as the establishment of Social Security, the adoption of Prohibition, a new child assistance program, or an employment training program, some people call such innovations "experiments." The word "experiment" is then being used in the sense of a new and sometimes tentative treatment. It is not being used in the sense of a scientific investigation. We try the innovation, and then if we don't care for it, we may change matters again. Since the word "experiment" is commonly used in this way, we need an expression for the social equivalent of the controlled scientific investigation. We shall call such investigations controlled field trials, and when they employ randomization, we shall prefix the word "randomized." The expression "field trial" is intended to emphasize the possibly substantial variation of effects from one place, person, or institution to another.

4. In *nonrandomized field trials*, the investigator initiates new treatments but without the use of randomization. For example, the investigator gives some people and not others treatment 1 and then compares the performance of those who got treatment 1 with that of others who got treatment 2. This nonrandomized method is a step forward from the observational study because the investigator rather than the social process chose the treatment, and so we can relate treatment and outcome. The difficulties of this procedure have to do with a variety of matters, but the key problem is that the effect of the treatment is not distinctive in all cases, so that the treatment cannot be proved to have caused the effect of interest. Selection effects and variability of previous experience have often led to biases and misinterpretations. In the famous Lanarkshire milk experiment ("Student," 1931), a controlled but nonrandomized study, the teachers tended to give the less robust children the milk, and so the value of the milk treatment was left uncertain. Biases arising from selection have on several occasions led to adopting therapies that seemed to have great prospects in the light of the nonrandomized study, but that have not proved out under randomized clinical trials. We document this point in Section V-B.

5. *Randomized controlled field trials* are currently our best device for appraising new programs. The word "trial" suggests the direct comparison of the effects of treatments. We shall also speak of these trials as "studies" because the investigators usually go beyond just the initial comparison of treatments. In these studies, the experimental units—individuals, families, school districts, whatever the unit—are randomly assigned to treatments or regimens and carefully followed to find out what the effect of the regimen might be. The randomization helps in several ways. First, it avoids the dangers of self-selection or of biased selection that we have mentioned earlier. It provides objectivity to outsiders. If we hand select the cases ourselves, then no matter how fair we may try to be, we may tend to choose on some basis that will confuse the effects of the variable of primary interest. If we use a random method, we assure the reader or consumer, as well as ourselves, that we have constructively protected against selectivity. (We still may want to examine the outcome for balance and perhaps adjust if nature

has given us a bad break.) Second, it helps us control for variables we may not otherwise be able to control. We explain this further in Section VI.

Since "randomized controlled field trials" is rather a mouthful, let us spell out its parts. The expression "field trial" implies that the treatment or treatments are being studied in the field rather than in the laboratory, and that they are being tried out in practice rather than through simulation or theory. A field trial might consist of one treatment only, but it could refer to several. For instance, a field trial of a new medication might be for the purpose of discovering side effects. "Controlled" refers to two matters: (1) that the choice of treatment for a site or an individual is primarily that of the investigator rather than the individual (once he agrees to participate) or the natural or market processes; (2) that at least two treatments are being compared. "Randomized" refers to the use of chance at some stage to choose which units get which treatments.

The purpose of randomized controlled field trials, like that of the other kinds of evaluative investigations we discuss, is marshalling information to aid decisions (Thompson, 1973). People tend to think of this device as especially important for the scientist rather than for the policy maker. This leaves us with the idea that a scientist needs a very fine tool to get information about a process, but the policy maker should be content with uncertain information. Although sometimes this may be true, one could argue that exactly the reverse holds: the policy maker needs not only fine tools, but also good efforts to develop better tools. This seems especially true in policy problems where large numbers of individuals are involved and large amounts of money are at stake or when lives and careers are being substantially affected.

E.   Large and small effects

When is it that weaker tools are adequate? We usually think that in the presence of "slam-bang" effects, weaker methods work. For example, if there is a well-established disease which once had a 100% chance of leading to death in a short time, and if someone begins to keep 30% of the patients alive and well for more than two years, we would say that a slam-bang effect was at work and that it looked as if the new treatment caused the cures.

This sort of dreamy situation is one that we tend to think of when we install new social programs. We will raise IQ by 20 or 30 points, advance education by four additional months per year of training, cut the death rate on the highways by 50%, and so on. These optimistic forecasts often play a crucial role in the political process that leads to a program being tried. These dreams lead people to suggest that if one has a first-class social program it will speak for itself. Statistics will not be needed. One cannot argue with this position, given its assumptions; such programs will indeed be beacons in the night. In the cold light of day, however, such slam-bang effects are few, as Section IV documents. For this reason we suggest that evaluations of these new social programs should be designed to document even modest effects, if they occur, so that new programs may be built upon these gains.

III. THREE INSTRUCTIVE EXAMPLES

For concreteness, we next give examples of three evaluations of medical and social innovations. These real-life cases give an opportunity to illustrate distinctions between randomized and nonrandomized controlled field trials, and also to focus on difficulties that arise in such evaluations.

A. The Salk vaccine trials[1]

The 1954 trial to test a new preventive medication for paralytic polio, the Salk vaccine, is most instructive. First, it exposed children to a new vaccine, and thereby showed that we as a nation have been willing to experiment on people, even our dearest ones, our children. Secondly, the preliminary arguments over the plan instructed us, as did the way it was actually carried out—in two parallel studies.

In the initial design—the *observed control method*—the plan was to give the vaccine to those second graders whose parents volunteered them for the study, to give nothing to the first and third graders, and then to compare the average result for the untreated first and third grade with the treated group in the second grade.

There are troubles here. In the more sanitary neighborhoods, polio occurs more frequently than in unsanitary neighborhoods, and the more sanitary regions are associated with higher income and better education. It is also a social fact that better educated people tend to volunteer more than less well educated ones. Consequently we could expect that the volunteers in the second grade would be more prone to have the disease in the first place than the average second grader, and than the average of the first and third graders. The comparison might well not be valid because of this bias. In addition, if only second graders got the vaccine, more of them might be suspected by physicians of having caught the disease because of possible exposure through the vaccine itself, and so there might well be differential frequencies of diagnoses in the volunteer and nonvolunteer groups. Another difficulty is that if an epidemic happened to confine itself largely to one of these school grade groups, this large-scale investigation might wind up an uninterpretable fiasco.

---

[1] Francis *et al.*, 1955; Meier, 1972; Brownlee, 1955.

Some state public health officials noticed these difficulties and recommended instead a second design, the *placebo control method*, which randomizes the vaccine among volunteers from all grade groups; that is, these officials recommended a randomized controlled field trial. Half the volunteers got the vaccine and half a salt water injection (placebo), so that the "blindness" of the diagnoses could be protected. Thus the physician could be protected from his expectations for the outcome in making a diagnosis. This meant that the self-selection effects and their associated bias would be balanced between the vaccinated and unvaccinated groups of volunteers, and that the hazards to validity from an epidemic in a grade would be insured against.

In actuality, both methods were used: one in some states and the other in others. The result has been carefully analyzed, and the randomized trial (placebo control) shows conclusively a reduction in paralytic polio rate from about 57 per hundred thousand among the controls to about 16 per hundred thousand in the vaccinated group. (See Table 1.)

In the states where only the second-grade volunteers were vaccinated, the vaccinated volunteers had about the same rate (17 per hundred thousand) as those vaccinated (16 per hundred thousand) in the placebo control areas. The expected bias of an increased rate for volunteers as compared to nonvolunteers appeared among the whole group. Among the

TABLE 1 SUMMARY OF STUDY CASES BY VACCINATION STATUS FOR SALK VACCINE EXPERIMENT.*

Study group	Study population (thousands)	Paralytic poliomyelitis cases: rate per hundred thousand
Placebo control areas: Total	749	36
Vaccinated	201	16
Placebo	201	57
Not inoculated†	339	36
Incomplete vaccinations	8	12
Observed control areas: Total	1,081	38
Vaccinated	222	17
Controls‡	725	46
Grade 2 not inoculated	124	35
Incomplete vaccinations	10	40

* Source: Paul Meier. "The biggest public health experiment ever: The 1954 field trial of the Salk poliomyelitis vaccine," in J. M. Tanur *et al.*, eds., *Statistics: A guide to the unknown.* San Francisco: Holden–Day, 1972, Table 1, p. 11.

† Includes 8,577 children who received one or two injections of placebo.

‡ First- and third-grade total population.

placebo controls, the volunteers who were not vaccinated had the highest rate (57 per hundred thousand) and those who declined to volunteer had 35 or 36 per hundred thousand. In the states using the observed control method, the first and third graders, who were not asked to volunteer and were not vaccinated, had a rate between the two extremes, 46 per hundred thousand.

Brownlee (1955), referring to the observed control study as 59% of the total investigation, says, "59% of the trial was worthless because of the lack of adequate controls" (p. 1013). This illustrates how one informed skeptic views the observed control study. Thus for him, the biases and lack of reliability destroyed this part of the study. Others might not be so harsh. Uncontrolled biases can make interpretation difficult because it becomes necessary for the interpreter to guess the size of the bias, and when its size may be comparable to that of the treatment effect, the interpreter is guessing the final result. In the Salk vaccine study we happened to have two investigations in parallel and they support each other. But this does not help us in the situation where the observed control study is performed alone.

These results then instruct us that the size of a study is not enough. We need randomization and controls. And we have to worry not only about biases, but about the possibility that uncertainty in the answers may make the results not very useful even when they happen to come out in the right direction and in approximately the right size, for we will not be confident that these events occurred. From the policy maker's point of view, he is less sure of the direction and size of the effect and so is less sure to make appropriate decisions.

B. The gamma globulin study[2]

The general success of the Salk vaccine randomized study can be contrasted with the results of a corresponding earlier study of gamma globulin which was carried out in a nonrandomized trial. In 1953, during the summer, 235,000 children were inoculated in the hope of preventing or modifying the severity of poliomyelitis. "The committee recognized that it would be very difficult to conduct rigidly controlled studies in the United States during 1953" (p. 3). They hoped to use mass inoculation in various places and compare differential attack rates at different sites, as well as to analyze other epidemiological data. In the end this approach turned out to be inconclusive, and the authors of that study describe the need for a more carefully controlled experiment. The general belief of Dr. Hammon, in commenting on the study, was that the gamma globulin was given too late, but that it seems to have an extremely limited application in the field of preventive

---

[2] U.S. Public Health Service, 1954.

medicine. If Hammon is right, the intended treatment may not have been given. This is a concern often raised about controlled social trials, as well.

What we have to recognize here is that whether or not gamma globulin was good for the purpose, the lack of randomization undermined the expert investigators' ability to draw firm conclusions, in spite of the large size of the study. The children were put at risk. Although it must be acknowledged that conducting randomized studies would have been difficult in 1953, those who argue today that randomized trials have ethical problems may wish to think about the problems of studies that put the same or greater numbers of people at risk without being able to generate data that can answer the questions being asked.

C. Emergency school assistance program[3]
The Emergency School Assistance Program (ESAP) was a federally funded program to assist desegregating schools to improve the quality of the education they offered. It was succeeded by the Emergency School Aid Act (ESAA), which has similar purposes. Both programs are intended, among other things, to improve academic performance. During 1971–72, a randomized controlled field study was performed under ESAP to see what benefits certain parts of the program had conferred.

This evaluation illustrates the possibility of a controlled field study being superimposed upon an ongoing large-scale program. In all, ESAP was distributing about $64,000,000. The funds going to the schools in the field trial amount to approximately $1,000,000 or less, perhaps about 1% of the total funds. The total funds available in ESAP were far from enough to distribute to all the schools and school districts that asked for aid (ESAP supported many kinds of programs, of which one kind was tested), and so it was not hard to justify a *randomized* controlled field study in which some schools did not get the funds and others did. Usually we prefer to compare two or more treatments, all of which are hoped to be beneficial, but here the comparison was between giving the funds and not giving the funds. The funds were used for two different purposes. First, all schools receiving funds (both elementary schools and high schools) used the money for teacher's aides, counseling, in-service education for trachers, and remedial programs. Second, in addition to these uses, the high schools also used some of the funds on programs intended to change the way the schools handled problems in race relations. Thus one difference between the elementary and the high school treatment was the program in race relations in the high school.

The designers of the field trial set up a rather straightforward plan whereby in the South 50 pairs of high schools and 100 pairs of grade schools

---

[3] National Opinion Research Center (NORC), 1973.

were candidates for ESAP grants. In each pair, one school was randomly chosen to get the funds and the other was not. The objections to participation in the controlled field study were reported to have been few. (There can be problems; for example, it may be hard for a school superintendent to convince his constituency that it is reasonable for one school to get and another not to get what looks like a valuable contribution. Developing an understanding that such a move can be not only fair but wise may be important for our society.)

The academic performance of the children in the schools receiving the funds was compared with that of those not receiving funds. Several groups were studied: males versus females, blacks versus whites, elementary schools versus high schools. The major positive finding was that black males in funded high schools improved by half a grade level compared to those in high schools without the funds. Other groups were not detected as improving. The researchers suppose, but not with as strong convictions as they have for the existence of the improvement itself, that the race relations programs may have influenced attitudes for the male blacks, leading to improved school performance.

Without going into the details of the other findings, we would like to emphasize that this is one of the very rare large-scale randomized controlled field studies in education that have been done so far. It was installed without much difficulty in the midst of an ongoing program, and we have some evidence about an improvement. The funds necessary for this investigation were largely those of a program that was already being administered; extra funding was not required. Even though billions have been spent in other educational programs, and tens of millions in evaluations, this is the only one where a substantial randomized controlled field trial has been carried out, and it gives us a definite notion of which groups improved their school achievement. One policy recommendation flowing from this study is the desirability of trying out programs in race relations in the elementary schools as well as in the high schools, because the presence of this element in the high school program was the main difference in treatment between the elementary school program and the high school program, and was the source of the positive effect in the latter.

In commenting upon this evaluation, the National Opinion Research Center experimenters say, "It is difficult to overstate the importance of the experimental design. Had there not been an experiment, we would have had to compare schools that were deemed worthy of ESAP funds to those that were not; no matter what statistical tricks we attempted to make the two groups comparable, the question of whether or not the differences we believed to be the result of ESAP were due to some other differences between the two schools would have always remained open" (Vol. I, p. ii). This uncertainty haunts nearly every attempt to reach firm conclusions from observational studies and nonrandomized field trials about the effects of social or medical programs, no matter how clever the analysts.

In addition to the positive finding, a number of findings indicated small or no effects, and so we know in what areas of schooling we need new thoughts if money is to benefit others in addition to black male high school students. An extra half a grade improvement is a large increment in performance for one year. An extra half a grade for students who have traditionally done poorly is more than a 50% improvement, perhaps as much as 70% over the expected gains in the same time period. And so we are discussing a very valuable effect.

Because such positive findings about school performance of black males came from a randomized study, there should be relatively few disagreements about the results themselves. Thus the value of randomization in this ESAP study was great, for it gave us firm inferences about a program that was adopted on a wide scale and worked.

How should we regard the rest of the money spent that does not seem to improve achievement? First, the funds went into the school system, and so they represented a redistribution of finances. Second, the findings tell us where we did not get substantial gains, as well as where we did.

Finally, this program is one of very few in education that provide firm evidence of a substantial effect. The study went forward without excessive difficulty and was imbedded as an integral part of the main program. Perhaps a little less effort debating the merits of randomized controlled field studies and a lot more spent on actually doing them might benefit society a great deal.

D. Afterword

The preceding three examples illustrate a variety of issues, at some length. In the next section we describe many studies, but usually much more briefly than those just given. Naturally, all such studies have complications and details that will be largely omitted in this short presentation.

After some of these studies, we remark on additional methodological points, but that is not the prime purpose of the section. Our primary purpose is to find out how often innovations are successful in carrying out their stated mission.

IV. RATINGS OF INNOVATIONS

In this section, we rate a substantial number of innovations. Our primary purpose is to find out something about how often innovations succeed and fail these days.

We include an innovation only if its evaluation seems well done and well documented. Each one involved a randomized controlled field trial. Furthermore, each trial is of sufficient size to reach some conclusion about the innovation it evaluates. For some studies the conclusion about the innovation has to be confined to the region, circumstances, or site where the trial was done. In others the study has been done in a broad enough way that its inferences may be more generalizable.

If all innovations worked well, the need for evaluations would be less pressing. If we forecast so nearly perfectly, the suggestion might even be made that we were not trying enough new things. Our findings in this section show that this happy state of affairs does not hold; they show, rather, that only a modest fraction of innovations work well. This finding makes clear that innovations need to have their performance assessed.

[Parts A and B are omitted.]

C. Our ratings of social innovations

We rate the innovations according to a five-point scale, from double plus (++), meaning a very successful innovation—it does well some of the major things it was supposed to do; to double minus (− −), meaning a definitely harmful innovation. A single minus (−) indicates a slightly harmful or negative innovation. A zero (0) means that the innovation does not seem to have much if any effect in either the positive or negative direction. It could mean also that the innovation has both small positive and small negative effects, neither overwhelming the other. A plus (+) means that the innovation seems to have a somewhat positive effect, but that one would have to weigh particularly carefully whether it was worth its price. We have not carried out detailed cost-benefit analyses here.

Several caveats are in order. The reader might disagree with our ratings, but this worry is not as substantial as one might at first suppose. We shall try to give enough detail as we go along so that the reader can get a feel for the studies. We doubt if any zeros would move up to double pluses, and we would be surprised if many single pluses moved up to double pluses. Similarly, we doubt if many double pluses would be reduced to single pluses. The double pluses are probably the items to watch especially. In a few studies we shall explain some special difficulties in making the ratings.

The surgical innovations are probably less subject to unreliability of ratings than the two other groups. The reason is twofold: first, the translation from the summaries of the original investigators' findings to the pluses or minuses is almost automatic; secondly, we have had expert surgical advice.

We wish to stress again that we are not rating the methodology of the field trial. All of the field trials we discuss were in our judgment of sufficient size and quality to give strong evidence of the efficacy of the innovation. Thus the rating applies to the *innovation* as measured by the field trial.

We are also not rating the study for its help in establishing a base line for future research, or for its dismissal of the innovation, or for some new approach discovered during the research. We merely rate as best we can whether the innovation itself, if cost-free, looks like a substantial success. When the innovation has multiple goals, we rate its success in achieving the primary goal. We regard all the *studies* as successes, even when the innovations they evaluate are not.

All told, we have in this section an observational study of randomized trials. Innovations that reach the stage of having a randomized trial have already gone through preliminary theoretical, intellectual, and pilot work. In general the trials we review were intended to be the final clinching documentation of the ability of the innovation to do its job. Every item in the list, therefore, was originally expected to be an absolute winner. Insofar as observational studies, pilot work, clinical practice, and theory can help, they already have made their contribution. The randomized field trial is the final hurdle. This is most important to bear in mind while reviewing these studies. We shall return to this point after discussing the studies themselves.

If two treatments perform equally well and one is much cheaper, then the latter would be preferred, especially if both treatments are helping society. We happen not to have examples of an innovation that did as well as the standard treatment but was cheaper. On the other hand, we have several where the innovation was more expensive and did no better than the standard treatment, which was sometimes "no treatment."

Similarly it is possible for two treatments to be equally beneficial, but for a certain innovation to be much preferred because the quality of life was substantially improved. For example, *if* a very limited operation helped patients with breast cancer as much as a radical operation, then the limited operation would be preferred. This particular issue (not among our lists of studies) is still under investigation, and we do not have any innovation in our group that falls into this category. The reader will readily appreciate that the decision as to what is especially beneficial in an innovation or a standard treatment is somewhat case-specific.

D. Social innovations

We turn now to our collection of evaluations of social innovations. The ESAP study given in Section III should be considered a member.

In giving descriptions of studies, we inevitably idealize and oversimplify. Some of these investigations have had whole books to describe them.

Infelicities trouble every substantial investigation. It is our hope that the reader will be provided with a much more extensive statement about each of these studies when Robert Boruch publishes his summaries of randomized field trials.

The reader who does not wish to read descriptions of the randomized trials and wants to move directly to summaries will find them in Section E for the social innovations, Section G for the socio-medical innovations, and Section I for medical innovations, while Section J provides a grand summary for our complete set of randomized controlled field studies.

1. The New Jersey graduated work incentive (negative income tax) experiment.[4] The purpose of the negative income tax experiment was to see what the labor response of the working poor might be to a system of support that added directly to their income. The idea was to give a guaranteed minimum income to such a working family, but the more the family earned, the less would be the contribution of the government. The family was allowed to keep part of what it earned itself according to a "tax" scale.

The experiment was carried out in New Jersey, using three levels of "taxation," 30, 50, and 70%, and several different sizes of guarantee. In the original year the poverty line was about $3300 for a family of four. The sizes of guarantees expressed in fractions of the poverty line were $\frac{1}{2}$, $\frac{3}{4}$, 1, and $1\frac{1}{4}$. Not all taxation levels were used with all guarantee levels—some pairs were omitted because the effect was believed to be too small for useful measurement. In addition to the several treatment groups involving originally 1,216 families with 141 added later, there was also a control group of 491 families that received no benefits, except that they were paid modest sums for filling out questionnaires from time to time.

Economic theory strongly suggested that the result of such a negative income tax would be a reduction in the number of working hours a family contributed, but the theory did not have much to say about the amount of that reduction. That was an important reason for doing the experiment. Some people argued that if the working poor had a guaranteed minimum income, they would stop working altogether. The experiment was completed in 1973, and the results are largely in (see Figure 1).

The most striking finding is that the reduction in hours worked is small—less than 10% for most groups. The work of the wives did decrease, in some cases a substantial percentage of their own total work, but since wives were not contributing a great deal in working hours outside the home (to qualify, all families had at least one able-bodied male worker), their contribution to this reduction was small in total effect. Even with the overall reduction in hours, the earnings remained about the same.

---

[4] Department of Health, Education and Welfare (HEW), 1973.

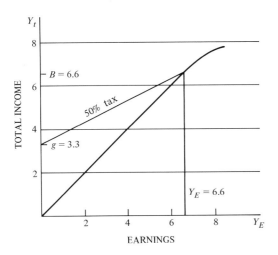

FIG. 1 *Relation between family earnings Y_E for a family of four, and the total income Y_T, when g (the guarantee) is $3300 (that is, g = 3.3) and the tax rate is 50%. When the family earns $Y_E = \$6600$, it receives no money from the program and its total income is B = $6600. The 45° line shows what the earnings would be if there were no negative income tax; it curves a bit to the right of $6600 because of ordinary income taxes.*

Thus the evidence is that a negative income tax to the working poor does not create a large reduction in work effort. Since many had feared that it would create a large reduction, the proposed innovation can be regarded as a considerable success; that is, a double plus. Again, let us emphasize that what is being rated here is the innovation, not the experiment, and the comparison is the observed small loss in work effort against the feared large losses.

We might mention that the assignment of the families to the various taxation-guarantee groups was designed to maximize the information received from the investigation (Conlisk and Watts, 1969); this was a very sophisticated randomized assignment. Inevitably and realistically, economists express concern that full-scale implementation of such a program may lead to consequences different from those of the trial.

RATING: ++

[*Part 2 is omitted.*]

3. Delinquent girls.[5] The investigators tried to reduce juvenile delinquency among teenage girls in two ways: first, by predicting which girls were likely to become delinquent; and secondly, by applying a combination of individual and group treatment to girls who exhibited potential problem behaviors. The population was four cohorts of girls entering a vocational high school; of these, approximately one quarter were screened into this study as indicating potential problems. These girls were randomly assigned to a treatment group which was given treatment at Youth Consultation Service (YCS), a social agency; and to a nontreatment group given no special services. The assignments were 189 to YCS, 192 to the nontreatment group.

The result was that in spite of the group and the individual counseling, delinquency was not reduced. The investigators were successful in identifying girls who were likely to become delinquent, but that was not the primary purpose of the study. They report that, "on all the measures . . . grouped together as school-related behavior . . . none of them supplies conclusive evidence of an effect by the therapeutic program" (p. 176). Similar findings were reported for out-of-school behavior.

We view this innovation as rating a zero, though the detection ability might be of value on another occasion.

RATING: 0

[*Part 4 is omitted.*]

5. Manhattan bail project.[6] The purpose of the Manhattan Bail Project experiment was to see whether arrested persons who have close ties to the community will return for trial even if they are not required to put up bail. Based upon interviews with the defendants prior to arraignment, staff of the Vera Foundation chose on the basis of a scoring system some thousands of defendants they thought were suitable to be recommended for release. (Persons arrested for very severe crimes were not eligible for Vera consideration.) Then they randomly split defendants deemed suitable for release into two groups, half (the recommended group) that they recommended to the court for release without bail, and half (the control group) for which no recommendation was made. The court followed 50% of the recommendations for release without bail in the recommended group, and in the control group it released 16%. Of all those released in this way, 15—that is, about 7/10 of 1%—failed to show up in court. We see here an example of a "slam-bang" effect. The result is so overwhelming that, as Botein says (p. 331), "One need not struggle with recondite statistics to gauge such results."

RATING: ++

---

[5] Meyer, Borgatta, and Jones, 1965.
[6] Botein, 1964–1965.

The idea of the bail bond innovation has been taken up all across the country. Vera has gradually increased from 28% to 65% its recommendation for release. The judges have increased to 70% their acceptance of the Vera recommendations, and the District Attorney's office increased its agreement from about 50% to 80%, all in a period of about four years (1961–64). It would be helpful if someone could gather the results of the many applications of the bail bond idea and give a continuing evaluation under the various changing uses.

With such large effects one might argue that a field trial was scarcely needed. But additional valuable information would probably not have been firmly gathered without the field trial. It turns out that in the recommended group 60% of recommended parolees were acquitted or had their cases dismissed, as opposed to 23% in the control group. Of those 40% of the parolees found guilty in the experimental group, about 16% were sentenced to prison, while 96% of those convicted in the control group were sentenced to prison. All told, then, we learned not only about the reliability of the word of those released, but also rather unexpectedly about the huge differential consequences of the treatments on the ultimate outcome of the case for the experimental and control groups.

The whole enterprise has been a most notable success, starting with an observational study on the lack on the part of the accused of available funds for bail, followed by the field trial just described, and then followed by further developmental exploration intended to improve the process of justice further. (See discussion of Dunn and George that follows.)

Although this pathbreaking work is most impressive in its own right, it is even more important as an illustration in one field of what can be done, and of the need to develop an investigational process. Botein (p. 320) quotes Abraham S. Goldstein of Yale: "Increasingly, law is seen as a decisional process in which men use institutions to shape norms, to interpret them and to enforce them. Inevitably, such an approach brings with it an effort to appraise legal institutions in terms of the functions they are called to play. And this can be done *only if more information is fed into the process...*" (emphasis ours). He goes on to point out that this drive has led us to "frame issues in ways which make empirical research essential if a meaningful body of scholarship is to grow" (p. 320). And Botein says that law students need to be trained to work with others who are better equipped to carry out field research. In commenting on these remarks, Botein emphasizes that a major impact of the Manhattan Bail Project has been generally overlooked; that is, "the spur and stimulus it has given to empirical experimentation and study in criminal law throughout the country" (p. 320).

We would emphasize more generally that these experiments are part of the current development of gathering data carefully and cumulatively for social problems.

A study of the applicability of pretrial release in Des Moines, Iowa used the questionnaire and the point system of the Manhattan Bail Project (Dunn & George, 1964). The investigators proposed to the judges the pretrial release without bond of 740 out of 940 prisoners. Of these 740, the judges released 716 with the following results: 98% appeared in court when they were supposed to; 10 people never showed up; and 6 people came to court several days late. Of the 10 who did not show up, 7 were charged with traffic violations, 2 with forgery, and 1 with breaking and entering. This is an example of a one-treatment observational study. For another site, it supports the idea that community-based arrestees will almost always return to court even without the requirement of bail.

[*Parts 6, 7, and 8 are omitted.*]

9. Harvard Project Physics.[7]   Project Physics was an effort to construct a new high school physics curriculum that would be both more interesting and more effective than traditional instruction. A national experiment in curriculum evaluation for Project Physics was carried out during academic year 1967–68. From among the 16,911 physics teachers listed by the National Science Teachers Association, a random sample of 136 teachers was drawn using random numbers, 124 being actually reached by registered mail. They were asked to participate and told that to participate they would have to be able to agree in advance to teach the experimental or control course, whichever they were chosen for. The experimental teachers further had to attend a 6-week course, the control teachers a two-day session. (This difference in amount of time devoted to training and attending to the teachers is one source of possible criticism of the investigation. This is not so much because of the actual physics training, since these teachers were continuing with their own course, but because of the additional enthusiasm and freshness of treatment and of examples that such a long session can produce. However, the two-day session seems much better than none.) Of the 124 teachers responding, 52 declined for various reasons (previous commitment, change in situation, lack of interest, and so on) and 72 accepted. Of the 72, 46 were randomly assigned to the experimental, 26 to the control group. Transfers, illness, and other events brought the final experimental group to 34 teachers and the control group to 19 teachers.

Welch and Walberg (1972) report that cognitive performance of students in the two groups was much the same, and so Project Physics seemed

---

[7] Welch, Walberg, and Ahlgren, 1969; Welch and Walberg, 1972.

not to reach one of its goals; namely, increased science-process understanding as compared with the standard physics course. We rate the gain in cognitive performance a zero. Project Physics students scored higher on a measure of course satisfaction, and thought the historical approach interesting, their text enjoyable to read, and physics understandable without an extensive mathematics background. Students in control courses more often found physics to be one of the most difficult courses and concluded that physics has to be difficult. We rate the gain in enthusiasm and palatability a double plus. We have therefore a program with multiple goals, the ratings for their achievement being very different. This shows the importance and feasibility of doing studies that evaluate programs with multiple goals.

In all the other investigations rated in Section IV, we were able to identify a single primary goal for the purpose of our ratings, but here we could not, and so this study does not fit smoothly into the summary we give below in Table 4.

The authors report that the added cost of this national randomized controlled field study, over and above the costs for a regional nonrandomized investigation, was less than $10,000 all told. They highly recommend (Welch & Walberg, 1972) such national studies, especially considering the millions often spent in the development phase of such curriculum work. So far such studies are rare in education itself, let alone in curriculum work.

RATING: 0 (cognitive performance)
++ (enthusiasm, palatability)

E. Summary for social innovations

Of the eight innovations rated for single goals in this section, we gave three double pluses—that is, three innvovations were recorded as definitely successful. These were the Emergency School Assistance Program, the Manhattan Bail Project, and the Negative Income Tax—one program from education, one from the legal area, and one from welfare. Of the other five, three received zeros and two a plus. Thus none of the social innovations seemed definitely harmful. We did not assess the costs of the innovations, and so for the zeros the total impact on society might be somewhat negative if a program receiving a zero is continued. Since our rating scale is so simple, it is reassuring to find only two where a simple summary is inadequate. The pretrial conference seemed to have pluses and minuses in sufficiently complicated and hard-to-evaluate directions that probably the rating must be tempered by further examination. Harvard Project Physics required two ratings: zero for cognitive gain; double plus for palatability. In a different direction, the Cottage Life program had such slight advantages that the reader may prefer to give it a zero rather than a plus, while the Los Angeles police training program may deserve a double rather than a single plus.

In the Negative Income Tax investigation we gave the double plus primarily because the beneficiaries continued to work nearly at the previous rate of hours, and because they earned as much as they did before. It had been feared that they would drastically reduce their working hours. The reader might wish to argue that we should evaluate the whole package on a cost benefit basis, but that is beyond our goals in this paper.

Since our rated innovations all come from published sources, there is probably an upward bias in successful outcomes compared to the population of innovations evaluated by randomized controlled field studies. That is, an evaluation of a clearly unsuccessful innovation may be less likely to be published than an evaluation that found a success. In laboratory experiments we observe a much higher failure rate than we observe here, and so even if the population rate of highly successful social innovations were only half of what was observed in this set, we could afford to be pleased.

F. Evaluations of socio-medical innovations

The next series of evaluations deals with innovations that have strong components of both social and medical treatment. Although the reader might prefer to recategorize a few of our studies, these categories are more for convenience in exposition than for making inferences to types of innovations. The third category—medical—does represent an exception to this remark because it has a more objective basis for selection.

1. Outpatient treatment.[8]

The Gorham Report pointed out that the general medical insurance practice of paying only for procedures done in the hospital was encouraging doctors to send their patients to the hospital when they did not require full hospitalization. To investigate the possibility of savings by paying for outpatient treatment, Blue Cross-Blue Shield set up a large field trial in Kansas to see what would happen by giving people, in addition to their usual policy, coverage that would pay for certain procedures done outside the hospital (Hill & Veney, 1970). An experimental group of 5,000 people was given the new coverage at no extra cost, and a control group of 10,000 had the regular coverage only.

After a year the amounts of hospitalization for the two groups were compared, and it was found that, contrary to expectation, the group with the new extended coverage had 16% more days in the hospital than they had had the year before, while the controls, without the new coverage, had increased only 3%. Thus the new program did not have the hoped-for overall effect. More was learned from the field trial, though. The extended

---

[8] Hill and Veney, 1970; Gorham Report, 1967; Alpert et al., 1968.

coverage group did indeed have 15% fewer short-stay admissions (supporting the idea in the Gorham Report), but this decrease was more than offset by additional long stays. The extra cost for the outpatient coverage was found to be about $40 per patient.

RATING: −

We rate this innovation minus since it did not have the savings in cost that were forecast. Indeed, it cost more, not less. It is interesting to note that the effect suggested by the Gorham Report did exist, so that if it had not been for the unforeseen effects on the longer stays, this change in coverage would have been a beneficial policy change. This illustrates the value to the decision makers of controlled field trials: the ideas in the Gorham Report warrant serious consideration, but instituting the new policy on a wide scale with the expectation of reduced costs would have been a serious fiscal mistake. Whether a sustained program of this kind would find that the long stays were reduced in later years would require a further evaluation, because part of the problem here may be due to the treatment of accumulated illnesses, as the following reference suggests.

In a related study, Alpert *et al.* (1968) reported pediatric experience comparing a comprehensive medical care service with regular medical service. This comparison was based on a randomized controlled field trial. They found that in the first six months, the hospitalization rate per hundred children was over twice as high in the comprehensive care group as in the regular medical group, but that in each of the next four six-month periods the rates were lower. The average rates for the 30 months, per six-month period, were for the comprehensive care children 2.8 and for the regular medical care 3.3. These data offer some support for the position that the costs associated with initial examination and treatment may be larger because of accumulated ills.

[*Part 2 is omitted.*]

G. Summary for socio-medical innovations

Of the eight innovations rated here, one on tonsillectomy was rated double plus. The two innovations treated here on psychiatric care were rated plus. The zeros included a training program for medical students in comprehensive medical care, an attempt at treatment of persons arrested for drunkenness through legal assignment to therapy, a physical training program for the elderly in caring for themselves, and a team approach to family medical care. The one innovation scoring a negative was the outpatient payments for people with medical insurance. These subscribers had more hospital days than those with the ordinary policies. It is possible that the long-run effect of such a program would be more positive, as we have noted in the text.

H. Evaluations of medical, mainly surgical, innovations

Ten of the twelve studies presented in this section were found through a systematic MEDLARS search of the surgical literature (see close of this introduction). Our surgical advisers, who checked the ratings, were somewhat uneasy about associating 0's with some of these evaluations even though they agreed in these instances that the innovation itself was no improvement. They asked us to be sure to emphasize that some of these investigations are milestones in surgery—landmark studies—and that current surgical research and practice are building on these important studies. Their point is, of course, quite general.

First, when one has a solid finding, one can reason from it for some distance with assurance. Second, the value of an evaluation comes not only from the appraisal of the innovation or program it reviews, but also from the related findings which can be used in later work. Elsewhere, we emphasize the value that a substantial body of information has for long-run policy. Third, when an innovation widely expected to be successful does not perform as anticipated, either as therapy or according to theory, such firm knowledge points researchers in new directions.

To these three ideas, we would add a fourth. On first realizing that our systematic method of collecting had produced several milestone studies in surgery, we felt quite lucky. But on second thought, perhaps randomized clinical trials described in medical journals are just where one finds landmark studies. Maybe well-done randomized clinical trials create landmark studies.

When discussing these evaluations with others, we were asked by many to describe the illnesses and the operations in everyday terms. We authors could not do this, and we are grateful to Bucknam McPeek, M.D. for providing these descriptions. His initials follow his descriptive paragraphs.

1. A prospective evaluation of vagotomy-pyloroplasty and vagotomy-antrectomy for treatment of duodenal ulcer.[9]

We do not have an exact understanding of the causes of duodenal ulcers, but most standard treatments for ulcers are aimed toward decreasing the production of stomach acid. A very common surgical treatment for serious ulcer disease involves cutting the vagus nerves in an effort to decrease acid production. This procedure, vagotomy, is almost always performed either in association with an operation to enlarge the exit through which food leaves the stomach, or

---

[9] Jordan and Condon, 1970.

as a part of an operation to remove the lower portion of the stomach where the bulk of acid production is located. These two operations are called vagotomy-drainage for the former or vagotomy-resection for the latter. This study attempted to compare these two forms of surgical treatment. (B. McP.)

Patients were assigned to one of two groups using a "randomized series held in the custody of the study secretary" (p. 547). The two groups were 108 patients who had vagotomy-drainage (V-D) and 92 patients who had vagotomy-resection (V-R). There were two operative deaths in the V-D group, whose causes were believed not relevant to the treatment. "It is concluded ... that vagotomy and antrectomy (V-R) is superior to vagotomy and drainage (V-D) ... in the majority of patients because of its lower recurrence rate without the association of increased morbidity or mortality" (p. 560). Eight patients were reoperated on for recurrence, all in the V-D group, and two of the three patients suspected of having recurrences were also in the V-D group.

RATING: ++

[*Parts 2–7 are omitted.*]

8. A controlled trial of inverting versus everting intestinal suture in clinical large-bowel surgery.[10] The standard method of joining two segments of bowel together is to suture the bowel together in such a fashion that the outside layer of both segments are approximated. Technically this is called inverting, as the cut edges are turned toward the center of the bowel. Recently some have advocated the reverse; i.e., joining the bowel in such a fashion that the inner layers are approximated with the cut edges being everted or directed toward the outer surface. This new method also used a different style of suturing. (B. McP.).

This trial was done to compare the new method, everting, to the old method of suturing the bowel, inverting. Thirty-five patients were assigned to each treatment at random, and the numbers of patients who developed wound infections, peritonitis, or overt fecal fistulation were observed. The conclusion was that "These experiences are considered to provide a clear condemnation of the use of an everting technique of suture in the large intestine in clinical practice" (p. 817). Thus the new technique was judged to be definitely poorer than the older one.

RATING: – –

[*Parts 9–11 are omitted.*]

---

[10] Goligher *et al.*, 1970.

12. Salk vaccine.[11] This study was described in Section III.

RATING: + +

I. Summary of medical ratings

The 10 randomized trials found through the MEDLARS search gave one double plus for a vagotomy operation, and two pluses, one for ampicillin and the other for radiation treatment of cancer of the bronchus. There were five zeros and two negatives, one being a double negative. Thus great successes were hard to find. To the ten trials found through the MEDLARS search we have added Gastric Freezing, a zero; and Salk Vaccine, a double plus. By excluding these two, we have a rather objectively drawn sample.

J. Summary of ratings

Table 2 summarizes the ratings of the 28 single-goal studies we have now described. We should make clear that some of these studies may have had more goals, but we chose to rate only the one that we regarded as central. Since the gamma globulin study and the Des Moines Bail Study were not randomized trials, we do not include them in the ratings. Harvard Project Physics also is not included in the table of ratings, because it required the rating of two goals.

Overall, six innovations, or about 21% of the total, were scored double plus. The rate of double pluses does not differ sharply among the three groups. The pile-up at zero, 13 out of 28, or 46%, suggests that we have a rather broad interval for zeros.

We warn again that there may be some upward bias owing to selective reporting and selective finding by our searches. Even so, when we consider the high rate of failure of laboratory innovations, we can take pleasure in a success rate as high as the one seen here.

Except for the surgical innovations where we have a rather solid description of our population, the skeptical reader may feel we have no grounds for discussing rates of successful innovations in the absence of a population and in the presence of several possible selection effects. The difficulty is not unique—if one wants to know the percentage of new products that succeed or the percentage of new businesses that succeed, the same problems of definition of population and success arise.

To repeat briefly our remarks in Section IV-A, we guess that a higher proportion of better studied programs with published reports are likely to be successful than those less well studied. Further, more successful programs are more likely to have come to our attention. Consequently, we believe that the estimate of about 21% successful innovations is high compared to what a census would yield.

---

[11] Francis *et al.*, 1955; Meier, 1972; Brownlee, 1955.

TABLE 2 SUMMARY OF RATINGS.

Rating	− −	−	0	+	+ +
Total 8 Social innovations	0	0	3 D2. Welfare workers D3. Girls at voc. high D7. Pretrial conf.	2 D4. Cottage life D6. L. A. police (or + +)	3 D1. Neg. income tax D5. Manhattan bail D8. ESAP
Total 8 Socio-medical innovations	0	1 F1. Kansas Blue-Cross	4 F3. Comp. med. care F4. Drunk probation F7. Nursing home F8. Family medical care	2 F5. Psychiatric after-care F6. Mental illness	1 F2. Tonsillec- tomy
Total 12 Medical innovations	1 H8. Everting	1 H10. Yttrium- 90	6 H2. Vagotomy (Cox) H3. Vagotomy (Kennedy) H5. Cancer H6. Portacaval shunt H9. Chlorhexi- dine H11. *Gastric freezing	2 H4. Bronchus (possibly + +) H7. Ampicillin	2 H1. Vagotomy (Johnson) E12. *Salk vaccine
Grand total 28	1	2	13	6	6

* These two studies did not emerge from the MEDLARS search. All the other medical innovations did.

Beyond the question of the adequacy of our sample, the programs in our series that have had little or no success are in themselves an important source for concern, since they each represent a serious but unsuccessful attempt to solve a problem.

We have pointed out how even successful innovations often lead to small gains, how important such gains are for building on in the future, and the value of a randomized controlled field trial for detecting these gains. It is worth noting further that small gains can come about in more than one way. For example, nearly everyone in a program may gain a little bit, leading to a modest but widespread overall average gain. Or, some fraction or subgroup of people in a program may gain substantially, while other subgroups and perhaps most participants show no gains. The ESAP investigation, where black males in high school were found to benefit substantially while other groups did not show improvement, illustrates this latter possibility. Society may find such information useful when deciding what programs to implement.

To sum up, the major findings of this section are that (1) among societal innovations studied here, about one in five succeeded; and (2) among those that succeeded, the gain was often small in size, though not in importance.

Both findings have important consequences for the policy maker considering methods of evaluation and for the attitudes toward programs that society needs to develop. We should treasure and try to strengthen programs that have even small gains. After we gather further information in later sections, the implications are taken up in Section X.

V. FINDINGS FROM NONRANDOMIZED STUDIES

A. Nonrandomized studies

Section IV treated ratings of innovations, ratings obtained from randomized controlled field trials. Next we explore the results of investigations that for the most part did not use randomization. We will see the consequences of this approach for both weakness of the findings and the ultimate time taken to gather firm information.

1. The Baltimore Housing Study.[12] D. M. Wilner *et al.* (1962) undertook a study to see what the effects of improved housing were on physical, mental, and social health of low-income families. These effects were regarded as *additional* possible benefits over and above the improved shelter, cooking, and toilet facilities. This was a landmark study involving a large number of investigators from different fields, the development of new instruments for measuring outcomes, and improved methods of data collection, as well as careful analysis of the results. The treatment group of 300 families was given public housing with improved room, heat, toilet, refrigeration, and garbage disposal facilities. The control group consisted of 300 families matched with treatment families on social and demographic background characteristics. This study was not a randomized trial. Housing was assigned by the

---

[12] Wilner *et al.*, 1962

Baltimore Housing Authority and the matched control group was picked from the waiting list. Over a three-year period the two groups were compared on housing quality, physical morbidity, social-psychological adjustment, and children's performance in school.

The results showed that on several outcome variables the group that received the better housing had improved life circumstances. Mortality was substantially lower in the housing group, and morbidity (illness) in the housing group was lower for persons under 35, although not for older people. Accidents in the housing group were reduced by one third. While the children in the housing group did not improve on standardized tests, they were more likely to be promoted on schedule and had better school attendance.

Overall the results of the housing can be described as a success, and if the evaluation of this innovation had been based upon a randomized controlled field trial, we would have included it in the examples given in the preceding section. The crux of our problem is that we do not know the effect of the criteria used by the housing authority to choose those most deserving of housing from their large field of applicants. If, for example, the perceived potential of the applicant to develop in other ways if relieved of the disadvantages of poor housing were a conscious or unconscious factor in choosing the families to get the new housing, the study would in large part be verifying this assessment rather than the effect of the housing. If, on the other hand, the assignment was to give the new housing to the applicants most in need, the effectiveness of housing on the social outcomes measured might be seriously understated by the data. And, of course, the reverse could occur using other criteria, such as first come, first served.

If selection procedures positively biased the Wilner study, society could be badly disappointed with the results of a social program based on its findings. Let us notice that by not having done the randomization to begin with, the study has made it more difficult for someone later to try to find out, because the original finding is so agreeable to our prejudices.

[*Parts 2 and 3 are omitted.*]

4. Performance contracting.[13] The idea of accountability for instruction in education led to the concept of performance contracting. This means essentially that those doing the teaching get paid in accordance with the amount the pupil learns. This idea is rather old and was used in England in the eighteen hundreds.

---

[13] Gramlich and Koshel, 1973

Recently some companies felt that they could teach children better than the public schools, at least in some subjects, and they were willing to contract to do so, being paid according to performance. The Office of Economic Opportunity found a number of school districts that were willing to participate in a field trial using such contractors. The contractors apparently believed that they could improve performance substantially—perhaps by gains of one or two hundred percent.

The Office of Economic Opportunity (OEO) did not do a randomized trial, but rather assigned schools to the contractors. (OEO might have randomized the schools as in our ESAP description, but probably could not randomize pupils directly.) Each contractor taught about 100 pupils. It turned out that the students assigned to the performance contractors were not initially achieving as well as those in the control groups because the experimental schools had lower averages. That is, the performance contractors were initially at a disadvantage. Thus the companies doing the performance contracting probably had more trouble teaching their children than the regular school groups did theirs. In addition, there was an even deeper problem. The OEO had decided to run the experiment for only one year. The companies had to begin teaching four months after they bid on the contract and two months after being informed that they had won. This is in very marked contrast to the two- or three-year period used in installing the programs in the Planned Variation studies of Head Start and Follow Through. One might have expected that the performance contracting idea would have been developed and implemented more gradually. In the end, as near as one can tell, the contractors did, after adjustment for initial inequality, a little better, perhaps 9%, than the control groups. Recall that the control groups were not rushed for installation, as they were already installed in existing schools. We do not feel strongly about the value of performance contracting, but we do think it unwise to start and stop experiments so rapidly. For instance, contractors had no time to adjust to the new set of financial incentives.

There were, of course, political problems with performance contracting. Most teachers' unions didn't like the idea. The companies had signed contracts that let them in for potentially large financial losses, and the possibility of only modest gains. (It is not clear why.) The rush to installation might have been caused by a now-or-never atmosphere in Washington (Gramlich & Koshel, 1973).

It is difficult to say with a high degree of confidence how well the contractors did. The analysis necessarily depends very heavily on adjustment methods because of the initial lack of randomization. Thus we see a study that inflicted all the pains of innovation and gathered little of the fruits of knowledge.

It could be argued, of course, that this is just an example where the political problems took precedence over careful development of findings. Whether they did or not, society missed out as far as firm findings were concerned. Furthermore, once people learn that a procedure is effective, the political system has a way of adapting so as to use the new procedure. For example, it appears that some of the school systems involved in the performance contracting study have now adapted some of the contractors' materials into their ongoing programs.

[*Parts 5 and 6 are omitted.*]

B. Nonrandomized studies in medicine

We have mentioned earlier the value for social investigators of learning from the medical experience. What we have been observing recently in medicine are systematic attempts to appreciate the interpretative difficulties in ordinary nonrandomized investigations as compared with randomized controlled clinical trials. Much experience is building up, and we can profit from a short review of very extensive work in a few medical areas.

About 1945 an operation called portacaval shunt was introduced to treat bleeding in the esophagus for certain patients, and this operation has been extended for other purposes. After 20 years of experience with this operation and 154 papers on the subject, it still was not clear (Grace, Muench, & Chalmers, 1966) what advice a physician should give to a patient with esophageal varices. In Section IV-H-6, we have already described this operation and an associated randomized controlled trial. That trial was performed several years after Grace, Muench, and Chalmers reviewed the literature to see whether they could resolve such questions as whether the operation would prevent further hemorrhage, what disabling side effects there might be, or what expectation of life went with the operation as compared with not having it.

They rated the investigations on two variables: degree of control in the investigation and degree of enthusiasm for the operation as expressed in the article reporting the trial. The degrees of enthusiasm after the study are: marked, moderate (with some reservations), and no conclusion or enthusiasm. The degrees of control are: (1) well-controlled—random assignment to treatment groups; (2) poorly controlled—selection of patients for treatment (compared with an unselected group or some other experience); and (3) uncontrolled—no comparison with another group of untreated patients.

For the physician, the details of the relationship for three types of shunt operations (emergency, therapeutic, and prophylactic) would have high

TABLE 3 DEGREE OF CONTROL VERSUS DEGREE OF INVESTIGATOR ENTHUSIASM FOR SHUNT OPERATION IN 51 STUDIES HAVING AT LEAST 10 PATIENTS IN THE SERIES.*

Degree of control	Degree of enthusiasm			
	Marked	Moderate	None	Totals
Well-controlled	0	3†	3†	6
Poorly controlled	10	3	2	15
Uncontrolled	24	7	1	32
Totals	34	13	6	53

* Source: Revised from N. D. Grace, H. Muench, and T. C. Chalmers, "The present status of shunts for protal hypertension in cirrhosis," *Gastroenterology* **50,** (1966), Table 2, p. 685. Copyright © 1966 The Williams & Wilkins Co., Baltimore.

† In the original source, the cell "well-controlled–moderate enthusiasm" had one entry, but Dr. Chalmers informed us by personal communication that two studies can now be added to that cell. Furthermore, he told us that the "well-controlled–moderate enthusiasm" group is associated with therapeutic shunts, and the "well-controlled–none" with prophylactic shunts.

interest, but for our purpose, it is enough to look at their grand total table, our Table 3, for studies with 10 or more patients.

Table 3 shows clearly that following their uncontrolled studies, investigators almost invariably express some enthusiasm for the shunt, and more than two thirds of the time express marked enthusiasm. Poorly controlled investigations have much the same outcome. On the other hand, in the six instances where the study was well-controlled, three investigators expressed moderate enthusiasm; the rest none. We assume that the investigators using the well-controlled field trials had better grounds for their degree of enthusiasm than did those with no controls or poor controls. (See footnote to Table 3 for more detail on the operations.)

Some other findings in the Grace, Muench, and Chalmers review of portacaval shunts were that after four years, the survival rates of patients undergoing elective therapeutic shunts were much the same as those who did not get them (the initial operative mortality was about 15%, based on 1244 patients). Although bleeding was reduced in the prophylactic group of operations, survival was not improved (the initial operative mortality was over 4%, based on 137 patients). We shall not go into the side effects problem here.

This investigation is informative because we can put the results of uncontrolled, poorly controlled, and well-controlled studies side by side. In all, the results of the investigation show that uncontrolled and poorly controlled studies led to greater enthusiasm than was warranted on the basis of the well-controlled studies. If the poorly controlled studies had suggested conclusions similar to those of the well-controlled trials, we, the surgeons, and policy makers, could be more comfortable with the results of related studies in similar contexts. But we see instead that the results are far from the same. By performing many poorly controlled trials we waste time and human experience and mislead ourselves as well. The argument that we do not have time to wait for well-controlled trials does not seem to have been applicable here.

C. Summary for section V

Now that we have reviewed a number of nonrandomized studies, what overall conclusions emerge? One characteristic of nonrandomized studies that shows up in context after context is that even after repeated studies had consistently gotten the same result, there was always room to doubt the validity of the finding. Indeed, in several medical areas—portacaval shunt, estrogen therapy, and gastric freezing—the findings were not backed up with the same degree of investigator enthusiasm when put to the test of a carefully controlled randomized trial. This weakness of uncontrolled trials poses a particularly difficult problem for the policy maker faced with what appears to be more and more evidence in favor of a particular course of action, when he knows that he may just be seeing the same biases again and again.

Nonrandomized trials may not only generate conclusions with doubtful validity—they may actually delay the implementation of better evaluations. If a series of nonrandomized studies indicates that a certain treatment is highly effective, some investigators will point out the ethical difficulties of withholding this apparently valuable treatment from some persons in a randomized trial. Yet the evidence in this section suggests that nonrandomized studies may often artificially inflate our estimate of a treatment's value. Whenever this happens, and a randomized trial is postponed as a consequence, an ineffective treatment or program may be administered for years. The opportunity cost of such a mistake can be high.

VI. ISSUES RELATED TO RANDOMIZATION

This section deals with topics in controlled field studies that are closely related to the matter of randomization.

A. The idea of a sample as a microcosm

In discussing both sample surveys and controlled trials, people often suggest that we not take random samples but that we build a small replica of the population, one that will behave like it and thus represent it. Then, to assess the effect of a treatment, the investigator would simply treat one small replica and not treat another, thereby getting a perfect measure of the treatment effect. This is such an attractive idea that we need to explain why it is not done more often, and to mention circumstances when it nearly can be done. We confine ourselves to discussing the construction of one small replica or microcosm because if we can make one we usually can make two.

When we sample from a population, we would like ideally a sample that is a microcosm or replica or mirror of the target population—the population we want to represent. For example, for a study of types of families, we might note that there are adults who are single, married, widowed, and divorced. We want to stratify our population to take proper account of these four groups and include members from each in the sample. Otherwise, perhaps by chance we would get none or too few in a particular group—such as divorced—to make a reliable analysis. This device of stratifying is widely used to strengthen the sample and bar chance from playing unfortunate tricks.

Let us push this example a bit further. Do we want also to take sex of individuals into account? Perhaps, and so perhaps we should also stratify on sex. How about size of immediate family (number of children: zero, one, two, three, . . .)—should we not have each family size represented in the study? And region of the country, and size and type of city, and occupation of head of household, and education, and income, and . . . . The number of these important variables is rising very rapidly, and worse yet, the number of categories rises even faster. Let us count them. We have four marital statuses, two sexes, say five categories for size of immediate family (by pooling four or over), say four regions of the country, and six sizes and types of city, say five occupation groups, four levels of education, and three levels of income. This gives us in all $4 \times 2 \times 5 \times 4 \times 6 \times 5 \times 4 \times 3 = 57,600$ different possible types, if we are to mirror the population or have a small microcosm; and one observation per cell may be far from adequate. We thus may need hundreds of thousands of cases! Clearly this approach is getting too fine for most purposes, and such an investigation will not be carried out except when enormous resources are available. We cannot have a microcosm in most problems. What we can do instead is pick a few of the most important and controllable variables, stratify on these few, and then randomly select from within each of the groups or cells thus formed. The randomization is intended to control (make other things equal on the average) for other variables on which we have not been able to stratify. It prevents bias that would arise if, for example, a treatment group and control group, or several treatment groups, were quite different with respect to an important background variable, such as age of participants. This feature of making other things equal on the average applies as well to variables we have not thought of as to those we have. Randomization thus makes possible certain mathematical tests that might not otherwise be readily justified.

Why isn't the microcosm idea used all the time? The reason is not that stratification doesn't work. Rather it is because we do not have generally a closed system with a few variables (known to affect the responses) having a few levels each, with every individual in a cell being identical. To illustrate, in a grocery store we can think of size versus contents, where size is 1 pound or 5 pounds and contents are a brand of salt or a brand of sugar. Then in a given store we would expect four kinds of packages, and the variation of the packages within a cell might be negligible compared to the differences in size or contents between cells. But in social programs there are always many more variables and so there is not a fixed small number of cells. The microcosm idea will rarely work in a complicated social problem because we always have additional variables that may have important consequences for the outcome.

One can readily think of some circumstances when randomization might not be needed. In a chemical investigation, if we want to treat several samples of the same liquid, all of whose components are miscible, there seems to be little need to pick and choose among several aliquots as to which gets which treatment. The homogeneity of the liquid equates the basic material.

In a metallurgical study, the investigator may cut a piece of metal into chunks and treat them. Although these chunks may not be quite as homogeneous as the liquid in the chemical example, still they may be so much alike compared with the effect of the treatment we are about to administer that there is little reason to worry about randomization.

As a general rule, randomization has less value when the effect of the treatment is large enough to dominate both the biases in selection and the natural variability from one group or cell to another. When dealing with social problems, we must usually cope with variability among regions, families, schools, hospitals, and neighborhoods, often from several sources simultaneously. Consequently, the randomization matters a great deal, as does getting enough replications so that averages are sufficiently stable to give us a good estimate of the effects of treatments.

In discussing random sampling we do not limit our consideration to the simplest case of drawing two samples (one called the treatment group and the other called the control group) randomly from the population. Many variants of this idea can strengthen inferences. For example, in the ESAP study described in Section III, schools were paired, and then one of each pair was randomly assigned the treatment. Such a step improves the reliability of inference because the treatment-no treatment comparison is made over many pairs. Other procedures that can strengthen inference include stratification of the sort mentioned earlier, and sequential treatments where the choice of treatment that the next person or site receives depends upon all the information received up to the present time. Although we do not go into all the details of such procedures here, we expect that they will be increasingly used in the future. It is adequate for our purposes to recognize that these methods are waiting in the wings, and are sometimes used now. For example, as mentioned earlier, the New Jersey Work Incentive Program allocated its families to treatment in a special way which, while randomized, was designed to maximize the information developed by the investigation.

B. Searching for small program effects

Sometimes it helps to distinguish between sampling errors and nonsampling errors in investigations. Sampling errors are the ones which would disappear if somehow we were able to take the entire population into the sample. Nonsampling errors arise from the various sorts of biases that occur from a variety of measurement and selectivity problems. For example, selectivity could bias the fractions of various kinds of individuals entering different treatment groups. Measurement error may produce biases because of poor recall, recording mistakes, nonresponse, and so on. In assessing small differences, as the sample grows, the biases from the nonsampling errors become more important, and then the big problems with assessment and evaluation have to do with these nonsampling errors.

This point is well illustrated by the Salk Vaccine trials described in Section III, where in the placebo control method the study was able to document selection effects by comparing the disease rate for nonvaccinated volunteers with that of those who declined to volunteer (57 versus 36 per hundred thousand). The bias amounts to about half the effect (57 versus 17 per hundred thousand) for volunteers. Increasing the size of the study would not have changed this effect substantially, if at all. It was only by comparing the two randomized groups that one obtained a good assessment of the treatment effect. As we search for smaller and smaller effects, it becomes more and more difficult to know whether these are due to the treatment or rather to some artifact or disturbance. Thus, a crucial property of randomization is the protection it offers from many sources of bias, some not even suspected of being important. Randomization greatly increases the confidence one can have in the results of a large trial, especially when treatment effects are small.

Let us now consider two circumstances when an investigation will require substantial numbers of participants. One is the case just discussed, where the occurrence of an event, such as poliomyelitis, is quite rare. Here, a large sample is needed simply to turn up a reasonable number of occurrences in either the treatment or nontreatment groups. The second case is when program effects are small. Here, whether or not an event is rare, small samples even in a randomized study may not have much chance of detecting small program effects.

What attitude might an investigator take when such small effects are found? We have noted earlier that when a social program is mounted, there is often great expectation for spectacular effects: gains of the order of a 50% improvement in performance, or a doubling in the rate of reading, or a drop of 50% in automobile fatalities. Our empirical study found, however, that for an innovation to achieve gains of such magnitude is an uncommon event. Let us think about this question of small gains a bit further.

To take an example from education, suppose that students exposed to an innovation were in general the poorer students in their school system, and that in the past their average gain score per academic year was in the neighborhood of 0.7 of a grade-equivalent unit. This is a realistic value. What kind of improvement for such students would we consider a "success"? Obviously, bringing about an enormous change, such as a doubling of the rate of gain, would be a wonderful achievement. Yet, in view of our empirical study of innovations, would not changing the gain rate incrementally, say by an additional 0.2 of a grade-equivalent unit, represent a valuable achievement? It is true that these students, who would now be gaining an average of 0.9 of a grade-equivalent unit per year, would on the average still be below the national norms. But their rate of gain, using the numbers just suggested, would have increased by 2/7, or better than 28%. Is a 28% annual increase in achievement educationally negligible? The authors believe not. This view would especially hold if the gain was achieved by students having the most trouble in school, and further served as a basis for additional future improvement. In the end, costs and alternative values decide whether society will pay a fair amount for this kind of progress, expecially when there is a paucity of alternative treatments available, expensive or inexpensive, known to assure such gains. And, once again, the sensitivity offered by a randomized field trial is necessary to get good estimates of such modest yet important gains.

[*Parts C, D, and E are omitted.*]

F. Does randomization imply coercion?
Let us suppose that in a social innovation three treatments are to be compared: A, B, and C. We have argued extensively that a randomized controlled field study is necessary to get sensitive results. This implies the need to assign treatments randomly among many sites. Does this also imply

coercion? Must some sites (cities, for example) be forced against their will to participate in the field study for randomization to do its good work?

The answer is NO; there is no need for any city, or school, or group, to accept a treatment that it does not find acceptable. Suppose, for example, that out of hundreds of cities contending for money to engage in the social program, a subset of 50 are willing to accept either treatment A or treatment B, but are absolutely opposed to C. In this event, a randomized comparison between the two treatments A and B is still possible.

Two points we have touched upon earlier tie in to this discussion. First, if only a total of two cities are willing to accept either A or B, then even random assignment of the two treatments between the two cities will not yield a comparison in which we have confidence. This is simply because of the tiny sample of cities involved. As more cities are willing to accept one of a subset of treatments, better estimates of the differential treatment effects can be developed. In addition, with more cities it becomes possible to estimate the city-to-city variation in outcome within any one treatment.

A second matter concerns the generalizability of treatment comparisons when some cities are willing to accept only a subset of treatments. Caution is required in generalizing results from a field study in a few cities to a larger population of cities. We are not in a good position to judge how a program would have fared in a school system that would not accept it as a possibility. Yet until they change their position, this is not as important as learning reliably how the program performs in systems that will accept it. These caveats notwithstanding, the major point here is that randomization can be used in field studies without any treatment recipient feeling he has been "coerced" into participating, provided some are willing to accept either of a pair of treatments. It is an attractive feature of controlled field studies, not just randomized ones, that they offer the opportunity of achieving a flexible mix between centralized control of an investigation and local site options as to what treatments are acceptable.

G. The ethics of controlled field studies

Although many social investigators are aware of the advantages of randomization for evaluating programs, a common reason offered for doing so few randomized studies focuses on the ethics of conducting such investigations. Some people think that using randomized trials implies that people will be abused or mistreated. They say, "You can't experiment with people!" Let us examine this position a little more carefully.

We change our social system—for example, our educational system— frequently and rather arbitrarily; that is, in ways ordinarily intended to be beneficial, but with little or no evidence that the innovation will work. These changes are routinely made in such an unsystematic way that no one can assess the consequences of these haphazard adjustments. By using this casual approach, we are frittering away the valuable experiences, good and bad, of the participants. This action devalues both their pleasure and suffering, to say nothing of their achievements and failures, by not learning from them for society's benefit; indeed, for the benefit of the participants themselves, their families, and their children.

This is not to say that all ethical and technical problems can be overcome. Far from it; there are important questions that for ethical reasons should not be investigated by controlled trials, randomized or not, on children or on adults. We stress, however, that for the same ethical reasons these same questions should not be investigated by haphazardly trying an innovation on a number of likely subjects to see how it works out.

Most people are willing to accept randomization when resources are limited. For example, if only 100 pills are available and 200 people volunteer for the treatment, a randomized assignment is relatively uncontroversial. However, even when a program has enough funds to benefit all, there is still plenty of room for the sort of study we are discussing because there may be many alternatives for program delivery. If one has a food distribution program, is it better to give out stamps, deliver the food to the poor, give people the money for food, or what? It would be good to know also whether under various circumstances people ate it themselves, sold it, fed it to cattle, or threw it away.

When we object to controlled field trials with people, we need to consider the alternatives—what society actually does. Instead of field trials, programs currently are instituted that vary substantially from one place to another, often for no very good reason. We do one thing here, another there in an unplanned way. The result is that we spend our money, often put people at risk, and learn little. This haphazard approach is not "experimenting" with people; instead, it is *fooling around with people.* It is most important that we appreciate the difference between these two ideas. We need to decide whether fooling around with people's lives in a catch-as-catch-can way that helps society little is a good way to treat our citizens, and we need to understand that in current practice this is the principal alternative to randomized controlled field trials.

H. Need to develop methodology
In looking forward to the contribution that randomized controlled field trials have to make to the administration and evaluation of social programs, we are hampered because there have been so few. Consequently we are still developing the necessary skills, techniques, and theory to facilitate and strengthen such field trials. Evaluators of social programs will have to devise their own special methods of applying randomization in the context of

ongoing and often shifting programs, just as agriculture, experimental laboratories, quality control departments, and opinion polls have each had to produce their own variations on the theme of randomization.

We cannot map from an easy chair just how such developments would go, since in large part this will depend upon the experience gained as more randomized trials are integrated with social programs. Thus we will be learning not only more about the effectiveness of programs but also how to integrate field trials smoothly into social programs with fewer problems and possibly at lower cost.

Shifts in the goals of a program, for whatever reason, will pose difficult problems for any evaluative process. Most of these problems are not specific to randomized trials. Their occurrence is a warning that the background and base-line data collected at the start of a project should be as broad as possible since this increases the chance that they will retain their relevance even after some changes in program goals.

I. Need for an ongoing capability for doing randomized controlled field studies

What should society think of carefully evaluated innovations that work well? First, it should be pleased to find a fair proportion of them working. Second, it needs a mature attitude toward both reforms and evaluations. It needs to accept, though not without grumbling, the variety of performances that new ideas provide, from very poor to very good. It needs to learn to tolerate this groping for solutions and the mistakes in the attempts. It is astounding how mature America has become about accepting mistakes in forecasts and estimates. For example, we continue to take a tolerant and constructive attitude toward polls in spite of the *Literary Digest* failure, the Truman-Dewey election, and the two Heath-Wilson "failures" in England (we use quotes because neither was very far off). Society understands that these measuring devices are fallible, just like weather forecasts, but that they nevertheless have their practical uses and their successes as well as failures.

The nation accepts the idea that a good deal of data about a problem can be routinely gathered through the sample survey approach. This positive attitude goes along with the existence of a substantial number of survey organizations which are able on very short notice to field an investigation for a client, helping him design and carry it out from start to finish. We are less used to the idea of the randomized controlled field study, and have less experience in carrying it out. Once people come to understand it and its role better, we can expect more appreciation for its utility.

This suggests that policy makers should push for the development of an ongoing capability to mount well-designed randomized field studies. This capability will be developed gradually over time, as several organizations gain experience in the conduct of such field studies. It may then become part of the normal course of events for policy makers to call on such organizations to provide information about program effectiveness and program improvement.

[*Part VII is omitted.*]

VIII. COSTS, TIMELINESS, AND RANDOMIZED FIELD STUDIES

The policy maker, when considering whether to evaluate a program with a randomized controlled field trial, will weigh a number of matters. Thoughtful views of costs and timeliness associated with randomized studies differ with the occasion, and we bring out in this section some implications for short-run policy implied by long-term needs.

A. Costs and benefits of doing randomized controlled field studies

A number of people have called for more controlled field trials, and it is instructive to ask why more such trials have not been done in recent social and medical work (Campbell [1969]; Cochrane [1972]; Gilbert & Mosteller [1972]; Lasagna [1969]; Light, Mosteller, & Winokur [1971]; Orcutt [1970]; Rivlin [1970, 1971, 1973]; Rutstein [1969]). Despite the advantages of randomly controlled trials, three objections often emerge: (1) randomly assigning treatments to sites or to people raises political problems (see Sections V-D and VII-C for discussion); (2) randomly controlled trials take too long; and (3) they are too expensive to conduct. Let us examine the question of cost.

How much should society be prepared to pay for an evaluation of a program that leads to firm and reliable inferences about how well the program is working? The answer to this difficult question depends upon many features of the program: its size, its importance to society, and the alternatives. The answer to a related question is clearer. How much should society be willing to pay for an evaluation that does *not* lead to firm inferences about how well a program is working? Not much. Yet for years we have been paying enormous amounts for evaluations of this second kind. Had we earmarked a small portion of the budget expended on these efforts for a few randomized field studies, we might have realized three benefits: first, we might have learned with greater reliability how well or how poorly a particular program was working; second, we might have spent less on overall evaluation expenses; and third, we might have been able to use the results of the field trials to improve the operation of the program, so that it could better serve its intended beneficiaries.

These three possible benefits are mentioned in a somewhat abstract context because they apply to many programs in both the social and medical fields. Let us focus on a particular set of social programs that illustrate these three points—*manpower training programs*. These have been developed in the past decade to train people to get and hold jobs. The bulk of such federal spending between 1963 and 1973 was distributed among four particular program groups: the Manpower Development and Training Act (MDTA), the Neighborhood Youth Corps (NYC), Job Opportunities in the Business Sector (JOBS), and the Work Incentive Program (WIN).

Between 1963 and 1971 the Federal Government spent 6.8 billion dollars for training 6.1 million people. By any yardstick, this is a huge expenditure on an important social enterprise. The average taxpayer might feel safe in concluding that these programs had obvious benefits for the trainees because so much money was spent over such a long period of time.

What are the findings of the evaluations of manpower training programs? A report of the National Academy of Sciences (1974) says that although a total of 180 million dollars has been spent on evaluating these programs, we still know little about the effect of the programs on the trainees' job seeking and job holding behavior. In the words of the report, "Manpower training programs have been in existence a little over a decade, yet, with the possible exception of the Manpower Development and Training programs, little is known about the educational or economic effects of manpower training programs. This is troublesome, especially in light of the fact that about $180 million have been spent over the past ten years in an attempt to evaluate these programs. There are several reasons for lack of clarity ... " (p. 1). The report goes on to document the methodological inadequacies of the evaluations, primarily case studies, involving nonrandom samples with data collected retrospectively. It concludes that, "In short, while reliable evaluation is badly needed, it does not exist even after ten years of study and the application of large amounts of public resources" (p. 2).

In a staff study prepared for the Subcommittee on Fiscal Policy of the Joint Economic Committee, United States Congress, Jon H. Goldstein (1972) reaches a similar conclusion: "Despite substantial expenditure of public funds for research and evaluation, there is only limited reliable information about the impact of training. Some of the largest and most important programs have been subjected only to crude, preliminary investigations" (p. 14).

These two carefully developed reports show that the average taxpayer would have been disappointed in his expectations. Apparently little is known about the effectiveness of these programs. Although the many manpower-training studies that have been carried out in the past ten years tend to suffer from the difficulties mentioned earlier, they seem to show that most of the time, most programs had essentially no or little positive effect upon the trainees.

Sifting through this literature leads us to a single randomized controlled field study conducted in the Cincinnati Neighborhood Youth Corps program (Robin, 1969). There were far more volunteers for the program than there were places. The evaluators randomly assigned the volunteers, female teenagers, between a treatment and a control group. The treatment consisted of monetary payments and work training for part-time work while the teenagers were still finishing high school. The outcome measure was how much these extra payments *reduced* the dropout rate of these girls from high school. After a year, the evaluators found that indeed a statistically significant difference had developed: the treatment girls were *more likely to drop out* of school than the controls.

There are some hints from just a few reported studies that selected manpower training programs may be highly effective in achieving their goals. But these can be viewed only as promising rather than convincing, because randomization of trainees between treatment and control groups was not employed. For example, Brazziel (1966) reports on a training program that offered general education and technical education, and compared the effects of these programs with two control groups. The general education training seemed highly effective, both during the training and after a one-year follow-up. The difficulty we have in generalizing such findings comes from the lack of any reported randomization of trainees among the several groups.

The accumulated evidence on manpower training programs told us little about their effectiveness, with the one exception of a small controlled field study that showed us an outcome in the opposite direction to that intended.

Manpower training programs thus exemplify an area where thoughtful public policy has broken down. The goal of these programs is laudable: to find a job for a person who doesn't have one and wants one. Society has found that it is not easy to train a person to get and keep a job; and therefore we need to learn more effective ways of delivering training services. Randomized controlled field studies might enable us to learn which, if any, versions of programs are succeeding in their mission, and might indicate good pairings between programs and kinds of trainees.

In the future, as a result of revenue sharing, new manpower training programs may be instituted by the states. They will want to consider what sorts of field trials they need to improve their own programs. Most states are now less well prepared for carrying out randomized controlled field trials than the federal government, and so the availability of organizations competent to carry out such trials would be crucial if evolutionary work is to succeed.

When thinking about the cost of a field trial embedded in an active program, we must realize that the entire cost of the field trial is not an extra expenditure. The people in the trial are part of the program. We need only think of the added cost associated with designing and monitoring the investigation, and analyzing its results—the marginal cost of the investigation.

Are randomized controlled field studies too expensive to embed in such large ongoing programs? No. The manpower training experience suggests that just the reverse is true: it is too expensive to pour large sums of money into programs, year after year, with no reliable indication of their value and no firm data on how to improve them.

[*Parts B and C are omitted.*]

IX. ISSUES THAT ARISE IN IMPLEMENTING INNOVATIONS
In addition to questions of feasibility and cost, evaluators and program developers alike face a series of questions that arise when field studies are implemented. We now turn to some of these.

[*Part A is omitted.*]

B. Field trials and policy inaction
Some evaluators become discouraged when information retrieved from field trials is not instantly acted upon by administrators or decision makers. We find this view politically naive. First, nothing happens in a moment. One good study may not be enough to satisfy the people in charge. There may be commitments in certain programs that preclude immediate changes of the sort that have been found to be especially beneficial. Evaluators have to understand that they are involved in a political process, and that the success and palatability of the total political process is a part of the evaluation system to which the evaluator of a particular program may not be tuned.

On the other hand, we find little reason to be discouraged. For one thing, so few strong evaluations exist that one can scarcely plead that the results are not being considered. To quote Donald Campbell (Salasin, 1973), "I don't see the store of redhot findings that are being neglected . . . [and] at the moment I'm not panicked by the failure to utilize them." It is true that the overall political situation does much to determine the next step in any program. But we have no reason to suppose that when a systematic body of knowledge has been acquired, the political system will ignore it. Inaction does not necessarily mean lack of consideration. There may, of course, be ways to help the political system appreciate new results, but the more urgent problem is to get them.

There is plenty of room for educating decision makers and policy workers by people who do studies—that is, room for helping to get the message of the results over to legislatures and agency heads. But when one has so few studies that are strongly based, it is hard to argue that decision makers are neglecting them. *Legislators should be asking, "Where are they?"* Not so much because any one study is invaluable to instant legislative decision, but because the overall process of gathering this information is what we need. We need to quit thinking in terms of the single evaluation of the single program and regard randomized studies as a way of life. Collecting such sets of good studies leads to accumulating patterns of information that are much more important and interpretable than the results of single investigations. With a collection of weak investigations it becomes hard to interpret any picture that emerges, particularly since few studies give adequate notice of their weaknesses.

A related point is a common criticism leveled against the very idea of evaluating social programs: that evaluations sometimes provide a political excuse for ending a program. How does this criticism tie in to the consequences of doing evaluations via randomized controlled field studies? We believe that if the stopping of a social program is due to political considerations, and independent of real program results, then no methodology will save this program. That is, if a program will be stopped independent of what an evaluation shows, then randomization will not lead to an evaluation's being an input into the policy process. Thus, there is no good argument that calling for randomized studies is a proxy for wanting to discontinue a program.

C. Political obstacles

Social innovations and hence their evaluations often have complicated political and legal implications. We recognize that sometimes political reasons exist for not having good evaluations. A detailed discussion of such political reasons falls outside the scope of this paper. Here we view the goal of evaluation as providing data for the political decision process, not as deciding the value of an innovation for society.

We have reviewed a variety of objections to good evaluations, randomized or nonrandomized, where complaints such as "the information won't be quite good enough." "it will take too long," "it costs too much," "the program is too complex," or "it won't be generalizable" are given for not carrying out a trial. A more fundamental reason that often underlies such objections is much more direct: a program manager simply may not wish to have his program evaluated. He may prefer poor information to good information, or no information at all to a modest amount. If a program manager has a career trajectory that depends more upon the size of the programs he controls than the effectiveness of those programs, his first interest may be in expanding a program, rather than considering its effectiveness for its clients.

D. T. Campbell (1969) has made the suggestion that to combat this difficulty, program managers should be rewarded less for the size or actual effectiveness of their program, and more on the quality of the procedures they employ for evaluation. This would encourage more widespread adoption of randomized trials, since generating good information would become a primary objective of the manager.

The history of program evaluations suggests that adopting Campbell's idea might change sharply the attitudes of program managers and their sponsoring agencies. Political expediency has in the past led to suppression of information about programs, and in some extreme cases even lying about what the effects were. An even more common occurrence, illustrated in the recent history of manpower training program evaluations and the early history of Head Start, involves program managers' commissioning evaluations that because of their retrospective nature are bound from their moment of inception to yield findings that are ambiguous. This will not surprise the politically sophisticated observer. To the extent that managers correctly perceive they will be rewarded only if their programs demonstrate a double plus rating, they are acting quite rationally in their self interest to either develop an evaluation that artificially inflates their program's success, or to commission an evaluation with a design that will not allow even the most competent investigator to pin down program effects with any reasonable degree of reliability. Until we find ways to reward them for good evaluations, only program managers who are totally confident that well-designed randomized field trials will show their programs to be big successes will find it in their self interest to commission such desirable evaluations.

We hope that these attitudes will change, and we see some evidence that they are beginning to change already. The public is demanding greater accountability for its tax monies, and large-scale programs being developed by government agencies are slowly but steadily beginning to build in the idea of embedding controlled field studies as integral parts of the program.

X. FINDINGS AND RECOMMENDATIONS

A. The results of innovations

To see how effectively new ideas for helping people worked out in practice, we have collected a series of innovations from social programs and medicine that have been well evaluated (Section IV-D, E, H). The overall findings are that 1) about a fifth of these programs were clear and substantial successes; 2) a similar number had some small to moderate position effects; and 3) most of the remaining programs either had no discernible effects or were mixed in their effects, while a few were even found to be harmful rather than beneficial. These proportions do not differ sharply among the social, medical, and socio-medical studies (Section IV-J and Table 4).

How should we interpret these findings? If most innovations had worked, one might well feel that we were not being expansive or broad enough in our attempts to ameliorate social problems. If hardly any had worked, one might conclude that not enough thought and planning were being put into these programs and that they were wasting society's resources. Although our results fall between these two extremes, we would have liked to see a higher proportion of successful innovations, particularly since we feel that the selection biases of our observational study are probably causing the data to overestimate the proportion of successful innovations rather than underestimate them. Thus it seems to us that the more successful innovations would be both more likely to have been well evaluated and more likely to have come to our attention (Section IV-A). If it is true that we are less apt to evaluate programs that are feared to have little effect, society should be concerned that so many very large programs have only been evaluated with nonrandomized studies if at all.

B. Findings for nonrandomized trials

Although we are often pushed to do them for reasons of expediency, uncontrolled trials and observational studies have frequently been misleading in their results. Such misdirection leads to the evaluations' being ineffective and occasionally even harmful in their role as tools for decision makers. This was well illustrated in the medical studies described in Section V-B, and we are concerned because similar troublesome features are present in many evaluations of social programs. Nonrandomized studies may or may not lead to a correct inference, but without other data the suspicion will persist that their results reflect selection effects, as we discussed in Wilner's study of housing (Section V-A-1). This suspicion leads to two difficulties for the decision maker. First, his confidence in the evaluation is limited, and even when he does believe in the result, he may be reluctant or unable to act because others are not convinced by the data. Second, because of this lingering suspicion, observational studies are rarely successful in resolving a controversy about causality (Section V-C). Though controversy about policy implications may of course persist, few controversies about the effects of new programs survive a series of carefully designed randomized controlled trials.

C. Beneficial small effects

The observation that many programs do not have slam-bang effects stresses the importance of measuring small effects reliably (Sections II-B, VI-B). Once small effects are found and documented, it may be possible to build improvements upon them. The banking and insurance businesses have built their fortunes on small effects—effects the size of interest rates. Ten percent per year doubles the principal in a little over seven years. Similarly, a small effect that can be cumulated over several periods—for example, the school life of a student—has the potential of mounting up into a large gain. Naturally, small effects require stronger methods for their accurate detection than do large ones. One must be sure that the observed effects are not due to initial differences between groups or to other spurious causes. Randomized controlled field trials are virtually essential for controlling these sources of bias, and so are necessary for the accurate measurement of small effects. The examples of randomized controlled field trials given in Section IV show that in practice when such trials have been carried out, they have been helpful for understanding the process, for bringing out the issues, and for suggesting policy implications.

D. Costs and time

Although it contradicts our intuition, the cost of randomized controlled field trials may well be less than the cost of nonrandomized methods or observational studies (Section VIII-A). Although the cost of a particular randomized trial may exceed that of an observational study, even repeated observational studies often yield unreliable results (Section V-B). In some situations it may take a few years to design, implement, and analyze a randomized study. But this is an extremely short time compared to the generations that problems such as poverty, unemployment, hunger, and poor education have been with us. We should also note that often randomized studies take no longer than nonrandomized studies. The cost of not doing randomized studies can be extremely high—we may never find out the effectiveness of our programs (Section VIII-E).

One must sympathize with the decision maker who suggests that information that will be available in a few years is not of much value for his immediate decisions. But looking a step ahead, we see that information that is *not* available in a few years will *not* be available for decisions even then, let alone now. As we have stressed, the problems these innovations are treating are the more permanent ones of society, and a few years from now matters could be even more urgent than they are now. This suggests that the discount rate for information may not reduce the value of future information, but rather increase it, and so we should be more willing to invest in such long-term studies.

E. Feasibility of randomized trials

We find that randomized controlled field trials can be and have been carried out in situations that were made complicated and difficult by both ethical and technical problems. The Salk Vaccine field trial shows that society is willing to apply randomization to its children when the issues at stake are well known (Section III-A). Naturally, we recognize the constraint that some field trials would be impractical or unethical (Section VI-D) and should not be set up, and fortunately we have regulations to protect the public. These will continue to be developed. Inevitably, political problems can also arise that make evaluations hard or even impossible to carry out (Section IX-C). We have suggested the use of appropriate incentives as one way to encourage participation (Section VII-B), but we do not treat political problems in detail in this paper. We have outlined some of the flexibility that is available when participating individuals, groups, or institutions are willing to accept either one of a pair of treatments (Section VI-F). Further, we believe that the dichotomy of centralized control versus local options is a complication that can often be solved by special study designs and careful planning. A randomized field trial can frequently be conducted in a manner consistent with local units' (such as cities or schools) having a complete veto on treatments they consider undesirable (Section VI-F).

By carrying out the trials in the field we often discover additional facts of considerable value. An example is the finding of the Manhattan Bail Project that there were very different legal outcomes for those released than for those jailed among comparable groups of arrestees (Section IV-D-5).

F. Evolutionary evaluations

We do not advocate holding back large-scale programs until randomized trials can be held. Our reasoning is that political pressures often make this position unrealistic. Instead, we encourage embedding the trials in the program (Section VIII-D). Programs often continue for quite a long time. This presents the opportunity for evolutionary improvement when good evaluations are done within the program itself (Section IX-A). The crucial point here is that such evaluations should be directed toward improvement rather than being restricted to "go, no-go" decisions. It is more realistic to measure progress in an ongoing program than in a pilot study, because larger-scale studies can detect small but valuable effects at a low marginal cost. Of course, when advance studies can be made, as in the New Jersey Work Incentive Program, we naturally regard the special opportunity as beneficial. And we do encourage the use of pilot studies, whenever possible.

In many programs Congress makes available money through "set-asides" for mandatory evaluations. More of these funds should be used for randomized controlled field trials designed to indicate how to improve the programs. Sometimes components of a program can be studied and improved without involving the whole effort. Boruch has suggested to us that such component investigations may reduce the threat to the program administrator and leave him more comfortable with the evaluators than he would be with total program evaluations (Section IX-A).

G. Long-run development

We need to develop a capability for doing randomized controlled field trials that will enable us to mount such trials as a natural part of new program development (Section VI-I). This facility exists today for carrying out excellent sample surveys, and we see no reason that similar capabilities could not be developed in the coming years to carry out randomized field trials. The existence of such institutions will not only enable us to set up field trials when appropriate, but in addition we will begin to accumulate substantial amounts of reliable data about social programs. As such experience and capability develop, the time required for doing randomized controlled studies may well be reduced. As part of this process, we must work on developing better incentives for participating in controlled trials, better methods of installing and assessing the installation of complex programs, and strategies for handling the problems associated with multiple goals. Over the past twenty years various organizations specializing in carrying out sample surveys have steadily improved their capability to conduct such surveys rapidly and accurately. They have accumulated experience and learned from mistakes that may have been made from time to time. As all policy makers know, survey organizations are now accepted as an important component of the information-gathering process in America. It is time to develop a similar place for groups carrying out controlled field trials (Section VI-H).

H. Controlled trials vs. fooling around

Ethical problems have often been cited as reasons for not carrying out well-controlled studies. As we have discussed (Section VI-G), this is frequently a false issue. The basic question involves comparing the ethics of gathering information systematically about our large scale programs with the ethics of haphazardly implementing and changing treatments as so routinely happens in education, welfare, and other areas. Since the latter approach generates little reliable information, it is unlikely to provide lasting benefits. Although they must be closely monitored, like all investigations involving human subjects, we believe randomized controlled field trials can give society valuable information about how to improve its programs. Conducting such investigations is far preferable to the current practice of "fooling around with people," without their informed consent.

REFERENCES

At the end of each reference are the numbers of the section(s) and subsection(s) where that reference is treated. For example, the Alpert reference is treated in subsection F-1 of section IV.

Alpert, J. J., Heagarty, M. C., Robertson, L., Kosa, J., & Haggarty, R. J. Effective use of comprehensive pediatric care. *American Journal of Diseases of Children*, 1968, **116,** 529–533. (IV-F-1)

Bissell, J. S. *Implementation of planned variation in Head Start: Review and summary of first year report.* Washington, D.C.: U.S. Department of Health, Education, and Welfare, Office of Child Development, 1971. (VI-C, VI-E)

Bissell, J. S. Planned variation in Head Start and Follow Through. In J. C. Stanley (Ed.), *Preschool programs for the disadvantaged* (Vol. 2). Baltimore: Johns Hopkins University Press, 1973. (VI-C)

Boruch, R. F. Abstracts of randomized experiments for planning and evaluating social programs. Compiled for the Social Science Research Council's Committee on Experimentation for Planning and Evaluating Social Programs and for the Project on Measurement and Experimentation in Social Settings at Northwestern University. Revised, Fall 1972. (Unpublished) (IV-A)

Boruch, R. F., & Davis, S. Appendix: Abstracts of controlled experiments for planning and evaluating social programs. In H. W. Riecken, *et al.*, *Social experimentation as a method for planning and evaluating social interventions.* In press. (IV-A)

Botein, B. The Manhattan Bail Project: Its impact on criminology and the criminal law processes. *Texas Law Review*, 1964–65, **43,** 319–331. (IV-D-5, X-5)

Box, G. E. P. Use and abuse of regression. *Technometrics*, 1966, **8,** 625–629. (II-C)

Box, G. E. P., & Draper, N. R. *Evolutionary operation. A statistical method for process improvement.* New York: John Wiley & Sons, 1969. (IX-A)

Brazziel, W. F. Effects of general education in manpower programs. *Journal of Human Resources.* Summer 1966, **1,** 39–44. (VIII-A)

Brownlee, K. A. Statistics of the 1954 Polio Vaccine Trials. *Journal of the American Statistical Association*, 1955, **50,** 1005–1013. (III-A)

Callow, A. D., Resnick, R. H., Chalmers, T. C., Ishihara, A. M., Garceau, A. J., & O'Hara, E. T. Conclusions from a controlled trial of the prophylactic portacaval shunt. *Surgery*, 1970, **67,** 97–103. (IV-H-6)

Campbell, D. T. Reforms as experiments. *American Psychologist*, 1969, **24,** 409–429. (VIII-A, IX-C)

Chalmers, T. C. Randomization and coronary artery surgery. *Annals of Thoracic Surgery*, 1972, **14,** 323–327. (V-B)

Chalmers, T. C., Block, J. B., & Lee, S. Controlled studies in clinical cancer research. *New England Journal of Medicine*, 1972, **287,** 75–78. (V-B)

Cicirelli, V. G., *et al. The impact of Head Start: An evaluation of the effects of Head Start on children's cognitive and affective development* (Vol. *1*). Westinghouse Learning Corporation and Ohio University (contractors). U.S. Department of

Commerce/National Bureau of Standards/Institute for Applied Technology. Distributed by Clearinghouse, Springfield, Va., PB 184 328, 12 June 1969. (V-A-3)

Cochrane, A. L. *Effectiveness and efficiency: Random reflections on health services.* London: The Nuffield Provincial Hospitals Trust, 1972. (VIII-A)

Conlisk, J., & Watts, H. A model for optimizing experimental designs for estimating response surfaces. In *American Statistical Association Proceedings of the Social Statistics Section, 1969.* Washington, D.C.: American Statistical Association. (IV-D-1)

Cox, A. G. Comparison of symptons after vagotomy with gastrojejunostomy and partial gastrectomy. *British Medical Journal,* 1968, **1,** 288–290. (IV-H-2)

Crosfill, M., Hall, R, & London, D. The use of chlorhexidine antisepsis in contaminated surgical wounds. *British Journal of Surgery,* 1969, **56,** 906–908. (IV-H-9)

Ditman, K. S., Crawford, G. G., Forgy, E. W., Moskowitz, H., & MacAndrew, C. A controlled experiment on the use of court probation for drunk arrests. *American Journal of Psychiatry,* August 1967, **124,** 160–163. (IV-F-4)

Dunn, M. R., & George, T. W. Des Moines pre-trial release project 1964–1965. *Drake Law Review,* 1964, **14,** 98–100. (IV-D-5)

Dwight, R. W., Higgins, G. A., & Keehn, R. J. Factors influencing survival after resection in cancer of the colon and rectum. *American Journal of Surgery,* 1969, **117,** 512–522. (IV-H-5)

Earle, H. H. *Police recruit-training: Stress vs. non-stress.* Springfield, Ill.: Charles C. Thomas, 1973. (IV-D-6, VI-E)

Elinson, J., with abstracts prepared by C. Gell, School of Public Health, Columbia University. The effectiveness of social action programs in health and welfare. Working paper. Ross Conference on pediatric research: "Problems of assessing the effectiveness of child health services," March 15–17, 1967. (IV-A)

Fairweather, G. W. (Ed.) *Social psychology in treating mental illness: An experimental approach.* New York: John Wiley & Sons, 1964. (IV-F-6)

Federal Bureau of Prisons. *Rational innovation: An account of changes in the program of the National Training School for boys from 1961 to 1964.* Washington, D.C.: Federal Bureau of Prisons, 1964. (IV-D-4)

Francis, T., Jr., Korns, R. F., Voight, R. B., Boisen, M., Hemphill, F. M., Napier, J. A., & Tolchinsky, E. An evaluation of the 1954 poliomyelitis vaccine trials. Summary Report. *American Journal of Public Health and The Nation's Health,* 1955, **45,** xii, 1–63. (III-A, VI-B, X-5)

Gamma globulin in the prophylaxis of poliomyelitis: An evaluation of the efficacy of gamma globulin in the prophylaxis of paralytic poliomyelitis as used in the United States in 1953. (Public Health Monograph No. 20, U.S. Public Health Service publication No. 358.) Washington, D.C.: U.S. Government Printing Office, 1954. (III-B)

Gilbert, J. P., & Mosteller, F. The urgent need for experimentation. In Mosteller, F., & Moynihan, D. P. (Eds.), *On equality of educational opportunity.* New York: Random House, 1972. (VIII-A)

Goldstein, J. H. The effectiveness of manpower programs. A review of research on the impact on the poor. In *Studies in public welfare.* Subcommittee on Fiscal Policy, Joint Economic Committee, Congress of the United States. Washington, D.C.: U.S. Government Printing Office, 1972. (VIII-A)

Goligher, J. C., Morris, C., McAdam, W. A. F., De Dombal, F. T., & Johnston, D. A controlled trial of inverting versus everting intestinal suture in clinical large-bowel surgery. *British Journal of Surgery,* 1970, **57,** 817–824. (IV-H-8)

[Gorham Report] *A report to the President on medical care price.* U.S. Department of Health, Education, and Welfare. Washington, D.C.: U.S. Government Printing Office, 1967. (IV-F-1)

Grace, N. D., Muench, H., & Chalmers, T. C. The present status of shunts for portal hypertension in cirrhosis. *Gastroenterology,* 1966, **50,** 684–691. (V-B)

Gramlich, E., & Koshel, P. *Social experiments in education: The case of performance contracting.* Washington, D.C.: Brookings Institution, December 1973. (V-A-4)

Hammond, K. R., & Kern, F. *Teaching comprehensive medical care.* Cambridge, Mass.: Harvard University Press, 1959. (IV-F-3)

Henderson, E. S. Treatment of acute leukemia. *Seminars in Hematology,* 1969, **6,** 271–319. (VIII-C)

Hill, D. B., & Veney, J. E. Kansas Blue Cross/Blue Shield Outpatient Benefits Experiment. *Medical Care,* 1970, **8,** 143–158. (IV-F-1)

Jordan, P. H., Jr., & Condon, R. E. A prospective evaluation of vagotomy-pyloroplasty and vagotomy-antrectomy for treatment of duodenal ulcer. *Annals of Surgery,* 1970, **172,** 547–560. (IV-H-1)

Kelman, H. R. An experiment in the rehabilitation of nursing home patients. *Public Health Reports,* 1962, **77,** 356–366. (IV-F-7)

Kennedy, T., & Connell, A. M. Selective or truncal vagotomy? A double-blind randomized controlled trial. *The Lancet,* May 3, 1969, 899–901. (IV-H-3)

Lasagna, L. Special subjects in human experimentation. *Daedalus,* Spring, 1969, 449–462. (VIII-A)

Lewis, C. E., & Keairnes, H. W. Controlling costs of medical care by expanding insurance coverage. Study of a paradox. *New England Journal of Medicine,* 1970, **282,** 1405–1412. (VII-A)

Light, R. J., Mosteller, F., & Winokur, H. S., Jr. Using controlled field studies to improve public policy. In *Federal Statistics: Report of the President's Commission* (Vol. 2). Washington, D.C.: U.S. Government Printing Office, 1971. (VIII-A)

Meier, P. The biggest public health experiment ever: The 1954 field trial of the Salk poliomyelitis vaccine. In J. M. Tanur *et al.* (Eds.) *Statistics: A guide to the unknown.* San Francisco: Holden-Day, 1972. (III-A)

Meyer, H. J., & Borgatta, E. F. *An experiment in mental patient rehabilitation: Evaluating a social agency program.* New York: Russell Sage Foundation, 1959. (V-A-6)

Meyer, H. J., Borgatta, E. F., & Jones, W. C. *Girls at vocational high: An experiment in social work intervention.* New York: Russell Sage Foundation, 1965. (IV-D-3)

Miao, L. Gastric freezing. In J. P. Bunker *et al.* (eds.), *Costs, risks, and benefits of surgery.* New York: Oxford University Press, 1977.

Miller, A. B., Fox, W., & Tall, R. Five-year follow-up of the Medical Research Council comparative trial of surgery and radiotherapy for the primary treatment of small-celled or oat-celled carcinoma of the bronchus. *The Lancet,* September 6, 1969, 501–505. (IV-H-4)

Nash, A. G., & Hugh, T. B. Topical ampicillin and wound infection in colon surgery. *British Medical Journal,* 1967, **1,** 471–472. (IV-H-7)

National Academy of Sciences. *Final report of the Panel on Manpower Training Evaluation. The use of Social Security earnings data for assessing the impact of manpower training programs.* Washington, D.C.: National Academy of Sciences, January, 1974. (VIII-A)

National Opinion Research Center [NORC]. *Southern schools. An evaluation of the effects of the Emergency School Assistance Program and of school desegregation* (Vol. 1). Prepared for the Office of Planning, Budgeting and Evaluation, U.S. Office of Education of the Department of Health, Education and Welfare. (NORC Report No. 124A.) Chicago: University of Chicago, National Opinion Research Center, October 1973. (III-C, IV-D-8, IV-J, VI-A, VIII-D)

Newhouse, J. P. *A design for health insurance experiment.* Santa Monica: RAND, November 1972. (VII-B)

Orcutt, G. H. Data research and government. *American Economic Review,* May, 1970, **60** (2), 132–137. (VIII-A)

Pinkel, D., Simone, J., Hustu, H. O., & Aur, R. J. A. Nine years' experience with "total therapy" of childhood acute lymphocytic leukemia. *Pediatrics,* 1972, **50,** 246–251. (VIII-C)

Rivlin, A. M. Systematic thinking and social action. Berkeley, California: H. Polan Gaither Lectures, January, 1970. (VIII-A)

Rivlin, A. M. *Systematic thinking for social action.* Washington, D.C.: Brookings Institution, 1971. (VIII-A)

Rivlin, A. M. How can experiments be more useful? *American Economic Review, Papers and Proceedings,* May 1974. (VIII-A)

Robin, G. D. An assessment of the in-public school Neighborhood Youth Corps Projects in Cincinnati and Detroit, with special reference to summer-only and year-round enrollees: Final Report. Philadelphia: National Analysts, Inc., February, 1969. (VIII-A)

Rosenberg, M. *The pretrial conference and effective justice. A controlled test in personal injury litigation.* New York: Columbia University Press, 1964. (IV-D-7)

Ruffin, J. M., Grizzle, J. E., Hightower, N. C., McHardy, G., Shull, H., & Kirsner, J. B. A co-operative double-blind evaluation of gastric "freezing" in the treatment of duodenal ulcer. *New England Journal of Medicine,* 1969, **281,** 16–19. (IV-H-11, V-B)

Rutstein, D. D. The ethical design of human experiments. *Daedalus,* Spring, 1969, 523–541. (VIII-A)

Salasin, S. Experimentation revisited: A conversation with Donald T. Campbell. *Evaluation*, 1973, **1** (3), 9–10. (IX-B)

Salcedo, J., Jr. Views and comments on the Report on Rice Enrichment in the Philippines. In *Food and Agriculture Organization of the United Nations* (Report No. 12). Rome, Italy: March 1954. (V-A-2)

Scriven, M. Evaluating educational programs. *The Urban Review*, February 1969, **3** (4), 20–22. (VII-A)

Sheldon, A. An evaluation of psychiatric after-care. *British Journal of Psychiatry*, 1964, **110,** 662–667. (IV-F-5)

Sherwin, C. W., & Isenson, R. S. Project Hindsight: A Defense Department study of the utility of research. *Science*, June 1967, **156,** 1571–1577. (VIII-C)

Silver, G. A. *Family medical care. A report on the family health maintenance demonstration.* Cambridge, Mass.: Harvard University Press, 1963. (IV-F-8)

Skipper, J. S., Jr., & Leonard, R. C. Children, stress and hospitalization: A field experiment. *Journal of Health and Social Behavior*, 1968, **9,** 275–287. (IV-F-2)

Smith, M. S. *Some short term effects of Project Head Start. A preliminary report on the second year of planned variation—1970–1971.* Cambridge, Mass.: Huron Institute, 1973. (IV-F-3, V-A-3)

Smith, M. S., & Bissell, J. S. Report analysis: The impact of Head Start. *Harvard Educational Review*, 1970, **40,** 51–104. (V-A-3)

Stewart, H. J., Forrest, A. P. M., Roberts, M. M., Chinnock-Jones, R. E. A., Jones, V., & Campbell, H. Early pituitary implantation with Yttrium-90 for advanced breast cancer. *The Lancet.* October 18, 1969, 816–820. (IV-H-10)

"Student." The Lanarkshire milk experiment. *Biometrika*, 1931, **23,** 398–406. (II-D-4)

Thompson, M. S. *Evaluation for decision in social programs.* Unpublished doctoral dissertation, Harvard University, 1973. (II-D-5)

U.S. Department of Health, Education, and Welfare [HEW]. Summary report. New Jersey graduated work incentive experiment: A social experiment in negative taxation sponsored by the Office of Economic Opportunity, U.S. Department of Health, Education, and Welfare. Mimeographed, December 1973. (IV-D-1, VI-A, VI-E, X-6)

Wallace, D. *The Chemung County research demonstration with dependent multi-problem families.* New York: State Charities Aid Association, 1965. (IV-D-2)

Wangensteen, O. H., Peter, E. T., Nicoloff, D. M., Walder, A. I., Sosin, H., & Bernstein, E. F. Achieving "physiological gastrectomy" by gastric freezing. A preliminary report of an experimental and clinical study. *Journal of the American Medical Association*, 1962, **180,** 439–444. (IV-H-11)

Weisberg, H. T. *Short term cognitive effects of Head Start programs: A report on the third year of planned variation—1971–1972.* Cambridge, Mass.: Huron Institute, September 1973. (V-A-3, VII-A)

Welch, W. W., & Walberg, H. J. A natural experiment in curriculum innovation. *American Educational Research Journal*, Summer 1972, **9** (3), 373–383. (IV-D-9)

Welch, W. W., Walberg, H. J., & Ahlgren, A. The selection of a national random sample of teachers for experimental curriculum evaluation. *School Science and Mathematics*, March 1969, 210–216. (IV-D-9)

White, R. R., Hightower, N. C., Jr., & Adalid, R. Problems and complications of gastric freezing. *Annals of Surgery*, 1964, **159,** 765–768. (V-B)

Wilner, D. M., Hetherington, R. W., Gold, E. B., Ershoff, D. H., & Garagliano, C. F. Databank of program evaluations. *Evaluation*, 1973, **1** (3), 3–6. (IV-A)

Wilner, D. M., Walkley, R. P., Pinkerton, T. C., Tayback, M., with the assistance of Glasser, M. N., Schram, J. M., Hopkins, C. E., Curtis, C. C., Meyer, A. S., & Dallas, J. R. *The housing environment and family life.* Baltimore: The Johns Hopkins Press, 1962. (V-A-1, X-2)

Wilson, J. O. Social experimentation and public policy analysis. *Public Policy*, Winter 1974, **22,** 15–38. (V-A-3)

ALLOCATING RESOURCES FOR POLICY RESEARCH: HOW CAN EXPERIMENTS BE MORE USEFUL?

ALICE M. RIVLIN

Less than a decade ago most economists—save a few mavericks like Guy Orcutt—viewed experimentation as a tool available to physical scientists and psychologists, but not to them. But interest in social experimentation grew rapidly in the late 1960's due at least partly to two developments. First, efforts to rationalize decision making at the Federal level brought economists and other analysts into important government posts and made them painfully aware of how little their traditional data sources allowed them to say about the likely effects of policy changes. Second, the tight Federal budget, the political split between the President and the Congress, and the widespread disillusionment with Great Society promises of rapid social change made expensive, new, untested social programs look unattractive even to dedicated liberals and made experimentation seem a more sensible alternative.

Thus far only a few major social experiments have been finished; one might well argue that it is therefore too soon to assess the usefulness of such experiments. But can we afford to wait? Compared with traditional ways of collecting data, experiments are costly and time consuming; and there is clearly some danger that the government will commit substantial resources to experiments that are poorly chosen, designed, or executed and do not yield useful results. The confidence of politicians and the public in a potentially powerful tool could be undermined if experimentation is clumsily used.

In what follows, therefore, I attempt to draw some tentative lessons from the social experimentation experience so far and suggest what kinds of future experiments might be most useful to policy makers. I start from the assumption that resources for experimentation are and will be severely

Reprinted with permission from *American Economic Review*, Vol. 64, No. 2 (May 1974), pp. 346–354.

limited, so that it will be particularly important to use experimental re-sources cost-effectively.

I. FOUR TYPES OF EXPERIMENTS

Various social experiments are addressed to distinct kinds of policy prob-lems and raise distinct kinds of design and execution problems.[1] Recent ones appear to fall into four groups, addressed to four types of policy questions.

Type 1

What is the response of individuals, households, or other micro units to a change in economic incentives?

This type of experiment attempts to estimate the effect of a change in a price, tax, or subsidy on the behavior of a large number of independent units such as individuals or households (or conceivably firms in a market with large numbers of small units). The "treatment" is a schedule of prices or taxes or subsidies. The outputs of interest are measures of economic activity (e.g., earnings, hours worked, or expenditures). The units are assumed not to influence each other.

Examples are: (1) The New Jersey and rural income-maintenance experiments (see Instit. for Res. on Poverty). Concern centered on finding out how hours worked and earnings were related to guarantee levels and the marginal tax rate. (2) The housing demand experiment (see Abt Assoc.). The need was to find out how household expenditures for housing were related to various forms and levels of housing allowance. (3) Health insur-ance experiments (see Joseph Newhouse). Concern centered on finding out how individual use of medical care relates to the coinsurance and deductible features of health insurance policies. (4) The income-maintenance experi-ments in Gary, Denver, and Seattle. These are not pure examples of this type of experiment because the participants are offered various types of services as well as money payments.

Problems of execution. Carrying out any social experiment successfully is a managerial tour de force, but Type 1 experiments present fewer problems of execution than other types. The treatment (negative tax schedule, housing allowance, etc.) can be exactly specified. Outputs (earnings, hours worked, etc.) can be identified and reasonably accurately measured. A probability sample of individuals or other micro units can be drawn and units can be

---

[1] Such experiments do have one thing in common: they all raise serious ethical and legal issues analogous to those encountered in biomedical and psychological experimentation on human subjects (Rivlin and Timpane, eds., forthcoming-a).

assigned to treatment and control groups on a random basis without serious difficulty.

Problems of inference. The validity of this type of experiment depends on the assumption that the behavior of the micro units in response to the treatment is independent. This assumption makes it possible to use a thin sample from a wide area rather than giving the treatment to everyone in a smaller area who would be eligible if the policy were in effect. But, of course, the assumption may be wrong. People may behave one way if they are the only ones on their block receiving a negative income tax or a housing allowance or a government health insurance plan and quite differently if all their friends and neighbors are subject to the same policy. The New Jersey experiment, for all its careful design and execution, may, in fact, tell us nothing about what would happen if all low-income families were eligible for negative income tax benefits.

Even with a thin sample there is still the question of whether to sample from the whole population or from a more limited geographical area. Limiting the area reduces some kinds of variability and greatly reduces the administrative costs of the experiment, but it also increases the chances that exogenous local events will overwhelm the results. This danger was clear and present when New Jersey changed its welfare law in the middle of the experiment and when Seattle's unemployment rate rose precipitously as the local experiment was getting under way.

Two other inference problems that plague Type 1 experiments are common to all experiments with human beings. First, do people behave in the face of a temporary policy in the same way they would in the face of a permanent one? This problem seems most serious in experiments that involve major long-run decisions—like the decision to buy a house or even to move to a different apartment. Some clues as to the importance of the problem may be obtained by splitting the sample in a given experiment, giving one group the policy treatment for a longer time than the other and seeing if their behavior differs, but some uncertainties about the validity of inference from a temporary experiment will still remain.

The second problem is the so-called Hawthorne effect. Do people really behave normally when they know their behavior is being observed?

Type 2
What is the market response to a change in economic incentives?

These experiments relate to the same kind of policy proposals that give rise to Type 1 experiments, but ask a different set of questions. The problem is to find out not how individuals respond to a policy change, but how a whole market responds. How do supply and price, say, of housing respond to a policy-induced change in demand? Or how do demand and price, say, for low-skill workers respond to a change in supply?

Examples are: (1) The housing supply experiment (see I. Lowry, ed.). The purpose of the experiment is to estimate how much housing supply would increase and how much rents and housing prices would rise in response to housing demand generated by a housing allowance. (2) Several similar experiments which have been discussed but not carried out—for example, experiments involving the impact of increased health insurance on the supply of health services; the impact of negative income taxes on wage rates; and the impact of day-care vouchers on the supply of care.

Problems of execution. These experiments are far more difficult to carry out than Type 1, mainly because here it is impossible to use a thin sample. It is necessary to saturate an area, giving the treatment to everyone who would be eligible under a national policy and seeing how the market responds. Saturation experiments are costly, unless the communities being saturated are so small as to be of little national interest. Moreover, they raise political difficulties. Community consent must be obtained, and this may be difficult if the relevant market encompasses several local jurisdictions. Some jurisdictions may refuse to participate; others may try to alter the experiment to their own ends. It may also be necessary to account for the behavior of institutions with market power (e.g., banks) as well as to measure the aggregate behavior of micro units in the market. The outputs themselves may be hard to measure (e.g., housing supply).

Problems of inference. The main problem with Type 2 experiments is that the cost of saturation limits the number of sites and it is risky to generalize about the behavior of markets from samples of one or two. The chances that exogenous local events will invalidate the experiment are even higher than for Type 1 experiments. It might be possible to compare the treatment sites with control sites, but one can hardly put confidence limits on the differences. It is not at all clear how control sites should be chosen or when two cities are really comparable. How would one know whether another city is "like Pittsburgh" in all the dimensions that might affect the results of a community-wide experiment?

Type 2 experiments also raise the familiar uncertainties as to whether responses are affected by the temporary nature of the treatment or by the fact that behavior is being observed. These problems are harder to deal with than in Type 1 experiments, and cannot be remedied, as in a Type 1 experiment, by sample-splitting.

Type 3
What is the production function of a public service, such as health, education, or manpower training?

These experiments arise from uncertainties about a different set of government programs—programs at all levels of government that provide services to people. The hope is that experiments can be used to uncover relationships between inputs and outputs so that the desired outputs can be produced more effectively.

Examples are: (1) Follow Through and Head Start planned variations (see Rivlin and Timpane, eds., forthcoming-b). These attempted to try out a variety of "models" of early childhood curricula and compare the effects of the models with each other and with the effects of regular schooling. (2) Similar experiments under discussion or in some cases carried out on a limited scale concerning health services, child care, family planning, manpower training, and bilingual education.

Problems of execution. Type 3 experiments are even harder to carry out than Type 2. Unlike Types 1 and 2, where the policy change of interest is a relatively simple tax or price schedule, the "treatments" to be compared in Type 3 are complex and hard to describe clearly. They are also likely to result in multiple outputs, and disagreements are bound to arise about how the outputs should be measured and which are most important.

One way of simplifying the problem is to agree on a set of measurable outputs (e.g., reading and math scores of children), then vary easily measurable inputs (e.g., class size) and try to estimate relationships between the inputs and the outputs that can be used to make the system more effective. This approach has been tried frequently in education, but has not yielded many significant results. Class size does not appear to predict test scores of children, which is hardly surprising. Presumably, what does matter is what happens in a class of a given size—what the curriculum is, how the teacher uses time, how he communicates with students, and what he expects of them.

It may be that education experimenters have so far failed to vary the inputs that really matter or to measure outputs appropriately. More miniexperiments should be tried in hopes of finding relationships between inputs that can be manipulated easily in existing schools and desired outputs. On the other hand, it may prove necessary to abandon simple experiments in education in favor of attempts to define more complex programs or models and test these.

The "planned variation" programs were undertaken to compare the effectiveness of disparate and complex models of early childhood education—an objective that proved extremely difficult to carry out in practice. Problems arose because the "models" were not well defined, could not readily be translated into specific directions for teachers to follow, and were changed and developed as the experiment went along. Models were implemented in varying degrees in different sites but no good measures were developed of the extent of implementation. There was little agreement on what output measures were appropriate or how to weight them. For want of better measures, standardized tests were used as outputs, despite the fact that standardized tests are poorly designed for comparing the effectiveness of different curricula and despite strong dissents from the identification of "success" in early childhood education with the acquisition of cognitive skills. Little theory (comparable to the microeconomic theory underlying Type 1 and 2 experiments) was available to indicate the direction, timing, or magnitude of the expected effects of the model curriculum. In addition, some rather rudimentary and avoidable errors made the planned variation results hard to interpret. Comparison groups, for example, were often drawn from less deprived populations than the treatment groups.

Correcting these problems while applying the planned variation approach to other areas would involve (1) developing and pretesting models more fully prior to large-scale experimentation; (2) developing measures of the extent to which a model is actually implemented in an experimental site; (3) developing more discriminating output measures and specifying the direction in which they are expected to move and criteria of "success"; and (4) selecting treatment and control samples from the same population, but not allowing the treatment to spill over into the control samples. All of this requires large resources and a period of several years' time both to develop the models and the measures and to conduct an experiment. It is not at all certain that such an ambitious plan could be carried out in the real world of bureaucracies at several levels of government. And when the answers were finally forthcoming, would they be to questions still considered relevant?

Problems of inference. Two questions about the planned variation approach concern whether one can hold a model of service delivery (e.g., a school curriculum with full specifications about how it is to be implemented) static long enough to test and evaluate it and whether it is even desirable to do so. It can certainly be argued that the *U.S.* system of highly decentralized decision making about services renders invalid attempts to test and compare a rigid set of models. In the real world the models would be altered by those who carried them out at the local level and would end up different from each other and from the original conception. To impose an artificial rigidity for the sake of experimentation can be regarded as stifling creativity and ingenuity.

Another problem is whether the communities (or schools, hospitals, day-care centers, etc.) that participate in an experiment should do so as volunteers. It seems necessary to use volunteers since communities dragooned into participating in a service delivery experiment will probably not cooperate fully or give the models a fair test. But the use of volunteers creates a problem of inference: the results can be generalized only to a population of other volunteer communities, or, indeed, only to communities that would volunteer to implement a particular model.

Type 4

How can incentives be altered in order to affect the production of a service and in turn to affect ultimate outcomes?

These experiments arise out of multistage hypotheses which assert that the way to affect the behavior of large systems (school systems, health delivery systems) is to change the incentives to which the systems respond. Type 4 is a mixture of the first three types and by far the most complicated.

Examples are: (1) Education vouchers (see Rand Corporation). The complex hypothesis behind education vouchers is that giving parents a choice of schools will induce schools to compete for students, which in turn will make schools choose more effective methods and teachers and will alter student outcomes in the directions desired by parents. The current demonstration of vouchers in Alum Rock, California, is limited to public schools, but other tests including private schools are under serious discussion. (2) Health maintenance organizations. Again the hypothesis is complex: that paying health providers for all the care a patient needs in a year (rather than service by service) will induce them to provide a different mix of care, which in turn will improve the patient's health (or lower the cost of the same health result). Tests involve the use of prepaid health-maintenance organizations to provide health care for low-income patients. (3) Performance contracting (see Gramlich and P. Koshel). This experiment grew out of another hypothesis about incentives: that school systems could contract with private firms to teach certain skills, reimbursing the firms on the basis of student performance, and that this in turn will induce the firms to choose effective methods and will result in higher student performance. The actual experiment did not last long enough to test the hypothesis; it showed only that performance contracting did not produce dramatic results in one year.

Problems of execution and inference. Type 4 experiments are the hardest to plan, execute, and interpret. One way to ease the difficulty would be to take a "black box" approach. For example, vouchers could be tried in a sample of communities, and student outcomes in those communities could be compared with outcomes in control communities without any attempt to monitor what happened inside the box—how the changes, if any, took place. But this approach is appropriate only if the main purpose of the experiment is to knock down a hypothesis that changing an incentive structure can have a significant and rapid effect on outcomes. If the government is serious about testing a change in incentives that is expected to be successful and might be widely adopted, it would seem desirable to look inside the black box and try to understand how the change works, what the essential ingredients of success are and how the results are related to changes in the nature of the incentive.

It should be recognized, however, that it may never be possible to try experiments (with multiple sites, controls, and other features required for statistical inference) with such complicated hypotheses. It may be necessary to settle for what can be learned from monitoring the experiences of a series of sites that volunteer to try the policy and adapt it to their own peculiar needs, values, and conditions.

II. CHOOSING USEFUL EXPERIMENTS

One of the big problems of social experimentation is the constant conflict between the pure research objectives of the experiment and other political and policy objectives. One manifestation of the conflict is the desire of the researcher to keep the treatment constant over the life of the experiment, so that he can make estimates of the parameters of some underlying model of the social system involved, and the desire of program operators and politicians to keep changing the treatment, to profit from experience, to increase the chances of a successful outcome, or to avoid public criticism and other difficulties that arise as the experiment progresses.

Researchers conducting Type 1 experiments seem able to stand their ground. To discover individual reactions to changes in incentives, it is clearly necessary to leave the policy constant for an appreciable period. It would not have made much sense to alter the guarantees or marginal tax rates in the middle of the New Jersey experiment; indeed, one can argue that three years of constant treatment were not enough. The goal of finding out how the behavior of individuals is related to policy parameters (e.g., marginal tax rates) can be attained by having additional treatment groups exposed to different values of the parameters, rather than by varying the parameters for the same treatment group over the life of the experiment.

Type 2 experiments, however, are so expensive that it is normally impossible to try multiple varieties of the policy instrument and observe how the market responses differ. It is necessary to choose one or two varieties. Then the question is whether to choose policies likely to cause a large shock to market (e.g., a high-level housing allowance likely to cause a big increase in demand for housing and strong upward pressure on rents) or one likely to cause less disruption. A third alternative is to phase the policy in slowly, endeavoring to minimize the disruption as one goes along. The answer really depends on the political purpose of the experiment—on whether the objective is to find what really happens in the case of a big policy change or to demonstrate that a policy can work smoothly if it is phased in carefully.

Type 3 experiments clearly need a pre-experimental period in which service delivery models are developed and adapted and during which learning from experience is allowed. In the interests of clean research findings, large-scale field tests should probably be delayed until the service delivery models are reasonably stable and able to be replicated, but, of course, it is hard to know when that stage has been reached. Indeed, interest in the innovation may have died before it reaches a stable state. The same observations apply to Type 4 experiments.

Alternatives to experimentation

Since experiments are expensive and time consuming, alternative ways of getting the information needed for policy purposes—e.g., surveys or data generated by natural-occurring (nonexperimental) events—should be considered in the hope that the needed information can be obtained faster or at less cost.

Rather than conduct Type 1 experiments, one might try to find natural changes in tax, price, or subsidy schedules for some groups in the population (e.g., changes in the terms of employee health insurance in a company) and to observe the behavior of individuals in the face of these changes. Sometimes, of course, no closely related policies exist.

As an alternative to Type 2 experiments, the possibility of finding naturally occurring shocks in comparable markets should be explored. For example, it might be possible to estimate the impact of an increase in demand for housing by observing what has happened in communities that have experienced an upsurge in demand. Such an upsurge might occur naturally where there is a sudden increase in income or employment in a local area.

As substitutes for Type 3 experiments, naturally occurring events are likely to be somewhat suspect—to involve unrepresentative samples or situations especially conducive to innovation in service delivery. Indeed, reliance on nonexperimental methods has produced so few clues to the nature of production functions in the social services that a strong prima facie case can be made for more systematic development and testing of models.

There is not likely to be any alternative to the Type 4 experiment. But it should be recognized that a true experiment is not likely to be possible, either.

III. PRESCRIPTIONS

Type 1. These experiments have been shown to be feasible and a good case can be made for increased use of them in the future to help policy makers predict the responses of households and other micro units to changes in taxes, prices, and subsidies. Such experiments might be used to help formulate policies with respect to user charges for public services, effluent charges to reduce pollution, higher education tuition and student aid policy, parking fees and other devices for reducing automobile use, student loan policy, as well as income maintenance, health-care financing, housing allowances, and even various forms of tax policy.

However, experimental data would be much more useful if they could be plugged in to the context of more extensive, continuing panel surveys. If the permanent panels advocated by Thomas Juster were available, subsamples of the panels could occasionally be used as experimental groups to test responses to particular policy changes. For example, panels of young people could be followed through the transition from school to work. These panels could also be used to measure responses to various forms of student aid. Subsamples of the panel could be offered student aid on different terms and the differences in their behavior could be measured.

Type 2. These experiments are probably also feasible, but should be used with considerably greater caution than Type 1. Saturation experiments are very expensive and difficult to interpret because controls are not really possible and special local circumstances may confound the results. Hence, they are more likely to be useful as a dry run for a policy whose adoption is imminent than as a way of estimating structural parameters of a market.

Type 3. It has to be recognized that we are not *now* able to carry out experiments with complex service-delivery models. The models are not well enough defined; outcome measures are not well enough developed. The planned variation experiments in education yielded few interpretable results because they were conducted without sufficient effort to define the models and develop measures of outcome and implementation. These mistakes should not be repeated. An experimental strategy may be worth the effort (especially since there are no obvious alternatives), but such a strategy is unlikely to pay off unless considerable time and resources are devoted to development before large-scale experiments are conducted.

Type 4. Field trials of policies to alter incentives of the large institutions (e.g., vouchers in a school system) can certainly be valuable, but it has to be recognized that the innovation will be developing as the trials go along. It may never be possible to do "experiments" on which firm statistical inferences can be based.

IV. CONCLUSIONS

The cautionary tone of this paper should emphatically not be construed as a rejection of experimentation as a tool for finding answers to policy questions. Experiments may be expensive compared with traditional forms of social research, but even the costs of major experiments are small compared with the costs of social policies that do not work or that might have been significantly more effective if experimental results had been available. I fully concur with Juster's position: economists and others who seek to improve the basis for policy formulation should devote far more attention and resources to data collection and measurement than they have in the past. Ever fancier statistical manipulation of inadequate data from traditional sources is unlikely to improve knowledge about policy choices significantly. The effort required to design and carry out both surveys and experiments may be painful and unglamorous, but it is the *sine qua non* of more rational and informed policy formulation.

The problem, of course, is not to choose between surveys and experiments, but to find the mix that will tell us the most. A reasonable strategy would seem to me to involve: (1) greatly increased resources for continuing panel surveys of many subpopulations whose behavior is of policy importance; (2) increased reliance on Type 1 experiments, often using part of a panel sample as the experimental or control group; (3) increased efforts to learn how to do Type 3 experiments with alternative methods of service delivery; and (4) very occasional use of Type 2 and 4 "experiments," mainly to develop or demonstrate a new policy and monitor results rather than rigorous experiments to yield policy parameters.

REFERENCES

E. Gramlich and P. Koshel, *Social Experiments in Education: The Case of Performance Contracting*, Brookings Instit., Washington forthcoming.

F. T. Juster, "The Use of Surveys for Policy Research," *Amer. Econ. Rev., Proc.*, May 1974, *64*.

I. Lowry, ed., *Housing Assistance Supply Experiment, General Design Report: First Draft*, Rand Corp., Santa Monica 1973.

J. Newhouse, *A Design for a Health Insurance Experiment*, Rand Corp., Santa Monica, Nov. 1972.

G. H. Orcutt, "Data Needs for Computer Simulation of Large-Scale Social Systems," *Proc. of the Conf. on Computer Methods in the Analysis of Large-Scale Social Systems*, Joint Center for Urban Studies, Mass. Instit. of Tech. and Harvard Univ., Cambridge, Mass. 1964.

A. Rivlin and M. Timpane, eds., *Legal and Ethical Issues in Social Experimentation*, Brookings Instit., Washington forthcoming-a.

——— and———, *Planned Variation in Education*, Brookings Instit., Washington forthcoming-b.

Abt Associates, *Housing Allowance Demand Experiment, Evaluation Design*, Cambridge, Mass. 1973.

Institute for Research on Poverty, *Final Report of the Graduated Work Incentives Experiment*, Madison, Dec. 1973.

Rand Corporation, *Technical Analysis Plan for Evaluation of the OEO Elementary Education Voucher Demonstration: Technical Dissertation*, Santa Monica, Feb. 1972.

PART V

DECISION MAKING

THE DECISION TO
SEED HURRICANES

*RONALD A. HOWARD, JAMES E. MATHESON,
and D. WARNER NORTH*

The possibility of mitigating the destructive force of hurricanes by seeding them with silver iodide was suggested by R. H. Simpson in 1961. Early experiments on hurricanes Esther (1961) and Beulah (1963) were encouraging (*1*), but strong evidence for the effectiveness of seeding was not obtained until the 1969 experiments on Hurricane Debbie (*2*). Debbie was seeded with massive amounts of silver iodide on 18 and 20 August 1969. Reductions of 31 and 15 percent in peak wind speed were observed after the seedings.

Over the last 10 years property damage caused by hurricanes has averaged $440 million annually. Hurricane Betsy (1965) and Hurricane Camille (1969) each caused property damage of approximately $1.5 billion. Any means of reducing the destructive force of hurricanes would therefore have great economic implications.

DECISION TO PERMIT OPERATIONAL SEEDING
In the spring of 1970 Stanford Research Institute began a small study for the Environmental Science Service Administration (ESSA) (*3*) to explore areas in which decision analysis (*4, 5*) might make significant contributions to ESSA, both in its technical operations and in its management and planning function. At the suggestion of Myron Tribus, Assistant Secretary of Commerce for Science and Technology, we decided to focus the study on the decision problems inherent in hurricane modification (*6*).

The objective of the present U.S. government program in hurricane modification, Project Stormfury, is strictly scientific: to add to man's

Reprinted with permission from *Science*, Vol. 176, No. 4040 (June 16, 1972), pp. 1191–1202. Copyright © 1972 by the American Association for the Advancement of Science.

knowledge about hurricanes. Any seeding of hurricanes that threaten inhabited coastal areas is prohibited. According to the policy currently in force, seeding will be carried out only if there is less than a 10 percent chance of the hurricane center coming within 50 miles of a populated land area within 18 hours after seeding.

If the seeding of hurricanes threatening inhabited coastal areas is to be undertaken, it will be necessary to modify the existing policies. The purpose of our analysis is to examine the circumstances that bear on the decision to change or not to change these existing policies.

The decision to seed a hurricane threatening a coastal area should therefore be viewed as a two-stage process: (i) a decision is taken to lift the present prohibition against seeding threatening hurricanes and (ii) a decision is taken to seed a particular hurricane a few hours before that hurricane is expected to strike the coast. Our study is concentrated on the policy decision rather than on the tactical decision to seed a particular hurricane at a particular time. It is also addressed to the experimental question: What would be the value of expanding research in hurricane modification, and, specifically, what would be the value of conducting additional field experiments such as the seedings of Hurricane Debbie in 1969?

Our approach was to consider a representative severe hurricane bearing down on a coastal area and to analyze the decision to seed or not to seed this "nominal" hurricane. The level of the analysis was relatively coarse, because for the policy decision we did not have to consider many geographical and meteorological details that might influence the tactical decision to seed. We described the hurricane by a single measure of intensity, its maximum sustained surface wind speed, since it is this characteristic that seeding is expected to influence (7). The surface winds, directly and indirectly (through the storm tide), are the primary cause of the destruction wrought by most hurricanes (8). The direct consequence of a decision for or against seeding a hurricane is considered to be the property damage caused by that hurricane. (Injuries and loss of life are often dependent on the issuance and effectiveness of storm warnings; they were not explicitly included in our analysis.)

However, property damage alone is not sufficient to describe the consequence of the decision. There are indirect legal and social effects that arise from the fact that the hurricane is known to have been seeded. For example, the government might have some legal responsibility for the damage caused by a seeded hurricane (9). Even if legal action against the government were not possible, a strong public outcry might result if a seeded hurricane caused an unusual amount of damage. Nearly all the government hurricane meteorologists that we questioned said they would seed a hurricane threatening their homes and families—if they could be freed from professional liability.

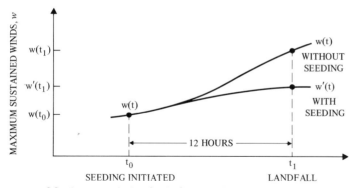

FIG. 1 *Maximum sustained winds over time.*

The importance of the indirect effects stems in large part from uncertainty about the consequences of taking either decision. A hurricane is complex and highly variable, and at present meteorologists cannot predict accurately how the behavior of a hurricane will evolve over time. The effect of seeding is uncertain also; consequently, the behavior of a hurricane that is seeded will be a combination of two uncertain effects: natural changes and the changes induced by seeding.

The seeding decision would remain difficult even if the uncertainty were removed. Suppose that, if the hurricane is not seeded, the surface wind intensifies as shown by the curve $w(t)$ in Figure 1 and that, if the hurricane is seeded, the behavior of the wind is that shown by the curve $w'(t)$. The effect of the seeding has been to diminish the wind, thus reducing property damage, yet the wind speed $w'(t_1)$ when the hurricane strikes land at time t_1 is higher than the wind speed when the seeding was initiated at time t_0. Even if the decision-maker were certain of $w(t_1)$ and $w'(t_1)$, he would still have a difficult choice. If he chooses not to seed, the citizens may have more property damage. On the other hand, if he chooses to seed, the citizens may not perceive themselves as better off because of his decision. Instead, they may perceive only that the storm became worse after the seeding and they may blame the decision-maker for his choice. The trade off between accepting the responsibility for seeding and accepting higher probabilities of severe property damage is the crucial issue in the decision to seed hurricanes.

DECISION UNDER UNCERTAINTY

The decision to seed a threatening hurricane would be taken about 12 hours before the hurricane is predicted to strike the coast. At this time the consequences are uncertain for both alternatives; the decision-maker does not know what amount of property damage will be sustained if the hurricane is

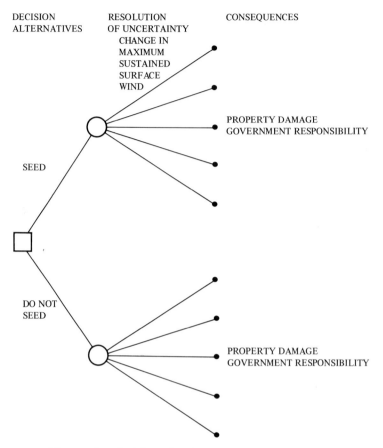

DECISION   RESOLUTION   CONSEQUENCES
ALTERNATIVES   OF UNCERTAINTY
                      CHANGE IN
                      MAXIMUM
                      SUSTAINED
                      SURFACE
                      WIND

SEED

                                              PROPERTY DAMAGE
                                              GOVERNMENT RESPONSIBILITY

DO NOT
SEED

                                              PROPERTY DAMAGE
                                              GOVERNMENT RESPONSIBILITY

FIG. 2 *The seeding decision: decision tree.*

seeded or is not seeded. We may illustrate the situation facing him in the form of
a decision tree, as shown in Figure 2. The decision-maker must select one of
the two alternatives, seeding or not seeding. The decision cannot be avoided for
inaction is equivalent to selecting the alternative of not seeding. Each alternative
leads to a set of possible consequences: property damage caused by the hurricane
and the responsibility incurred by the government. These consequences are,
in turn, related to the intensity of the hurricane and whether or not it was
seeded. The consequences for each alternative are uncertain at the time the
decision is made; the uncertainty will be resolved after the decision-maker
selects his choice. This decision under uncertainty may be examined according to the usual procedures of a decision analysis. We use the information
that is currently available to develop a probability distribution over changes
in the intensity of the hurricane as measured by its maximum sustained

surface wind speed for each of the two decision alternatives. Then we use data from past hurricanes to infer a relation between wind speed and property damage. By assessing the consequences in property damage and government responsibility and the probability that these consequences will be achieved, we are able to determine which of the decision alternatives is the preferred choice.

UNCERTAINTY IN HURRICANE WIND CHANGES

We began our analysis by considering the change in maximum sustained surface winds over a 12-hour period for a hurricane that is not seeded. If enough data had been available on the changes in hurricane wind speeds with time, a probability distribution for wind changes could have been based largely on these past data. Wind-change data were not available, but data were available for changes over time in the central pressure of hurricanes. The central pressure and the maximum wind speed of a hurricane are closely related; Holliday has shown that the available data can be summarized fairly well by a linear relation (*10*). We combined this relation with observations of the change in central pressure over a 12-hour period, using the assumption that the discrepancies from the Holliday relation are independent over a 12-hour period and independent of the change in central pressure. These assumptions imply a probability distribution on wind changes over a 12-hour period that is normal with a mean of zero and a standard deviation of 15.6 percent (*11*).

Therefore, present information is consistent with rather large natural changes in hurricane intensity over a 12-hour period. There is about one chance in six that a hurricane whose maximum sustained wind speed is 100 miles per hour will intensify over a 12-hour period to a maximum wind speed of over 115 miles per hour; there is also about one chance in six that the winds would naturally diminish to less than 85 miles per hour. In assessing these probabilities only general historical and meteorological information has been used. In a specific hurricane situation additional meteorological information might indicate that the hurricane would be more likely to intensify or more likely to diminish.

EFFECT OF SEEDING

The next step is to develop a probability distribution for the wind speed if the hurricane is seeded. The change in wind speed over 12 hours would then be a combination of the natural change occurring in the hurricane and the change caused by seeding. With the limited data available it is reasonable to assume that the two effects would be independent of each other and act in an additive fashion; for example, if the natural change is an intensification such that the maximum sustained wind speed is increased from 100 to $(100 + x)$ percent, and if the effect of seeding is to diminish the maximum sustained wind speed from 100 to $(100 - y)$ percent, the net observed change over 12 hours is from 100 to $(100 + x - y)$ percent. A probability distribution has already been assigned for natural changes; we need to assign a probability distribution for the change caused by seeding. In developing this probability distribution it is necessary to distinguish between the effect of seeding on one hurricane and the average effect of seeding on many hurricanes. The effect of seeding on a particular hurricane might be quite different from its average effect.

After discussion with meteorologists associated with Project Stormfury, we concluded that the major uncertainty about the effect of seeding would be resolved if we knew which of the following mutually exclusive and collectively exhaustive hypotheses described the effect of seeding:

1. H_1, the "beneficial" hypothesis. The average effect of seeding is to reduce the maximum sustained wind speed.

2. H_2, the "null" hypothesis. Seeding has no effect on hurricanes. No change is induced in maximum sustained wind speed.

3. H_3, the "detrimental" hypothesis. The average effect of seeding is to increase the maximum sustained wind speed.

The scientific basis for the "beneficial" hypothesis, H_1, had its origins in the original Simpson theory (1). It has been modified and strengthened by Project Stormfury studies involving a computer model of hurricane dynamics (1, 12). This hypothesis, in fact, motivated the formation of the Project Stormfury research program. A possible basis for the "null" hypothesis, H_2, is that seeding does not release enough latent heat to affect the dynamics of the hurricane. The "detrimental" hypothesis, H_3, has been added to complete the set. Meteorologists do not have a basis in physical theory for H_3 that is comparable to that for H_1 or H_2.

Even if we know which of the hypotheses is true, there remain uncertainties about the effects of seeding. We now describe the approach we followed in creating a model to formalize existing knowledge about these uncertainties. Then we shall return to the hypotheses.

Let us suppose we have access to a clairvoyant who can tell us which hypothesis, H_1, H_2, or H_3, represents the actual effect of seeding on hurricanes. What probability would we assign to the 12-hour change in the maximum sustained winds of a seeded hurricane for each of his three possible answers? If the clairvoyant says H_2 is true, the assignment process is simple. Seeding has no effect, and the same probabilities are assigned to the wind speed w' if the hurricane is seeded as to the wind speed w if the hurricane is not seeded (*13*).

$$P(w'|H_2) = P(w) = f_N(100\%, 15.6\%) \tag{1}$$

If H_1 is the clairvoyant's answer, the process is more difficult. The average effect is known to be a reduction in storm intensity, but the amount of this average reduction is uncertain. The Simpson theory and the computer studies indicate that a reduction of 10 to 20 percent in wind speed should be expected, with 15 percent as the most likely value. This information was summarized by assigning to the change in wind speed a normal probability distribution with a mean of −15 percent and a standard deviation of 7 percent. An average reduction greater than 15 percent is considered as likely as an average reduction less than 15 percent, and the odds are about 2 to 1 that the average reduction will lie between 22 and 8 percent rather than outside this interval.

The effect of seeding on an individual hurricane would be uncertain even if the average effect of seeding were known. Odds of about 2 to 1 were considered appropriate that the effect of seeding would not differ from the average effect by more than about 7 percent; thus, a normal distribution centered at the average value with a standard deviation of 7 percent was judged an adequate summary of the information available on fluctuations in seeding effects. Combining the uncertainty about fluctuations with the uncertainty about the average effect leads to a probability distribution for the effect of seeding a specific hurricane that is normal with a mean equal to −15 percent and a standard deviation of 10 percent (*14*).

Adding the natural change in the hurricane over a 12-hour period to the change resulting from seeding gives the total 12-hour change occurring in a seeded hurricane if hypothesis H_1 is true. The probability distribution assigned to w' is then normal with a mean of 85 percent and a standard deviation of 18.6 percent (*15*):

$$P(w'|H_1) = f_N(85\%, 18.6\%) \tag{2}$$

The development of a probability distribution for w', if it is considered that H_3 is true, proceeds in a similar way. The average change effected by seeding is described by a normal probability distribution with a mean of +10 percent and a standard deviation of 7 percent. The fluctuations expected when an individual hurricane is seeded are normally distributed around the average with a standard deviation of 7 percent. Combining these uncertainties with the uncertainty about the natural change in the hurricane over a 12-hour period, we obtain a probability distribution for w' that is normal with a mean of 110 percent and a standard deviation of 18.6 percent:

$$P(w'|H_3) = f_N(110\%, 18.6\%) \tag{3}$$

We have now developed probability distributions for the wind speed w' over a 12-hour period following the initiation of seeding for each of the three hypotheses. To obtain the probability distribution for w' that represents present information about the change in a seeded hurricane, we multiply each of the above distributions by the probability that is presently assigned to each of the hypotheses being true and sum over the three hypotheses:

$$P(w') = \sum_{i=1}^{3} P(w'|H_i)P(H_i) \qquad (4)$$

ASSIGNING PROBABILITIES TO THE HYPOTHESES

The last element in developing a probability distribution for w' is to assign the probabilities $P(H_1)$, $P(H_2)$, and $P(H_3)$. These probabilities should take into account both present meteorological information and meteorological information before the results of the 1969 Debbie experiments. The models we have just constructed allow us to examine the effect of experimental observations, such as the Debbie results, in revising the probabilities assigned to the three hypotheses. If a wind speed $w' = u$ has been observed after a seeding experiment, the posterior probabilities $P(H_i|u)$ are related to the probabilities $P(H_i)$ assigned before the experiment by Bayes' equation (5, 16, 17):

$$P(H_i|u) = \frac{P(u|H_i)P(H_i)}{P(u)} \qquad (5)$$

where the denominator is

$$P(u) = P(w' = u) = \sum_{i=1}^{3} P(w' = u|H_i)P(H_i) \qquad (6)$$

The extension to several independent experiments is straightforward. The Debbie results are considered as two independent experiments in which reductions of 31 and 15 percent in wind speed were observed over a 12-hour period. The posterior probabilities assigned to the hypotheses are computed by multiplying together the appropriate values of two normal probability density functions. The probability density function for the Debbie results if hypothesis H_i is true, $P(u_1 = 69$ percent, $u_2 = 85$ percent$|H_i)$, is

$$P(69\%, 85\%|H_1) = 1.50 \times 2.14 = 3.21$$
$$P(69\%, 85\%|H_2) = 0.372 \times 1.64 = 0.61 \qquad (7)$$
$$P(69\%, 85\%|H_3) = 0.195 \times 0.886 = 0.173$$

These numbers can be used to compute the posterior probabilities appropriate after the Debbie results from any set of probabilities assigned to the hypotheses before the Debbie results were known. For example, suppose that before the Debbie experiments the three hypotheses H_1, H_2, and H_3 were considered to be equally likely, that is, each had a probability of 1/3. Then, after the Debbie results are incorporated through Bayes' equation, the corresponding posterior probabilities assigned to the hypotheses are

$$P(H_1|\text{Debbie}) = \frac{3.21 \times 1/3}{3.21 \times 1/3 + 0.61 \times 1/3 + 0.173 \times 1/3} = .81$$

$$P(H_2|\text{Debbie}) = .15 \tag{8}$$

$$P(H_3|\text{Debbie}) = .04$$

However, meteorologists did not believe that H_1, H_2, and H_3 were equally likely before the Debbie experiments. They thought that seeding was unlikely to have any effect but that, if seeding did have an effect, it was more likely to be a reduction in wind speed than an increase, because a reduction was expected from both the Simpson theory and the computer model studies. Further, the four field experiments that were conducted before Debbie all led to no change or to reductions in the maximum wind speeds (*1*).

We determined probability assignments for the three hypotheses to reflect present information by two conditions: (i) Before Debbie, meteorologists believed that H_1 was more likely than H_3 if seeding had any effect on a hurricane. (ii) Since Debbie, meteorologists believe that H_1 and H_2 are equally likely.

These conditions led us to use the probabilities

$$P(H_1) = .49$$
$$P(H_2) = .49 \tag{9}$$
$$P(H_3) = .02$$

in our analysis. These posterior probabilites correspond to the pre-Debbie probabilities

$$P(H_1) = .15$$
$$P(H_2) = .75 \tag{10}$$
$$P(H_3) = .10$$

This set of probability assignments implies that prior to Debbie the odds were 3 to 1 that seeding would have no effect but that, if seeding did have an effect, the odds were 3 to 2 for wind reduction rather than wind intensification. Since the Debbie results, the chance of seeding causing an average intensification of hurricanes is assessed at 1 in 50, and the "null" hypothesis, H_2, of no effect and the "beneficial" hypothesis, H_1, of an average reduction are judged equally likely.

The probability assignments (Eq. 9) representing present information were reviewed with Project Stormfury officials before being used in the analysis. However, the results of the analysis are not particularly sensitive to the specific numbers, as we discuss below.

PROBABILITY DISTRIBUTIONS ON WIND SPEED

We now can compute the probability distributions on wind speed for the seeding and not-seeding alternatives (from Eqs. 1–4 and Eq. 9). These distributions are plotted in Figure 3 as complementary cumulative distribution functions. By reading the ordinate values corresponding to an initial wind intensity of 100 percent, we find that the probability assigned to intensification if a hurricane is seeded is .36; if the hurricane is not seeded, the probability is .50. The probability of intensification by 10 percent or more is .18 if a hurricane is seeded and .26 if it is unseeded. For any particular wind speed, the probability that this speed will be exceeded is always greater if the hurricane is unseeded than if it is seeded, because the complementary cumulative distribution function for the not-seeding alternative is always above the curve for the seeding alternative. This result is called stochastic dominance of the seeding alternative.

We have now specified the uncertainties about the outcome of the decision to seed. The same methods could be applied if the outcome were specified by several variables rather than simply by the relative change in

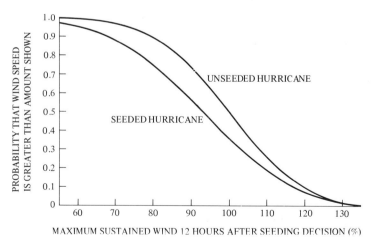

FIG. 3 *Probability distributions on 12-hour wind changes for the seeded and unseeded hurricanes.*

maximum sustained wind speed. Much of the uncertainty in the outcome is the result of uncertainty about the natural change in hurricane behavior, not about the effect of seeding. This characteristic holds even more strongly if other aspects of hurricane behavior are examined, such as the trajectory of a hurricane or the precipitation it generates. Although it is considered unlikely that seeding would have a significant effect on these features of hurricanes, substantial variations may occur from natural causes.

The uncertainty about the natural behavior of a hurricane makes the issue of government responsibility of paramount importance. The intensification after seeding illustrated in Fig. 1 is a distinct possibility. Even if further experiments confirm that the "beneficial" hypothesis, H_1, is true, there would still be about one chance in ten that a seeded hurricane will intensify by 10 percent or more. Meteorological advances and improved computer models may eventually allow many of the natural changes in a hurricane to be predicted accurately, but this capability may require many years to achieve.

WIND CHANGES AND PROPERTY DAMAGE

The winds of a hurricane cause property damage directly and indirectly, the latter by creating a high storm tide that can flood low-lying coastal areas. The data available for past hurricanes do not distinguish wind and storm-tide damage; consequently, a detailed basis is lacking for a causal model relating wind and property damage. In our analysis, we assumed a general power law of the form

$$d = c_1 w^{c_2} \tag{11}$$

where d is property damage in millions of dollars, w is the maximum sustained wind speed in miles per hour, and c_1 and c_2 are empirical constants to be determined from historical data on hurricanes. We estimated c_2 from data obtained from the American Red Cross on residential damage from 21 hurricanes. Since the Red Cross data were available for counties, we could isolate the damage caused by precipitation-induced flooding rather than by the wind or the storm tide by assuming that such damage occurred well inland. (The Red Cross data are the only statistics available that permit even this crude distinction between causes of damage.) Corrections for construction cost inflation and population growth were included, and c_2 was determined as 4.36 by a linear least-squares fit of the logarithms (Figure 4). Thus, a change in the wind speed by a factor x implies a change in property damage by the factor x to the power 4.36. If x is 0.85, corresponding to a 15 percent reduction in maximum wind speed, the corresponding reduction in property damage is 51 percent (*18*).

The approximations of this method and the limited data indicate that broad limits are appropriate in a sensitivity analysis. If c_2 is 3, the reduction in damage corresponding to a 15 percent reduction in wind speed is 39 percent; if c_2 is 6, the corresponding damage reduction is 62 percent.

Since the probability assignments to wind changes were made on relative rather than absolute changes in maximum sustained wind speeds, the scaling factor c_1 can be assigned as the last step in the analysis. We assume a nominal hurricane whose maximum wind speed at the time of the seeding decision is such that, if no change occurs in the 12 hours before landfall, the property damage will be $100 million. The analysis for a more or a less severe hurricane can be obtained by a suitable change in scale factor (*19*).

Using this relationship between property damage and maximum wind speed, we can develop the probability distributions for property damage for the nominal hurricane, whether seeded or unseeded. Figure 5 shows that the seeding alternative stochastically dominates the not-seeding alternative: the

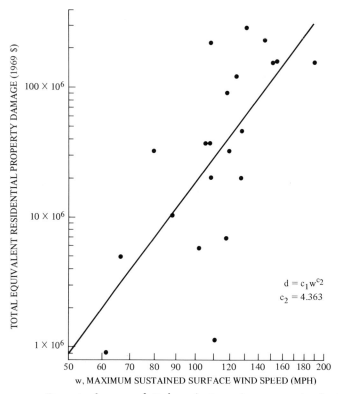

FIG. 4 *Property damage plotted against maximum sustained wind speed.*

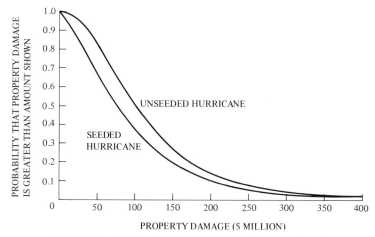

FIG. 5 *Probability distributions on property damage for the seeded and unseeded hurricanes.*

probability of exceeding a particular amount of property damage is always greater if the hurricane is not seeded than if it is seeded. Hence, if property damage is the criterion, the better alternative is to seed.

FURTHER ANALYSIS OF THE DECISION TO SEED

The decision to seed is shown in the form of a decision tree in Figure 6. The decision to seed or not to seed is shown at the decision node denoted by the small square box; the consequent resolution of the uncertainty about wind change is indicated at the chance nodes denoted by open circles. For expository clarity and convenience, especially in the later stages of the analysis, it is convenient to use discrete approximations to the probability distributions for wind change (*20*) (Table 1).

As a measure of the worth of each alternative we can compute the expected loss for each alternative by multiplying the property damage for each of the five possible outcomes by the probability that the outcome will be achieved and summing over the possible consequences. The expected loss for the seeding alternative is $94.33 million (including a cost of $0.25 million to carry out the seeding); the expected loss for the not-seeding alternative is $116 million; the difference is $21.67 million or 18.7 percent.

These results should be examined to see how much they depend on the specific assumptions in the model. Stochastic dominance is a general result that does not depend on the specific form of the relationship between property damage and maximum wind speed (see Eq. 11); rather, it depends on the probabilities assigned to hypotheses H_1, H_2, and H_3. The probability of H_3 must be raised to .07 before stochastic dominance no longer holds. Even if the probability of H_3 is raised much higher, seeding still results in the least expected property damage. If $P(H_1)$ is .40, $P(H_2)$ is .40, and $P(H_3)$ is .20, the expected loss for the seeding alternative is $107.8 million—7 percent less than for the not-seeding alternative. Variation of the exponent c_2 from 3 to 6 does not change the decision: if c_2 is 3, the expected property damage with seeding is 14 percent less; if c_2 is 6, the expected reduction in damage is 22 percent. If the criterion of expected cost is replaced by a

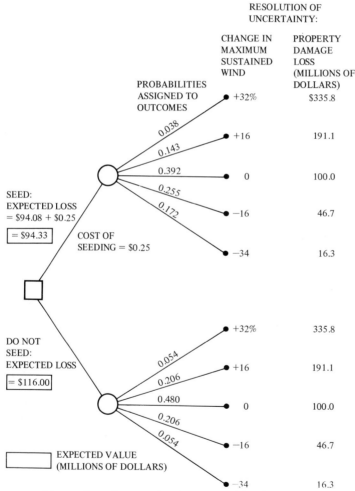

FIG. 6 *The seeding diagram for the nominal hurricane.*

TABLE 1 PROBABILITIES ASSIGNED TO WIND CHANGES OCCURRING IN THE 12 HOURS BEFORE HURRICANE LANDFALL. DISCRETE APPROXIMATION FOR FIVE OUTCOMES.

Interval of changes in maximum sustained wind	Representative value in discrete approximation (%)	Probability that wind change will be within interval	
		If seeded	If not seeded
Increase of 25% or more	+32	.038	.054
Increase of 10 to 25%	+16	.143	.206
Little change, +10 to −10%	0	.392	.480
Reduction of 10 to 25%	−16	.255	.206
Reduction of 25% or more	−34	.172	.054

nonlinear utility function reflecting aversion to risk, the relative advantage of the seeding alternative is even greater (*21*). The results of extensive sensitivity analysis may be summarized as follows: The expected loss in terms of property damage appears to be about 20 percent less if the hurricane is seeded. Varying the assumptions of the analysis causes this reduction to vary between 10 and 30 percent but does not change the preferred alternative.

GOVERNMENT RESPONSIBILITY

The analysis in the section above indicates that, if minimizing the expected loss in terms of property damage (and the cost of seeding) is the only criterion, then seeding is preferred. However, an important aspect of the decision—the matter of government responsibility—has not yet been included in the analysis. We have calculated a probability of .36 that a seeded hurricane will intensify between seeding and landfall and a probability of .18 that this intensification will be at least 10 percent. This high probability is largely the result of the great natural variability in hurricane intensity. It is advisable to consider both the legal and the social consequences that might occur if a seeded hurricane intensified.

The crucial issue in the decision to seed a hurricane threatening a coastal area is the relative desirability of reducing the expected property damage and assuming the responsibility for a dangerous and erratic natural phenomenon. This is difficult to assess, and to have a simple way of regarding it we use the concept of a government responsibility cost, defined as follows. The government is faced with a choice between assuming the responsibility for a hurricane and accepting higher probabilities of property damage. This situation is comparable to one of haggling over price: What increment of property-damage reduction justifies the assumption of responsibility entailed by seeding a hurricane? This increment of property damage is defined as the government responsibility cost. The government responsibility cost is a means of quantifying the indirect social, legal, and political factors related to seeding a hurricane. It is distinguished from the direct measure—property damage—that is assumed to be the same for both modified and natural hurricanes with the same maximum sustained wind speed.

We define the government responsibility cost so that it is incurred only if the hurricane is seeded. It is conceivable that the public may hold the government responsible for not seeding a severe hurricane, which implies that a responsibility cost should also be attached to the alternative of not seeding. Such a cost would strengthen the implication of the analysis in favor of permitting seeding.

The assessment of government responsibility cost is made by considering the seeding decision in a hypothetical situation in which no uncertainty is present. Suppose the government must choose between two outcomes:

1. A seeded hurricane that intensifies 16 percent between the time of seeding and landfall.
2. An unseeded hurricane that intensifies more than 16 percent between the time of seeding and landfall. The property damage from outcome 2 is x percent more than the property damage from outcome 1.

If x is near zero, the government will choose outcome 2. If x is large, the government will prefer outcome 1. We then adjust x until the choice becomes very difficult; that is, the government is indifferent; that is, the government is indifferent to which outcome it receives. For example, the indifference point might occur when x is 30 percent. An increase of 16 percent in the intensity of the nominal hurricane corresponds to property damage of $191 million, so that the corresponding responsibility cost defined by the indifference point at 30 percent is (.30) ($191 million), or $57.3 million. The responsibility cost is then assessed for other possible changes in hurricane intensity.

The assessment of government responsibility costs entails considerable introspective effort on the part of the decision-maker who represents the government. The difficulty of determining the numbers does not provide an excuse to avoid the issue. Any decision or policy prohibiting seeding implicitly determines a set of government responsibility costs. As shown in the last section, seeding is the preferred decision unless the government responsibility costs are high.

Let us consider an illustrative set of responsibility costs. The government is indifferent, if the choice is between:

1. A seeded hurricane that intensifies 32 percent and an unseeded hurricane that intensifies even more, causing 50 percent more property damage.

2. A seeded hurricane that intensifies 16 percent and an unseeded hurricane that causes 30 percent more property damage.

3. A seeded hurricane that neither intensifies nor diminishes (0 percent change in the maximum sustained wind speed after the seeding) and an unseeded hurricane that intensifies slightly, causing 5 percent more property damage.

4. A seeded hurricane that diminishes by more than 10 percent and an unseeded hurricane that diminishes by the same amount. (If the hurricane diminishes after seeding, everyone agrees that the government acted wisely; thus, responsibility costs are set at zero.)

The analysis of the seeding decision with these government responsibility costs included is diagramed in Figure 7. Even with these large responsibility costs, the preferred decision is still to seed.

The responsibility costs needed to change the decision are a substantial fraction of the property damage caused by the hurricane. For the $100-million hurricane chosen as the example for this section, the average responsibility cost must be about $22 million to change the decision. If the hurricane were in the $1-billion class, as Camille (1969) and Betsy (1965) were, an average responsibility cost of $200 million would be needed. In other words, an expected reduction of $200 million in property damage would be foregone if the government decided not to accept the responsibility of seeding the hurricane.

The importance of the responsibility issue led us to investigate the legal basis for hurricane seeding in some detail. These investigations were carried out by Gary Widman, Hastings College of the Law, University of California. A firm legal basis for operational seeding apparently does not now exist. The doctrine of sovereign immunity provides the government only partial and unpredictable protection against lawsuits, and substantial grounds for bringing such lawsuits might exist (22). A better legal basis for government seeding activities is needed before hurricane seeding could be considered other than as an extraordinrary emergency action. Specific congressional legislation may be the best means of investing a government agency with the authority to seed hurricanes threatening the coast of the United States.

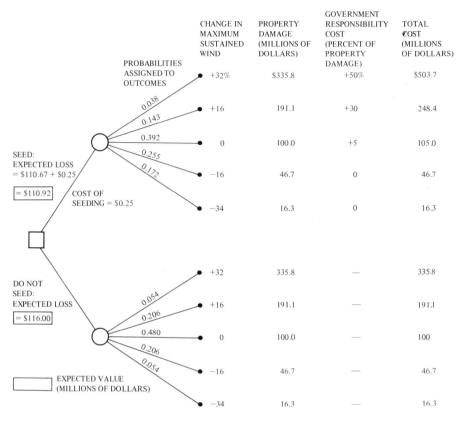

FIG. 7 *The seeding decision for the nominal hurricane (government responsibility cost included).*

VALUE OF INFORMATION

One of the most important concepts in decision analysis is the value of information: How much it would be worth to make the decision after rather than before uncertainty is resolved? In the case of hurricane modification, how much should the government pay to learn which of the three hypotheses, H_1, H_2, or H_3, is actually true (23)? We imagine that the government has access to a clairvoyant who has this information and is willing to sell it to the government, if he is paid before he makes the information available. It is easiest to understand the calculation in terms of the decision to seed one hurricane threatening a coastal area.

Let us consider the choice between the two decision situations shown in Figure 8. The government can choose to buy the information and make the decision after it has learned which hypothesis is true, or it can choose not to

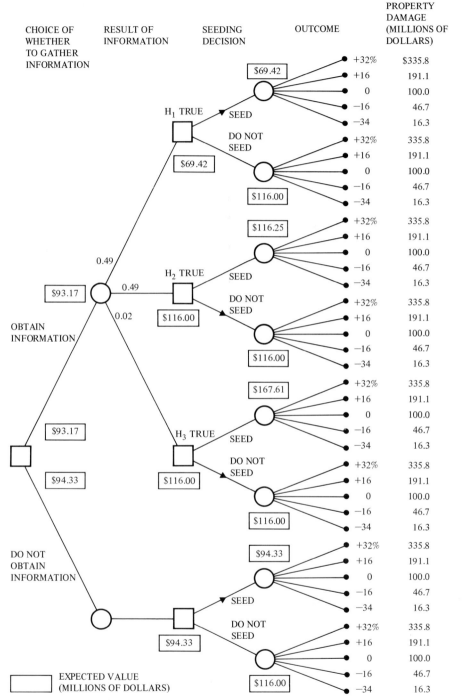

FIG. 8 *Expected value of the clairvoyant's information—which hypothesis describes the effect of seeding? (There is no government responsibility cost.)*

buy the information and can make the seeding decision on the basis of the present uncertainty.

Let us, for the moment, consider only property damage and the cost of seeding and disregard government responsibility costs. If H_1 is true, the preferred decision is to seed because the expected loss is $69.42 million compared with a loss of $116.00 million for the alternative of not seeding. If H_2 is true, then by choosing not to seed, the government saves the $0.25-million cost of seeding; the loss expected from property damage is the same for both alternatives: $116.00 million. If H_3 is true, seeding is a poor choice; the expected loss from property damage is $167.61 million, $51.61 million more than for the alternative of not seeding. At the present time, the government does not know what the clairvoyant will say, but probabilities have been assigned to his answers:

$$P(H_1) = .49$$
$$P(H_2) = .49 \qquad\qquad (12)$$
$$P(H_3) = .02$$

The expected loss corresponding to the decision situation in Figure 8 is then computed by multiplying the probability of each of the clairvoyant's answers by the expected loss associated with that answer and summing over the three possible answers:

$$(.49)(\$69.42) + (.49)(\$116.00) + (.02)(\$116.00) = \$93.17 \text{ million} \qquad (13)$$

Comparing this with the expected loss for the best alternative (seed) without the clairvoyant's information, which was $94.33 million, we see that it is $1.16 million less. This difference represents the expected value of the clairvoyant's information in allowing the government to make a better decision. It is a relatively small number compared with the expected losses because the information is not expected to be of much value—the probability assignments indicate that seeding is already a good idea. Without the clairvoyant's information the government should seed; with the clairvoyant's information, with probability .49, the government will save the cost of seeding ($0.25 million), and with the low probability .02 it will avert the potentially disastrous intensification expected from H_3, saving $167.61 million −$116 million = $51.61 million. By this reasoning we get the same answer as before for the value of information

$$(.49)(\$0.25) + (.02)(\$51.61) = \$1.16 \text{ million} \qquad (14)$$

and we can see that the value is very sensitive to the small probability assigned to H_3.

Now suppose that the government responsibility costs assumed previously are included. The expected value of perfect information is then much higher because, if H_2 is true, the government responsibility costs can be saved by not seeding. If the decision without perfect information is to seed, the expected saving from engaging the clairvoyant is

$$(.49)(\$0.25 + \$23.28) + (.02)(\$51.61 + \$53.57) = \$13.63 \text{ million} \qquad (15)$$

This figure represents 11.75 percent of the expected property damage if the alternative of not seeding is taken for the nominal hurricane.

The value of information largely derives from the fact that it allows the government to avoid the responsibility for seeding if seeding turns out to have no effect. The large increase over the value computed in Eq. 13 is due to the contribution of the government responsibility costs. Most of the increase of \$12.47 million, namely \$11.41 million, comes from the first or H_2 term.

The value of information depends on the extent to which the government is willing to assume responsibility for seeding a hurricane. If responsibility were not an issue, the government would seed operationally now, and information would have a comparatively low value in the context of this decision. The value of information is greatest when the government responsibility costs are large enough to make the decision essentially even between seeding and not seeding. Still higher responsibility costs cause the value of information to decrease (24).

VALUE OF FURTHER SEEDING EXPERIMENTS

The analysis of the value of a seeding experiment is similar to the determination of the value of the clairvoyant's information. The difference is that the resolution of uncertainty is only partial. The information obtained in the experiment is used in Bayes' equation (Eq. 5) to revise the prior probability assignments to the hypotheses. The original decision is then reevaluated with the posterior probabilities (Figure 9). The result of the experiment is uncertain when the decision to experiment is made; consequently, the value of experimentation must be computed as an expectation over the possible posterior decision situations. The situation can be diagramed in tree form as shown in Figure 9.

The analysis for two experimental seedings is given in Table 2 (25). The values assumed above for the government responsibility costs have been used. The expected value of the experiment in improving one operational seeding decision is \$5.39 million, slightly less than twice the value of a single experimental seeding and more than ten times the assumed experimental cost, \$0.50 million. This value represents 4.7 percent of the expected

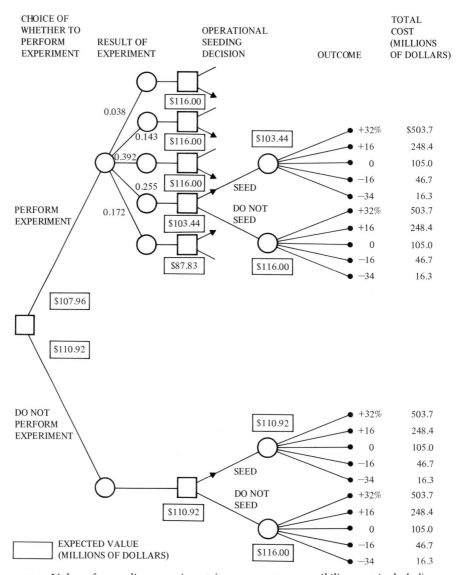

| CHOICE OF WHETHER TO PERFORM EXPERIMENT | RESULT OF EXPERIMENT | OPERATIONAL SEEDING DECISION | OUTCOME | TOTAL COST (MILLIONS OF DOLLARS) |

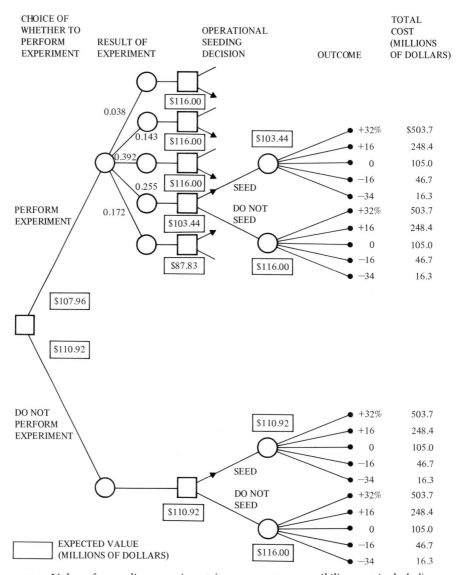

FIG. 9 *Value of a seeding experiment (government responsibility cost included).*

property damage if the alternative of not seeding is taken. In the discrete version used in the analysis, one of five possible values (see Table 1) is taken as representative of the observed change in hurricane intensity over a 12-hour period following seeding: −34, −16, 0, +16, and +32 percent. The order in which the results are obtained is not significant, and a total of 15 pairs of results could be obtained with two experiments (Table 2). These pairs might be placed in three groups: favorable, unfavorable, and mixed results. The probability of obtaining a pair of favorable results (-34, -34; -34, -16; -34, 0; and -16, -16 percent) (26) in the two experimental seedings is .327; a pair of results in this group would provide substantial confirmation of hypothesis H_1.

TABLE 2 EVALUATION OF A FUTURE EXPERIMENT WITH TWO (INDEPENDENT) EXPERIMENTAL SEEDINGS. GOVERNMENT RESPONSIBILITY COST IS INCLUDED.

Observed change in wind speed		Prior probability of observation	Posterior probability of hypotheses			Subsequent operational seeding decision expected values (million dollars)		
u_1	u_2		H_1	H_2	H_3	Loss with seeding alternative	Loss with the better alternative	Posterior value of perfect information
-34	-34	.0441	.97	.03	<.005	79.87	79.87	0.80
-34	-16	.1009	.89	.11	<.005	84.67	84.67	2.68
-34	0	.1140	.77	.22	<.005	92.11	92.11	5.64
-16	-16	.0684	.69	.30	<.005	97.08	97.08	7.53
		.3274						
-34	$+16$	.0324	.65	.34	.01	100.16	100.16	9.06
-34	$+32$	.0078	.60	.37	.03	105.27	105.27	12.10
-16	0	.1915	.49	.51	.01	110.25	110.25	12.78
-16	$+16$	.0651	.34	.64	.02	120.07	116.00	13.05
0	0	.1610	.28	.70	.02	123.37	116.00	10.81
-16	$+32$	.0167	.29	.65	.06	126.05	116.00	11.15
0	$+16$	.1229	.18	.79	.03	131.35	116.00	6.78
		.5974						
0	$+32$	.0332	.14	.77	.09	138.02	116.00	5.51
$+16$	$+16$	.0251	.10	.83	.07	138.62	116.00	3.98
$+16$	$+32$	.0145	.08	.75	.17	148.37	116.00	3.02
$+32$	$+32$	.0024	.05	.59	.36	165.72	116.00	1.98
		.0752						

Value of seeding decision with prior information	110.92
Expected value of seeding decision with seeding experiments	105.53
Value of experiment	5.39
Cost of experiment	0.50
Net expected value of experiment	4.89

For example, a repetition of the pair of results obtained with Debbie in 1969 (−34, −16 percent in the discrete approximation) would lead to posterior probabilities of .89 for H_1, .11 for H_2, and less than .005 for H_3. A probability of .075 is computed for a pair of strongly unfavorable results (0, +16; +32; +16, +16; +16, +32; +32, +32 percent); in this case the probability assigned to H_1 would be revised strongly downward. The remaining mixed pairs of results do not significantly confirm or deny H_1, and these results have a total probability of .595. Within this group a small probability (.055) is accorded to conflicting results in the two experiments (−34, +16; −34, +32; −16, +16; −16, +32 percent).

ANOTHER APPROACH TO DETERMINING THE VALUE OF SEEDING EXPERIMENTS

The preceding discussion indicates that the value of experiments is sensitive to the government responsibility costs that are assumed in the analysis. We may wish to determine the value of experiments in a different manner in which the issue of government responsibility is treated implicitly.

Suppose that operational seeding will be permitted only after another successful result is obtained in a pair of experiments of the Debbie type. This approximation gives a lower bound to the value of experiments because only a successful experimental result is regarded as valuable. Even if wind reductions are not observed, knowledge gained about the effects of seeding may have implications for future successful operational seeding.

The probability of a favorable pair of results in two experimental seedings of a hurricane was computed as .327. If favorable experimental results are obtained and a subsequent hurricane is seeded operationally, the expected reduction in property-damage losses is $37.88 million. Even if government responsibility costs are included, the reduction in expected losses is $26.80 million. Since these reductions occur with a probability of .327, the expected value of the experiment in improving one operational decision is $12.40 million if only the property damage is considered and $8.77 million if the decrease in property damage is partially offset by the government responsibility costs. The figures $8.77 million and $12.40 million represent 7.6 and 10.7 percent, respectively, of the $116-million property damage expected from the not-seeding alternative in the seeding decision for the nominal hurricane.

We see that the value of experiments is considerably higher than the values computed earlier. This difference results from the high responsibility costs implicit in the decision not to seed on the basis of present information. It may be a reasonable assumption that a bad outcome for the first seeding of a hurricane threatening a coastal area would have much less severe legal and social consequences if it were preceded by another successful experiment. Therefore, lowering the government responsibility costs may be appropriate after another successful field experiment.

GENERALIZING THE VALUE OF ADDITIONAL INFORMATION

The preceding discussions are directed specifically toward updating our information about which hypothesis, H_1, H_2, or H_3, describes the effect of seeding on the maximum sustained wind speed of a hurricane. The analysis has been done for a single seeding decision for a moderately intense hurricane threatening a coastal area. Perfect information applies not only to a single hurricane but to all hurricanes that might be seeded operationally. The numerical results for the single nominal hurricane are summarized in the extreme left column of Table 3 and are extended to multiple hurricanes in the remaining columns.

Even if only half the hurricanes could be seeded because of tactical considerations having to do with precipitation, hurricane trajectory, and so on, the expected annual benefit from perfect information is $26 million. If we assume that only half the hurricanes could be seeded and discount the expected benefits of perfect information for all future hurricane seasons at a discount rate of 7 percent, we arrive at $370 million. This figure represents

TABLE 3 SUMMARY OF THE VALUE OF ADDITIONAL INFORMATION ON THE EFFECT OF SEEDING. ONLY THE 50 PERCENT OF HURRICANES THAT ARE ASSUMED TO BE POSSIBLE CANDIDATES FOR SEEDING ON THE BASIS OF TACTICAL CONSIDERATIONS ARE CONSIDERED. IF ALL HURRICANES ARE ASSUMED TO BE CANDIDATES FOR OPERATIONAL SEEDING, THE FIGURES OF THE LAST TWO COLUMNS SHOULD BE DOUBLED.

Item	Nominal hurricane used in analysis		Single hurricane season (million dollars)	All future hurricane seasons, discounted at 7% (million dollars)
	Million dollars	Percentage		
Expected property damage without seeding	116.0	100	220.0	3142
Expected value of perfect information	13.6	11.8	26.0	370
Expected value of a field experiment consisting of two experimental seedings	5.4	4.7	10.2	146
Expected value of field experiments:*				
With government responsibility costs	8.8	7.6	16.6	238
Government responsibility costs = 0	12.4	10.7	23.5	335

* If it is assumed that prior operational seeding is not permitted.

the value of a "perfect" experiment that would determine whether H_1 is true.

A single repetition of the 1969 Hurricane Debbie experiment has an expected value of $5.39 million in the context of the nominal hurricane, or about 4.7 percent of expected property damage. For the decision to seed a single hurricane in the billion-dollar range, the expected value of the experiment is ten times as high, about $50 million. For one hurricane season the value is 4.7 percent of $220 million, or $10.2 million (it is assumed again that various tactical considerations might preclude seeding in half of the cases). For all future hurricane seasons, with a discount rate of 7 percent, the value is $146 million compared with an experimental cost of about $500,000. The benefit to cost ratio is therefore about 300. Even if only a single hurricane season is considered, the expected benefits are 20 times greater than the cost of the experiment and ten times the present annual budget for Project Stormfury.

EXPERIMENTAL CAPABILITY DECISION
The occurrence of hurricanes is a random phenomenon. Therefore, it is uncertain whether there will be an opportunity for an experimental seeding before the arrival of a threatening storm that might be operationally seeded. Opportunities for experimental seeding have been scarce. In the last few years there have been only six experimental seedings, and these have been conducted on three hurricanes, Esther (1961), Beulah (1963), and Debbie (1969) (7). Experimental seedings have been limited to a small region of the Atlantic Ocean accessible to aircraft based in Puerto Rico, and few hurricanes have passed through this region.

There are many other regions of the ocean where hurricanes might be found that satisfy the present criterion for experimental seeding—that is, the hurricane will be seeded only if the probability is less than .10 that it will come within 50 miles of a populated land area within 18 hours after seeding. However, a decision to expand the present experimental capability of Project Stormfury would need to be made well before the experiment itself. Whereas the seeding itself requires only that an aircraft be fitted with silver iodide pyrotechnic generators, the monitoring of the subsequent development of the hurricane requires other aircraft fitted with the appropriate instrumentation. The requirements in equipment, crew training, and communications and support facilities are substantial. In addition, permission may be needed from nations whose shores might be threatened by the seeded hurricane. The experimental decision, then, involves an investment in the capability to perform an experimental seeding. Whether an experiment is performed depends on the uncertain occurrences of hurricanes in the experimental areas.

The expected time before another experimental opportunity for Project Stormfury's present capability is about one full hurricane season. There was no opportunity during 1970. Preliminary estimates of the cost of a capability to seed hurricanes in the Pacific are about $1 million (27). The incidence of experimentally seedable hurricanes in the Pacific appears to be more than twice that in the Atlantic (28). Therefore, it appears advisable to develop a capability to conduct experimental hurricane seeding in the Pacific Ocean since the benefits expected from this capability outweigh the costs by a factor of at least 5 (29).

CONCLUSIONS FROM THE ANALYSIS

The decision to seed a hurricane imposes a great responsibility on public officials. This decision cannot be avoided because inaction is equivalent to a decision not to permit seeding. Either the government must accept the responsibility of a seeding that may be perceived by the public as deleterious, or it must accept the responsibility for not seeding and thereby exposing the public to higher probabilities of severe storm damage.

Our report to the National Oceanic and Atmospheric Administration recommended that seeding be permitted on an emergency basis. We hope that further experimental results and a formal analysis of the tactical decision to seed a particular hurricane will precede the emergency. However, a decision may be required before additional experimental or analytical results are available. A hurricane with the intensity of Camille threatening a populous coastal area of the United States would confront public officials with an agonizing but unavoidable choice.

The decision to seed hurricanes can not be resolved on strictly scientific grounds. It is a complex decision whose uncertain consequences affect many people. Appropriate legal and political institutions should be designated for making the hurricane-seeding decision, and further analysis should be conducted to support these institutions in carrying out their work.

ROLE OF DECISION ANALYSIS

The results of a decision analysis depend on the information available at the time it is performed. Decision analysis should not be used to arrive at a static recommendation to be verified by further research, rather it should be used as a dynamic tool for making necessary decisions at any time. Various sensitivity analyses included here indicate how new information might be expected to influence policy recommendations. However, the advent of a severe hurricane will necessitate a decision on the basis of the information then available.

The analysis of hurricane modification points up a difficulty that is common in public decision-making on complex technological issues. When the consequences of deploying new technology are uncertain, who will make the choice? While many individuals or groups may share responsibility, decision analysis conceptually separates the roles of the executive decision-maker, the expert, and the analyst. The analyst's role is to structure a complex problem in a tractable manner so that the uncertain consequences of the alternative actions may be assessed. Various experts provide the technical information from which the analysis is fashioned. The decision-maker acts for society in providing the basis for choosing among the alternatives. The analysis provides a mechanism for integration and communication so that the technical judgments of the experts and the value judgments of the decision-maker may be seen in relation to each other, examined, and debated. Decision analysis makes not only the decision but the decision process a matter of formal record. For any complex decision that may affect the lives of millions, a decision analysis showing explicitly the uncertainties and decision criteria can and should be carried out.

REFERENCES AND NOTES

1. R. H. Simpson and J. S. Malkus, *Sci. Amer.* **211,** 27 (Dec. 1964).

2. R. C. Gentry, *Science* **168,** 473 (1970).

3. Now incorporated in the National Oceanic and Atmospheric Administration.

4. R. A. Howard, *Proceedings of the Fourth International Conference on Operational Research* (Wiley, New York, 1966).

5. ———, *IEEE Trans. Syst. Sci. Cybern. 4* (1968), p. 211.

6. A detailed discussion of the research is to be found in the project's final report [D. W. Boyd, R. A. Howard, J. E. Matheson, D. W. North, *Decision Analysis of Hurricane Modification* (Project 8503, Stanford Research Institute, Menlo Park, Calif., 1971)]. This report is available through the National Technical Information Service, U.S. Department of Commerce, Washington, D.C., accession number COM-71-00784.

7. The meteorological information leading to this approximation is discussed in detail in the SRI project final report (6), especially appendix B. Meteorologists connected with Project Stormfury believe it highly improbable that seeding will cause any substantial change in the course of the hurricane, and other important consequences of seeding are not foreseen at this time. We wish to stress that our role in the decision analysis of hurricane modification has been to provide the methodology for analyzing a complex decision with uncertain consequences. The specific assumptions have been provided by the hurricane meteorologists associated with Project Stormfury and by other experts in relevant fields. Because of space limitations these assumptions cannot be discussed in detail in this article; the interested reader is advised to consult the project's final report or communicate directly with the authors. The type of seeding is assumed to be the same as that used in the Hurricane Debbie experiments: massive multiple seeding of the clouds in the outer eyewall region with silver iodide. During September 1971, Project Stormfury conducted seeding experiments of a different type on Hurricane Ginger (R. C. Gentry, internal communication, National Oceanic and Atmospheric Administration, October 1971). The Ginger experiment involved the seeding of clouds in the rain bands well outside the eyewall region. This "rainsector" experiment was selected because Ginger had a large and poorly formed eyewall and was judged not to be a good subject for eyewall-region seeding. Although some changes in cloud structure and wind field occurred at a time when they might have been caused by seeding, these changes were minor compared with the dramatic changes that occurred in Hurricane Debbie after seeding. Because of the difference in type of seeding, the Ginger results do not imply a need for revision of the analysis or data presented in this article.

8. In some hurricanes, such as Diane (1955) and Camille (1969), precipitation-induced inland flooding has also been an important cause of property damage. Seeding might cause some increase in precipitation. In considering the policy decision to permit seeding we ignored these precipitation effects, but they might sometimes be important in the decision to seed a specific hurricane.

9. Throughout the analysis it is assumed that seeding would be authorized and carried out by some agency of the federal government.

10. C. Holliday, *Technical Memorandum WBTM SR-45* (Environmental Science Service Administration, Washington, D.C., 1969).

11. The details of the derivation of this probability distribution are given in appendix B of (6). The indirect approach of using the Holliday relation combined with pressure-change observations was first suggested by R. C. Sheets of the National Hurricane Research Laboratory.

12. S. L. Rosenthal, *Technical Memorandum ERLTM-NHRL 88* (Environmental Science Service Administration, Washington, D.C., 1970). See also *Project Stormfury Annual Report 1970* (National Hurricane Reseach Laboratory, Miami, 1971).

13. A probability distribution on an uncertain quantity x will be denoted $P(x)$ whether x takes on discrete or continuous values. If x is discrete, $P(x)$ will be the probability mass function; if x is continuous, $P(x)$ will be the probability density function. A probability distribution of the normal or Gaussian family specified by its mean m and standard deviation σ will be denoted $f_N(m, \sigma)$.

14. The average effect of seeding and the fluctuation from the average may be regarded as (independent) normal random variables whose sum represents the effect of seeding on a specific hurricane. According to well-known results in probability theory, this sum will be normally distributed with a mean equal to the sum of the two means and a standard deviation equal to the square root of the sum of the squares of the two standard deviations.

15. The effect of seeding and the natural change in the storm are described as independent normal random variables and the total change is their sum. The independence assumption is judged an appropriate summary of present knowledge; sensitivity to this assumption is examined in (6). Important assumptions such as this one were reviewed with Project Stormfury meteorologists. A letter to us from R. C. Gentry (October 1970) stated, "while seeding may affect different hurricanes by different amounts, we are not yet prepared to predict these differences." The assumption of independence does not deny that there may be a relationship between the natural change occurring in a hurricane and the effect of modification. When information about this relationship becomes available, it should be incorporated into the analysis and the independence assumption should be withdrawn.

16. H. Raiffa, *Decision Analysis: Introductory Lectures on Choices Under Uncertainty* (Addison-Wesley, Reading, Mass., 1968); M. Tribus, *Rational Descriptions, Decisions, and Designs* (Pergamon, New York, 1969).

17. D. W. North, *IEEE Trans. Syst. Sci. Cybern. 4* (1968), p. 200.

18. The details of the calculation of c_2 are given in (6). Similar relationships between maximum sustained wind speed and property damage have been stated by other investigators [R. L. Hendrick and D. G. Friedman, in *Human Dimensions in Weather Modification*, W. R. Derrick Sewell, Ed. (Univ. of Chicago Press, Chicago, 1966), pp. 227–246]. In November 1971, D. G. Friedman communicated to us some results from analyzing insurance claim data. He finds an exponent of 6.7; this value would lead to much larger reductions in property damage than were assumed in our analysis. Other investigators have suggested an equation of the form $d = c_1(w - w_0)^2$, where c_1 and w_0 are empirical constants (R. C. Gentry, private communication). This equation would give results essentially equivalent to ours.

19. This procedure is an approximation, which depends on the fact that seeding costs are small compared with costs of property damage.

20. It is shown in (6) that the results are not sensitive to the discrete approximation.

21. For example, if an exponential utility function with a risk aversion coefficient of $\gamma = 0.001$ is used, the difference between the certain equivalents for the two alternatives increases from $21.67 million to $24.2 million. Because of stochastic dominance, any risk attitude will always leave seeding as the preferred alternative. Further discussion on risk preference may be found in (5) and (17).

22. These issues are discussed in detail in appendixes E and F of (6).

23. In answering this question we assume that the government is willing to pay up to $1 to avoid $1 of property damage.

24. It is possible for the responsibility costs to be so high that a hurricane would not be seeded even if it were certain that H_1 is true. This amount of responsibility cost implies that the government would prefer an unseeded hurricane to a seeded hurricane that caused only half as much property damage.

25. For these calculations a system of computer programs for evaluating large decision trees, developed by W. Rousseau of Stanford Research Institute, was used.

26. These discrete outcomes correspond to a reduction of 10 percent or more. The discrete approximation simplifies the analysis by restricting the number of possible experimental results. Earlier we considered the revision of probabilites based on the results of the 1969 Hurricane Debbie experiments. There the discrete approximation was not used, but it would have given equivalent results.

27. R. C. Gentry, personal communication. In arriving at this figure it was assumed that military aircraft based in the Pacific could be used in the seeding.

28. *Project Stormfury Annual Report 1968* (National Hurricane Research Laboratory, Miami, 1969).

29. The details of this calculation are given in (6).

30. This article summarizes research performed for the National Oceanic and Atmospheric Administration, U.S. Department of Commerce, contract 0–35172; the project leader is D. W. North. The authors acknowledge the substantial contribution of Dr. Dean W. Boyd. The authors also wish to acknowledge Professor Gary Widman of Hastings College of the Law, University of California, San Francisco, for legal research supporting the project and Dr. Cecil Gentry, Dr. Robert Simpson, Dr. Joanne Simpson, and many others who have been associated with Project Stormfury for their assistance and cooperation. The findings and conclusions presented are the sole responsibility of the authors and do not necessarily reflect the views of the U.S. government or any of the individuals mentioned above.

LETTERS

Seeding hurricanes

Howard, Matheson, and North, in their article "The decision to seed hurricanes" (16 June, p. 1191), provide a good framework for an initial consideration of this important subject. They do not, however, include the effect of seeding on the hurricane rainfall rate—only the effects on the maximum sustained wind and on the wind-related storm tide.

While these latter effects may be paramount for coastal areas, in the light of the floods that accompanied hurricane Agnes, the storm rainfall should also be considered a decision factor when further studies are made of the seeding of hurricanes that threaten coastal areas. As seeding could conceivably increase the storm rainfall, both at the coastline and inland, the increased damage from flooding would then have to be balanced against the hoped-for reduction in damage from wind and storm tide.

Research on the control of hurricane direction, as well as on the reduction of wind intensity, appears indicated. If directional control were feasible—and, for example, some control of the rate of release of latent heat in different storm sectors is technically available now—this would be an attractive option in the case of storms approaching coastal areas.

The question of loss of life in seeded hurricanes, not covered in the article, must eventually be faced. The parallel question of seeding in war (News and Comment, 16 June, p. 1216), could also benefit from the same kind of rational and orderly analysis as that begun by Howard *et al.* To be fully useful, a study should attempt to separate the military from the civil

Reprinted with permission from *Science*, Vol. 179 (February 23, 1973), pp. 744–747. Copyright © 1973 by the American Association for the Advancement of Science.

effects, and the value judgments should be founded on an analysis of war as a moral problem.

BERNARD A. POWER
255 Touzin Avenue,
Dorval, Qu°bec, Canada

The article by Howard, Matheson, and North is an elegant decision-making analysis (within a Bayesian framework) that considers the consequences of both property damage and government responsibility of seeding versus nonseeding of hurricanes in terms of change in maximum sustained surface wind. Within this somewhat constrained analysis (surface wind as a surrogate for a complex physical phenomenon, property damage, and government responsibility are the only effects considered), a thorough range of possible outcomes is examined, including the three key hypotheses that seeding is beneficial, ineffective, or detrimental to the goal of reducing the social cost of hurricanes. The central conclusion is that "On the basis of present information, the probability of severe damage is less if a hurricane is seeded" and that seeding should be permitted on an emergency basis and encouraged on an experimental basis. But beyond this recommendation, the analysis itself is suggested as a model for "any complex decision that may affect the lives of millions, a decision analysis showing explicitly the uncertainties and decision criteria [that] can and should be carried out."

Among social scientists working at the boundaries of atmospheric science, the Howard *et al.* analysis has been received with critical enthusiasm. Some 6 years ago, along with Sewell, I suggested a process of analyzing social impacts akin to this analysis (*1*) and undertook with Julian and Sewell (*2*) a modest field survey to determine the expectations of leading atmospheric scientists about the viability of a range of weather modification technologies.

In the spirit of decision analysis, I question the use of the Howard *et al.* analysis and offer three alternative hypotheses to be used in the context of the current social, political, and scientific milieu when such questions as the decision to seed hurricanes are being dealt with.

1) Hypothesis H_1. Decision analysis is a rational method of analysis that systematically precludes in nonrandom fashion significant aspects of the problem, because these aspects are either not known, poorly understood, have low a priori estimates of probability, or seem inappropriate to the terms of reference.

2) Hypothesis H_2. Decision analysis is a rational method of analysis which will be used in an "arational" way.

3) Hypothesis H_3. Decision analysis is a rational method of analysis employed rationally for amoral purposes.

The first hypothesis emphasizes the problem of where to make the cut in systems analysis. Howard *et al.* have so constrained their analysis as to ignore the beneficial and detrimental effects of hurricanes on the water balance of the areas affected (*3*). They also seem unaware of the counterintuitive effects, well documented from other forms of hazard control (*4*), in which the knowledge of seeding may increase the damage toll by influencing negatively other human responses, such as evacuation, preventive measures, and so forth. And there is no mention of the low-probability outcomes, for example, the potentially negative environmental impacts of large-scale injection of silver iodide particles into the atmosphere. Such analyses are always constrained by time, effort, and imagination and must systematically exclude many considerations. And indeed many are missing from the article.

Under the second hypothesis, the use of the analysis serves as justification for decisions made on other more transscientific grounds. Thus if a decision is taken on the basis of considerations extraneous to the analysis (for example, the bureaucratic ambition of an organization for its own growth), will "arational" analysis be used to buttress the decision and give an unwarranted gloss of respectability? How often are even negative results ignored in such cases, with the comforting statement, "Oh, we had Stanford Research Institute carefully study the question." The precedents for this misuse are ample. The most extensive use of rational analysis to date, benefit-cost analysis in water resource development (less elegant than decision analysis, but relevant nonetheless) has served for 35 years to justify a program of water resource development that many feel has served the public less well than it could have if such analysis had been absent (*5*). In another instance of rational analysis, the results of cloud-seeding experiments in Texas, Arizona, and Florida were quickly used to justify operational cloud-seeding programs before adequate control experiments were made in dry periods.

As for the final hypothesis, one need only follow the recent reports in *Science* (News and Comment, 16 June, p. 1216; 21 July, p. 239; 1 Sept., p. 776; 13 Oct., p. 144) concerning the massive use of environmental modification, including weather control, in Southeast Asia to consider that the experience gained in peaceful geophysical modification can be quickly turned to other purposes less helpful to mankind.

To the extent that any one of these hypotheses is valid, the social scientist committed both to rational analysis and to responsibility for his or her actions is in a dilemma. If the limits of the analysis or its possible misuse are great, would society be better off without it? I think in some cases the answer must be yes, as much in social science as in new technology. Indeed to the extent that social science becomes important (that is, people really take it seriously) social scientists must be as self-critical and responsible about their methods and their possible abuse and misuse as technologists should be about their inventions. In some cases where uncertainty is very great, it may be as irresponsible to advocate a decision-making methodology that does nothing to really reduce the uncertainty or to control its use as it is to build an SST. At the very least, until we can take into account both the limits and unintended use of decision analysis, we should be cautious in its advocacy. And in areas of great scientific unknowns, such as weather modification, where heavy pressure exists for its "arational" use and some pressure for its amoral use, extreme caution is indicated.

ROBERT W. KATES
Graduate School of Geography,
Clark University,
Worcester, Massachusetts 01610

References

1. R. W. Kates and W. R. D. Sewell, *Human Dimensions of Weather Modification* (Department of Geography Research Paper No. 105, University of Chicago, Chicago, 1966), pp. 347–362.
2. P. R. Julian, R. W. Kates, W. R. D. Sewell, *Water Resour. Res.* 5, 215 (1969).
3. L. M. Hartman, D. Hilland, M. Giddings, *ibid.*, p. 555.
4. Taskforce on Federal Flood Control Policy, *A Unified National Program for Managing Flood Losses,* House Document 465, 89th Congr., 2nd sess. (Government Printing Office, Washington, D.C., 1966).
5. G. F. White, in *Water Research*, A. V. Kneese and S. C. Smith, Eds. (Johns Hopkins Press, Baltimore, Md., 1966), pp. 251–273.

Power is correct in suggesting that rainfall and steering effects are important issues in hurricane seeding. Another important factor is storm tide, which can be affected significantly by coastal geography. These effects might be of critical importance in the tactical decision to seed a particular hurricane. As the full report referenced in our article shows, present knowledge concerning these factors is consistent with our strategic recommendation to permit, as an emergency measure, the seeding of some hurricanes threatening a coastal area.

It is possible to conduct a decision analysis to determine the value of research on hurricane steering. However, our discussions with meteorologists have indicated that while the ability to steer hurricanes would be valuable, this ability is unlikely to result from a research program. Consequently, it is not clear that the decision analysis of steering research would demonstrate that the research has a high value.

On the question of loss of life, we found that, given the effective hurricane warnings provided by the U.S. Weather Service, the expected number of lives lost in a present-day hurricane is relatively small. If these lives are valued for decision-making purposes in a range from $100,000 to $300,000 each, they constitute an expected loss of only about one-tenth the expected property damage for the hurricane. Furthermore, since storms that damage less property also tend to kill fewer people, the case for removing the prohibition against seeding is only strengthened by including human loss.

We direct our commentary on Kates's letter to the three hypotheses he suggests for the nature of decision analysis.

Hypothesis H_1 is that decision analysis systematically excludes significant aspects of the problem because they are uncertain or improbable. Anyone familiar with decision analysis knows that its procedures involve not excluding, but discovering and emphasizing, significant aspects of the problem. In fact, decision analysis is uniquely concerned with assessing probabilities and their implications. Kates presents no evidence that our recommendations would be changed by additional analysis of any of the factors he mentions.

Hypothesis H_2 is that decision analysis might be misused. We agree that anything from hammers to medicine may be misused, but we find no logical argument that they should be unused. Moreover, Kates presents no evidence that our hurricane analysis has been or will be misused.

Hypothesis H_3 is that decision analysis might be used for amoral purposes. Presuming that amoral means immoral, we can only reiterate that the fact that hammers and medicine can be instruments of crime is no argument for discontinuing their production. Kates presents no evidence that our analysis has been or will be used for immoral purposes.

But Kates's hypotheses do not form a collectively exhaustive set. We would like to include a fourth hypothesis, H_4: Decision analysis is a rational method for displaying and balancing the important uncertain, complex, and dynamic factors that surround a decision. We leave it to others to judge whether this hypothesis is supported by our work.

RONALD A. HOWARD
Department of Engineering–Economic Systems, Stanford University, Stanford, California 94301

JAMES E. MATHESON
D. WARNER NORTH
Decision Analysis Group, Stanford Research Institute, Menlo Park, California 94025

Hurricane seeding analysis

In the article "The decision to seed hurricanes" by Howard *et al.* (*1*) it is stated in the subtitle that "On the basis of present information, the probability of severe damage is less if a hurricane is seeded." In my opinion present

Reprinted with permission from *Science*, Vol. 181 (September 14, 1973), pp. 1072–1073. Copyright © 1973 by the American Associatiion for the Advancement of Science.

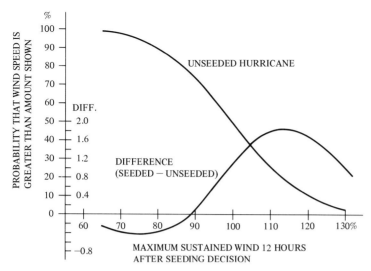

FIG. 1 *Probability distribution on 12-hour wind changes for the unseeded hurricane, and the difference in probability distributions between the seeded and the unseeded hurricane.*

knowledge does not support such a statement because the results of studies of this problem do not provide a unique answer. Consequently, no conclusions can presently be made about the economic effects resulting from seeding hurricanes.

The data available from seeding experiments (such as those from Hurricane Debbie and possibly Hurricane Ginger) are too few for a statistical analysis to yield confident conclusions. Furthermore, the results of the numerical model studies referred to by Howard *et al.* conflict with results which I reported (*2*). In fact, if the method of Howard *et al.* is applied to my results, the conclusion reached is the opposite of that reached by Howard *et al.*, as I show in Fig. 1.

The standard deviations adopted here are the same as those in Howard *et al.* for all three hypotheses concerning the effect of seeding (H_1, reduction of the maximum wind; H_2, no effect; H_3, increase of the maximum wind). The probability distribution for the wind speed if the hurricane is seeded, w', if H_2 is true, is the same as that of Howard *et al.* (*3*):

$$P'(w'|H_2) = P(w'|H_2) = P(w) = f_N(100\%, 15.6\%) \qquad (1)$$

where w is the wind speed of the unseeded hurricane (*4*).

Using the results of the numerical experiments presented in (*2*) I assign the following probability distribution to w' for the case that H_3 is true

$$P'(w'|H_3) = f_N'(107\%, 18.6\%) \qquad (2)$$

The probability distribution employed for w', if it is considered that H_1 is true, is

$$P'(w'|H_1) = f_N'(95\%, 18.6\%) \tag{3}$$

Therefore the probability density function for the Debbie results, if hypothesis H_i is true, now becomes

$$P'(69\%, 85\%|H_i) = \begin{cases} 1.4996 & i = 1 \\ 0.5716 & i = 2 \\ 0.2827 & i = 3 \end{cases} \tag{4}$$

Now, considering the deductions made in (2)—on the basis of physical reasoning and the results of numerical model experiments which definitely indicate an effect of intensification by seeding—I assign the pre-Debbie probabilities

$$P'(H_1) = .0227$$
$$P'(H_2) = .7500 \tag{5}$$
$$P'(H_3) = .2273$$

whereas in Howard *et al.* the corresponding set is

$$P(H_1) = .15$$
$$P(H_2) = .75$$
$$P(H_3) = .10$$

Hence, the pre-Debbie odds that seeding has no effect are the same in set 5 as in Howard *et al.* However, $P'(H_3)$ is taken to be one order of magnitude larger than $P'(H_1)$ to reflect that, if seeding affects the intensity at all, an increase of the maximum wind is expected.

When sets 4 and 5 are introduced in Bayes' equation the posterior probabilities become

$$P'(H_1) = .0647$$
$$P'(H_2) = .8131 \tag{6}$$
$$P'(H_3) = .1222$$

whereas in Howard *et al.*

$$P(H_1) = .49$$
$$P(H_2) = .49$$
$$P(H_3) = .02$$

Set 6 implies that, since the Debbie results, the odds are about 4 to 1 that seeding has no effect, and if seeding does have an effect the odds are 2 to 1 for wind intensification rather than wind reduction.

Finally, I can compute the probability distribution on wind speed [from Eqs. 1, 2, 3, and 6 above and equation 4 in (1)]. The difference in probability between the seeding and not-seeding alternatives is so small that it is hard to show it in a plot of the complementary cumulative distribution functions of those two alternatives. Instead, I plot this function for the not-seeding alternative and the difference (the function for seeding minus the function for not-seeding) in Figure 1. I find that the probability for intensification (wind speed more than 100 percent of the initial wind speed) if a hurricane is seeded is .511; if the hurricane is not seeded the probability is .500 [in (1) these values are .36 and .50, respectively]. The probability of intensification by 10 percent or more is .278 if a hurricane is seeded and .261 if it is not seeded [.18 and .26, respectively, in (1)].

Furthermore, for any particular wind speed larger than 88 percent of its initial value, the probability that this speed will be exceeded is greater if the hurricane is seeded than if it is not seeded. For wind speeds less than 88 percent of their initial values the situation is reversed; however, the difference in this interval is much smaller in magnitude than it is in the former interval.

Since the analysis given above may be considered to be as soundly based as that in (1), it shows that the available data are too sparse to yield a statistical basis for conclusive statements. I suggest that the method of statistical analysis (possibly somewhat modified) should be used to investigate the requirements on reliability and volume of results from model studies and field experiments in order to permit confident conclusions and recommendations.

HILDING SUNDQVIST
Institute of Meteorology, University of Stockholm
Stockholm 19, Sweden

References and notes

1. R. A. Howard, J. E. Matheson, D. W. North, *Science* **176**, 1191 (1972).

2. H. Sundqvist, *Tellus* **24** (No. 1), 6 (1972).

3. The same notation is used here as in (1). For convenience, some of the data given in (1) are repeated; the probabilities from that article are designated by P and those of the treatment given here by P'.

4. As in Howard *et al.* [reference 13 in (1)] a probability distribution on a quantity x is denoted $P(x)$, and a probability distribution of the normal or Gaussian family specified by its mean m and standard deviation σ is denoted $f_N(m, \sigma)$.

31 October 1972; revised 1 June 1973

In the concluding section of our article we stated: "The results of a decision analysis depend on the information available at the time it is performed. Decision analysis should not be used to arrive at a static recommendation to be verified by further research, rather it should be used as a dynamic tool for making necessary decisions at any time." We are pleased that Sundqvist finds our analysis a useful format in which to present his views regarding the results of hurricane modification. He has succinctly summarized his opinion in the form of a prior probability distribution and then used the Debbie experimental results to develop consequent probability distributions for the wind speed, both with and without seeding. His pre-Debbie probability assignment was that there was a 75 percent chance of no seeding effect, and that if there were an effect, the odds were 10 to 1 that it would be deleterious. The Debbie experiment is not sufficient to overcome this pessimistic prior probability distribution: a decision-maker who subscribed to Sundqvist's view would not wish to attempt operational hurricane seeding at this time.

Our analysis was based on the best information we could obtain from U.S. hurricane modification experts. As decision analysts we cannot comment on Sundqvist's differing opinion, except to say that our information sources were aware of his work and did not subscribe to his views. Further dialogue between Sundqvist and the community of U.S. hurricane modification experts would be appropriate to determine whether the latter see any new reason to modify their judgments.

RONALD A. HOWARD
Department of Engineering–Economic Systems, Stanford University, Stanford, California 94305

JAMES E. MATHESON
D. WARNER NORTH
Decision Analysis Group, Stanford Research Institute, Menlo Park, California 94025

A CASE STUDY OF GRADUATE ADMISSIONS: APPLICATION OF THREE PRINCIPLES OF HUMAN DECISION MAKING[1]

ROBYN M. DAWES[2]

Applications for postgraduate education are growing at an ever-increasing rate; the Council of Graduate Schools estimates that there were slightly over 7 million such applications last year.[3] This application rate has forced almost all graduate departments to be selective in their admissions, with ratios of applicants to admitted students ranging as high as 50 or 100:1 for some of the "top" graduate departments. The criteria used for selection are usually undergraduate grades, aptitude test scores, and letters of recommendation; these criteria are often combined in some inexplicit way by the admissions committee of the department, and some resulting rate or ranking of the applicants is used to invite them until the department's quota of first-year students is filled. Occasionally, a department (or an individual concerned with admissions procedures) will do an empirical study to determine which if any of these criteria predict some outcome variable—such as graduate grades, attainment of a PhD, faculty ratings of promise, salary, or future productivity. These studies have revealed disappointing predictive validity for the standard admissions criteria (cf. Hoyt, 1966; Hyman, 1957; Lannholm, 1968; Mehrabian, 1969; Newman, 1968; Platz, McClintock, & Katz, 1959; Rawls, Rawls, & Harrison, 1969; Robertson & Hall, 1964; Robertson & Nielsen, 1961; Sedlacek & Hutchins, 1966; Tully, 1962; Watters & Patterson, 1953).

The focus of the present article is not on the validity of the usual selection criteria considered singly—which on purely logical grounds can be expected to be low.[4] Rather, the focus is on the way in which these criteria are combined by the members of admissions committees in order to reach an overall rating of the applicant. Reaching such an overall evaluation has

From *American Psychologist*, Vol. 26, No. 2 (February 1971), pp. 180–188. Copyright © 1971 by the American Psychological Association. Reprinted by permission.

been studied extensively in the domains of psychological and medical diagnosis. Certain principles established in those domains can be applied *mutatis mutandis* to the decision-making problem of evaluating graduate applicants. This article outlines and discusses three major principles that have been established by previous studies, and shows how these principles can be applied to the admissions decisions of one department of psychology over the past several years. The result is a case study, in that only one department's actions are studied. It may, however, be of general interest— because two of the principles to be discussed have previously been established by a large body of literature, and their applications to this particular department's admissions decisions demonstrate how they could be profitably applied to the decisions of other departments. Thus, the present report differs in two important respects from previous articles; first, it is concerned with the decision-making process, rather than with the validities of the criteria on which the decision is based. Second, the predictions tested in the article are derived from past theory and research.

This theory and research concern the ways in which psychologists combine information to arrive at psychological diagnoses and predictions. (These psychologists have been studied by other psychologists.) The initial focus of this work was on the question of whether psychologists make better diagnoses and predictions than can be made by an actuarial analysis of the data on which their predictions are based. In his influential 1954 book, Meehl proposed that they cannot. In that book, he reviewed the literature and concluded that almost all of it showed that when actuarial methods were pitted against the judgment of the clinician, the actuarial methods won the contest, or both methods tied. Since that book was published, there have been a plethora of additional studies oriented toward the question of whether the clinical judgment is superior to the actuarial combination (Sawyer, 1966), and some of these studies have been quite extensive (Goldberg, 1965). But Meehl was able to conclude almost 15 years after his book was published that there was only a single example in the literature showing clinical judgment to be superior (Meehl, 1965), and this conclusion was immediately disputed by Goldberg (1968a) on the grounds that even that example did not show such superiority.

It should not be surprising that actuarial methods are superior to clinical prediction. In principle, such methods have to be superior—for, in principle, it should always be possible to devise an actuarial method that simulates the clinician's behavior; thus, in principle, there is at least one method that does as well as the clinician, and there may always be one that is better. What is striking is that the only actuarial method considered in most of the research is that of linear combination of criterion variables—and this very simple actuarial method consistently does better than clinical judgment. Each criterion variable is scored in some way (usually such that higher numbers are indicative of higher scores on the outcome, or of membership in the diagnostic category), and the weights to be attached to these variables are determined by orthodox multiple-regression techniques. Cross products, powers, and other configuration terms are not considered. The first principle to be examined in this article, then, is that a simple linear combination of the criteria the admissions committee considers will do a better job of predicting performance in graduate school than will the admissions committee itself.

Roughly five years after Meehl's book was published, Hoffman (1960) proposed that simple linear models could not only be used to predict outcome variables, but that they could be used to predict clinical judgment as well. Hoffman termed the linear model he used to predict the clinician's judgment a "paramorphic representation" of such judgment. This term was chosen because Hoffman did not mean to imply that the actual psychological process involved in making the judgment was that of weighing various variables, but rather that the judgmental process could be simulated by such a weighting. There are many cases where the simulation is clearly inappropriate in that it predicts qualitative aspects of the judgemental process that are not in fact correct; the simulation is regarded as a good paramorphic representation, however, if overall, the judgments it makes correspond to the judgments the clinician makes. (For example, consider a linear model meant to represent the decisions of a draft board; clearly, such a model has certain qualitative characteristics that are incorrect; for example, once an individual "flunks" any physical or psychological criterion of the draft board, then his performance on the other criteria is irrelevant— while a linear model is always sensitive to changes in values on all criteria that are given nonzero weight; nevertheless, it is possible to construct a linear model that does a "reasonable" job of simulating draft board behavior.[5])

Since Hoffman's initial paper, a number of studies have been conducted—most of which have supported the proposal that clinical judgment may be represented (paramorphically) by linear models. These studies have been conducted primarily by three groups of psychologists— one at Colorado (Hammond, Hirsch, & Todd, 1964; Hirsch, Hammond, & Hirsch, 1964), one at Purdue (Dudycha & Naylor, 1966; Naylor & Wherry, 1965; Schenck & Naylor, 1968; Wherry & Naylor, 1966), and one at the Oregon Research Institute (ORI) (Goldberg, 1968b; Hoffman, Slovic, & Rorer, 1968; Slovic, 1969; Wiggins & Hoffman, 1968)—although there has been work done at other places as well (Anderson, 1968; Beach, 1967; Christal, 1968; Tucker, 1964; Yntema & Torgerson, 1961). Most of these studies have been conducted in analogue experimental situations, and it is reasonable to ask whether the situations were constructed in such a way that the linear model works, but are not representative of real-world decision-making situations. This question has been raised by Dawes (1964), who pointed out that many important social decisions are based on multiple-cut models or on disjunctive models. More recently, however, Einhorn (1970) has demonstrated that the type of decision models proposed by Dawes can in fact be approximated by the linear model when an appropriate transformation is made on the input variables. Hence, since paramorphic representation is meant only to approximate the behavior of the decision maker, Einhorn's observations support the contention that the linear model is a good paramorphic representation.[6]

Thus, the second principle to be examined is that behavior of the admissions committee studied can be simulated by a linear combination of the criteria it considers. If it can (and it can), then the paramorphic representation may be used in place of the admissions committee to make certain crude distinctions—such as screening out a large number of applicants whom the admissions committee would clearly reject. To anticipate, it turns out that 55% of the applicants the admissions committee considered could have been screened out on this basis *without rejecting a single individual whom the admissions committee actually admitted.*

The third principle is that under certain circumstances the paramorphic representation of the judge may be more valid than is the judge himself; that is, the paramorphic representation may be used to simulate the judge's behavior, and the results of the simulation may be more predictive of the outcome criterion than is the judge. This principle has been investigated at some length at ORI, where it has been termed "bootstrapping." Goldberg (1970) has demonstrated the existence of such bootstrapping in judgments of whether the Minnesota Multiphasic Personality Inventory (MMPI) profiles are from psychotic or neurotic individuals.

At first, bootstrapping appears to be paradoxical. How can a model (linear or any other sort) based on an individual's behavior do a better job of what the individual is trying to do than does the individual himself? The answer is that a mathematical model, by its very nature, is an abstraction of the process it models; hence, if the decision maker's behavior involves following valid principles but following them poorly, these valid principles will be abstracted by the model—as long as the deviations from these principles are not systematically related to the variables the decision maker is considering. For example, a decision maker may be weighting aptitude, past performance, and motivation correctly in predicting performance in graduate school and beyond, yet he may be influenced by such things as fatigue, headaches, boredom, and so on; in addition, he will be influenced by whether the most recent applications he has seen are particularly strong or weak. A paramorphic representation of his behavior would not be affected by these extraneous variables, and as long as these variables are not systematically related to the relevant variables of aptitude, past performance, and motivation, the model will attach the appropriate weights to these relevant variables.[7]

Bootstrapping can occur in contexts in which the true judgmental model may be approximated by a linear model. And research at ORI has indicated that such approximation is possible whenever the true model is monotone in each argument (see Footnote 6). Since the admissions problem is one in which it is always clearly better to have more aptitude than less, higher grades than lower grades, and better references than worse, it is reasonable to conclude that bootstrapping may occur in this context. The third principle to be examined in this article, therefore, is that the paramorphic representation of the admissions committee's judgments should be more valid than those judgments themselves.

DETAILS OF THE STUDY

For the past several years, the admissions committee of the Department of Psychology at the University of Oregon has followed roughly the same procedure for inviting students into its doctoral program. (There is no master's program as such.) The committee has required all applicants to take some form of aptitude test (in 1969, the Graduate Record Examination [GRE] became mandatory), to provide the committee with a transcript of past work, and to obtain letters of recommendation from three professors or work supervisors. Once this information was supplied to the committee, each of the four members separately rated the applicants on a rating scale; the scale used most often had the following verbal labels attached to each point: (1) reject now, (2) defer rejection but looks weak, (3) defer, (4) defer acceptance but looks strong, (5) accept now, and (6) offer a National Defense Education Act or other fellowship. The numerical values of this scale were averaged in order to obtain an overall rating of the applicant. After all of the applicants had been evaluated, those with the highest overall ratings in each subarea of psychology were invited, and as some applicants declined the invitation, the applicants with the next highest ratings were invited; the process was continued until the positions available for first-year students in each of the subareas were filled. All students invited were guaranteed jobs.[8]

The average rating of the admissions committee will be regarded as its judgment of how well the applicant will do in graduate school. It is this rating that is studied, both with respect to how well it predicts graduate performance and with respect to how well it alone can be paramorphically represented by a linear model of the variables on which it is based.

Actual performance in graduate school was assessed by faculty ratings collected in the spring of 1969 for all students who had been admitted between fall of 1964 and fall of 1967, and who had not dropped out of the program for nonacademic reasons (e.g., marriage).

The following rating scale was used: 5, outstanding; 4, above average; 3, average; 2, below average; 1, dropped out of the program in academic difficulty. Each faculty member was asked to rate only those students whom he felt competent to judge. One reason for using such overall ratings is that subjective impressions of faculty members are a major determinant of the job (if any) a student obtains after leaving graduate school, and—according to the current mythology—the nature of this job is of crucial importance in the student's later career.[9]

One hundred and eleven students remained in the sample; the number of faculty members rating each of these students ranged from 1 to 20, with the mean number being 5.67 and the median being 5. To determine the reliability of these ratings, they were subjected to a one-way analysis of variance in which each student being rated was regarded as a treatment. If there is substantial agreement between raters, the resulting between-treatment variance ratio (η^2) should be both significant and large. This variance ratio, which may also be regarded as the squared Pearson product-moment correlation between each observation and its treatment mean, is equal to .67; it is significant well beyond the .001 level. (The F ratio with 110 and 518 degrees of freedom is equal to 9.79.) The magnitude of η^2 is quite impressive when it is realized that the within-treatment variance (i.e., disagreement between raters) reflects not only the faculty members' disagreement about the student's performance, but also their differential use of the crude rating scale.

It turned out that there was, nevertheless, substantial disagreement among the faculty members concerning who had left the program while in academic difficulty. The ratings were therefore "purified" by finding out from the department head exactly which students had been in difficulty when they left. Such students were automatically assigned the rating 1, and all 1 ratings given to other students were deleted. (It should be kept in mind that this purification was made after the reliability of the ratings was assessed.) The mean faculty rating (FR) assigned to a given student (irrespective of the number of judgments on which it was based) is the measure of performance in graduate school used in this study.

The applications of each of the 111 students in this sample were examined, and four variables were analyzed: overall undergraduate grade-point average (GPA), a crude index of the quality of the undergraduate institution (QI),[10] the total raw score GRE (i.e., the sum of the raw score on the verbal part and that on the quantitative part), and the average rating (AR) made by the admissions committee at the time the applicant was accepted.

The correlations between all the variables are given in Table 1; the parentheses indicate the sample size on which these correlations are based (since not all variables were available for all subjects).[11] Note that GPA and QI taken alone correlate more highly with later faculty ratings than does the rating of the admissions committee. Yet the admissions committee had

TABLE 1 CORRELATIONS BASED ON SELECTED STUDENTS.

Variable	GRE	GPA	QI	AR
GRE	—			
GPA	−.13 (77)	—		
QI	.30 (80)	−.33 (93)	—	
AR	.05 (23)	.54 (23)	.19 (23)	—
FR	.11 (86)	.21 (96)	.25 (103)	.19 (23)

Note. Parentheses indicate the sample size. Abbreviations: GRE = Graduate Record Examination; GPA = grade-point average; QI = quality of the undergraduate institution; AR = average rating; FR = faculty rating.

access to the information contained in both these variables and much other information as well.

When a multiple-regression analysis is performed using GRE, GPA, and QI, the multiple R is .40. In order to evaluate the multiple correlation without "capitalization on chance," the sample was randomly divided into two subsamples, and the standard double cross-validation procedure was employed. The average cross-validated correlation was .38. This correlation is substantially higher than that between the admissions committee rating and the faculty rating—although the two correlations cannot be compared directly for statistical significance since they are based on different subparts of the sample.

In order to evaluate the success of the paramorphic representation of the committee's behavior and of the possibility of bootstrapping, it was necessary to collect an additional sample—one of applicants, rather than one of students who had been selected into the program. Three hundred and eighty-four applicants for fall of 1969 who had completed their applications prior to April 15, 1969, were studied. The same variables previously evaluated were coded, the main difference between this study and the previous one being that the dependent variable of interest is now the average rating of the admissions committee rather than later faculty evaluation. The intercorrelations between the variables are presented in Table 2.

The multiple correlation predicting the admissions committee rating from GPA, GRE, and QI is .78. More importantly, as mentioned previously, when the weights given the three predictor variables are applied to obtain the appropriate linear combination, it is possible to find a cut point on this combination having the property that no one who scores below it was invited by the admissions committee. *Fifty-five percent of the applicants scored below this point, which means that they could have been eliminated on*

TABLE 2 CORRELATIONS BASED ON APPLICANTS.

Variable	GRE	GPA	QI
GRE	—		
GPA	.18 (353)	—	
QI	.29 (381)	−.12 (354)	—
AR	.64 (381)	.55 (354)	.21 (384)

Note. Parentheses indicate the sample size. Abbreviations: GRE = Graduate Record Examination; GPA = grade-point average; QI = quality of the undergraduate institution; AR = average rating.

the basis of the paramorphic representation of the admissions committee's behavior without a single error being committed.[12]

Does bootstrapping work? When the weights used to predict the admissions committee behavior are applied to the sample of selected students, the resulting linear combination correlates .25 with the later faculty ratings. While this correlation is higher than that between the admissions committee's ratings and the later faculty ratings, it must be kept in mind that the admissions committees were different across the years, and hence no statistical evaluation of this bootstrapping is possible. The results are, however, in the predicted direction.

Bootstrapping was also evaluated by correlating the paramorphic representation with the spring 1970 evaluation of the students actually selected from the applicant population. At the time of this evaluation, each student was discussed first by a graduate student progress committee and then by the entire staff. The major emphasis of discussion was on whether the student had done satisfactorily in the first-year "core" program and hence should be told he is expected to obtain the PhD—or whether the student should be advised to take a terminal MA degree. (Neither decision is irrevocable.) As well as making this crude distinction, however, the staff made further differentiations among the students. Specifically, one student was given special commendation for his performance, five students were "passed with distinction," eight students were "passed," two students were granted a "provisional pass," and three students were advised to take a terminal master's degree. Hence, the 19 students evaluated can be ranked into five categories corresponding to the staff's evaluation of their performance. This categorical student ranking (SR) was then compared with: (*a*) the paramorphic representation (PR) of the admissions committee and (*b*) the average rating (AR) of the admissions committee. The statistic used to evaluate these correlations was the Spearman rank correlation coefficient corrected for ties (Siegel, 1956, pp. 206–210). These correlations are presented in Table 3.

TABLE 3 CORRELATIONS BASED ON
ACCEPTED APPLICANTS AT END OF
FIRST YEAR.

Variable	SR	PR
SR	—	
PR	.51	—
AR	.10	.54

Note.   Abbreviations: SE = student
ranking; PR = paramorphic representation; AR = average rating.

Clearly, bootstrapping has occurred. The paramorphic representation of the admissions committee's judgment predicts the first-year evaluation better than does the judgment itself; in fact, the representation accounts for approximately 25 times as much variance as does the judgment per se. (The correlation between the representation and the first-year evaluation is significant beyond the .05 level, and very close to the .01 level; the significance of the difference between the two correlations cannot be tested because the assumption of normality for evaluating the significance of the difference between two correlations based on the same sample (Guilford, 1956, p. 194) is inappropriate in the case of rank orders.)

The weights used to predict the faculty ratings are presented in Equation 1, while those used to predict the admissions committee ratings are presented in Equation 2.

$$.0006 \, GRE + \ .76 \, GPA + .2518 \, QI \qquad (1)$$
$$.0032 \, GRE + 1.02 \, GPA + .0791 \, QI \qquad (2)$$

It is of passing interest to note that the admissions committee does not place sufficient weight on the quality of the undergraduate academic institution. In fact, this quality index is the best single predictor of later faculty ratings.[13] The interpretation made here of this finding, however, is not that all admissions committees everywhere should place more weight on the variable of undergraduate institutional quality, but rather that such quality became a good predictor among the selected group by virtue of the fact that the admissions committee tended to ignore it.

COST–BENEFIT ANALYSIS

It has been argued that the federal government is concerned about the financial gains of social research (Lepkowski, 1969). Consider, now, the cost benefit that would accrue if a paramorphic representation of admissions committee's behaviors across the country could be used to eliminate 55% of the applicants without screening out any who would be in fact admitted by the committee. First, there would be the cost of establishing such a representation for each committee. This cost is negligible, since it involves only a computation of correlation coefficients (by computer) and the construction of regression equations. In contrast, however, the monetary benefits would be striking. If four professionals each spend 10 minutes looking at an application, then there are 40 minutes of professional time spent on each applicant. Since people on admissions committees tend not to be the most senior or eminent members of their profession, let us suppose that the average salary of each committee member is roughly $7 an hour, or $14,000 for a total year. Then, $4.67 of professional time is spent on each application, which comes to a total of roughly $32.7 million per year (see Footnote 3). If 55% of this effort could be saved, the resulting savings in professional time would be approximately $18 million per year. (All this, of course, is based on the idea that the professionals on admissions committees could do something else that is valuable with their time.) In addition, there are the costs saved to the student involving the preparation of his application, and there are costs to other professionals, who are recommending the student for a position that he is certain not to obtain. In addition to the monetary costs, there are psychological costs—both in terms of dreariness to the professional evaluating the applicant and in terms of heartache to the applicant who mistakenly hopes that he can be admitted to a certain institution.

DEHUMANIZING EFFECT OF A REGRESSION EQUATION
The author and his colleagues feel a certain uneasiness about evaluating graduate applicants on the basis of a regression equation—whether one meant to predict later faculty ratings, or one meant to predict the admissions committee's own behavior. Surely, the applicant deserves the personal attention of the committee. To be screened out on the basis of certain conventional (and white middle-class) criteria without even having come to the attention of the admissions committee is infuriating and demeaning. Surely other qualities are more important than grades and aptitude scores and college prestige. (Even the current research demonstrates that these conventional criteria are poor predictors.) So how can the use of a paramorphic representation be justified?

First, there is nothing in the above proposal that constrains any admissions committee to use the paramorphic representation for all decisions, or to apply it to all applicants. For example, the Psychology Department at the University of Oregon will not use the representation when considering black, Mexican-American, or American Indian applicants (both for reasons of social justice and because the equations were constructed on a sample of white—presumably middle-class—applicants).

Second, there probably are criteria that predict graduate success better than do the three considered in the regression equation. The problem is that the admissions committee does not know what they are (except perhaps on a vague verbal level). And it has no way of assessing them. Since the clinical judgment of the admissions committee is not even as good as two of the conventional variables considered singly, it can only be concluded that the attempt of the admissions committee to assess these other presumably important variables decreases rather than increases the validity of its judgments. What is needed is *research* concerning the determinants of graduate success. (And, throughout, it must be remembered that the fact that a certain well-defined and extensively studied predictor does not do a good job does not imply that a variable the judge makes up out of his own intuition—for example, his "assessment of the student's motivation"—will do a better job.)

Finally, the fact that the judgments are made systematically by the paramorphic representation of the regression equation does not mean that it is not the policy of the admissions committee that is being applied. We cannot escape the ethical responsibility for the decision making simply because we make it systematically. Nor, on the other hand, does the fact that it is made systematically—for example, by computer—mean that it is not our decision.

So the fact that certain decisions may be made systematically and economically with the aid of a computer does not mean that the decisions have been made in a "dehumanized" manner. The research presented here indicates that such decisions may be less capricious and more valid than those made by the decision maker relying on his own intuitions. Such decisions are more human.

REFERENCES

Anderson, N. H. A simple model for information integration. In R. P. Abelson, E. Aronson, W. J. McGuire, T. M. Newcomb, M. J. Rosenberg, & P. H. Tannenbaum (Eds.), *Theories of cognitive consistency: A sourcebook.* Chicago: Rand McNally, 1968.

Beach, L. R. Multiple regression as a model for human information utilization. *Organizational Behavior and Human Performance*, 1967, **2**, 274–289.

Cass, J., & Birnbaum, M. *Comparative guide to American colleges.* New York: Harper & Row, 1968.

Christal, R. E. Selecting a harem—and other applications of the policy-capturing model. *Journal of Experimental Education*, 1968, **36**, 35–41.

Dawes, R. M. Social selection based on multidimensional criteria. *Journal of Abnormal and Social Psychology*, 1964, **68,** 104–109.

Dudycha, A. L., & Naylor, J. C. The effect of variations in the cue R-matrix upon the obtained policy equations of judges. *Educational and Psychological Measurement*, 1966, **26,** 583–603.

Einhorn, H. J. The use of nonlinear, noncompensatory models in decision making. *Psychological Bulletin*, 1970, **3,** 221–230.

Goldberg, L. R. Diagnosticians vs. diagnostic signs: The diagnosis of psychosis vs. neurosis from the MMPI. *Psychological Monographs*, 1965, **79**(9, Whole No. 602).

Goldberg, L. R. Seer over sign: The first "good" example? *Journal of Experimental Research in Personality*, 1968, **3,** 168–171. (a)

Goldberg, L. R. Simple models or simple processes? Some research on clinical judgments. *American Psychologist*, 1968, **23,** 483–496. (b)

Goldberg, L. R. Man versus model of man: A rationale, plus some evidence, for a method of improving on clinical inferences. *Psychological Bulletin*, 1970, **73,** 422–432.

Guilford, J. P. *Fundamental statistics in psychology and education*. New York: McGraw-Hill, 1956.

Hammond, K. R., Hirsch, C, J., & Todd, F. J. Analyzing the components of clinical inference. *Psychological Review*, 1964, **71,** 438–456.

Hansen, W. L. Prediction of graduate performance in economics. Department of Economics, University of Wisconsin, February 1969. (Mimeo)

Hirsch, C. J., Hammond, K. R., & Hirsch, J. L. Some methodological considerations in multiple-cue probability studies. *Psychological Review*, 1964, **71,** 42–60.

Hoffman, P. J. The paramorphic representation of clinical judgment. *Psychological Bulletin*, 1960, **57,** 116–131.

Hoffman, P. J., Slovic, P., & Rorer, L. G. An analysis-of-variance model for the assessment of configural cue utilization in clinical judgment. *Psychological Bulletin*, 1968, **69,** 338–349.

Hoyt, D. P. College grades and adult achievement: A review of the literature. *The Educational Record*, 1966, **47,** 70–75.

Hyman, S. R. The Miller Analogies Test and University of Pittsburg PhDs in psychology. *American Psychologist*, 1957, **12,** 35–36.

Lannholm, G. V. Review of studies employing GRE scores in predicting success in graduate school 1952–67. (Graduate Record Examinations Special Report No. 68-1) Princeton, N.J.: Educational Testing Service, 1968.

Lepkowski, W. Washington science outlook. *Scientific Research*, 1969, **4**(21), 16.

Meehl, P. E. *Clinical versus statistical prediction: A theoretical analysis and review of the literature*. Minneapolis: University of Minnesota Press, 1954.

Meehl, P. E. Seer over sign: The first good example. *Journal of Experimental Research in Personality*, 1965, **1,** 27–32.

Mehrabian, A. Undergraduate ability factors in relationship to graduate performance. *Educational and Psychological Measurement*, 1969, **29,** 409–419.

Naylor, J. C., & Wherry, R. J., Sr. The use of simulated stimuli and the "JAN" technique to capture and cluster the policies of raters. *Educational and Psychological Measurement*, 1965, **25,** 969–986.

Newman, R. I. GRE scores as predictors of GPA for psychology graduate students. *Educational and Psychological Measurement*, 1968, **28,** 433–436.

Platz, A., McClintock, C., & Katz, D. Undergraduate grades and the Miller Analogies Test as predictors of graduate success. *American Psychologist*, 1959, **14,** 285–289.

Rawls, J. R., Rawls, D. J., & Harrison, C. W. An investigation of success predictors in graduate school in psychology. *The Journal of Psychology*, 1969, **72,** 125–129.

Robertson, M., & Hall, E. Predicting success in graduate school. *The Journal of General Psychology*, 1964, **71,** 359–365.

Robertson, M., & Nielsen, W. The Graduate Record Examination and selection of graduate students. *American Psychologist*, 1961, **16,** 648–650.

Sawyer, J. Measurement *and* prediction, clinical *and* statistical. *Psychological Bulletin*, 1966, **65,** 178–200.

Schenck, E. A., & Naylor, J. C. A cautionary note concerning the use of regression analysis for capturing the strategies of people. *Educational and Psychological Measurement*, 1968, **28,** 3–7.

Sedlacek, W. E., & Hutchins, E. G. An empirical demonstration of restriction of range artifacts in validity studies of the Medical College Admissions Test. *Journal of Medical Education*, 1966, **41,** 222–229.

Siegel, S. *Nonparametric statistics for the behavioral sciences.* New York: McGraw-Hill, 1956.

Slovic, P. Analyzing the expert judge: A descriptive study of a stockbroker's decision processes. *Journal of Applied Psychology*, 1969, **53,** 255–263.

Thorndike, R. L. *Personnel selection: Tests and measurement techniques.* New York: Wiley, 1949.

Tucker, L. R. A suggested alternative formulation in the developments by Hirsch, Hammond, & Hirsch, and by Hammond, Hirsch, & Todd. *Psychological Review*, 1964, **71,** 528–530.

Tully, G. E. Screening applicants for graduate study with the aptitude test of the Graduate Record Examinations. *College and University*, 1962, **38,** 51–60.

Watters, D. V., & Patterson, D. G. Miller Analogies Test scores and ratings of PhD's in psychology. *American Psychologist*, 1953, **8,** 89–90.

Wherry, R. J., Sr., & Naylor, J. C. Comparison of two approaches—JAN and PROF—for capturing rater strategies. *Educational and Psychological Measurement*, 1966, **26,** 267–286.

Wiggins, N., & Hoffman, P. J. Three models of clinical judgment. *Journal of Abnormal Psychology*, 1968, **73,** 70–77.

Yntema, D. B., & Torgerson, W. S. Man-computer cooperation in decisions requiring common sense. *IRE Transactions of the Professional Group on Human Factors in Electronics*, 1961, HFE-2(1), 20–26.

NOTES

[1] This study was supported in part by Grant No. MH 12972 from the National Institute of Mental Health, United States Public Health Service, and in part by Grant No. 5SO5-FRO7080-03 from the United States Public Health Service. The author thanks Judy Boylan and Linda Mushkatel for their assistance in data collection and Molly Stafford for her assistance in data analysis.

[2] Requests for reprints should be sent to Robyn M. Dawes, Oregon Research Institute, Eugene, Oregon 97403.

[3] Gustave O. Arlt, personal communication, 1969.

[4] Only selected applicants can be studied. The resulting restrictions in the range of talent attenuates correlations (Thorndike, 1949, pp. 170–173). In addition, there is the fact that whatever vague methods are used by admissions committees for combining criteria, these methods tend to be compensatory. Thus, an individual who has an extremely low undergraduate grade-point average will be admitted only if he has extremely high aptitude scores. It follows that those people with low grades (aptitude) tend to be those with high aptitude (grades), but not the converse—which means that people with low values in one criterion should be expected to do well on the basis of other criteria.

[5] This conclusion is based on an informal study by the author; information is available from him.

[6] In addition, recent simulation studies by L. G. Rorer and the present author indicate that the linear model is a very good model of other models—provided that the other models are monotone in each variable. That is, as long as the judgmental situation is one in which a higher value at any criterion is at least as good as a lower value, then a linear approximation of the actual function being used to predict the outcome measure will do reasonably well.

[7] The process may be conceptualized as one in which random error is applied to some valid score that is approximated by a linear combination of criterion variables. A moment's thought, or an extensive computer simulation, will reveal that a multiple-regression analysis of the valid score plus error on the predictor variables will yield the correct *relative* weights for these variables.

[8] There were two minor departures from this procedure. First, if in the judgment of the chairman of the admissions committee an applicant would clearly be rejected, only one or two other members of the committee were asked to rate that applicant; this policy was formalized in 1969, when the study of the previous years' behavior of the admissions committee indicated that no applicant with one rating of 4 or below and one rating below 4 was invited. Further, if it was clear that an applicant would be among those first invited, the invitation was made prior to evaluating all other applicants.

[9] Perhaps better measures could have been devised had the sample been composed of much older people who had been out of graduate school longer; unfortunately, however, the admissions situation was much different when these older people entered graduate school, and there were no thorough records of the criteria on which they were admitted. (In fact, many were probably admitted without being required to supply all the information that current applicants supply.)

[10] This index was based on Cass and Birnbaum's (1968) rating of selectivity given at the end of their book, *Comparison Guide to American Colleges.* The verbal categories of selectivity were given numerical values according to the following rule: most selective, 6; highly selective, 5; very selective (+), 4; very selective, 3; selective, 2; not mentioned, 1.

[11] The small number of students who had overall admissions committee ratings is due to the unhappy fact that the rating scale used changed slightly from year to year. The finding that such ratings are less predictive than are linear combinations of the variables on which they are based is, however, well documented in past literature. The reader who is justly skeptical of a conclusion based on an N of 23 is referred to that literature. As mentioned in the body of this article, its primary purpose is to illustrate how established principles can be applied to the graduate admissions problem—not to present inductive evidence for these principles.

[12] Another variable investigated was an average rating given by people writing letters of recommendation for the applicant. Inclusion of this variable in the multiple-regression analysis did not appreciably increase the multiple correlation; in fact, the proportion of applicants who could be screened out actually diminished rather than increased. People writing letters of recommendation differed appreciably in their overall tendency to say that applicants were average to superior (none was said to be below average), and hence these letter ratings were often quite misleading.

[13] Hansen (1969) has also discovered that quality of undergraduate institution is the best predictor of his outcome measure, which is first-year grades in the Economics Department at the University of Wisconsin.

JUDGMENT UNDER UNCERTAINTY: HEURISTICS AND BIASES

AMOS TVERSKY and DANIEL KAHNEMAN

Many decisions are based on beliefs concerning the likelihood of uncertain events such as the outcome of an election, the guilt of a defendant, or the future value of the dollar. These beliefs are usually expressed in statements such as "I think that ...," "chances are ...," "it is unlikely that ...," and so forth. Occasionally, beliefs concerning uncertain events are expressed in numerical form as odds or subjective probabilities. What determines such beliefs? How do people assess the probability of an uncertain event or the value of an uncertain quantity? This article shows that people rely on a limited number of heuristic principles which reduce the complex tasks of assessing probabilities and predicting values to simpler judgmental operations. In general, these heuristics are quite useful, but sometimes they lead to severe and systematic errors.

The subjective assessment of probability resembles the subjective assessment of physical quantities such as distance or size. These judgments are all based on data of limited validity, which are processed according to heuristic rules. For example, the apparent distance of an object is determined in part by its clarity. The more sharply the object is seen, the closer it appears to be. This rule has some validity, because in any given scene the more distant objects are seen less sharply than nearer objects. However, the reliance on this rule leads to systematic errors in the estimation of distance. Specifically, distances are often overestimated when visibility is poor because the contours of objects are blurred. On the other hand, distances are often underestimated when visibility is good because the objects are seen sharply. Thus, the reliance on clarity as an indication of distance leads to common biases. Such biases are also found in the intuitive judgment of

Reprinted with permission from *Science*, Vol. 185 (September 27, 1974), pp. 1124–1131. Copyright © 1974 by the American Association for the Advancement of Science.

probability. This article describes three heuristics that are employed to
assess probabilities and to predict values. Biases to which these heuristics
lead are enumerated, and the applied and theoretical implications of these
observations are discussed.

REPRESENTATIVENESS

Many of the probabilistic questions with which people are concerned belong
to one of the following types: What is the probability that object A belongs
to class B? What is the probability that event A originates from process B?
What is the probability that process B will generate event A? In answering
such questions, people typically rely on the representativeness heuristic, in
which probabilities are evaluated by the degree to which A is representative
of B, that is, by the degree to which A resembles B. For example, when A is
highly representative of B, the probability that A originates from B is
judged to be high. On the other hand, if A is not similar to B, the
probability that A originates from B is judged to be low.

For an illustration of judgment by representativeness, consider an
individual who has been described by a former neighbor as follows: "Steve
is very shy and withdrawn, invariably helpful, but with little interest in
people, or in the world of reality. A meek and tidy soul, he has a need for
order and structure, and a passion for detail." How do people assess the
probability that Steve is engaged in a particular occupation from a list of
possibilities (for example, farmer, salesman, airline pilot, librarian, or physician)? How do people order these occupations from most to least likely? In
the representativeness heuristic, the probability that Steve is a librarian, for
example, is assessed by the degree to which he is representative of, or
similar to, the stereotype of a librarian. Indeed, research with problems of
this type has shown that people order the occupations by probability and by
similarity in exactly the same way (*1*). This approach to the judgment of
probability leads to serious errors, because similarity, or representativeness,
is not influenced by several factors that should affect judgments of
probability.

Insensitivity to prior probability of outcomes

One of the factors that have no effect on representativeness but should have
a major effect on probability is the prior probability, or base-rate frequency,
of the outcomes. In the case of Steve, for example, the fact that there are
many more farmers than librarians in the population should enter into any
reasonable estimate of the probability that Steve is a librarian rather than a
farmer. Considerations of base-rate frequency, however, do not affect the

similarity of Steve to the stereotypes of librarians and farmers. If people evaluate probability by representativeness, therefore, prior probabilities will be neglected. This hypothesis was tested in an experiment where prior probabilities were manipulated (*1*). Subjects were shown brief personality descriptions of several individuals, allegedly sampled at random from a group of 100 professionals—engineers and lawyers. The subjects were asked to assess, for each description, the probability that it belonged to an engineer rather than to a lawyer. In one experimental condition, subjects were told that the group from which the descriptions had been drawn consisted of 70 engineers and 30 lawyers. In another condition, subjects were told that the group consisted of 30 engineers and 70 lawyers. The odds that any particular description belongs to an engineer rather than to a lawyer should be higher in the first condition, where there is a majority of engineers, than in the second condition, where there is a majority of lawyers. Specifically, it can be shown by applying Bayes' rule that the ratio of these odds should be $(.7/.3)^2$, or 5.44, for each description. In a sharp violation of Bayes' rule, the subjects in the two conditions produced essentially the same probability judgments. Apparently, subjects evaluated the likelihood that a particular description belonged to an engineer rather than to a lawyer by the degree to which this description was representative of the two stereotypes, with little or no regard for the prior probabilities of the categories.

The subjects used prior probabilities correctly when they had no other information. In the absence of a personality sketch, they judged the probability that an unknown individual is an engineer to be .7 and .3, respectively, in the two base-rate conditions. However, prior probabilities were effectively ignored when a description was introduced, even when this description was totally uninformative. The responses to the following description illustrate this phenomenon:

> Dick is a 30 year old man. He is married with no children. A man of high ability and high motivation, he promises to be quite successful in his field. He is well liked by his colleagues.

This description was intended to convey no information relevant to the question of whether Dick is an engineer or a lawyer. Consequently, the probability that Dick is an engineer should equal the proportion of engineers in the group, as if no description had been given. The subjects, however, judged the probability of Dick being an engineer to be .5 regardless of whether the stated proportion of engineers in the group was .7 or .3. Evidently, people respond differently when given no evidence and when given worthless evidence. When no specific evidence is given, prior probabilities are properly utilized; when worthless evidence is given, prior probabilities are ignored (*1*).

Insensitivity to sample size

To evaluate the probability of obtaining a particular result in a sample drawn from a specified population, people typically apply the representativeness heuristic. That is, they assess the likelihood of a sample result, for example, that the average height in a random sample of ten men will be 6 feet (180 centimeters), by the similarity of this result to the corresponding parameter (that is, to the average height in the population of men). The similarity of a sample statistic to a population parameter does not depend on the size of the sample. Consequently, if probabilities are assessed by representativeness, then the judged probability of a sample statistic will be essentially independent of sample size. Indeed, when subjects assessed the distributions of average height for samples of various sizes, they produced identical distributions. For example, the probability of obtaining an average height greater than 6 feet was assigned the same value for samples of 1000, 100, and 10 men (2). Moreover, subjects failed to appreciate the role of sample size even when it was emphasized in the formulation of the problem. Consider the following question:

> A certain town is served by two hospitals. In the larger hospital about 45 babies are born each day, and in the smaller hospital about 15 babies are born each day. As you know, about 50 percent of all babies are boys. However, the exact percentage varies from day to day. Sometimes it may be higher than 50 percent, sometimes lower.
>
> For a period of 1 year, each hospital recorded the days on which more than 60 percent of the babies born were boys. Which hospital do you think recorded more such days?
>
> > The larger hospital (21)
> >
> > The smaller hospital (21)
> >
> > About the same (that is, within 5 percent of each other) (53)

The values in parentheses are the number of undergraduate students who chose each answer.

Most subjects judged the probability of obtaining more than 60 percent boys to be the same in the small and in the large hospital, presumably because these events are described by the same statistic and are therefore equally representative of the general population. In contrast, sampling theory entails that the expected number of days on which more than 60 percent of the babies are boys is much greater in the small hospital than in the large one, because a large sample is less likely to stray from 50 percent. This fundamental notion of statistics is evidently not part of people's repertoire of intuitions.

A similar insensitivity to sample size has been reported in judgments of posterior probability, that is, of the probability that a sample has been drawn from one population rather than from another. Consider the following example:

> Imagine an urn filled with balls, of which $\frac{2}{3}$ are of one color and $\frac{1}{3}$ of another. One individual has drawn 5 balls from the urn, and found that 4 were red and 1 was white. Another individual has drawn 20 balls and found that 12 were red and 8 were white. Which of the two individuals should feel more confident that the urn contains $\frac{2}{3}$ red balls and $\frac{1}{3}$ white balls, rather than the opposite? What odds should each individual give?

In this problem, the correct posterior odds are 8 to 1 for the 4:1 sample and 16 to 1 for the 12:8 sample, assuming equal prior probabilities. However, most people feel that the first sample provides much stronger evidence for the hypothesis that the urn is predominantly red, because the proportion of red balls is larger in the first than in the second sample. Here again, intuitive judgments are dominated by the sample proportion and are essentially unaffected by the size of the sample, which plays a crucial role in the determination of the actual posterior odds (2). In addition, intuitive estimates of posterior odds are far less extreme than the correct values. The underestimation of the impact of evidence has been observed repeatedly in problems of this type (3, 4). It has been labeled "conservatism."

Misconceptions of chance

People expect that a sequence of events generated by a random process will represent the essential characteristics of that process even when the sequence is short. In considering tosses of a coin for heads or tails, for example, people regard the sequence H-T-H-T-T-H to be more likely than the sequence H-H-H-T-T-T, which does not appear random, and also more likely than the sequence H-H-H-H-T-H, which does not represent the fairness of the coin (2). Thus, people expect that the essential characteristics of the process will be represented, not only globally in the entire sequence, but also locally in each of its parts. A locally representative sequence, however, deviates systematically from chance expectation: it contains too many alternations and too many runs. Another consequence of the belief in local representativeness is the well-known gambler's fallacy. After observing a long run of red on the roulette wheel, for example, most people erroneously believe that black is now due, presumably because the occurrence of black will result in a more representative sequence than the occurrence of an additional red. Chance is commonly viewed as a self-correcting process in which a deviation in one direction induces a deviation in the opposite direction to restore the equilibrium. In fact, deviations are not "corrected" as a chance process unfolds, they are merely diluted.

Misconceptions of chance are not limited to naive subjects. A study of the statistical intuitions of experienced research psychologists (5) revealed a lingering belief in what may be called the "law of small numbers," according to which even small samples are highly representative of the populations from which they are drawn. The responses of these investigators reflected the expectation that a valid hypothesis about a population will be represented by a statistically significant result in a sample—with little regard for its size. As a consequence, the researchers put too much faith in the results of small samples and grossly overestimated the replicability of such results. In the actual conduct of research, this bias leads to the selection of samples of inadequate size and to overinterpretation of findings.

Insensitivity to predictability

People are sometimes called upon to make such numerical predictions as the future value of a stock, the demand for a commodity, or the outcome of a football game. Such predictions are often made by representativeness. For example, suppose one is given a description of a company and is asked to predict its future profit. If the description of the company is very favorable, a very high profit will appear most representative of that description; if the description is mediocre, a mediocre performance will appear most representative. The degree to which the description is favorable is unaffected by the reliability of that description or by the degree to which it permits accurate prediction. Hence, if people predict solely in terms of the favorableness of the description, their predictions will be insensitive to the reliability of the evidence and to the expected accuracy of the prediction.

This mode of judgment violates the normative statistical theory in which the extremeness and the range of predictions are controlled by considerations of predictability. When predictability is nil, the same prediction should be made in all cases. For example, if the descriptions of companies provide no information relevant to profit, then the same value (such as average profit) should be predicted for all companies. If predictability is perfect, of course, the values predicted will match the actual values and the range of predictions will equal the range of outcomes. In general, the higher the predictability, the wider the range of predicted values.

Several studies of numerical prediction have demonstrated that intuitive predictions violate this rule, and that subjects show little or no regard for considerations of predictability (1). In one of these studies, subjects were presented with several paragraphs, each describing the performance of a student teacher during a particular practice lesson. Some subjects were asked to *evaluate* the quality of the lesson described in the paragraph in percentile scores, relative to a specified population. Other subjects were asked to *predict*, also in percentile scores, the standing of each student teacher 5 years after the practice lesson. The judgments made under the two conditions were identical. That is, the prediction of a remote criterion (success of a teacher after 5 years) was identical to the evaluation of the information on which the prediction was based (the quality of the practice lesson). The students who made these predictions were undoubtedly aware of the limited predictability of teaching competence on the basis of a single trial lesson 5 years earlier; nevertheless, their predictions were as extreme as their evaluations.

The illusion of validity

As we have seen, people often predict by selecting the outcome (for example, an occupation) that is most representative of the input (for example, the description of a person). The confidence they have in their prediction depends primarily on the degree of representativeness (that is, on the quality of the match between the selected outcome and the input) with little or no regard for the factors that limit predictive accuracy. Thus, people express great confidence in the prediction that a person is a librarian when given a description of his personality which matches the stereotype of librarians, even if the description is scanty, unreliable, or outdated. The unwarranted confidence which is produced by a good fit between the predicted outcome and the input information may be called the illusion of validity. This illusion persists even when the judge is aware of the factors that limit the accuracy of his predictions. It is a common observation that psychologists who conduct selection interviews often experience considerable confidence in their predictions, even when they know of the vast literature that shows selection interviews to be highly fallible. The continued reliance on the clinical interview for selection, despite repeated demonstrations of its inadequacy, amply attests to the strength of this effect.

The internal consistency of a pattern of inputs is a major determinant of one's confidence in predictions based on these inputs. For example, people express more confidence in predicting the final grade-point average of a student whose first-year record consists entirely of B's than in predicting the grade-point average of a student whose first-year record includes many A's and C's. Highly consistent patterns are most often observed when the input variables are highly redundant or correlated. Hence, people tend to have great confidence in predictions based on redundant input variables. However, an elementary result in the statistics of correlation asserts that, given input variables of stated validity, a prediction based on several such inputs can achieve higher accuracy when they are independent of each other than when they are redundant or correlated. Thus, redundancy among inputs decreases accuracy even as it increases confidence, and people are often confident in predictions that are quite likely to be off the mark (1).

Misconceptions of regression

Suppose a large group of children has been examined on two equivalent versions of an aptitude test. If one selects ten children from among those who did best on one of the two versions, he will usually find their performance on the second version to be somewhat disappointing. Conversely, if one selects ten children from among those who did worst on one version, they will be found, on the average, to do somewhat better on the other version. More generally, consider two variables X and Y which have the same distribution. If one selects individuals whose average X score deviates from the mean of X by k units, then the average of their Y scores will usually deviate from the mean of Y by less than k units. These observations illustrate a general phenomenon known as regression toward the mean, which was first documented by Galton more than 100 years ago.

In the normal course of life, one encounters many instances of regression toward the mean, in the comparison of the height of fathers and sons, of the intelligence of husbands and wives, or of the performance of individuals on consecutive examinations. Nevertheless, people do not develop correct intuitions about this phenomenon. First, they do not expect regression in many contexts where it is bound to occur. Second, when they recognize the occurrence of regression, they often invent spurious causal explanations for it (1). We suggest that the phenomenon of regression remains elusive because it is incompatible with the belief that the predicted outcome should be maximally representative of the input, and, hence, that the value of the outcome variable should be as extreme as the value of the input variable.

The failure to recognize the import of regression can have pernicious consequences, as illustrated by the following observation (1). In a discussion of flight training, experienced instructors noted that praise for an exceptionally smooth landing is typically followed by a poorer landing on the next try, while harsh criticism after a rough landing is usually followed by an improvement on the next try. The instructors concluded that verbal rewards are detrimental to learning, while verbal punishments are beneficial, contrary to accepted psychological doctrine. This conclusion is unwarranted because of the presence of regression toward the mean. As in other cases of repeated examination, an improvement will usually follow a poor performance and a deterioration will usually follow an outstanding performance, even if the instructor does not respond to the trainee's achievement on the first attempt. Because the instructors had praised their trainees after good landings and admonished them after poor ones, they reached the erroneous and potentially harmful conclusion that punishment is more effective than reward.

Thus, the failure to understand the effect of regression leads one to overestimate the effectiveness of punishment and to underestimate the effectiveness of reward. In social interaction, as well as in training, rewards are typically administered when performance is good, and punishments are typically administered when performance is poor. By regression alone, therefore, behavior is most likely to improve after punishment and most likely to deteriorate after reward. Consequently, the human condition is such that, by chance alone, one is most often rewarded for punishing others and most often punished for rewarding them. People are generally not aware of this contingency. In fact, the elusive role of regression in determining the apparent consequences of reward and punishment seems to have escaped the notice of students of this area.

AVAILABILITY

There are situations in which people assess the frequency of a class or the probability of an event by the ease with which instances or occurrences can be brought to mind. For example, one may assess the risk of heart attack among middle-aged people by recalling such occurrences among one's acquaintances. Similarly, one may evaluate the probability that a given business venture will fail by imagining various difficulties it could encounter. This judgmental heuristic is called availability. Availability is a useful clue for assessing frequency or probability, because instances of large classes are usually recalled better and faster than instances of less frequent classes. However, availability is affected by factors other than frequency and probability. Consequently, the reliance on availability leads to predictable biases, some of which are illustrated below.

Biases due to the retrievability of instances

When the size of a class is judged by the availability of its instances, a class whose instances are easily retrieved will appear more numerous than a class of equal frequency whose instances are less retrievable. In an elementary demonstration of this effect, subjects heard a list of well-known personalities of both sexes and were subsequently asked to judge whether the list contained more names of men than of women. Different lists were presented to different groups of subjects. In some of the lists the men were relatively more famous than the women, and in others the women were relatively more famous than the men. In each of the lists, the subjects erroneously judged that the class (sex) that had the more famous personalities was the more numerous (6).

In addition to familiarity, there are other factors, such as salience, which affect the retrievability of instances. For example, the impact of seeing a house burning on the subjective probability of such accidents is probably greater than the impact of reading about a fire in the local paper. Furthermore, recent occurrences are likely to be relatively more available than earlier occurrences. It is a common experience that the subjective probability of traffic accidents rises temporarily when one sees a car overturned by the side of the road.

Biases due to the effectiveness of a search set

Suppose one samples a word (of three letters or more) at random from an English text. Is it more likely that the word starts with r or that r is the third letter? People approach this problem by recalling words that begin with r (road) and words that have r in the third position (car) and assess the relative frequency by the ease with which words of the two types come to mind. Because it is much easier to search for words by their first letter than by their third letter, most people judge words that begin with a given consonant to be more numerous than words in which the same consonant appears in the third position. They do so even for consonants, such as r or k, that are more frequent in the third position than in the first (6).

Different tasks elicit different search sets. For example, suppose you are asked to rate the frequency with which abstract words (thought, love) and concrete words (door, water) appear in written English. A natural way to answer this question is to search for contexts in which the word could appear. It seems easier to think of contexts in which an abstract concept is mentioned (love in love stories) than to think of contexts in which a concrete word (such as door) is mentioned. If the frequency of words is judged by the availability of the contexts in which they appear, abstract words will be judged as relatively more numerous than concrete words. This bias has been observed in a recent study (7) which showed that the judged frequency of occurrence of abstract words was much higher than that of concrete words, equated in objective frequency. Abstract words were also judged to appear in a much greater variety of contexts than concrete words.

Biases of imaginability

Sometimes one has to assess the frequency of a class whose instances are not stored in memory but can be generated according to a given rule. In such situations, one typically generates several instances and evaluates frequency or probability by the ease with which the relevant instances can be constructed. However, the ease of constructing instances does not always reflect their actual frequency, and this mode of evaluation is prone to biases. To illustrate, consider a group of 10 people who form committees of k members, $2 \leq k \leq 8$. How many different committees of k members can be formed? The correct answer to this problem is given by the binomial coefficient $\binom{10}{k}$ which reaches a maximum of 252 for $k = 5$. Clearly, the number of committees of k members equals the number of committees of

$(10 - k)$ members, because any committee of k members defines a unique group of $(10 - k)$ nonmembers.

One way to answer this question without computation is to mentally construct committees of k members and to evaluate their number by the ease with which they come to mind. Committees of few members, say 2, are more available than committees of many members, say 8. The simplest scheme for the construction of committees is a partition of the group into disjoint sets. One readily sees that it is easy to construct five disjoint committees of 2 members, while it is impossible to generate even two disjoint committees of 8 members. Consequently, if frequency is assessed by imaginability, or by availability for construction, the small committees will appear more numerous than larger committees, in contrast to the correct bell-shaped function. Indeed, when naive subjects were asked to estimate the number of distinct committees of various sizes, their estimates were a decreasing monotonic function of committee size (6). For example, the median estimate of the number of committees of 2 members was 70, while the estimate for committees of 8 members was 20 (the correct answer is 45 in both cases).

Imaginability plays an important role in the evaluation of probabilities in real-life situations. The risk involved in an adventurous expedition, for example, is evaluated by imagining contingencies with which the expedition is not equipped to cope. If many such difficulties are vividly portrayed, the expedition can be made to appear exceedingly dangerous, although the ease with which disasters are imagined need not reflect their actual likelihood. Conversely, the risk involved in an undertaking may be grossly underestimated if some possible dangers are either difficult to conceive of, or simply do not come to mind.

Illusory correlation

Chapman and Chapman (8) have described an interesting bias in the judgment of the frequency with which two events co-occur. They presented naive judges with information concerning several hypothetical mental patients. The data for each patient consisted of a clinical diagnosis and a drawing of a person made by the patient. Later the judges estimated the frequency with which each diagnosis (such as paranoia or suspiciousness) had been accompanied by various features of the drawing (such as peculiar eyes). The subjects markedly overestimated the frequency of co-occurrence of natural associates, such as suspiciousness and peculiar eyes. This effect was labeled illusory correlation. In their erroneous judgments of the data to which they had been exposed, naive subjects "rediscovered" much of the common, but unfounded, clinical lore concerning the interpretation of the draw-a-person test. The illusory correlation effect was extremely resistant to contradictory data. It persisted even when the correlation between symptom and diagnosis was actually negative, and it prevented the judges from detecting relationships that were in fact present.

Availability provides a natural account for the illusory-correlation effect. The judgment of how frequently two events co-occur could be based on the strength of the associative bond between them. When the association is strong, one is likely to conclude that the events have been frequently paired. Consequently, strong associates will be judged to have occurred together frequently. According to this view, the illusory correlation between suspiciousness and peculiar drawing of the eyes, for example, is due to the fact that suspiciousness is more readily associated with the eyes than with any other part of the body.

Lifelong experience has taught us that, in general, instances of large classes are recalled better and faster than instances of less frequent classes; that likely occurrences are easier to imagine than unlikely ones; and that the associative connections between events are strengthened when the events frequently co-occur. As a result, man has at his disposal a procedure (the availability heuristic) for estimating the numerosity of a class, the likelihood of an event, or the frequency of co-occurrences, by the ease with which the relevant mental operations of retrieval, construction, or association can be performed. However, as the preceding examples have demonstrated, this valuable estimation procedure results in systematic errors.

ADJUSTMENT AND ANCHORING
In many situations, people make estimates by starting from an initial value that is adjusted to yield the final answer. The initial value, or starting point, may be suggested by the formulation of the problem, or it may be the result of a partial computation. In either case, adjustments are typically insufficient (4). That is, different starting points yield different estimates, which are biased toward the initial values. We call this phenomenon anchoring.

Insufficient adjustment
In a demonstration of the anchoring effect, subjects were asked to estimate various quantities, stated in percentages (for example, the percentage of African countries in the United Nations). For each quantity, a number between 0 and 100 was determined by spinning a wheel of fortune in the subjects' presence. The subjects were instructed to indicate first whether that number was higher or lower than the value of the quantity, and then to estimate the value of the quantity by moving upward or downward from the given number. Different groups were given different numbers for each quantity, and these arbitrary numbers had a marked effect on estimates. For

example, the median estimates of the percentage of African countries in the United Nations were 25 and 45 for groups that received 10 and 65, respectively, as starting points. Payoffs for accuracy did not reduce the anchoring effect.

Anchoring occurs not only when the starting point is given to the subject, but also when the subject bases his estimate on the result of some incomplete computation. A study of intuitive numerical estimation illustrates this effect. Two groups of high school students estimated, within 5 seconds, a numerical expression that was written on the blackboard. One group estimated the product

$$8 \times 7 \times 6 \times 5 \times 4 \times 3 \times 2 \times 1$$

while another group estimated the product

$$1 \times 2 \times 3 \times 4 \times 5 \times 6 \times 7 \times 8$$

To rapidly answer such questions, people may perform a few steps of computation and estimate the product by extrapolation or adjustment. Because adjustments are typically insufficient, this procedure should lead to underestimation. Furthermore, because the result of the first few steps of multiplication (performed from left to right) is higher in the descending sequence than in the ascending sequence, the former expression should be judged larger than the latter. Both predictions were confirmed. The median estimate for the ascending sequence was 512, while the median estimate for the descending sequence was 2,250. The correct answer is 40,320.

Biases in the evaluation of conjunctive and disjunctive events

In a recent study by Bar-Hillel (9) subjects were given the opportunity to bet on one of two events. Three types of events were used: (i) simple events, such as drawing a red marble from a bag containing 50 percent red marbles and 50 percent white marbles; (ii) conjunctive events, such as drawing a red marble seven times in succession, with replacement, from a bag containing 90 percent red marbles and 10 percent white marbles; and (iii) disjunctive events, such as drawing a red marble at least once in seven successive tries, with replacement, from a bag containing 10 percent red marbles and 90 percent white marbles. In this problem, a significant majority of subjects preferred to bet on the conjunctive event (the probability of which is .48) rather than on the simple event (the probability of which is .50). Subjects also preferred to bet on the simple event rather than on the disjunctive event, which has a probability of .52. Thus, most subjects bet on the less likely event in both comparisons. This pattern of choices illustrates a general finding. Studies of choice among gambles and of judgments of probability indicate that people tend to overestimate the probability of conjunctive events (*10*) and to underestimate the probability of disjunctive events. These biases are readily explained as effects of anchoring. The stated probability of the elementary event (success at any one stage) provides a natural starting point for the estimation of the probabilities of both conjunctive and disjunctive events. Since adjustment from the starting point is typically insufficient, the final estimates remain too close to the probabilities of the elementary events in both cases. Note that the overall probability of a conjunctive event is lower than the probability of each elementary event, whereas the overall probability of a disjunctive event is higher than the probability of each elementary event. As a consequence of anchoring, the overall probability will be overestimated in conjunctive problems and underestimated in disjunctive problems.

Biases in the evaluation of compound events are particularly significant in the context of planning. The successful completion of an undertaking, such as the development of a new product, typically has a conjunctive character: for the undertaking to succeed, each of a series of events must occur. Even when each of these events is very likely, the overall probability of success can be quite low if the number of events is large. The general tendency to overestimate the probability of conjunctive events leads to unwarranted optimism in the evaluation of the likelihood that a plan will succeed or that a project will be completed on time. Conversely, disjunctive structures are typically encountered in the evaluation of risks. A complex system, such as a nuclear reactor or a human body, will malfunction if any of its essential components fails. Even when the likelihood of failure in each component is slight, the probability of an overall failure can be high if many components are involved. Because of anchoring, people will tend to underestimate the probabilities of failure in complex systems. Thus, the direction of the anchoring bias can sometimes be inferred from the structure of the event. The chain-like structure of conjunctions leads to overestimation, the funnel-like structure of disjunctions leads to underestimation.

Anchoring in the assessment of subjective probability distributions

In decision analysis, experts are often required to express their beliefs about a quantity, such as the value of the Dow-Jones average on a particular day, in the form of a probability distribution. Such a distribution is usually constructed by asking the person to select values of the quantity that correspond to specified percentiles of his subjective probability distribution. For example, the judge may be asked to select a number, X_{90}, such that his subjective probability that this number will be higher than the value of the Dow-Jones average is .90. That is, he should select the value X_{90} so that he is just willing to accept 9 to 1 odds that the Dow-Jones average will not exceed it. A subjective probability distribution for the value of the

Dow-Jones average can be constructed from several such judgments corresponding to different percentiles.

By collecting subjective probability distributions for many different quantities, it is possible to test the judge for proper calibration. A judge is properly (or externally) calibrated in a set of problems if exactly Π percent of the true values of the assessed quantities falls below his stated values of X_Π. For example, the true values should fall below X_{01} for 1 percent of the quantities and above X_{99} for 1 percent of the quantities. Thus, the true values should fall in the confidence interval between X_{01} and X_{99} on 98 percent of the problems.

Several investigators (11) have obtained probability distributions for many quantities from a large number of judges. These distributions indicated large and systematic departures from proper calibration. In most studies, the actual values of the assessed quantities are either smaller than X_{01} or greater than X_{99} for about 30 percent of the problems. That is, the subjects state overly narrow confidence intervals which reflect more certainty than is justified by their knowledge about the assessed quantities. This bias is common to naive and to sophisticated subjects, and it is not eliminated by introducing proper scoring rules, which provide incentives for external calibration. This effect is attributable, in part at least, to anchoring.

To select X_{90} for the value of the Dow-Jones average, for example, it is natural to begin by thinking about one's best estimate of the Dow-Jones and to adjust this value upward. If this adjustment—like most others—is insufficient, then X_{90} will not be sufficiently extreme. A similar anchoring effect will occur in the selection of X_{10}, which is presumably obtained by adjusting one's best estimate downward. Consequently, the confidence interval between X_{10} and X_{90} will be too narrow, and the assessed probability distribution will be too tight. In support of this interpretation it can be shown that subjective probabilities are systematically altered by a procedure in which one's best estimate does not serve as an anchor.

Subjective probability distributions for a given quantity (the Dow-Jones average) can be obtained in two different ways: (i) by asking the subject to select values of the Dow-Jones that correspond to specified percentiles of his probability distribution and (ii) by asking the subject to assess the probabilities that the true value of the Dow-Jones will exceed some specified values. The two procedures are formally equivalent and should yield identical distributions. However, they suggest different modes of adjustment from different anchors. In procedure (i), the natural starting point is one's best estimate of the quantity. In procedure (ii), on the other hand, the subject may be anchored on the value stated in the question. Alternatively, he may be anchored on even odds, or 50-50 chances, which is a natural starting point in the estimation of likelihood. In either case, procedure (ii) should yield less extreme odds than procedure (i).

To contrast the two procedures, a set of 24 quantities (such as the air distance from New Delhi to Peking) was presented to a group of subjects who assessed either X_{10} or X_{90} for each problem. Another group of subjects received the median judgment of the first group for each of the 24 quantities. They were asked to assess the odds that each of the given values exceeded the true value of the relevant quantity. In the absence of any bias, the second group should retrieve the odds specified to the first group, that is, 9:1. However, if even odds or the stated value serve as anchors, the odds of the second group should be less extreme, that is, closer to 1:1. Indeed, the median odds stated by this group, across all problems, were 3:1. When the judgments of the two groups were tested for external calibration, it was found that subjects in the first group were too extreme, in accord with earlier studies. The events that they defined as having a probability of .10 actually obtained in 24 percent of the cases. In contrast, subjects in the second group were too conservative. Events to which they assigned an average probability of .34 actually obtained in 26 percent of the cases. These results illustrate the manner in which the degree of calibration depends on the procedure of elicitation.

DISCUSSION

This article has been concerned with cognitive biases that stem from the reliance on judgmental heuristics. These biases are not attributable to motivational effects such as wishful thinking or the distortion of judgments by payoffs and penalties. Indeed, several of the severe errors of judgment reported earlier occurred despite the fact that subjects were encouraged to be accurate and were rewarded for the correct answers (2, 6).

The reliance on heuristics and the prevalence of biases are not restricted to laymen. Experienced researchers are also prone to the same biases—when they think intuitively. For example, the tendency to predict the outcome that best represents the data, with insufficient regard for prior probability, has been observed in the intuitive judgments of individuals who have had extensive training in statistics (1, 5). Although the statistically sophisticated avoid elementary errors, such as the gambler's fallacy, their intuitive judgments are liable to similar fallacies in more intricate and less transparent problems.

It is not surprising that useful heuristics such as representativeness and availability are retained, even though they occasionally lead to errors in prediction or estimation. What is perhaps surprising is the failure of people to infer from lifelong experience such fundamental statistical rules as regression toward the mean, or the effect of sample size on sampling variability. Although everyone is exposed, in the normal course of life, to numerous examples from which these rules could have been induced, very few people discover the principles of sampling and regression on their own. Statistical principles are not learned from everyday experience because the relevant instances are not coded appropriately. For example, people do not discover that successive lines in a text differ more in average word length than do successive pages, because they simply do not attend to the average word length of individual lines or pages. Thus, people do not learn the relation between sample size and sampling variability, although the data for such learning are abundant.

The lack of an appropriate code also explains why people usually do not detect the biases in their judgments of probability. A person could conceivably learn whether his judgments are externally calibrated by keeping a tally of the proportion of events that actually occur among those to which he assigns the same probability. However, it is not natural to group events by their judged probability. In the absence of such grouping it is impossible for an individual to discover, for example, that only 50 percent of the predictions to which he has assigned a probability of .9 or higher actually came true.

The empirical analysis of cognitive biases has implications for the theoretical and applied role of judged probabilities. Modern decision theory (12, 13) regards subjective probability as the quantified opinion of an idealized person. Specifically, the subjective probability of a given event is defined by the set of bets about this event that such a person is willing to accept. An internally consistent, or coherent, subjective probability measure can be derived for an individual if his choices among bets satisfy certain principles, that is, the axioms of the theory. The derived probability is subjective in the sense that different individuals are allowed to have different probabilities for the same event. The major contribution of this approach is that it provides a rigorous subjective interpretation of probability that is applicable to unique events and is embedded in a general theory of rational decision.

It should perhaps be noted that, while subjective probabilities can sometimes be inferred from preferences among bets, they are normally not formed in this fashion. A person bets on team A rather than on team B because he believes that team A is more likely to win; he does not infer this belief from his betting preferences. Thus, in reality, subjective probabilities determine preferences among bets and are not derived from them, as in the axiomatic theory of rational decision (12).

The inherently subjective nature of probability has led many students to the belief that coherence, or internal consistency, is the only valid criterion by which judged probabilities should be evaluated. From the standpoint of the formal theory of subjective probability, any set of internally consistent probability judgments is as good as any other. This criterion is not entirely satisfactory, because an internally consistent set of subjective probabilities can be incompatible with other beliefs held by the individual. Consider a person whose subjective probabilities for all possible outcomes of a coin-tossing game reflect the gambler's fallacy. That is, his estimate of the probability of tails on a particular toss increases with the number of consecutive heads that preceded that toss. The judgments of such a person could be internally consistent and therefore acceptable as adequate subjective probabilities according to the criterion of the formal theory. These probabilities, however, are incompatible with the generally held belief that a coin has no memory and is therefore incapable of generating sequential dependencies. For judged probabilities to be considered adequate, or rational, internal consistency is not enough. The judgments must be compatible with the entire web of beliefs held by the individual. Unfortunately, there can be no simple formal procedure for assessing the compatibility of a set of probability judgments with the judge's total system of beliefs. The rational judge will nevertheless strive for compatibility, even though internal consistency is more easily achieved and assessed. In particular, he will attempt to make his probability judgments compatible with his knowledge about the subject matter, the laws of probability, and his own judgmental heuristics and biases.

SUMMARY

This article described three heuristics that are employed in making judgments under uncertainty: (i) representativeness, which is usually employed when people are asked to judge the probability that an object or event A belongs to class or process B; (ii) availability of instances or scenarios, which is often employed when people are asked to assess the frequency of a class or the plausibility of a particular development; and (iii) adjustment from an anchor, which is usually employed in numerical prediction when a relevant value is available. These heuristics are highly economical and usually effective, but they lead to systematic and predictable errors. A better understanding of these heuristics and of the biases to which they lead could improve judgments and decisions in situations of uncertainty.

REFERENCES AND NOTES

1. D. Kahneman and A. Tversky, *Psychol. Rev.* **80,** 237 (1973).

2. ———, *Cognitive Psychol.* **3,** 430 (1972).

3. W. Edwards, in *Formal Representation of Human Judgment,* B. Kleinmuntz, Ed. (Wiley, New York, 1968), pp. 17–52.

4. P. Slovic and S. Lichtenstein, *Organ. Behav. Hum. Performance* **6,** 649 (1971).

5. A. Tversky and D. Kahneman, *Psychol. Bull.* **76,** 105 (1971).

6. ———, *Cognitive Psychol.* **5,** 207 (1973).

7. R. C. Galbraith and B. J. Underwood, *Mem. Cognition* **1,** 56 (1973).

8. L. J. Chapman and J. P. Chapman, *J. Abnorm. Psychol.* **73,** 193 (1967); *ibid.*, **74,** 271 (1969).

9. M. Bar-Hillel, *Organ. Behav. Hum. Performance* **9,** 396 (1973).

10. J. Cohen, E. I. Chesnick, D. Haran, *Br. J. Psychol.* **63,** 41 (1972).

11. M. Alpert and H. Raiffa, unpublished manuscript; C. A. S. von Holstein, *Acta Psychol.* **35,** 478 (1971); R. L. Winkler, *J. Am. Stat. Assoc.* **62,** 776 (1967).

12. L. J. Savage, *The Foundations of Statistics* (Wiley, New York, 1954).

13. B. De Finetti, in *International Encyclopedia of the Social Sciences*, D. E. Sills, Ed. (Macmillan, New York, 1968), vol. 12, pp. 496–504.

14. This research was supported by the Advanced Research Projects Agency of the Department of Defense and was monitored by the Office of Naval Research under contract N00014-73-C-0438 to the Oregon Research Institute, Eugene. Additional support for this research was provided by the Research and Development Authority of the Hebrew University, Jerusalem, Israel.

PART VI

STATISTICAL MODELS IN
LEGAL SETTINGS

.

EVALUATING THE "SMALL" PROBABILITY OF A CATASTROPHIC ACCIDENT FROM THE MARINE TRANSPORTATION OF LIQUEFIED NATURAL GAS

WILLIAM B. FAIRLEY

I. INTRODUCTION

Applications have been made to the Federal Power Commission (FPC) for permission to import liquefied natural gas (LNG) from Algeria into United States ports with investments on the order of $10 billion envisioned for facilities and specially built tankers. However, a large spill of LNG in port could result in a catastrophic fire whose consequences are of the same order of magnitude in lives and property loss as a major accident in a nuclear power plant. This article is a review of problems in estimates of the probability of a large spill of LNG and a catastrophic accident therefrom that were developed in written testimony and cross-examination in proceedings at the Federal Power Commission (1). The purpose is not to argue one way or the other about the outcome of the technical debate in the proceedings. It is rather to draw from the experience several tentative criteria or guidelines for evaluating catastrophic accident probabilities in new problems.

Although the points made are illustrated by the LNG experience, they have analogues in other fields of accidents as well, especially where the safety of a relatively new and complex technological system is in question (2). Nuclear power plant safety is an important example (3). There too, statistical models, data analysis, and judgment have been used to estimate "small" probabilities of a catastrophic accident. The adjective "small" is in quotes because it is arguable whether the probability cumulated over several years would be regarded as small by the ordinary citizen.

This paper appeared in David Okrent, ed., "Risk-Benefit Methodology and Application: Some Papers Presented at the Engineering Foundation Workshop, September 22–26, 1975, Asilomar, California, UCLA-ENG-7498, December 1975. The author gratefully acknowledges the help of the following people in preparing this discussion: James A. Fay; Thomas A. Arnold; Bruce J. Terris; Michael O. Finkelstein; Frederick Mosteller; James Harlan; Stuart Sessions; Theodore Xiarhos.

This article explores some of the issues of modeling, of use of data, and of judgment that such estimation of small probabilities raises. It should be regarded as a case study of issues that arise in applying statistical and probabilistic thinking to similar problems.

Consideration of the risk of a catastrophic LNG fire formed part of the Final Environmental Impact Statement issued by the FPC in July 1974 for the construction and operation of an import terminal for LNG on Staten Island, New York. The applicant was the Distrigas Corporation, a subsidiary of the Cabot Corporation of Boston (4). In the Final Environmental Impact Statement, a principal basis for the finding that the proposed movement of LNG tankers and LNG barges in New York harbor posed an acceptable risk were commissioned reports done for the FPC and for the applicant by consultants (5).

We will refer to the studies done for the FPC as the "Commission reports," to those done for the Distrigas Corporation as the "Applicant reports," and to both together as the "LNG risk reports" or sometimes simply as the "reports." The reports are similar in the general approach taken to estimating the probability of a large LNG spill or of a major accident arising from such a spill, although there are many important differences in detail (6A).

The present article draws attention to a number of problems in estimating small probabilities in a real application—problems that are illustrated by or in the reports. The purpose is not to be critical of these reports, which attack a new problem area with many useful and suggestive ideas, but rather to highlight the problems in a concrete setting. Many of these problems have no obvious best solution or no obvious solution at all. The guidelines are not presented as a complete list in any sense, but rather as a group of morals that could usefully be drawn from consideration of the risk reports on LNG marine transportation.

II. SUMMARY OF THE LNG RISK REPORTS

The Distrigas proposal called for tanker movement from the Atlantic through New York harbor to the terminal on Staten Island. Some of the LNG unloaded at the terminal would be piped to customers in New Jersey, and some would be reloaded onto barges for movement through the harbor and up the East River for delivery to the Brooklyn Union Gas Company and Consolidated Edison. Parallel studies of the risks of LNG tanker and barge movements were done in the Commission reports and the Applicant reports.

The Commission reports estimated the probability of a major LNG accident over the course of a ten-year period from all the tanker movement combined to be on the order of 1 in 4000 and the same probability from the barge movement to be on the order of 1 in 400.

Because accidents involving large spills of LNG in harbors have not occurred, or at least have not been reported, the reports sought data on accidents such as collisions, groundings, and rammings occurring to other types of big ships, including tankers, and barges. For example, in the Commission reports, United States Coast Guard data on reported accidents to tankers in New York harbor over the period 1969–1973 were used to estimate a base rate of accidents (but not necessarily involving spills) for vessels thought to be similar in relevant ways to LNG tankers. A total of 49 accidents in an estimated 86,400 transits were discovered for this period, and following an upward adjustment of the estimated rate to allow for sampling variations in the accident count, a rate of 8 accidents per 10,000 transits was chosen as the estimated base rate.

An estimate of the probability of an accident occurring to an LNG tanker was now obtained by taking various features of LNG tanker navigation into account on a judgmental basis, including new proposed Coast Guard rules and regulations covering the conditions of LNG tanker movement, which rules were thought to make these movements relatively safer than those of ordinary tankers. Such items as Coast Guard escort, daylight travel, and use of special navigational equipment were included. On the basis of these considerations, the accident rate of 8/10,000 was reduced by a factor of 5 to 8/50,000.

The second stage of the analysis in the reports was to estimate the chance that a large spill would occur once an accident had happened. The product of this rate and the rate of accidents yields an estimated rate of accidents *that also involve a large spill*. The reports developed models to estimate the chance of a spill. Two of these models were based on detailed physical consideration of LNG tankers and barges, one was based on the relation of the chance of a spill to the chance of monetary damages exceeding a threshold value, and a fourth was an inferential model based on the observation of zero "massive" spills from 50 barge accidents reported in New York harbor over a period. These models incorporated either implicitly or explicitly a factor of reduction for the chance of an LNG spill as compared to the chance of a spill of most other types of cargo. For example, in the Commission report on LNG tankers the chance of a spill from an ordinary tanker was estimated at 1 in 100, and this figure was reduced by factors of 3/2 and 5 for an LNG spill.

Multiplying together all the factors in the Commission report on tankers yields an estimated rate of 1 in 4,664,179 per transit for a major LNG spill, and multiplying again by the assumed number of trips in a ten-year period yields an estimated rate of 1 in 3746 or approximately 1 in 4000.

III. SOME GUIDELINES FOR ESTIMATION OF ACCIDENT PROBABILITIES

A.   Estimates of "the" probability of an accident must include, explicitly or implicitly, contributions from all the possible sources of the accident

A probability will be underestimated to the extent that possible sources are excluded, and so a downwardly biased estimate is the consequence of omitting relevant sources of risk. The underestimation is likely to be a serious concern only to the degree to which the probability of the omitted sources might be of the same order of magnitude as the included sources.

In the LNG risk reports, the case of a collision of the LNG vessel with others was analyzed extensively, but a number of other scenarios also leading to a spill were not included; or if they were mentioned, no quantitative estimate or bound on their size was supplied. Discussion of "the" probability of an LNG spill in massive operations may, consequently, have been misleading because of these omissions (6B).

Every list of accident sources must contain an "other" or "miscellaneous" category that includes sources unidentified as yet. The "other" category may include, for example, sequences of events within a complex technological system and events involving the interaction of human operators with the system.

The existence of these possibilities means there is some minimum value below which a small estimate of the probability of an event is not credible. Since these events are possible, we must assign some probability to them, and the size of the probability attached to them taken as a group provides a minimum value or range of minimum values to any overall estimate of the probability of an accident. In some cases this minimum is larger, maybe considerably larger, than the value estimated from the list of identified risk sources.

An example from a very different context illustrates this point. A royal flush, consisting of an ace through ten all of one suit in a dealer's poker hand, has a small probabiluty, but the chance that such a hand is the result of cheating would sometimes be accorded a much higher probability. Thus, what is the chance of seeing a royal flush in the the real world? It is the chance of seeing it arise naturally plus the chance that it arises from cheating. The chance that it arises will be the sum of the probabilities assigned to these two events, if we use the most natural assumptions.

A royal flush can be an ace through ten in clubs, hearts, diamonds, or spades: 4 different hands. The total number of possible poker hands is the number of different ways of selecting 5 cards out of 52, which can be shown to be 2,598,960. If every hand were equally likely to be dealt, then the dealer would have 4 chances in 2,598,960 to get a royal flush, or 1 chance in 649,740.

Now suppose that successful cheating to reach a royal flush was given the probability of 1 in 10,000. What is the probability of a royal flush? It is equal to 1/10,000 plus 1/649,740, which is just a little over 1 in 10,000. The value of 1 in 10,000 is then a minimum value to any realistic estimate of the probability of a royal flush.

Would not the 1 in 10,000 figure for the probability of cheating be a guess? No doubt it would, even though some evidence and argument could be used to support it or some other figure. Poker players could ask themselves how many times in 10,000 hands of play they believed they had been cheated. They could ask how many times a dealer had pulled a royal flush. Perhaps data could be gathered on this frequency. Would not the number be poorly determined in the end?

We would have to hear arguments from informed persons and collect and review whatever evidence we could (7). In the end we still might find considerable disagreement, ranging perhaps from persons who thought the probability approached more than 50% to persons who thought the fears were greatly exaggerated. However, even the latter person might be unwilling to assign a value below 1 in 1000 or 1 in 10,000 per hand for the event—both of which, after all, are small probabilities. In the end we might find general agreement on some minimum value, even though many people believed the actual probability was higher. This minimum value could be one or more orders of magnitude larger than the original estimate (8). Some of the LNG risk estimates appear to be smaller than the probabilities that some observers at least would assign to unfamiliar or unexpected sources of LNG accidents. For example, the Applicant's barge report estimates an annual probability of 1/15,000 for an LNG spill during the 70 barge transits between Rossville and Greenpoint. Is the probability alone of a sabotage of that operation leading to a spill possibly greater than 1 in 15,000 in a year? My purpose is not to speculate upon whether or not it is greater, but to make the point that the estimates of probabilities made for identifiable and analyzed sources have to be considered *together with* the probability of an accident arising from all other sources.

Does the historical record of accidents analyzed in the reports already include the possibilities of unusual or unidentified events, and therefore do the estimates in these reports already include an allowance for such possibilities? No, because there may be entirely new phenomena involved concerning LNG transportation. Experience with new LNG vessel designs with their safety features, and with the entire developing cryogenic technology is thin. Other things that are new include, for example, recent international experience with bombings, hijackings, and the like. New technology and a new historical situation make it necessary to continually reassess sources of risk. Finally, a rate of unusual events is not reliably estimated from a brief span of experience.

B. The widest related base of potential accident experience (exposure) should be surveyed for indications about the probability of an accident for a particular kind of experience

In a new technology the problem posed for the would-be analyst of accident probabilities is the absence of a significant historical record of operating experience with which to estimate accident rates. In particular the inference that can be drawn about the maximum accident rate given a record of zero occurrences of accident rates of some type, say of catastrophic proportions, is very limited at best.

For example, LNG marine experience to date is consistent with much higher rates than estimated. The Commission's Final Environmental Impact Statement finds that the "accident-free" experiences of LNG tankers in some 800 voyages in worldwide operations to date provides "significant" evidence of the safety of these operations (9). No definition of "accident" and no evidence of a search of the record for a finding of zero accidents was given to support the claim. Suppose, however, that it *were* verified that there had been literally zero accidents during this experience.

Then we can ask what values of a probability of an accident per voyage would be ruled out by a record of zero accidents in 800 voyages and what values would be consistent with such a record. We can reason intuitively that the evidence should rule out very high values. If the probability of an accident per voyage were 1/2 then the number of accidents "expected" would be half of 800 or 400. However, 400 is only an average. The actual figure would most likely be somewhat above or below 400.

Following this line of reasoning in examining expected values, we can see that a probability of 1/100 also does not seem to be consistent with the evidence, because it would imply an expected or average number of 8 accidents. Of course, since 1/100 is a probability, we could by chance observe zero accidents even though 8 were expected.

A value of 1/800 for the probability per voyage would imply an expected or average number of accidents of exactly 1. Now there is a considerable chance of observing zero accidents in 800 even though the expected number was 1.

If the accident probability per voyage were really 1 in 8,000, then the expected number of accidents in a year would be only 0.1, and the chance of observing zero accidents in 800 would be even larger.

So we see that very low values of a probability per trip are certainly consistent with the assumed record of zero accidents in 800 voyages. But on the other hand, a value as high as 1 in 100 or 1 in 200 would also be consistent with the record. That the record is consistent with very low values does not prove that the values are low (10).

Returning to the criterion stated at the beginning of this section that the widest possible base of experience should be surveyed, we first point out the corollary that the place to begin is at home. That is, the experience that *is* available for the given technology should be carefully considered. Careful consideration will involve a thorough survey of the history of operating experience. Sometimes claims are made that are not substantiated in this fashion.

For example, the Applicant barge report states that "the routine shipment of LNG by tanker in and out of European, North African, Asian, and Alaskan ports without incident over the past decade has demonstrated that the water transport of LNG can be accomplished safely." (11). To document the nonoccurrence of a single "incident" as claimed, we would need supporting documentation from official records and probably also from private casualty records. We would also need to know the definition of an "incident" to ascertain to what events the claim extends (12).

How far afield from the particular technology or experience whose accident probability is in question should accident experience be gathered? This question cannot be given any universal answer, but in each instance there is likely to be analogous or partially analogous experience that could be considered, even if it is later determined not to be relevant.

In the case of marine LNG safety, the accident records of ships carrying other liquefied gases would appear to be partly relevant. Accidents have occurred to ships carrying other liquefied gases. The following account appears in Noel Mostert's *Supership* (13):

> Experience is the only guide and there is one particularly disturbing experience with a liquid gas carrier, as recounted in his article in *Safety at Sea* by Captain Bayley. In the autumn of 1968 a small Swedish gas tanker named *Claude*, carrying 900 tons of liquefied butane gas, was sailing down Southampton water in foggy weather. She was in charge of a pilot. The *Claude* collided with an inbound British freighter. "Seconds after the collision," Captain Bayley writes, "the pilot of the *Claude* found himself alone on the bridge of the stricken ship, the rest of the crew having jumped into the fog-shrouded water. The gas tanker's engine was left turning with slight reverse pitch on the propeller! The pilot knew nothing of the cargo beneath him, but figuring that the crew knew what was best for their own skins, he too abandoned ship." The abandoned *Claude* drifted back the way she had come, assisted by her propeller and the tide, and went aground. The drama however did not end there. The ship was towed to a refinery and a Portuguese gas ship was chartered to take off the *Claude*'s cargo. During the transfer operation one of the hoses sprang a leak and a "vast cloud of gas was carried on the wind towards the refinery and the city of Southampton." "In a fine display of panic," Captain Bayley writes, "the Portuguese tanker steamed away, ignoring the rupturing of hoses and pipelines, inestimably increasing the risk of explosion. The rapid evaporation of the liquid gas caused ice to form and volunteers working without gas masks...had a hard job to close the valves left open by the departing gentlemen of Portugal."

On November 9, 1974, the tanker *Yuyo Maru*, which was carrying liquefied butane gas and other cargo collided with a freighter in Tokyo Bay, starting a large fire and killing 19 crewmen with 14 missing (*14*). An investigation might well show other casualties involving the marine transportation of liqufied gases.

The accident record of LNG operations on land may have some relevance to particular types of accidents that occur with LNG on the water. While there are unique features of marine operations with LNG, there must also be features in common with or related to operations with LNG on land. For example, some fire-fighting equipment or pipe materials might be similar on land and water, while tanker hull construction might have no parallel on land. Some hazards associated with earthquakes and pipelines might be similar.

The land record may offer some lessons about the predictability of safety with new technology, even if it cannot be taken in any direct way as a guide to the future marine record. Furthermore, while each particular accident may have unique features that are unlikely to be repeated, the record needs to be reviewed for whatever lessons it may have about the possibilities and likelihoods of a kind of accident, keeping in mind that particular details are unlikely to be predictable.

There are unfortunate major accidents with LNG on land, the principal ones being the Cleveland disaster of 1944 that took 133 lives and the 1973 Staten Island storage tank fire that killed 40 (*15*).

An important statistical point about selectivity in gathering data requires emphasis when considering the use of related experience. It is almost always possible to define the experience so narrowly that no major accidents have occurred. Thus major LNG accidents have occurred but not major LNG *marine* accidents. Significant gas tanker accidents have occurred but not significant *LNG* tanker accidents. This may be due to the greater safety of LNG tankers, but it may also be due to luck.

A related point is potential selectivity in choosing the source of data or the geographical or time coverage of the data for a particular class of experience. It is possible, quite inadvertently, to choose a data set of origin and scope that gives a biased estimate of accident rates. In any statistical investigation, it is good practice to discuss the availability of alternative data sets and the reasons for choosing the set or sets used in preference to others.

While related experience should not be ignored, neither can it be taken as a direct source of estimates for accident rates in the particular technology or experience of interest. There may be substantial differences in rates associated with differences in the source of experience (as between land and sea), in different locations, in different times, and with variations in technology. In the absence of explicit theory about these differences in rates, we will have to exercise judgment about the relation of accident rates in related experience to the accident rate of primary interest.

Wherever possible, data should be analyzed to either substantiate constancy of rates or to exhibit the degree of variability present. Where constancy is found, there is some justification for using the wider data base for estimating a common rate. Where variability is found, some information may thereby be provided about the uncertainty in the observed rate of principal interest.

The LNG risk reports have assumed LNG vessels to be like other classes of vessels for the purpose of estimating a base rate of accidents, but they have then noted *differences* between LNG vessels and others in order to reduce the expected LNG accident and spill rate below the base rate by factors of 5 or 25. Data and analysis are needed to show that the base rate had suitable constancy over different years, ports, cargoes, ship types, etc. The ways in which LNG vessels might be *more* dangerous than others need attention. For example there may be positive contributions to the chance of an accident arising from the unique or incompletely understood features of LNG technology and marine transportation—such things as the new designs of tankers, new use of materials in construction, new systems for fire fighting with LNG, effects of small spills, or the trains of events in different accident scenarios. Mostert's account of the mishaps of the *Claude* indicate a source of potentially greater danger, namely greater apprehensiveness by crew and officers of the vessel (*16*).

The possible need for inflating factors can be explained in a slightly different way. What is the base situation to which various safety measures are applied? Is it correct to take the reported frequency of accidents of ordinary vessels as the estimated probability of an accident for an LNG vessel if (1) that vessel did not have the special safety features it is presumed to have and if (2) it were operated just like any other vessel? This is the assumption underlying the procedure of the risk reports. The safety measures may only restore the *status quo ante*; that is, they make what would otherwise be a dangerous LNG vessel as safe as other vessels but no safer. It is possible that this is partially true so that the reduction factors in the reports are too great.

The size of the underestimate of the risk that could result from such a one-sided consideration is great. The Commission reports each use two reduction factors of 5—one for the presumed greater safety in navigation and one for the presumed greater safety in design of LNG vessels—yielding combined reduction factors of 25. Without these two factors the Commission estimate of a major LNG barge accident in ten years might be 1 in 16, not 1 in 400.

C. The combination of estimates of probability in parts of a system to reach overall estimates of probability is subject to subtle errors and must be carefully reviewed

In the LNG reports, the final estimate of a probability of a spill in each of the reports is reached by multiplying rate of accidents expected for LNG vessels (for example, 5 in 50,000 for LNG barges) times rate of spills expected in accidents (for example, 9 in 500 for LNG barges). The product of the two rates is then said to be a rate of spills expected for LNG vessels. This product, however, is correct only if the kinds of accidents used in the two rates are the same. The second rate, or spill rate in an accident, must be the spill rate in those accidents that could occur to an LNG vessel. Now in the Applicant barge report and in both of the Commission reports, it is assumed that because of the special navigational rules and aids for LNG vessels only 20% of all accidents that occur to ordinary barges could occur to LNG vessels. That is, the rate of 5 accidents in 50,000 transits for LNG barges is based on taking one-fifth of 20% of the observed (adjusted) rate of 5 per 10,000 for ordinary barges. If the 20% were no more productive of spills than the whole population of accidents, then the spill rate for LNG vessels in these accidents would be the same as the spill rate for LNG vessels in all accidents. Without evidence that the 20% is not more productive or less productive of spills, we do not know if the rate of accidents times the rate of spills given accidents yields an overall rate of spills. The assumption that the spill rate for the 20% category of accidents is the same as the rate for all accidents is equivalent to assuming that the spill rate is independent of the accident category.

Another example of combinations of estimates involving unargued independence assumptions occurred in developing the reduction factors of 5 in the LNG risk reports. The Applicant barge report assumes that the several navigational rules and aids have independent effects on accident reduction. Let us assume for the moment that each of the preventive actions taken alone would cause the reduction in accidents that is claimed; this does not imply that the combined effect of all the actions can be computed by multiplying reduction factors together. These actions may be duplicative of each other in the sense that they eliminate the same set of accidents, or the accidents that one eliminates include all the ones that the other does (*17*).

Personal judgment can easily err in combining the effects of several individual factors used in combination. Combination is especially difficult on an intuitive basis. A highly interesting discussion of the difficulties people have with forming judgments of probabilities of complex events when unaided by formal methods of analysis is given in the previous article in this book.

D. Possible sources of error and uncertainty in estimates should be explicitly considered and, wherever possible, estimated quantitatively
It is common to estimate sampling error and make adjustments for that, but not uncommon to see much larger potential sources of nonsampling error overlooked. Thus the LNG risk reports seemed not to take into account the

possible existence of unreported marine accidents and inaccuracies in the reported amounts of damage. The reports do not make a distinction between actual and reported rates and amounts, discussing "numbers of accidents" not "reported numbers of accidents." We know in every field of data collection that the numbers of events reported to authorities and officially recorded by the latter may differ substantially from the actual frequency of these events (*18*).

The Commission barge report uses two different Coast Guard data sets on reported barge accidents. Appendix A, said to cover accidents in New York harbor, includes accidents located some distance from that harbor: Philadelphia, Pennsylvania; Snake Hill, Pennsylvania; Peekskill, New York; and Erie Basin, New York, for example. Table 2.3 involves only accidents in New York harbor. The note to Appendix A reads:

> Note: The data base employed for Appendix A is somewhat different from the data base of Table 2.3. In particular, a slightly different set of fiscal years is involved. The geographical area may also be somewhat different.

This note reveals that the geographical boundaries of the data are not well understood. No explanation is given of the uncertainties involved or of why no better definition could be supplied (*19*). Such reports would be improved by including explanations of complications in the data. This is a general principle for statistical reports, not just for accident studies.

In problems of this kind, sampling error may not be dealt with as conservatively as it seems to be. For the LNG data the rates of reported accidents in New York harbor over recent 4-year periods as computed in the Commission reports were 1 per 1763 transits for tankers (or 5.67 per 10,000) and 1 per 3055 transits (or 3.27 per 10,000) for barges.

Instead of taking these as the estimates of accident probabilities for vessels, the higher values of 1 per 1250 and 1 per 2000 for tankers and for barges, respectively, were chosen to allow for the possibility that the lower reported frequencies were the result of chance fluctuations below normal values. These adjusted rates are about 50% higher than the reported rates. An upward adjustment is definitely conservative. How conservative were the sizes of the upward adjustments? The reports say that the sizes were chosen to give only a 1% chance that, very roughly speaking, the adjustments should be any larger.

Whether the adjustments were conservative depends on the assumption that was made about the character of the chance fluctuations of reported accident rates about a true or normal value. The assumption made was that these fluctuations occur with probabilities given by a Poisson distribution (*20*).

What is the evidence for this assumption? The Commission tanker report says: "Since the number of accidents is a count, it should follow the

Poisson distribution." (21). The understood premise is that every count is Poisson or that every count of accidents is Poisson, neither of which is true. Many examples of count data are not Poisson. And, although the Poisson has a long history of use for accident data, so do other distributions like the negative binomial, the Polya, and various "mixture" distributions (22). Unless the assumption of a Poisson distribution is supported, we do not have a basis for believing that the sizes of the adjustments are as conservative as believed.

Other distributions would be likely to produce greater variability in the numbers of accidents than a Poisson. The consequence of greater variability in the number of accidents observed for any given expected or normal rate of accidents is that large fluctuations from the expected value are more likely. Therefore, to attain a given degree of conservatism, larger upward adjustments would have to be made in such a case than if the fluctuations followed the Poisson distribution. Witness the fact that in attempting to control the quality of manufactured product, quality-control engineers regard the Poisson distribution as an ideal state to be achieved by gaining control over all aspects of the process, not something that comes automatically with counts of defects or of defectives. Initially they expect additional uncontrolled variation because of differences in such variables as operators, machines, raw materials, lighting, and even day of the week. Corresponding variation in the LNG problem might depend on weather, time of year, amount of traffic, and state of international relations. An illustration of an unusual event is a "boat parade" when boats and ships welcome an arrival like a replica of the *Santa Maria*. The sudden appearance of hundreds of boats where handfuls previously sailed can change accident probabilities considerably.

What are the possible numerical consequences of such matters in the LNG risk reports for estimates of probabilities of a spill or a major LNG accident? It is helpful to group important sources of error and of uncertainty in the estimates of probabilities of a spill or major accident in six categories and to discuss how each might increase the final estimates. Tables 1 and 2 apply this discussion quantitatively to the Commission reports.

The discussion that follows does not suggest new estimates for accident rates. Rather it gives a set of reminders of what these rates might well be in the light of the information presented in the reports. What is needed beyond this, in accident assessment problems, is a comprehensive discussion of sources of error and uncertainty that would analyze the separate sources, their interrelationships, and the possibilities of setting upper and lower bounds on their effects.

Reporting error refers to errors in the basic data used. The existence of unreported accidents means that the (adjusted) rates of 8 accidents per 10,000 transits for tankers and 5 accidents per 10,000 transits for barges

TABLE 1 SOURCES OF ERROR AND UNCERTAINTY IN COMMISSION TANKER REPORT BASED ON TABLE 3, ATTACHMENT 2, ESTIMATE OF THE PROBABILITY OF AN UNDESIRABLE LNG EVENT.

Factor	1 Symbol	2 Commission report estimate	3 Source of error or uncertainty in estimate	4 Possible upward correction factor for estimate (Multiply times Column 2)
Number of trips	A	1245^a		
Historical probability of a tankship or tank barge accident	B	8/10,000	Reporting error Extrapolation to LNG vessels	2 to 5 2 to 5
LNG navigation reduction factor	C	1/5	Speculatively based estimate	5
Right tail area of damage distribution	D	1/100	Unsubstantiated theory	2 or more
Probability that damage occurs in tank area	E	2/3	Definitional error	3/2
Probability of spillage for a tankship or tank barge	F	1	—	—
Reduction factor engineering design of an LNG vessel as compared to a tankship or tank vessel	G	1/5	Speculatively based estimate	5
Probability of an undesirable event given the foregoing	H	1	—	—
Probability of an undesirable LNG event in 10 years (product of factors A through H)		1/3746		
Single trip probability (product of factors B through H)		1/4,664,179		

^{a} Trips in 10 years to Staten Island and Providence

found in the Commission reports may be underestimates of the true rates. It seems possible in the light of Captain Hill's remarks (*17*) that the underestimate could be somewhere between 200 and 500 percent; that is, the factor of underestimate might be between 2 and 5. Multiplying the rate of 8 for tankers by 2 and by 5, we see that the true rate might be between 16 and 40

TABLE 2 SOURCES OF ERROR AND UNCERTAINTY IN COMMISSION BARGE REPORT BASED ON TABLE 2.1, ATTACHMENT 4, ESTIMATE OF THE PROBABILITY OF AN UNDESIRABLE LNG EVENT.

Factor	1 Symbol	2 Commission report estimate	3 Source of error or uncertainty in estimate	4 Possible upward correction factor for estimate (Multiply times Column 2)
Number of trips	A	1380[a]		
Historical probability of a tank barge accident	B	5/10,000	Reporting error Extrapolation to LNG vessels	2 to 5 2 to 5
LNG navigation reduction factor	C	1/5	Speculatively based estimate	5
Historical probability of massive spillage given an accident	D	9/100	Unsubstantiated theory	2 or more
Reduction factors for engineering design of an LNG barge as compared to a conventional tank barge	E	1/5	Speculatively based estimate	5
Probability of an undesirable event given a massive spill	F	1	—	—
Probability of an undesirable LNG event in 10 years (product of factors A through F)		$\overline{1/403}$		
Single trip probability (product of factors B through F)		1/555,555		

[a] Trips in 10 years to Consolidated Edison and Brooklyn Union.

per 10,000. Multiplying the barge rate of 5 by 2 and by 5 gives a rate of 10 to 25 per 10,000.

Extrapolation to LNG vessels refers to the uncertainty inherent in extrapolating from average rates of accidents for certain classes of vessels to a rate of accident for particular LNG vessels. LNG vessels may have peculiar dangers and characteristics that are generally associated with higher risk. And because a direct study of LNG vessel accidents has not been made, because claims of incident-free experience are unsubstantiated, and finally because the accident rates in related experience have not been reviewed, it is difficult to say how much higher the accident rates of LNG vessels could be. We do know that there are considerable variations among the reported rates of accidents for at least some distinguishable classes of vessels. Further investigation of these variations could suggest a reasonable range of conjectured factors. In the absence of such an investigation, I can only express the opinion that actual accident rates for LNG vessels of between 2 and 5 times that of, say, all tankers or tank barges could not be ruled out on the basis of present knowledge. (Later experience may change all this.)

Speculatively based estimates refer to reduction factors selected on the basis of personal judgment that has been shown either to be inadequately supported by relevant information or to be fallacious. An example of the latter is the use of assumptions of independence between individual preventive actions. Because there is countervailing speculation as to ways in which LNG vessels and navigation could be more dangerous, there seems to be no basis at present for reductions. It would seem to be conservative to remove these reduction factors.

Definitional error refers to an error in the definition of a rate, such as that in the definition of spill rate in the Commission barge report. Because it reduces the spill rate to about half what it should be, a correction factor of 2 is required to correct it. The tank area factor of 2/3 in the Commission tanker report also appears to be an example of definitional error (*23*).

Unsubstantiated theory refers to the uncertainty in an estimate derived from an imperfect or inadequately verified theory—in this case the theory of spills in an accident. It is most difficult to set reasonable conjectured ranges for possible factors of underestimation, and as I have noted, the reports do not supply an analysis themselves of what the uncertainties might be. A factor of 2 or more could be conjectured, but there is no particular basis for this choice. The reports themselves give different estimates for accident probabilities that differ by factors of roughly between 2 and 10 between estimates for barges and tankers, between Commission and Applicant estimates for a barge, and between Commission and Applicant estimates for a tanker.

What are the numerical implications of this discussion for the final estimates of probabilities of spills or of accidents in the reports? To find the combined effect would take a detailed analysis that should be done as part of an original investigation, so it is not clear how the estimates would be changed.

However, based on the information supplied in the reports, it is reasonable to point out that very substantial increases in the estimates could occur. We noted that the estimate of a probability of 1 in 400 for a major LNG accident in the Commission barge report would be 1 in 16 if the two reduction factors of 5 were omitted. Suppose the spill rate error introduces an upward correction factor of 2. That might justifiably make the estimate 1 in 8, or twice as high. Then there is the reporting error and the possible error in the spill rate theory. If all of these errors were present, the estimate might be as much as 1 in 2. Finally, for the twenty-year period of the application, the chance moves above 3 in 4.

The Commission barge report does not necessarily lead to an estimate for the probability of a major LNG accident near 1 (that is, that an accident is very likely to happen), but the report by no means rules out a high estimate based upon its own analysis. Since the Commission tanker report and both of the Applicant reports share many of the same possible errors and uncertainties, high estimates would be compatible with their analyses also.

E. Estimates of probabilities should be reported in ways not likely to mislead

Rates quoted directly as fractions and translated into expected numbers of accidents over a given period of time seem less likely to mislead than a quotation in terms of expected number of years until the first occurrence.

As an example, the event of a barge accident whose estimated probability is 1/7000 in a year has been reported in the Applicant barge report as having an estimated expected time of 7000 years to the first occurrence. While mathematically correct under the usual probability model assumed, this formulation readily lends itself to false interpretations or implications (24).

Many people would very naturally give interpretations to an expected value of 7000 years that are not in fact implied by it. Some would think that an accident would not occur before 7000 years and that, if it did not occur exactly in the 7000th year, at least it would occur somewhere nearby. In this particular application, the probabilities attached to the different years for the first occurrence of an accident are spread so far from the year 7000 that the quotation of this "expected" value is even more misleading than ordinarily.

Is there then any probability attached to the first accident occurring in the first few years of the application if the estimated "expected time to the first accident" is 7000 years? There is, because the 7000-year figure was itself originally derived from the estimate of a probability of 1/7000 of an accident in every year, including the first. The chance that the first accident would occur within the first 10 years is somewhat greater than 10 times 1/7000, or 1/700, and in the first 20 years it is about twice that, or 1/350.

Is there not, at least, any bunching of the probabilites around the year 7000, so that the first accident is more likely to be in the vicinity of 7000 years from now rather than earlier or later? There is no bunching of probabilities at all around the year 7000. In fact, the only place where the probabilities can be said to be bunched is at the beginning. And the single most likely, or modal, time for the first accident is in the first year. After the first year the probabilities for subsequent years decline geometrically (25). A nonmathematical reason for thinking that the chance of an accident is more likely in early years is that we have little experience then. Some initial mistakes get corrected later.

Is the statistic of 7000 years to an accident an appropriate choice for describing the probability of an accident? In the context of the discussion of LNG vessel accidents, it is not appropriate. It is common in statistics to describe the variability of a quantity about its average value by its "standard deviation." The standard deviation of the quantity "time to first accident" is actually just as large as its expected value (26). When a standard deviation is this large, we have another indication that there is a good deal of probability attached to the occurrence of accidents in years that are far away from the expected value.

It is desirable to choose a measure whose standard deviation is small relative to its expected value and whose standard deviation, furthermore, becomes smaller as more data are accumulated, so that the measure becomes more precise as more data are gathered. Neither of these properties is true of the measure "expected time to the first accident." This measure may influence people to believe erroneously that the risk is far in the future.

We began with a statement that the expected waiting time before an accident was 7000 years, only to find that even if this is so, there is more than one chance in 350 of an accident within 20 years.

Language used to describe probabilites can be vague and misleading. Thus the chance of a major LNG marine accident occurring has been said to be "extremely small" and the vessels described as "inherently safe" (27). Such formulations are not particularly helpful, because different people mean different things by these words and these differences may be practically significant. For example, the practical difference between a probability of 1/4000 and 1/400 may be great, although both values are small and might be described by the same terms.

Choice of words may encourage the belief that events with probabilities as small as this could never happen. But a small probability is not a zero probability. Even incredible and completely unexpected events do happen.

Care must also be taken to consider the precise events whose probability is said to be extremely small. In the Commission reports, a 10-year period is used for quoting probabilities of a major LNG accident to tankers and barges. The LNG import applications are for 20- and 22-year periods. If the Commission reports chose 20 years, this would roughly double the final probabilities of accidents if the probability was small. For example, the probability of a major barge accident becomes 1 in 200 in 20 years instead of 1 in 400 in 10 years.

During cross-examination, the choice of a 10-year period for reporting accident probabilities was defended on the grounds that the probabilities might be different after 10 years and that therefore it would be wrong to simply extrapolate to 20 years. The premise that the probabilities may be different is sound, but it seems more informative to have the probability quoted for the life of the application with the assumption of a given probability per year clearly labelled. It is possible that in a few years we would want to revise our estimates of accident probabilities per year upward or downward.

Another way to report the accident probability while calling attention to the uncertainty in the figure for 20 years would be to report a high, a middle, and a low estimate depending on the assumption made about how the probability estimates in the second 10 years would compare with those in the first.

The LNG risk reports analyze only trips for a few selected tanker and barge routes, mainly in New York harbor. Readers of these reports should therefore be advised that to analyze the probabilities of an accident due to the total number of LNG-laden vessels that would use American harbors if several applications were permitted they would want to know the total number of trips of LNG-laden vessels during the life of the applications.

While any particular year of operation with vessels on a particular route may yield what is regarded as a very small probability of an accident, the chance of an accident in, for example, 20 years on 20 different routes might be on the order of 400 times the given value for operating for one year on one route. Thus if the probability were 1 in 4000 per year at one site, it might be 400 times this, or 1 in 10, for 20 years at 20 sites, since 400 times 1/4000 is 1/10.

F. Judgmental estimates of accident probabilities face difficulties of reasoned substantiation and provide numerous opportunities for bias. Their basis in evidence may not be explicit but should be free of mistakes and clear biases

The Commission reports reduce the probability of a massive LNG tanker or barge spill by two factors of 5, one by virtue of the special Coast Guard navigation regulations and aids that it is believed will be in use and one by virtue of the presumed unusually safe design of LNG vessels. These factors are critical to the assertion that accidents are "unlikely."

Factors that are so critical to the final probability estimates require careful discussion. The Commission reports contain only brief paragraphs in each case. The tanker report contains no indication of what navigation controls or design features are being relied upon. Like the tanker report, the barge report does not mention the design features relied upon. It says that "it is reasonable to assume" that Coast Guard regulations might include a list of six controls but gives no reason to believe that these controls have actually been adopted (*28*).

There is no discussion of how much any of the design features or navigation controls might reduce the probability of accidents. Neither report discusses the different causes and types of tanker and barge accidents to determine which ones might or might not be affected by the LNG vessel design features or by the special navigation rules and aids.

The judgmental reduction factors have been introduced, not on the basis of a direct study of observed frequencies of accidents and of spills following the introduction of these various safety measures, but on the basis of personal judgment about how these various measures would be thought to affect these frequencies.

We are all aware of how differently things can turn out in practice—often for unsuspected reasons. An example is pertinent to the present discussion. In June of 1967 a traffic separation scheme was imposed in the Dover Straits in the hope of reducing collisions in that body of water. MacDuff analyzed reported accident experience in the Dover Straits 5 years before and 5 years after June 1967 (*29*). He found the "total number of major happenings," including collisions and strandings, to be little changed in the two periods (73 and 70 before and after, respectively), while traffic was "materially constant." Though head-on collisions were cut 2 to 1, other types of accidents increased or remained constant. Anyone who supposed that a separation scheme would reduce head-on collisions to near zero has evidently been disappointed, as has anyone who supposed an overall reduction in major happenings would result. Actual experience can be very different from anticipated experience, and only a careful review of the record can inform us about the extent of these differences.

IV. SUMMARY

The guidelines for estimating "small" accident probabilities have been derived from a consideration of catastrophic risk analyses for LNG marine transportation. Although not a complete list in any sense, they form at least a partial checklist with which to review proposed estimates of accident probabilities, especially the presumably small probabilities associated with catastrophic events. The guidelines apply with certain modifications to estimates of probabilities of events other than accidents. To recapitulate, they are:

A. Estimates of "the" probability of an accident must include, explicitly or implicitly, contributions from all the possible sources of the accident.

B. The widest related base of potential accident experience (exposure) should be surveyed for indications about the probability of an accident for a particular kind of experience.

C. The combination of estimates of probability in parts of a system to reach overall estimates of probability is subject to subtle errors and must be carefully reviewed.

D. Possible sources of error and uncertainty in estimates should be explicitly considered and, wherever possible, estimated quantitatively. (Major types of sources of error and uncertainty are reporting error, extrapolation, speculatively based estimates, definitional error, and unsubstantiated theory.)

E. Estimates of probabilities should be reported in ways not likely to mislead.

F. Judgmental estimates of accident probabilities face difficulties of reasoned substantiation and provide numerous opportunities for bias. Their basis in evidence may not be explicit but should be free of mistakes and clear biases.

NOTES AND REFERENCES

1. I appeared as an expert witness on behalf of the Union of Concerned Scientists, Cambridge, Massachusetts, and United States Representative John M. Murphy of Staten Island. Other interveners included the Attorney General's Office of the State of New York, the State of New Jersey Department of the Public Advocate, and the City of New York.

2. The article will not deal with assessing the consequences of an LNG spill nor with the acceptability of the risk of LNG accidents.

3. See United States Nuclear Regulatory Commission, *Reactor Safety Study*, Wash-1400, October 1975. Also see American Physical Society, *Report by the Study Group on Light-Water Reactor Safety*, 28 April, 1975; and Henry W. Kendall and Sidney Moglewer, *Preliminary Review of the AEC Reactor Safety Study*, Joint Review Committee of Sierra Club and Union of Concerned Scientists, November 1974.

4. United States Federal Power Commission, Distrigas Corporation, *et al.*, Docket Nos. CP73-132, *et al.*

5. Horner, Theodore W., "Probability Assessment of LNG Accidents on New York Barge Transits from Staten Island to Newtown Creek and Steinway Creek," Attachment 4, *Final Environmental Impact Statement: For the Construction and Operation of an LNG Terminal at Staten Island, New York*, Vol. II, July 1974, Federal Power Commission, Washington, D.C. Referred to in this article as "Commission's barge report."

    ——— and Ecosystems, Inc., "Probability Assessment of LNG Ship Accidents in the New York and Providence Harbors," Attachment 2, *Final Environmental Impact Statement*, Vol. II, July 1974, Federal Power Commission, Washington, D.C. Referred to in this article as "Commission's tanker report."

    Arthur D. Little Co., "Analysis of Probability of Collisions, Rammings, and Groundings of the LNG Barge *Massachusetts*," October 1974. Appears as Exhibit 50 in the FPC proceedings. Referred to in this article as "Applicant's barge report."

    Brown, A. A., "Probabilities of Collision and Damage Affecting the *Ben Franklin*," Arthur D. Little Co., Docket No. CP73-78 *et al.* Appears as Exhibit 18 in the FPC proceedings. Referred to in this article as "Applicant's tanker report."

6A. Dr. Horner's reports assumed, for purpose of argument, that a "massive" LNG spill in port would cause a large fire with attendant loss of life and property. The Little reports stopped short of this assumption and dealt only with probabilities of a significant spill of LNG. The distinction is not always maintained in this article.

6B. The Applicant report on the tanker *Ben Franklin* did not analyze ramming and grounding, and the Applicant report on the barge *Massachusetts* also did not include these in its estimate of a spill probability. The Applicant reports do not include in their calculations of a spill probability the risk of a collision with a vessel when it is docked. Such collisions are acknowledged to be "possible" for the barge *Massachusetts* in the Applicant barge report (p. 4), and in Appendix C (p. 2) the risk is apparently considered significant enough to recommend imposition of a speed limit near two of the LNG terminals.

The Applicant reports do not include in their calculations the risk of a spill due to grounding. The tanker report, Appendix A (p. 2), states only that "the potential of LNG spills due to a grounding collision is very small." There were a number of groundings listed in the accident data for 51 barge accidents in 1970–1973 in the Commission barge report.

The Applicant barge report does not include in its calculation the risk that the LNG barge will be struck by another tug or barge. Appendix A (p. 2) acknowledges that "unusually large vessels of these types" could cause a spill at "expected" transit speeds. Tugs and barges may not always travel at or below expected speeds.

Other hazards that have not been included in the risk calculations in the Applicant reports include the risk from explosions on board, spillage due to design, construction, or equipment failures, spills during unloading, and collision with another vessel that itself catches fire or explodes.

7. That the probability of an unconventional or unexpected event is not well determined does not mean that it is zero. In this connection I am personally fond of the dictum of my former economics teacher, Joseph Conard, who liked to say that he would rather be vaguely right than precisely wrong.

8. A discussion of minimum credible values for small estimates of probabilities appears in the book by Frederick Mosteller and David L. Wallace, *Inference and Disputed Authorship: The Federalist*, Addison-Wesley, 1964, pp. 90–91, under the title of "outrageous events." An application to a famous legal case is made in William B. Fairley and Frederich Mosteller, "A Conversation about *Collins*," appearing in this book.

9. *Final Environmental Impact Statement*, Vol. I, *op. cit.*, pp. 3–33.

10. Another attempt to draw an inference about a rate given zero occurrences of the numerator event was made in the Commission barge report. There an estimate of the probability of a spill given an accident was obtained despite the fact that no "massive" spills, by Dr. Horner's definition, were observed in the 50 reported barge accidents.

To do this the report postulates that massive spills occur in a certain unknown fraction of accidents. It finds that no accidents in a sample of 50 had massive spills and asks how large this unknown fraction could be if it were to be at all consistent with an observed frequency as low as zero out of 50. The largest value deemed consistent is chosen as an estimate of the probability of a spill given an accident.

To obtain an estimate of the probability that differs from zero, which is the observed frequency of such spills, some assumptions are required. The assumptions used are that each accident has a constant probability of being the spill-producing type and that spills in successive accidents are independent of each other. If these assumptions were true, then the argument of the report for estimating this probability to be no greater than 0.09, or 9%, would be a reasonable approach. However, if accidents vary considerably in their spill-producing likelihoods, and this seems plausible, the calculation of 0.09 made on the assumption of a constant probability is not correct. In that event, the probability of a spill given an accident would be underestimated in the calculation made in the report.

An extreme example is provided by Bertrand Russell's paradox of the chicken who increases the probability of survival each day as the sun rises only to find himself at the chopping block precisely at the end of his fattening period. Suddenly the probability that appeared to be increasing plummets to zero. A more technologically oriented example would be increasing failure probabilities of equipment with age.

11. Arthur D. Little Co., *op. cit.*, p. 4.

12. A second example drawn from the LNG risk reports is that in only one of the four reports was a factual investigation of the frequency and origin of spills of various sizes reported, even though the probability of a spill is the principal object of study. Such an investigation should seek data from as wide a span of time and reports as possible, and it must pay special attention to the occurrence of unreported spills.

The Applicant reports and the Commission report on tankers treat spills almost entirely from a theoretical point of view, without looking at actual data on spills *per se*. Although the data sets on reported accidents employed in the reports do include instances of spills, these sets were not systematically collected for the purpose of analyzing spills and empirical or factual analysis of the frequencies of spills in harbors is not given. The Commission report on barges examines one data set to determine that there were no "massive" spills. However, no definition of a "massive spill" is given. Therefore it is possible for the report to say that no massive spills occur in the data set with 50 reported accidents even though the first accident listed in the set involved a spill of 3000 barrels. The latter spill would equal approximately 500 cubic meters, or about 10% of the capacity of the LNG barge *Massachusetts*.

The conclusion we draw from the experience reported here is that data most relevant to the risks analyzed should be sought out and used. Theoretical formulations that bypass use of data should be a second choice or adopted as a complement to examination of the data. It has been proposed that the relevant data bases be mutually agreed upon by all participants in a proceeding. See Michael O. Finkelstein, "Regression Models in Administrative Proceedings," *Harvard Law Review*, Vol. 86, No. 8 (June 1973), pp. 1442–1475.

13. Mostert, Noel, *Supership*, Knopf, 1974, pp. 325–326. Copyright © 1974 by Alfred A. Knopf, Inc. Reprinted with permission.

14. *Japan Times*, November 11, 1974.

15. Juillerat, Ernest E., "Cleveland LNG Explosion, October 20, 1944," *Fireman*, October 1969. *Fire Journal*, May 1974, pp. 71–72.

16. The Commission reports do not analyze the possibility that any reduction in accident probabilities due to navigation controls and design features may be offset, at least in part, by factors that would *increase* the probabilities. To illustrate the point, we can at least imagine the possibility that special navigation rules would result in the crew being less alert for unusual events than they would tend to be under ordinary navigational rules.

    The fact that new technology is involved in LNG vessel design raises the possibility that, whether designed to be safer or not, the ships are in fact less safe than the average oil tanker and barge. The unique features of LNG ships and their cargo may introduce additional dangers. It has been asserted that LNG can, for example, cause brittle fracture of a ship's hull if spilled, that dangerous pressure can build up within the tanks from the vapor, that the vapor can catch fire more easily than oil, that the draft of the LNG tanker is greater than the depth of portions of the channel, and that the LNG ships' riding higher out of the water may reduce maneuverability. Whether or not these claims are true is not the point. The point is that LNG vessels are treated in these reports as different from other vessels only in being safer.

17. For example, Appendix B (p. 5) of the Applicant report reduces the likelihood of collisions by 50% for the vessel traffic system and then by 15% for the Bridge-to-Bridge Radiotelephone Act. Let us assume these reductions are appropriate if the vessel traffic system and bridge-to-bridge communications are introduced alone. This does not imply that, if both are introduced, collisions will be reduced first by a reduction factor of 50% and then by a factor of 15% more, yielding a final total of 42.5% of the original. *Both actions may eliminate the same collisions.* Consequently the resulting reduction may still be only 50% or close to 50%. Indeed, it is not impossible that a combination of two factors can actually be less effective than either one used alone. They might interfere with each other, for example. A combination of two factors *could* even increase accidents, though each one alone reduced them! Therefore the "reduction" factor could actually turn into an "inflation" factor.

    Another illustration of this problem is the reduction of 50% of the accidents deemed caused by human error because of special training of the tug crew (see Appendix B, p. 7). If it were the accidents caused by human error that were reduced by the vessel traffic system and bridge-to-bridge communications, then the accidents caused by human error would be being eliminated over and over again.

    The assumption of independence is even more serious when one is considering a long series of preventive actions rather than just two. The Applicant barge report (Appendix B) does not provide a basis for estimating what the combined effect of all the individual options will be. The combined effect might be thought to lie somewhere between 50%, which is the amount of the largest reduction for a single action, and the 80% claimed, but even this is not guaranteed.

    The same report reduces the likelihood of collision by 50% because of a vessel traffic system and by 15% because of the Bridge-to-Bridge Radiotelephone Act. However, according to an article by Captain R. C. Hill of the Coast Guard ("Collisions and Groundings: Preventing the Preventable," *U.S. Naval Institute Proceedings*, December 1974, pp. 42–47) and an article by Rear Admiral W. M. Benkert and then Commander Hill ("U.S. Coast Guard Vessel Traffic System," in *Proceedings of the Marine Safety Council*, July 1972), bridge-to-bridge communications are part of a vessel traffic system. The probability of collisions has apparently been reduced twice for the same events. If true, this is an extreme example of the lack of independence between preventive actions.

    In addition, Captain Hill states in his 1974 article that "radiotelephone equipment has been used on a voluntary basis in most major U.S. ports and waterways to varying degrees for many years." To the extent that this is true of the ports that formed the basis for the report's estimate of a 15% reduction, this reduction overestimates the net or additional reduction that could be expected. Since the degree of use of bridge-to-bridge radiocommunications at the time of the collisions in the data base is not given, there is no basis for determining whether the 15% reduction is valid or whether the appropriate reduction is 0 percent or any figure between 0 and 15%. The same is equally true of the reduction for the use of radar on p. 6 of Appendix B.

18. On p. 45 of "Collisions and Groundings" (*op. cit.*), Captain Hill indicates the possible size of bias in damage amounts that may be involved: "According to U.S. Coast Guard marine casualty statistics, the number of collisions and groundings in U.S. waters rose from 1,342 cases in fiscal year 1958 to 1,460 in fiscal year 1971. The average annual 'reported' losses to vessels, cargo, and property from these

casualties exceeds $40 million. A recent study of the Coast Guard marine casualty reports suggests that owing to unreported casualties and understimates of the dollar losses for those casualties that are reported, the actual annual dollar losses probably exceed five times that amount or $200 million per year."

19. In itself accident data from a wide geographical area is laudable, because if it were obtained in a planned way it could form the basis for geographical comparisons.

20. The Poisson distribution is often used as a theoretical distribution for the probabilities of given numbers of accidents (zero, one, two, three, etc.) occurring within a stated period of time. A discussion of the definition and principal properties of the Poisson together with a famous application to the frequency of occurrence of fatal horse kick accidents to men in the Prussian cavalry is given in Frederick Mosteller and Robert E. K. Rourke, *Sturdy Statistics*, Reading, Mass.: Addison-Wesley, 1973, pp. 125–133.

21. Horner, Attachment 2, *op. cit.*, p. 12.

22. Arbous, A. and J. Kerrich, "Accident Statistics and the Concept of Accident-Proneness," *Biometrics*, 7, (December 1951), pp. 340–432. Ferreira, Joseph, Jr., "Driver Accident Models and Their Use in Policy Evaluation," in *Analysis of Public Systems*, Alvin W. Drake, Ralph L. Keeney, and Philip M. Morse, eds., Cambridge, Mass.: The MIT Press, 1972.

23. Horner, Attachment 2, *op. cit.*, p. 22.

24. The probability model is the geometric distribution of the number of years to a first occurrence.

25. The conditional probability of an accident in each year given no accident in a previous year is assumed to be constant, say p, whereas the unconditional probability at time zero that the first accident occurs in year x is $(1 - p)^{x-1}p$. At the beginning of each year the probability is 1/7000 for an accident in that year. However, this is not the same thing as saying the probability is 1/7000 that the *first* accident would occur in, say, the second year from that date, or that 1/7000 is the probability that the first accident will occur in the third year, or that it is 1/7000 for the fourth, and so on. The reason is that for the first accident to occur in the *second* year, it cannot occur in the first year; for the first accident to occur in the *third* year, it cannot occur in the first two years; and so forth. The same reasoning shows why the first year is most likely and each successive year less likely—because the event of a first accident in each successive year requires successive conditions of nonoccurrence in preceding years.

26. The expected value is exactly equal to $1/p$, and the standard deviation is exactly $(1 - p)^{1/2}/p$, which is very nearly equal to $1/p$ when p is small.

27. Arthur D. Little Co., *op. cit.*, p. 5; and A. A. Brown, *op. cit.*, p. 1.

28. Horner, Attachment 4, *op. cit.*, p. 19.

29. MacDuff, T., "The Probability of Vessel Collision," *Ocean Industry*, September 1974.

PEOPLE V. COLLINS

THE SUPREME COURT OF CALIFORNIA

Defendants were convicted before the Superior Court, Los Angeles County, Maurice C. Sparling, J., of second-degree robbery, and one defendant appealed. The Supreme Court, Sullivan, J., held that admission, over objection, of testimony of college mathematics instructor pertaining to mathematical theory of probability of persons with defendants' distinctive characteristics having committed robbery, without adequate evidentiary foundation or adequate proof of statistical independence, and without furnishing any guidance to jury on crucial issue as to which, of admittedly few couples matching defendants' characteristics, was guilty of committing robbery involved, constituted prejudicial error, especially in view of closeness of case.

Judgment reversed.
McComb, J., dissented.

1. Criminal Law ⚷ 472
Application of mathematical techniques in proof of facts, particularly in criminal case, must be critically examined in view of substantial unfairness to defendant which may result from ill conceived techniques with which trier of fact is not technically equipped to cope.

2. Criminal Law ⚷ 486, 1169(9)
Admission over objection, of testimony of college mathematics instructor pertaining to mathematical theory of probability of persons with defendants'

Reprinted with permission from *California Reporter*, Vol. 66, West Publishing Company, St. Paul, Minn., 1968, pp. 242–253. Copyright © 1968 by West Publishing Company.

distinctive characteristics having committed robbery, without adequate evidentiary foundation or adequate proof of statistical independence, and without furnishing any guidance to jury on crucial issue as to which, of admittedly few couples matching defendants' characteristics, was guilty of committing robbery involved, constituted prejudicial error, especially in view of closeness of case. West's Ann.Pen.Code, §§ 211, 211a, 1096.

Rex K. DeGeorge, Beverly Hills, under appointment by the Supreme Court, for defendant and appellant.

Thomas C. Lynch, Atty. Gen., William E. James, Asst. Atty. Gen., and Nicholas C. Yost, Deputy Atty. Gen., for plaintiff and respondent.

SULLIVAN, JUSTICE

We deal here with the novel question whether evidence of mathematical probability has been properly introduced and used by the prosecution in a criminal case. While we discern no inherent incompatibility between the disciplines of law and mathematics and intend no general disapproval or disparagement of the latter as an auxiliary in the fact-finding processes of the former, we cannot uphold the technique employed in the instant case. As we explain in detail *infra*, the testimony as to mathematical probability infected the case with fatal error and distorted the jury's traditional role of determining guilt or innocence according to long-settled rules. Mathematics, a veritable sorcerer in our computerized society, while assisting the trier of fact in the search for truth, must not cast a spell over him. We conclude that on the record before us defendant should not have had his guilt determined by the odds and that he is entitled to a new trial. We reverse the judgment.

A jury found defendant Malcolm Ricardo Collins and his wife defendant Janet Louise Collins guilty of second degree robbery (Pen.Code, §§ 211, 211a, 1157). Malcolm appeals from the judgment of conviction. Janet has not appealed.[1]

On June 18, 1964, about 11:30 a.m. Mrs. Juanita Brooks, who had been shopping, was walking home along an alley in the San Pedro area of the City of Los Angeles. She was pulling behind her a wicker basket carryall containing groceries and had her purse on top of the packages. She was using a cane. As she stooped down to pick up an empty carton, she was suddenly pushed to the ground by a person whom she neither saw nor heard approach. She was stunned by the fall and felt some pain. She managed to look up and saw a young woman running from the scene. According to Mrs. Brooks the latter appeared to weigh about 145 pounds, was wearing "something dark," and had hair "between a dark blond and a light blond," but lighter than the color of defendant Janet Collins' hair as it appeared at trial. Immediately after the incident, Mrs. Brooks discovered that her purse, containing between $35 and $40, was missing.

About the same time as the robbery, John Bass, who lived on the street at the end of the alley, was in front of his house watering his lawn. His attention was attracted by "a lot of crying and screaming" coming from the alley. As he looked in that direction, he saw a woman run out of the alley and enter a yellow automobile parked across the street from him. He was unable to give the make of the car. The car started off immediately and pulled wide around another parked vehicle so that in the narrow street it passed within six feet of Bass. The latter then saw that it was being driven by a male Negro, wearing a mustache and beard. At the trial Bass identified defendant as the driver of the yellow automobile. However, an attempt was made to impeach his identification by his admission that at the preliminary hearing he testified to an uncertain identification at the police lineup shortly after the attack on Mrs. Brooks, when defendant was beardless.

In his testimony Bass described the woman who ran from the alley as a Caucasian, slightly over five feet tall, of ordinary build, with her hair in a dark blond ponytail, and wearing dark clothing. He further testified that her ponytail was "just like" one which Janet had in a police photograph taken on June 22, 1964.

On the day of the robbery, Janet was employed as a housemaid in San Pedro. Her employer testified that she had arrived for work at 8:50 a.m. and that defendant had picked her up in a light yellow car[2] about 11:30 a.m. On that day, according to the witness, Janet was wearing her hair in a blonde ponytail but lighter in color than it appeared at trial.[3]

There was evidence from which it could be inferred that defendants had ample time to drive from Janet's place of employment and participate in the robbery. Defendants testified, however, that they went directly from her employer's house to the home of friends, where they remained for several hours.

In the morning of June 22, Los Angeles Police Officer Kinsey, who was investigating the robbery, went to defendants' home. He saw a yellow Lincoln automobile with an off-white top in front of the house. He talked with defendants. Janet, whose hair appeared to be a dark blonde, was wearing it in a ponytail. Malcolm did not have a beard. The officer explained to them that he was investigating a robbery specifying the time and place; that the victim had been knocked down and her purse snatched; and that the person responsible was a female Caucasian with blonde hair in a ponytail who had left the scene in a yellow car driven by a male Negro. He requested that defendants accompany him to the police station at San Pedro and they did so. There, in response to police inquiries as to defendants' activities at the time of the robbery, Janet stated, according to Officer Kinsey, that her husband had picked her up at her place of employment at 1 p.m. and that they had then visited at the home of friends in Los Angeles. Malcolm confirmed this. Defendants were detained for an hour or two, were photographed but not booked, and were eventually released and driven home by the police.

Late in the afternoon of the same day, Officer Kinsey, while driving home from work in his own car, saw defendants riding in their yellow Lincoln. Although the transcript fails to disclose what prompted such action, Kinsey proceeded to place them under surveillance and eventually followed them home. He called for assistance and arranged to meet other police officers in the vicinity of defendants' home. Kinsey took a position in the rear of the premises. The other officers, who were in uniform and had arrived in a marked police car, approached defendants' front door. As they did so, Kinsey saw defendant Malcolm Collins run out the back door toward a rear fence and disappear behind a tree. Meanwhile the other officers emerged with Janet Collins whom they had placed under arrest. A search was made for Malcolm who was found in a closet of a neighboring home and also arrested. Defendants were again taken to the police station, were kept in custody for 48 hours, and were again released without any charges being made against them.

Officer Kinsey interrogated defendants separately on June 23 while they were in custody and testified to their statements over defense counsel's objections based on the decision in *Escobedo* and our first decision in *Dorado*.[4] According to the officer, Malcolm stated that he sometimes wore a beard but that he did not wear a beard on June 18 (the day of the robbery), having shaved it off on June 2, 1964.[5] He also explained two receipts for traffic fines totalling $35 paid on June 19, which receipts had been found on his person, by saying that he used funds won in a gambling game at a labor hall. Janet, on the other hand, said that the $35 used to pay the fines had come from her earnings.[6]

On July 9, 1964, defendants were again arrested and were booked for the first time. While they were in custody and awaiting the preliminary hearing, Janet requested to talk with Officer Kinsey. There followed a lengthy conversation during the first part of which Malcolm was not present. During this time Janet expressed concern about defendant and inquired as to what the outcome would be *if* it appeared that she committed the crime and Malcolm knew nothing about it. In general she indicated a wish that defendant be released from any charges because of his prior criminal record and that if someone must be held responsible, she alone would bear the guilt. The officer told her that no assurances could be given, that if she wanted to admit responsibility disposition of the matter would be in the hands of the court and that if she committed the crime and defendant knew nothing about it the only way she could help him would be by telling the truth. Defendant was then brought into the room and participated in the rest of the conversation. The officer asked to hear defendant's version of the matter, saying that he believed defendant was at the scene. However, neither Janet nor defendant confessed or expressly made damaging admissions although constantly urged by the investigating officer to make truthful statements. On several occasions defendant denied that he knew what had gone on in the alley. On the other hand, the whole tone of the conversation evidenced a strong consciousness of guilt on the part of both defendants who appeared to be seeking the most advantageous way out. Over defense counsel's same objections based on *Escobedo* and *Dorado,* some parts of the foregoing conversation were testified to by Officer Kinsey and in addition a tape recording of the entire conversation was introduced in evidence and played to the jury.[7]

At the seven-day trial the prosecution experienced some difficulty in establishing the identities of the perpetrators of the crime. The victim could not identify Janet and had never seen defendant. The identification by the witness Bass, who observed the girl run out of the alley and get into the automobile, was incomplete as to Janet and may have been weakened as to defendant. There was also evidence, introduced by the defense, that Janet had worn light-colored clothing on the day in question, but both the victim and Bass testified that the girl they observed had worn dark clothing.

In an apparent attempt to bolster the identifications, the prosecutor called an instructor of mathematics at a state college. Through this witness he sought to establish that, assuming the robbery was committed by a Caucasian woman with a blond ponytail who left the scene accompanied by a Negro with a beard and mustache, there was an overwhelming probability that the crime was committed by any couple answering such distinctive characteristics. The witness testified, in substance, to the "product rule," which states that the probability of the joint occurrence of a number of *mutually independent* events is equal to the product of the individual probabilities that each of the events will occur.[8] *Without presenting any statistical evidence whatsoever in support of the probabilities for the factors selected,* the prosecutor then proceeded to have the witness *assume*[9] probability factors for the various characteristics which he deemed to be shared by the guilty couple and all other couples answering to such distinctive characteristics.[10]

Applying the product rule to his own factors the prosecutor arrived at a probability that there was but one chance in 12 million that any couple possessed the distinctive characteristics of the defendants. Accordingly, under this theory, it was to be inferred that there could be but one chance in 12 million that defendants were innocent and that another equally distinctive couple actually committed the robbery. Expanding on what he had thus purported to suggest as a hypothesis, the prosecutor offered the completely unfounded and improper testimonial assertion that, in his opinion, the factors he had assigned were "conservative estimates" and that, in reality "the chances of anyone else besides these defendants being there, . . . having every similarity, . . . is somewhat like one in a billion."

Objections were timely made to the mathematician's testimony on the grounds that it was immaterial, that it invaded the province of the jury, and that it was based on unfounded assumptions. The objections were "temporarily overruled" and the evidence admitted subject to a motion to strike. When that motion was made at the conclusion of the direct examination, the court denied it, stating that the testimony had been received only for the "purpose of illustrating the mathematical probabilities of various matters, the possibilities for them occurring or re-occurring."

Both defendants took the stand in their own behalf. They denied any knowledge of or participation in the crime and stated that after Malcolm called for Janet at her employer's house they went directly to a friend's house in Los Angeles where they remained for some time. According to this testimony defendants were not near the scene of the robbery when it occurred. Defendants' friend testified to a visit by them "in the middle of June" although she could not recall the precise date. Janet further testified that certain inducements were held out to her during the July 9 interrogation on condition that she confess her participation.

Defendant makes two basic contentions before us: First, that the admission in evidence of the statements made by defendants while in custody on June 23 and July 9, 1964, constitutes reversible error under the rules announced in the *Escobedo* and *Dorado* decisions;[11] and second, that the introduction of evidence pertaining to the mathematical theory of probability and the use of the same by the prosecution during the trial was error prejudicial to defendant. We consider the latter claim first.

As we shall explain, the prosecution's introduction and use of mathematical probability statistics injected two fundamental prejudicial errors into the case: (1) The testimony itself lacked an adequate foundation both in evidence and in statistical theory; and (2) the testimony and the manner in which the prosecution used it distracted the jury from its proper and requisite function of weighing the evidence on the issue of guilt, encouraged the jurors to rely upon an engaging but logically irrelevant expert demonstration, foreclosed the possibility of an effective defense by an attorney apparently unschooled in mathematical refinements, and placed the jurors and defense counsel at a disadvantage in sifting relevant fact from inapplicable theory.

We initially consider the defects in the testimony itself. As we have indicated, the specific technique presented through the mathematician's testimony and advanced by the prosecutor to measure the probabilities in question suffered from two basic and pervasive defects—an inadequate evidentiary foundation and an inadequate proof of statistical independence.

First, as to the foundation requirement, we find the record devoid of any evidence relating to any of the six individual probability factors used by the prosecutor and ascribed by him to the six characteristics as we have set them out in footnote 10, *ante*. To put it another way, the prosecution produced no evidence whatsoever showing, or from which it could be in any way inferred, that only one out of every ten cars which might have been at the scene of the robbery was partly yellow, that only one out of every four men who might have been there wore a mustache, that only one out of every ten girls who might have been there wore a ponytail, or that any of the other individual probability factors listed were even roughly accurate.[12]

The bare, inescapable fact is that the prosecution made no attempt to offer any such evidence. Instead, through leading questions having perfunctorily elicited from the witness the response that the latter could not assign a probability factor for the characteristics involved,[13] the prosecutor himself suggested what the various probabilities should be and these became the basis of the witness' testimony (see fn. 10, *ante*). It is a curious circumstance of this adventure in proof that the prosecutor not only made his own assertions of these factors in the hope that they were "conservative" but also in later argument to the jury invited the jurors to substitute their "estimates" should they wish to do so. We can hardly conceive of a more fatal gap in the prosecution's scheme of proof. A foundation for the admissibility of the witness' testimony was never even attempted to be laid, let alone established. His testimony was neither made to rest on his own testimonial knowledge nor presented by proper hypothetical questions based upon valid data in the record. (See generally: 2 Wigmore on Evidence (3d ed. 1940) §§ 478, 650–652, 657, 659, 672–684; Witkin, Cal. Evidence (2d ed. 1966) § 771; McCormick on Evidence pp. 19–20; Evidence: Admission of Mathematical Probability Statistics Held Erroneous for Want of Demonstration of Validity (1967) Duke L.J. 665, 675–678, citing People v. Risley (1915) 214 N.Y. 75, 85, 108 N.E. 200; State v. Sneed (1966) 76 N.M. 349, 414 P.2d 858.) In the *Sneed* Case, the court reversed a conviction based on probabilistic evidence, stating: "We hold that mathematical odds are not admissible as evidence to identify a defendant in a criminal proceeding *so long as the odds are based on estimates, the validity of which have* [*sic*] *not been demonstrated.*" (Italics added.) (414 P.2d at p. 862.)

But, as we have indicated, there was another glaring defect in the prosecution's technique, namely an inadequate proof of the statistical independence of the six factors. No proof was presented that the characteristics selected were mutually independent, even though the witness himself acknowledged that such condition was essential to the proper application of the "product rule" or "multiplication rule." (See Note, supra, Duke L.J. 665, 669–670, fn. 25.)[14] To the extent that the traits or characteristics were not mutually independent (e.g., Negroes with beards and men with mustaches obviously represent overlapping categories[15]), the "product rule" would inevitably yield a wholly erroneous and exaggerated result even if all of the individual components had been determined with precision. (Siegel, Nonparametric Statistics for the Behavioral Sciences (1956) 19; see generally Harmon, Modern Factor Analysis (1960).)

In the instant case, therefore, because of the aforementioned two defects—the inadequate evidentiary foundation and the inadequate proof of statistical independence—the technique employed by the prosecutor could only lead to wild conjecture without demonstrated relevancy to the issues presented. It acquired no redeeming quality from the prosecutor's statement that it was being used only "for illustrative purposes" since, as we shall point out, the prosecutor's subsequent utilization of the mathematical testimony was not confined within such limits.

We now turn to the second fundamental error caused by the probability testimony. Quite apart from our foregoing objections to the specific technique employed by the prosecution to estimate the probability in question, we think that the entire enterprise upon which the prosecution embarked, and which was directed to the objective of measuring the likelihood of a random couple possessing the characteristics allegedly distinguishing the robbers, was gravely misguided. At best, it might yield an estimate as to how infrequently bearded Negroes drive yellow cars in the company of blonde females with ponytails.

The prosecution's approach, however, could furnish the jury with absolutely no guidance on the crucial issue: *Of the admittedly few such couples, which one, if any, was guilty of committing this robbery?* Probability theory necessarily remains silent on that question, since no mathematical equation can prove beyond a reasonable doubt (1) that the guilty couple *in fact* possessed the characteristics described by the People's witnesses, or even (2) that only *one* couple possessing those distinctive characteristics could be found in the entire Los Angeles area.

As to the first inherent failing we observe that the prosecution's theory of probability rested on the assumption that the witnesses called by the People had conclusively established that the guilty couple possessed the precise characteristics relied upon by the prosecution. But no mathematical formula could ever establish beyond a reasonable doubt that the prosecution's witnesses correctly observed and accurately described the distinctive features which were employed to link defendants to the crime. (See 2 Wigmore on Evidence (3d ed. 1940) § 478.) Conceivably, for example, the guilty couple might have included a light-skinned Negress with bleached hair rather than a Caucasian blonde; or the driver of the car might have been wearing a false beard as a disguise; or the prosecution's witnesses might simply have been unreliable.[16]

The foregoing risks of error permeate the prosecution's circumstantial case. Traditionally, the jury weighs such risks in evaluating the credibility and probative value of trial testimony, but the likelihood of human error or of falsification obviously cannot be quantified; that likelihood must therefore be excluded from any effort to assign a *number* to the probability of guilt or innocence. Confronted with an equation which purports to yield a numerical index of probable guilt, few juries could resist the temptation to accord disproportionate weight to that index; only an exceptional juror, and indeed only a defense attorney schooled in mathematics, could successfully keep in mind the fact that the probability computed by the prosecution can represent, *at best*, the likelihood that a random couple would share the characteristics testified to by the People's witnesses—*not necessarily the characteristics of the actually guilty couple.*

As to the second inherent failing in the prosecution's approach, even assuming that the first failing could be discounted, the most a mathematical computation could *ever* yield would be a measure of the probability that a random couple would possess the distinctive features in question. In the present case, for example, the prosecution attempted to compute the probability that a random couple would include a bearded Negro, a blonde girl with a ponytail, and a partly yellow car; the prosecution urged that this probability was no more than one in 12 million. Even accepting this conclusion as arithmetically accurate, however, one still could not conclude that the Collinses were probably *the* guilty couple. On the contrary, as we explain in the Appendix, the prosecution's figures actually imply a likelihood of over 40 percent that the Collinses could be "duplicated" by at least *one other couple who might equally have committed the San Pedro robbery.* Urging that the Collinses be convicted on the basis of evidence which logically establishes no more than this seems as indefensible as arguing for the conviction of X on the ground that a witness saw either X or X's twin commit the crime.

Again, few defense attorneys, and certainly few jurors, could be expected to comprehend this basic flaw in the prosecution's analysis. Conceivably even the prosecutor erroneously believed that his equation established a high probability that *no* other bearded Negro in the Los Angeles area drove a yellow car accompanied by a ponytailed blonde. In any event, although his technique could demonstrate no such thing, he solemnly told the jury that he had supplied mathematical proof of guilt.

Sensing the novelty of that notion, the prosecutor told the jurors that the traditional idea of proof beyond a reasonable doubt represented "the most hackneyed, stereotyped, trite, misunderstood concept in criminal law." He sought to reconcile the jury to the risk that, under his "new math" approach to criminal jurisprudence, "on some rare occasion ··· an innocent person may be convicted." "Without taking that risk," the prosecution continued, "life would be intolerable ··· because ··· there would be immunity for the Collinses, for people who chose not to be employed to go down and push old ladies down and take their money and be immune because how could we ever be sure they are the ones who did it?"

[1] In essence this argument of the prosecutor was calculated to persuade the jury to convict defendants whether or not they were convinced of their guilt to a moral certainty and beyond a reasonable doubt. (Pen.Code, § 1096.) Undoubtedly the jurors were unduly impressed by the mystique of the mathematical demonstration but were unable to assess its relevancy or value. Although we make no appraisal of the proper applications of mathematical techniques in the proof of facts (see People v. Jordan (1955) 45 Cal.2d 697, 707, 290 P.2d 484; People v. Trujillo (1948) 32 Cal. 2d 105, 109, 194 P.2d 681; in a slightly differing context see Whitus v. State of Georgia (1967) 385 U.S. 545, 552, fn. 2, 87 S.Ct. 643, 17 L.Ed.2d 599; Finkelstein, The Application of Statistical Decision Theory to the Jury Discrimination Cases (1966) 80 Harv. L. Rev. 338, 338–340), we have strong feelings that such applications, particularly in a criminal case, must be critically examined in view of the substantial unfairness to a defendant which may result from ill conceived techniques with which the trier of fact is not technically equipped to cope. (See State v. Sneed, supra, 414 P.2d 858; Note, supra, Duke L.J. 665) We feel that the technique employed in the case before us falls into the latter category.

[2] We conclude that the court erred in admitting over defendant's objection the evidence pertaining to the mathematical theory of probability and in denying defendant's motion to strike such evidence. The case was apparently a close one. The jury began its deliberations at 2:46 p.m. on November 24, 1964, and retired for the night at 7:46 p.m.; the parties stipulated that a juror could be excused for illness and that a verdict could be reached by the remaining 11 jurors; the jury resumed deliberations the next morning at 8:40 a.m. and returned verdicts at 11:58 a.m. after five ballots had been taken. In the light of the closeness of the case, which as we have said was a circumstantial one, there is a reasonable likelihood that the result would have been more favorable to defendant if the prosecution had not urged the jury to render a probabilistic verdict. In any event, we think that under the circumstances the "trial by mathematics" so distorted the role of the jury and so disadvantaged counsel for the defense, as to constitute in itself a miscarriage of justice. After an examination of the entire cause, including the evidence, we are of the opinion that it is reasonably probable that a result more favorable to defendant would have been reached in the absence of the above error. (People v. Watson (1956) 46 Cal.2d 818, 836; 299 P.2d 243.) The judgment against defendant must therefore be reversed.

In view of the foregoing conclusion, we deem it unneccessary to consider whether the admission of defendants' extrajudicial statements constitutes error under the rules announced in *Escobedo* and *Dorado*. Upon retrial, the admissibility of these or any other extrajudicial statements sought to be introduced by the prosecution must be determined in the light of the rules set forth in Miranda v. State of Arizona (1966) 384 U.S. 436, 86 S.Ct. 1602, 16 L.E.2d 694. (People v. Doherty (1967) 67 A.C. 1, 4, 9–13, 59 Cal.Rptr. 857, 429 P.2d 177.) As we have pointed out, the trial herein took place between our first and second *Dorado* decisions (see fn. 4, *ante*). Although defense counsel was commendably alert in basing objections to the admission of the statements upon the decisions in *Escobedo* and *Dorado*, he of course did not have the benefit of our numerous decisions beginning with the second *Dorado* decision expounding various facets of the exclusionary rule. In the event any extrajudicial statements made by defendant are offered in evidence on retrial, the parties will have an opportunity to make a record on pertinent issues subject to prior determination by the court in the light of *Miranda* rules before such statements are received in evidence. It would be fruitless for us to essay such a task at this point when such record does not yet exist.

The judgment is reversed.

TRAYNOR, C. J., and PETERS, TOBRINER, MOSK and BURKE, JJ., concur.

McCOMB, Justice.
I dissent. I would affirm the judgment in its entirety.

APPENDIX

If "*Pr*" represents the probability that a certain distinctive combination of characteristics, hereinafter designated "*C*," will occur jointly in a random couple, then the probability that *C* will *not* occur in a random couple is $(1 - Pr)$. Applying the product rule (see fn. 8, *ante*), the probability that *C* will occur in *none* of *N* couples chosen at random is $(1 - Pr)^N$, so that the probability of *C* occurring in *at least one* of *N* random couples is $[1 - (1 - Pr)^N]$.

Given a particular couple selected from a random set of *N*, the probability of *C* occurring in that couple (i.e., *Pr*), multiplied by the probability of *C* occurring in none of the remaining $N - 1$ couples (i.e., $(1 - Pr)^{N-1}$) yields the probability that *C* will occur in the selected couple and in no other. Thus the probability of *C* occurring in any particular couple, and in that couple alone, is $[(Pr) \times (1 - Pr)^{N-1}]$. Since this is true for each of the *N* couples, the probability that *C* will occur in precisely *one* of the *N* couples, without regard to which one, is $[(Pr) \times (1 - Pr)^{N-1}]$ added *N* times, because the probability of the occurrence of one of several *mutually exclusive* events is equal to the *sum* of the individual probabilities. Thus the probability of *C* occurring in *exactly one* of *N* random couples (*any* one, but *only* one) is $[(N) \times (Pr) \times (1 - Pr)^{N-1}]$.

By subtracting the probability that C will occur in *exactly one* couple from the probability that C will occur in *at least one* couple, one obtains the probability that C will occur in *more than one* couple: $[1-(1-Pr)^N - [(N)\times(Pr)\times(1-Pr)^{N-1}]$. Dividing this difference by the probability that C will occur in at least one couple (i.e., dividing the difference by $[1-(1-Pr)^N]$) then yields *the probability that C will occur more than once in a group of N couples in which C occurs at least once.*

Turning to the case in which C represents the characteristics which distinguish a bearded Negro accompanied by a pony-tailed blonde in a yellow car, the prosecution sought to establish that the probability of C occurring in a random couple was 1/12,000,000—i.e., that $Pr = 1/12,000,000$. Treating this conclusion as accurate, it follows that, in a population *of N* random couples, the probability of C occurring *exactly once* is $[(N)\times(1/12,000,000)\times(1-1/12,000,000)^{N-1}]$. Subtracting this product from $[1-(1-1/12,000,000)^N]$, the probability of C occurring in *at least one* couple, and dividing the resulting difference by $[1-(1-1/12,000,000)^N]$, the probability that C will occur in at least one couple, yields the probability that C will occur more than once in a group of N random couples of which at least one couple (namely, the one seen by the witnesses) possesses characteristics C. In other words, the probability of *another* such couple in a population of N is the quotient A/B, where A designates the numerator $[1-(1-1/12,000,000)^N]-[(N)\times1/12,000,000)\times(1-1/12,000,000)^{N-1}]$, and B designates the denominator $[1-(1-1/12,000,000)^N]$.

N, which represents the total number of all couples who might conceivably have been at the scene of the San Pedro robbery, is not determinable, a fact which suggests yet another basic difficulty with the use of probability theory in establishing identity. One of the imponderables in determining N may well be the number of N-type couples in which a single person may participate. Such considerations make it evident that N, in the area adjoining the robbery, is in excess of several million; as N assumes values of such magnitude, the quotient A/B computed as above, representing the probability of a second couple as distinctive as the one described by the prosecution's witnesses, soon exceeds 4/10. Indeed, as N approaches 12 million, this probability quotient rises to approximately 41 percent. We note parenthetically that if $1/N = Pr$, then as N increases indefinitely, the quotient in question approaches a limit of $(e-2)/(e-1)$, where "e" represents the transcendental number (approximately 2.71828) familiar in mathematics and physics.

Hence, even if we should accept the prosecution's figures without question, we would derive a probability of over 40 percent that the couple observed by the witnesses could be "duplicated" by at least one other equally distinctive interracial couple in the area, including a Negro with a beard and mustache, driving a partly yellow car in the company of a blonde with a ponytail. Thus the prosecution's computations, far from establishing beyond a reasonable doubt that the Collinses were the couple described by the prosecution's witnesses, imply a very substantial likelihood that the area contained *more than one* such couple, and that a couple *other* than the Collinses was the one observed at the scene of the robbery. (See generally: Hoel, Introduction to Mathematical Statistics (3d ed. 1962); Hodges & Lehmann, Basic Concepts of Probability and Statistics (1964); Lindgren & McElrath, Introduction to Probability and Statistics (1959).)

NOTES

[1] Hereafter, the term "defendant" is intended to apply only to Malcolm, but the term "defendants" to Malcolm and Janet.

[2] Other witnesses variously described the car as yellow, as yellow with an off-white top, and yellow with an egg-shell white top. The car was also described as being medium to large in size. Defendant drove a car at or near the times in question which was a Lincoln with a yellow body and a white top.

[3] There are inferences which may be drawn from the evidence that Janet attempted to alter the appearance of her hair after June 18. Janet denies that she cut, colored or bleached her hair at any time after June 18, and a number of witnesses supported her testimony.

[4] Escobedo v. State of Illinois (378 U.S. 478, 84 S.Ct. 1758, 12 L.Ed.2d 977.) was decided on June 22, 1964, four days after the robbery. The investigation was carried on both before and after *Escobedo* but before our first decision in People v. Dorado filed on August 31, 1964. Defendants' trial took place in November 1964 after we granted a rehearing in *Dorado* on September 24, 1964, but before our decision on rehearing filed January 29, 1965. (62 Cal.2d 338, 42 Cal. Rptr. 169, 398 P.2d 361.)

[5] Evidence as to defendant's beard and mustache is conflicting. Defense witnesses appeared to support defendant's claims that he had shaved his beard on June 2. There was testimony that on June 19 when defendant appeared in court to pay fines on another matter he was bearded. By June 22 the beard had been removed.

[6] The source of the $35, being essentially the same amount as the $35 to $40 reported by the victim as having been in her purse when taken from her the day before the fines were paid, was a significant factor in the prosecution's case. Other evidence disclosed that defendant and Janet were married on June 2, 1964, at which time they had only $12, a portion of which was spent on a trip to Tiajuana. Since the marriage defendant had not worked, and Janet's earnings were not more than $12 a week, if that much.

[7] Included in the conversation are the following excerpts from Janet's statements:
"If I told you that he didn't know anything about it and I did it, would you cut him loose?"
"I just want him out, that's all, because I ain't never been in no trouble. I won't have to do too much [time], but he will."
"What's the most time I can do?"
"Would it be easier if I went ahead and said, if I was going to say anything, say it now instead of waiting till court time?"
Defendant indicated that he should "go and have trust in [the officer], but maybe I'd be wrong. I mean, this is a little delicate on my behalf."
At another point defendant stated: "I'm leaving it up to her."
Defendant expressed concern during the conversation that any statement by Janet would not necessarily relieve him because he admittedly had been with her all that day since 11:30 a.m. The conversation closed when defendants indicated that they wished more time to think it over.

[8] In the example employed for illustrative purposes at the trial, the probability of rolling one die and coming up with a "2" is $\frac{1}{6}$, that is, any one of the six faces of a die has one chance in six of landing face up on any particular roll. The probability of rolling two "2's" in succession is $\frac{1}{6} \times \frac{1}{6}$, or $\frac{1}{36}$, that is, on only one occasion out of 36 double rolls (or the roll of two dice), will the selected number land face up on each roll or die.

[9] His argument to the jury was based on the same gratuitous assumptions or on similar assumptions which he invited the jury to make.

[10] Although the prosecutor insisted that the factors he used were only for illustrative purposes—to demonstrate how the probability of the occurrence of mutually independent factors affected the probability

that they would occur together—he nevertheless attempted to use factors which he personally related to the distinctive characteristics of defendants. In his argument to the jury he invited the jurors to apply their own factors, and asked defense counsel to suggest what the latter would deem as reasonable. The prosecutor himself proposed the individual probabilities set out in the table below. Although the transcript of the examination of the mathematics instructor and the information volunteered by the prosecutor at that time create some uncertainty as to precisely which of the characteristics the prosecutor assigned to the individual probabilities, he restated in his argument to the jury that they should be as follows:

Characteristic	Individual probability
A. Partly yellow automobile	1/10
B. Man with mustache	1/4
C. Girl with ponytail	1/10
D. Girl with blond hair	1/3
E. Negro man with beard	1/10
F. Interracial couple in car	1/1000

In his brief on appeal defendant agrees that the foregoing appeared on a table presented in the trial court.

[11] Escobedo v. State of Illinois (1964) 378 U.S. 478, 84 S.Ct. 1758, 12 L.Ed. 2d 977; People v. Dorado (1965) 62 Cal.2d 338, 42 Cal.Rptr. 169, 398 P.2d 361.

[12] We seriously doubt that such evidence could ever be compiled since no statistician could possibly determine after the fact which cars, or which individuals, "might" have been present at the scene of the robbery; certainly there is no reason to suppose that the human and automotive populations of San Pedro, California, include all potential culprits—or, conversely, that all members of these populations are proper candidates for inclusion. Thus the sample from which the relevant probabilities would have to be derived is itself undeterminable. (See generally Yaman, Statistics, An Introductory Analysis (1964), ch. I.)

[13] The prosecutor asked the mathematics instructor: "Now, let me see if you can be of some help to us with some independent factors, and you have some paper you may use. Your specialty does not equip you, I suppose, to give us some probability of such things as a yellow car as contrasted with any other kind of car, does it? * * * I appreciate the fact that you can't assign a probability for a car being yellow as contrasted to some other car, can you? A. No, I couldn't."

[14] It is there stated that: "A trait is said to be independent of a second trait when the occurrence or non-occurrence of one does not affect the probability of the occurrence of the other trait. The multiplication rule cannot be used without some degree of error where the traits are not independent." (Citing Huntsberger, Elements of Statistical Inference (1961) 77; Kingston & Kirk, The Use of Statistics in Criminalistics (1964) 55 J. Crim.L., C. & P.S. 516.) (Note, supra, Duke L.J. fn. 25, p. 670.)

[15] Assuming *arguendo* that factors B and E (see fn. 10, *ante*), were correctly estimated, nevertheless it is still arguable that most Negro men with beards *also* have mustaches (exhibit 3 herein, for instance, shows defendant with both a mustache and a beard, indeed in a hirsute continuum); if so, there is no basis for multiplying $\frac{1}{4}$ by $\frac{1}{10}$ to estimate the proportion of Negroes who wear beards *and* mustaches. Again, the prosecution's technique could *never* be meaningfully applied, since its accurate use would call for information as to the degree of interdependence among the six individual factors. (See Yamane, op. cit. supra.) Such information cannot be compiled, however, since the relevant sample necessarily remains unknown. (See fn. 10, *ante*.)

[16] In the instant case, for instance, the victim could not state whether the girl had a ponytail, although the victim observed the girl as she ran away. The witness Bass, on the other hand, was sure that the girl whom he saw had a ponytail. The demonstration engaged in by the prosecutor also leaves no room for the possibility, although perhaps a small one, that the girl whom the victim and the witness observed was, in fact, the same girl.

A CONVERSATION
ABOUT *COLLINS*

WILLIAM B. FAIRLEY and
FREDERICK MOSTELLER

People who wish to apply probability, statistics, and mathematics to legal work find careful analyses of the facts in specific cases rewarding. *People v. Collins*[1] is a particularly good case for such study, because the prosecution used a probabilistic argument to try to establish an identification. Unfortunately, students tend to point out an initial difficulty in the prosecutor's argument and then dismiss the case. As the court recognized, however, the issues involved are deeper and deserve far more attention. Professor Hans Zeisel is famed for his ability to give clear explanations of very difficult statistical ideas. In his honor, we shall try to emulate him by discussing some of the issues raised by this case in a dialogue between a lawyer and a statistician. Neither of the participants presumes the other to have a specialist's knowledge of his field.[2]

The dialogue is intended to discuss three points. First, it considers the question of whether dependent or independent probabilities were the basis for the prosecutor's argument in *Collins* and offers an interpretation more favorable to the prosecution than that usually given. Next, it suggests that data could have been assembled to make a reasonable estimate of the order of magnitude of the probability. The prosecution, however, did not provide any such evidence, and the court considered the consequences of accepting the prosecution's unsupported numbers. The court, in an appendix to its

Reprinted with permission from *The University of Chicago Law Review*, Vol. 41, No. 2 (Winter 1974), pp. 242–253. The authors are indebted to Lloyd Weinreb for numerous helpful comments. We also wish to acknowledge helpful comments from Jack Appleman, Michael Brown, Byron Burnett, Stephen Fienberg, Michael Finkelstein, Richard Hill, David Hoaglin, Nan Hughes, Charles Kagay, Don Karl, Joel Kleinman, Gilbert Kujovich, Alan Lederman, David Oakes, James Reeds, Karen Reeds, and Bernard Rosner. The work was partially aided by a National Science Foundation Grant (GS 32327XI).

opinion, developed a probabilistic model intended to show that the identification was weak even if the prosecution's numbers were accepted. The court apparently concluded that if a random item sampled from a large population belongs to a rare type, then the probability of at least one more item of that type in the population is about 0.41. The third goal of this dialogue is to consider the validity of the model that gave rise to this number. The conclusion reached in *Collins* deserves to be reviewed with some care. More than one valid model, and more than one interpretation, is possible; our treatment is intended to provoke further discussion of these matters.

I. PREFATORY NOTE ON *PEOPLE v. COLLINS*

Janet and Malcolm Collins were convicted in a jury trial in Los Angeles of second-degree robbery. Malcolm appealed his conviction to the Supreme Court of California, and the conviction was reversed. The court described the events of the robbery as follows:[3]

> On June 18, 1964, about 11:30 a.m. Mrs. Juanita Brooks, who had been shopping, was walking home along an alley in the San Pedro area of the City of Los Angeles. She was pulling behind her a wicker basket carryall containing groceries and had her purse on top of the packages. She was using a cane. As she stooped down to pick up an empty carton, she was suddenly pushed to the ground by a person whom she neither saw nor heard approach. She was stunned by the fall and felt some pain. She managed to look up and saw a young woman running from the scene. According to Mrs. Brooks the latter appeared to weigh about 145 pounds, was wearing "something dark," and had hair "between a dark blond and a light blond," but lighter than the color of defendant Janet Collins' hair as it appeared at trial. Immediately after the incident, Mrs. Brooks discovered that her purse, containing between $35 and $40, was missing.

> About the same time as the robbery, John Bass, who lived on the street at the end of the alley, was in front of his house watering his lawn. His attention was attracted by "a lot of crying and screaming" coming from the alley. As he looked in that direction, he saw a woman run out of the alley and enter a yellow automobile parked across the street from him. He was unable to give the make of the car. The car started off immediately and pulled wide around another parked vehicle so that in the narrow street it passed within six feet of Bass. The latter then saw that it was being driven by a male Negro, wearing a mustache and beard. At the trial Bass identified defendant as the driver of the yellow automobile. However, an attempt was made to impeach his identification by his admission that at the preliminary hearing he testified to an uncertain identification at the police lineup shortly after the attack on Mrs. Brooks, when defendant was beardless.

> In his testimony Bass described the woman who ran from the alley as a Caucasian, slightly over five feet tall, of ordinary build, with her hair in a

dark blond ponytail, and wearing dark clothing. He further testified that her ponytail was "just like" one which Janet had in a police photograph taken on June 22, 1964.

At the trial, following testimony by a college mathematics instructor, the prosecutor introduced a table in which he hypothesized the following probabilities of occurrence of the reported characteristics of the two people involved in the crime:[4]

Characteristic	Individual probability
A. Partly yellow automobile	1/10
B. Man with mustache	1/4
C. Girl with ponytail	1/10
D. Girl with blond hair	1/3
E. Negro man with beard	1/10
F. Interracial couple in car	1/1000

The prosecutor multiplied these individual probabilities and arrived at a figure of 1/12,000,000, which represented the probability "that any couple possessed the distinctive characteristics of the defendants."[5] In his summation, the prosecutor repeated this analysis and emphasized the extreme unlikelihood—"somewhat like one in a billion"—that a couple other than the defendants had all these characteristics.

II. A CONVERSATION ABOUT *COLLINS*

Lawyer: The California Supreme Court made a lot out of the prosecutor's unproven assumption that each of the six characteristics was "statistically independent." Will you explain that to me?

Statistician: Statistical independence between X and Y means that it is neither more nor less likely that Y happens whether or not X happens. For example, in drawing a card from an ordinary pack of playing cards, let X mean the card is an ace and Y mean the card is black. The probability that the card drawn is black (rather than red) is 1/2, whether or not the card is an ace.

L: Then the prosecutor's assumption was not merely unproven, it was almost certainly wrong. For example, it must be much more likely that a man has a mustache if he has a beard than if he does not. Beards and mustaches tend to run together. And, if you have a "girl with blond hair" and a "Negro man with a beard," the chance that you have an "interracial couple" must be close to 1000 times greater than the estimate of 1/1000. Right?

S: Yes, everyone notices these dependencies.

L: I don't believe that the prosecutor could have blundered that badly.

S: The court seems to have thought that he did. The 1/12,000,000 figure was certainly consistent with treating each of the characteristics as statistically independent and, according to the product rule, multiplying the probabilities of each to get the probability of all together.

L: What is the product rule?

S: You use it yourself all the time. What are the odds of getting heads if you toss a coin?

L: Fifty-fifty.

S: Yes, that makes the probability one in two or one-half. And if you toss it again?

L: Same.

S: Right. What is your chance of getting heads both times?

L: One in four.

S: Right; one-half times one-half. That's the product rule. The prosecutor may have arrived at 1/12,000,000 by multiplying all of the individual probabilities of each characteristic occurring alone.

L: But if there is dependence that wouldn't be right.

S: Yes, but I will explain how the individual probabilities used in the case are also consistent with an interpretation that is more favorable for the prosecutor.

L: What is that?

S: He may have been employing the product rule for dependent events. If we work backward in the table from (F) to (A) and appropriately define the characteristics, this interpretation is at least plausible. For (F), at the time of the trial, 1 in 1000 might have been an accurate frequency for interracial couples who sometimes drive cars. For (E), among interracial couples who sometimes drive, perhaps 1 in 10 had a Negro man with a beard.

L: In 1964 beards were much rarer than in 1974.

S: For (D), among couples having both of these characteristics, one can argue that 1 in 3 has a woman with blond hair. We could go on, interpreting each of the individual probabilities as a conditional probability, that is, given all of the preceding characteristics. If the individual probabilities were constructed in this manner, and if they were numerically correct, then their product would give the probability of the joint occurrence of the separate events or characteristics—those no longer regarded as independent. Of course I don't know if that's what the prosecutor had in mind, but it's a lot more plausible than the assumption of independent events.

L: But the resulting figure is the same either way.[6]

S: Yes.

L: Will you explain that?

S: Ordinarily we would have two different sets of probabilities for the characteristics, one representing the unconditional probabilities of events and the other representing the conditional probabilities for the characteristics in the order we choose for computation. If the probabilities in the table are the approximately correct conditional probabilities, then they are not likely to be the correct unconditional probabilities. For example, consider (E), "Negro man with beard." The population proportion of Negroes would be 10 or 12 percent, and the proportion of Negro males would be 5 or 6 percent; the proportion of Negro males with beards would be smaller still, say 2 percent. For (E) in 1964, the unconditional probability might therefore be about 1/50, rather than 1/10. If we change all of the probabilities to unconditional probabilities in this manner, then their product will not—except by a fluke—equal 1/12,000,000.

L: In this case, if you used unconditional probabilities as if there were independence, that would be a mistake, wouldn't it?

S: Yes; but if the separate probabilities given in the table are conditional probabilities, then the product rule for dependent probabilities would have been correctly used if we multiplied them together as we described.[7]

L: So the prosecutor may have been basically correct in getting an order of magnitude estimate for the frequency of couples with the characteristics of the robbers.

S: Possibly.

L: Still, even if the prosecutor intended to use the product rule for dependent events, he had not verified the individual probabilities he quoted.

S: But he could have taken some small steps in this direction. Suppose he had a small sample survey; this technique is sometimes used, though not always accepted by courts.[8] He could then have estimated the proportion of white girls with ponytails, the proportion of yellow cars, the proportion of black men with beards, and so on.

L: Since these numbers would have been just estimates, would the court have accepted them?

S: I don't know; that's your field, not mine.[9] But it would have at least had a chance to consider whether the method of gathering the data was adequate for the purpose. Remember that this analysis was an order of magnitude argument, and the court might have been sympathetic to a carefully made one. The court certainly suggested this attitude by developing its own mathematical model. Indeed, part of the court's complaint was that there was no effort by the prosecution to connect the numbers with the real world.

L: You mean he might just go out and count numbers of people of different types passing corners near the scene of the robbery at about 11:30 in the morning? Or ask the Registrar of Motor Vehicles to tell him what fraction of cars were yellow?

S: Yes, at a minimum. He might do better than that—but let's not get very far into the possible designs of his sample survey.

L: How could he handle the dependence problem?

S: By looking at pairs and triples of characteristics in his sample. For example, he might have counted 1,000 cars in the relevant neighborhood at the relevant time. He might have seen no cars with a couple like the one described, and he might have seen a few having as many as three of the required characteristics. Then he might be able to assess the rarity of the separate combinations of characteristics. Although it might be hard to determine a single collective probability, he would be able to define ranges of possible answers. The prosecution would then have a solidly based estimate of the rarity of the couple's characteristics. There are special statistical tools for handling probabilities of several characteristics that are not independent.[10] It would be an uncertain estimate, for example, fixing the probability between 1/10,000 and 1/100,000.

L: Would he be estimating conditional probabilities or unconditional ones?

S: He would estimate the probability that all of the relevant characteristics are found in a randomly drawn couple. That probability is the figure that all of these calculations are intended to estimate.

L: I'm intrigued by the court's claim that "the prosecution's figures actually imply a likelihood of over 40 percent that the Collinses could be 'duplicated' by at least *one other couple who might equally have committed the San Pedro robbery.*"[11] What bothers me, I suppose, is the idea that a mathematical appendix could prove something about the likelihood of the existence of couples of a certain type. That's an empirical question. I'd have thought that a sample survey or a census would be the only way to find out how many couples sharing a given set of characteristics were in the area of the robbery.

S: It certainly is an empirical question, and we have discussed in principle how the data needed to answer the question might be gathered. The court, however, was trying to show what could be said without any data. They said, in effect, "Let's assume with the prosecution that the probability that a random couple would share the robbers' characteristics is 1 in 12,000,000."

L: And then the court imagines randomly selecting some number of couples from all of the couples who could have committed the crime, one of whom (the defendants) was observed by the police to have the listed characteristics.

S: Yes. Let's call this number N. If we independently select N couples, each with a probability of 1 in 12,000,000 of sharing the robbers' characteristics, we can then calculate the probabilities of selecting none or one or more couples with these characteristics. If we put all those probabilities together, we get what's called the probability distribution of the number of such couples. Among the N couples.

L: How do you find these probabilities?

S: That calculation is made within probability theory, that is, these probabilities can be computed from a formula using the assumptions the court made. But we can carry out a simulation of the selection process that would illustrate these probabilities.

L: How?

S: We would randomly select N couples from the general population and record the number of couples selected that have the unusual characteristics. We would perform this selection process a number of times—perhaps a thousand—and the relative frequency of times we found no couples, one couple, two couples, and so on, would approximate the respective probabilities of finding, among N couples, no couples, one couple, two couples, and so on, with the unusual characteristics.

L: The court discusses conditional probabilities of different numbers of such couples. What are those?

S: The court says that the defendants are one couple with the characteristics of the robbers. According to the court, we should therefore be interested in probabilities that are conditional on that fact. That is, instead of asking for the chances of none or one or more, ask: if one, what are the chances of more than one? What is the probability of at least one more couple having the robbers' characteristics, given that there is one?[12]

L: I suppose that you could also simulate that probability.

S: We could go back to our earlier simulation and pick out all those selections of N couples having at least one couple with the required characteristics. We would then group these selections into those in which exactly one couple with the characteristics was selected and those in which more than one were selected. Of course, we ordinarily use a formula to make the calculation—as the court did.

L: So the court was saying that, in our case, if we collect all the selections of N in which at least one couple like the robbers was chosen, 41 percent of them will have more than one such couple. Is that right?

S: Yes. You understand the court perfectly. But in fact the court was wrong. A crucial point at which the appendix is mistaken is that the conditional probability of there being more than one couple like the robbers, given that there was at least one, is 0.41 only if N is about 12,000,000.[13] And the court itself recognized that we don't know what number N really is.[14]

L: How did the court go wrong?

S: I don't know. To reach its conclusion the court had to believe that N was 12,000,000. And it says it didn't believe that.

L: Doesn't the 1 in 12,000,000 figure that the court took from the prosecutor imply a selection of at least 12,000,000 couples?

S: No. Suppose we flip a coin ten times. There are 1,024 possible outcomes; if heads and tails have equal chances of coming up on each toss, then each possible outcome has an equal chance, 1/1,024, of occurring. In this instance the probability comes from the product rule, which is applicable because each flip of the coin is an independent event. We might have only one set of 10 tosses yielding only one outcome, yet we have a probability for that outcome of 1 in 1,024. So there is no need to have anything like a thousand flips.

L: So there's no special case for N being 12,000,000 just because the probability of each selection is 1/12,000,000. Suppose we try a small N, perhaps because we believe the robbers must have come from a small area in San Pedro near the scene of the robbery. Try 250,000 instead of 12,000,000.

S: O.K. We can get the answer to this question from the general formula given by the court that shows how the conditional probability varies with N.[15] When N is 250,000, assuming that the probability of any couple having the robbers' characteristics is still 1/12,000,000, the probability of finding more than one couple if there is at least one is about 0.01.[16]

L: That's about one-fortieth of the court's figure.

S: Yes.

L: No wonder we have that quote from Disraeli about liars, damn liars, and statisticians.

S: Actually, the original saying referred to expert witnesses, not statisticians.[17]

Your common sense is basically right about this aspect of the problem. A couple could have such rare properties that it wouldn't be observed once in a month of Sundays. We all know this. Further, we know that the fact that there is one such couple, does not imply there are more. There may be, and the court's model is one way to think about it. But we should not get carried away with the details of the model or the implication of the court's example. The court's example is somewhat misleading. It suggests that when probabilities are small and we observe one rare object, there are quite likely two or more of them, in fact, 41 percent likely.

L: Earlier, I chose a number for N that made it likely that the defendants were the robbers. Couldn't the actual numbers have favored them even more than the court's example?

S: Certainly. If there are 250,000 couples and the probability that a given couple has the required characteristics is, for example, 1/25,000 instead of 1/12,000,000, then the odds are overwhelming[18] that there is at least one more couple with those characteristics.

L: So, if I understand you, the court's argument—that the prosecution's probability of 1/12,000,000 implied a probability of 0.41 for a second couple having the robbers' characteristics—is true only if N equals 12,000,000, an assumption that the court rejected because N was, in its words, "not determinable."

S: That sums it up accurately.

L: I'd like to clear up the meaning of these "selections" of N couples used by the court. I can understand the meaning of the probabilities we have discussed if I think of Los Angeles as a large goldfish bowl—which I am told it is—and imagine selecting N couples at random from the bowl and noting their characteristics. But how do we connect it all to *Collins*?

S: I think of it a little differently. I think of Los Angeles as generating couples who go out into the San Pedro area, different sets of couples each day, or even each hour. We could find out roughly how many couples there are in the area during a short time period around the robbery, and that figure could be regarded as the number of couples. Some days there would be no couples of a given unusual type, some days one, and so on. If we used the court's formula, we would estimate the probability of a couple having the robbers' characteristics, and then apply the N that is appropriate for the place and time of day.[19]

L: Wouldn't there be a tendency for a given region to have the same couples every day?

S: Yes, and for that reason we might want to use a somewhat more complicated model than that presented by the court, but let's save that for another time.

L: In addition to the unknown N, I don't know what to do with the 1 in 12,000,000 frequency figure, or even a 1 in 12,000 figure. In either case we are likely to find a substantial possibility of one or more other couples having the robbers' characteristics. In the first case there may be only one other couple, whereas in the second there may be a thousand. But the logical point of our discussion is that, without any other evidence, the chance that there was only one couple like the robbers is now something between 100 to 1 in favor and 2,200 to 1 against.

S: Yes, and that shows how important it is to get a fair estimate of the proportion of robber-like couples and the number of eligible couples. Before you heard this logical point, the unusual observed characteristics seemed telling, didn't they?

L: Yes, and that is what is puzzling me now. Reading all the facts, including the evidence in addition to that included in the probability model, I thought I saw a strong case against the defendants, but now I have doubts, and I can't justify that earlier view or intuition.

S: If we had time, I would discuss with you a way to think about the odds that takes into account the unusual characteristics and the other evidence in the case. I'd also like to discuss the implications of possible errors of observation by the eyewitnesses to the robbery.[20] There is also the fact that the particular characteristics in this case were selected, and omitted, in a post hoc way, and that might have made a difference.[21] Finally, we have suggested the need for somewhat more complicated models than those we have discussed.

L: Perhaps these models should be discussed in another conversation.

S: No doubt it will take more than one conversation. The *Collins* court, in its opinion and appendix, took a big step towards moving the ideas of probability into legal discussion in such cases. A first step into new territory is rarely the last.

NOTES

[1] 68 Cal. 2d 319, 438 P.2d 33, 66 Cal. Rptr. 497 (1968).

[2] We call upon specialist knowledge in only one or two footnotes, and these notes may be passed over. For a discussion by a lawyer of *Collins* that presents an extensive exposition of elementary probability theory, see Cullison, *Identification by Probabilities and Trial by Arithmetic* (*A Lesson for Beginners in How to be Wrong with Greater Precision*), 6 HOUSTON L. REV. 471 (1969).

[3] 68 Cal. 2d at 321, 438 P.2d at 34, 66 Cal. Rptr. at 498.

[4] *Id.* at 325–26 n. 10, 438 P.2d at 37, 66 Cal. Rptr. at 501.

[5] *Id.* at 327, 438 P.2d at 37, 66 Cal. Rptr. at 501.

[6] Charles Kingston has made an illustrative calculation of the probability of the joint occurrence of characteristics (A) through (F) that gives a figure close to 1/12,000,000. He made explicit assumptions about dependencies among the characteristics and, in addition, used a revised list of characteristics that removes the ambiguities and overlaps in the original list. Kingston, *Probability and Legal Proceedings*, 57 J. CRIM. L.C. & P.S. 93 (1966).

[7] A simple example may clarify things. Suppose we have two young men and three old men; suppose also that one of the old men is a plumber and none of the other men are. The probability that a man drawn at random is a plumber is 1/5; the probability that a man drawn at random is old is 3/5. The assumption of independence between being older and being a plumber would give us the probability of selecting an older man who is a plumber as 3/5 times 1/5, or 3/25, which is clearly wrong. A correct attack would be to note that the probability of drawing an older man from this group is 3/5. Given that a man is old, the probability of that person also being a plumber is 1/3. We multiply 3/5 times 1/3 to get the correct probability, 1/5, of drawing an old man who is a plumber. This last approach is an application of the product rule for dependent events.

More generally, if P(A) is the probability of event A occurring, and P(B|A) is the probability that event B occurs given that A occurs, then the probability of both A and B occurring is given by the product:

$$P(A \text{ and } B) = P(A)[P(B|A)].$$

[8] *Cf.* Hans Zeisel, *Statistics as Legal Evidence*, 15 INTERNATIONAL ENCYCLOPEDIA OF THE SOCIAL SCIENCES 246 (1968); Zeisel & Diamond, "*Convincing Empirical Evidence*" *on the Six-Member Jury*, 41 U. CHI. L. REV. 281, 293 n. 52 (1974).

[9] *See* Zeisel, *The Uniqueness of Survey Evidence*, 45 CORNELL L. Q. 322 (1960). *See also* Sprowls, *The Admissibility of Sample Data into a Court of Law: A Case History*, 4 U.C.L.A. L. REV. 222 (1957).

[10] *Cf.* Y. BISHOP, S. FIENBERG, & P. HOLLAND, DISCRETE MULTIVARIATE ANALYSIS (MIT Press, in press).

[11] 68 Cal. 2d at 331, 438 P.2d at 40, 66 Cal. Rptr. at 504 (emphasis in original).

[12] The issue stressed here is whether there is more than one couple. One could note that, even when there is more than one couple, each couple has a chance of being the couple of interest. The total probability that the defendants are the couple in question would then be a sum. The sum is composed of the probability that there was exactly one couple like the robbers plus part of the probability that there are exactly two, and so on. We shall not go into this aspect of the problem here. For a discussion of the probability of duplication and the probability of identity, see Kingston, *Applications of Probability Theory in Criminalistics*, 60 J. AM. STAT. ASS'N 70 (1965). *See also* Cullison, *supra* note 2.

[13] The court formulated a model leading it to compute a binomial probability where the number of trials (couples) is N and the probability of a success (picking a robber-like couple) on any one trial is p. The court gives the well-known general formula for solving this problem, which we do not reproduce here. *See* 68 Cal. 2d at 334, 438 P.2d at 42, 66 Cal. Rptr. at 507. In the general formula p need not be 1/N, but the court used p as 1/12,000,000 to follow up the prosecutor's argument. The expected number of successes in N trials is Np. Because N is large and p is small, Poisson probabilities closely approximate the binomial probabilities, where Np is the mean of the approximating Poisson distribution. If we denote

Np by m, the conditional probability sought is

$$\frac{\text{probability of more than one}}{\text{probability of one or more}}$$

$$= 1 - \frac{\text{probability of exactly one}}{\text{probability of one or more}}$$

$$= 1 - \frac{me^{-m}}{1 - e^{-m}}$$

$$= 1 - \frac{m}{e^{m} - 1}.$$

The number e is the base of the natural logarithm and has an approximate value of 2.71828.

Here e^{-m} is the probability of zero couples sharing the characteristics of the robbers, $1 - e^{-m}$ the probability of one or more such couples, and me^{-m} the probability of exactly one. When m is small the required conditional probability is approximated by

$$m/2.$$

For m = 1, this approximation gives 0.5 instead of the more nearly exact value of 0.41. When p is taken as 1/N, then m = 1 and we get the court's results. But p might not be 1/N and thus m need not be 1; it could be much smaller or much larger.

[14] "N, which represents the total number of all couples who might conceivably have been at the scene of the San Pedro robbery, is not determinable . . . ." *Id.* at 335, 438 P.2d at 43, 66 Cal. Rptr. at 507.

[15] *Id.* at 334, 438 P.2d at 42, 66 Cal. Rptr. at 507.

[16] Using m = Np = (250,000) × (1/12,000,000) = 1/48 ~ 0.02, we get m/2 ~ 0.01.

[17] "There is probably no department of human inquiry in which the art of cooking statistics is unknown, and there are skeptics who have substituted 'statistics' for 'expert witnesses' in the well-known saying about classes of false statements. Miss Nightingale's scheme for Uniform Hospital Statistics seems to require for its realization a more diffused passion for statistics and a greater delicacy of statistical conscience than a voluntary and competitive system of hospitals is likely to create." SIR EDWARD COOK, THE LIFE OF FLORENCE NIGHTINGALE 433–34 (1913).

[18] Under this assumption, the odds are about 2,200 to 1. The simple approximation technique used above cannot be used here, because m, or Np, is not small. *See* notes 13 & 16 *supra.*

[19] The Collinses were identified as having been in San Pedro at the time of the robbery, 68 Cal. 2d at 322, 438 P.2d at 34, 66 Cal. Rptr. at 498, so the question remains: given one, what is the probability of more than one?

[20] These questions are taken up in Fairley, *Probabilistic Analysis of Identification Evidence*, 2 J. LEGAL STUDIES (1973). *See also* Finkelstein & Fairley, *A Bayesian Approach to Identification Evidence*, 83 HARV. L. REV. 489 (1970): Tribe, *Trial by Mathematics: Precision and Ritual in the Legal Process*, 84 HARV. L. REV. 1329 (1971); Finkelstein & Fairley, *A Comment on "Trial by Mathematics,"* 84 HARV. L. REV. 1801 (1971); Tribe, *A Further Critique of Mathematical Proof*, 84 HARV. L. REV. 1810 (1971).

[21] Cullison remarks that "the prosecutor's descriptions seem to do a better job of describing the defendants than of describing what was fairly established about the robbers." Cullison, *supra* note 2, at 503.

A COMMENT ON "TRIAL BY MATHEMATICS"

MICHAEL O. FINKELSTEIN and
WILLIAM B. FAIRLEY

In an article published last year in this *Review*,[1] we proposed the use of Bayes' theorem as an aid to evaluating certain types of statistical identification evidence. Professor Laurence H. Tribe, in *Trial by Mathematics: Precision and Ritual in the Legal Process*,[2] attacked this proposal; after a lengthy analysis, he concluded that use of a Bayesian approach, or any similar technique would be fundamentally unsound in the trial context. We feel compelled to comment because Professor Tribe supposes a use of Bayes' theorem which goes beyond anything we would think suitable, and thus finds difficulties that would not exist if the technique were confined to its proper setting. Unfortunately, he uses these difficulties not to argue for limitation, but to support his claim that any use of Bayesian techniques in the trial context should be precluded.

We illustrated our theme with a simple hypothetical:[3]

> [A] woman's body is found in a ditch in an urban area. There is evidence that the deceased had a violent quarrel with her boyfriend the night before. He is known to have struck her on other occasions. Investigators find the murder weapon, a knife which has on the handle [an incriminating] latent [right hand] palm print similar to defendant's print. The information in the print is limited so that [a fingerprint] expert can say only that such prints appear in no more than one case in a thousand [in the general population].

Did the defendant leave the print? The evidence of his relationship to the deceased suggests that the print may be his, although this evidence alone is far from conclusive. The one-in-a-thousand statistic greatly strengthens our belief that the print is the defendant's, but the evidentiary force of this statistic is not intuitively obvious. Bayes' theorem is a mathematical technique for combining the evidence apart from the palm print with the statistical

Reprinted with permission from *Harvard Law Review*, Vol. 84, No. 8 (June 1971), pp. 1801–1809. Copyright © 1971 by the Harvard Law Review Association.

palm print information to generate a final estimate of the probability that the print belonged to the defendant.[4] We argued that use of Bayes' theorem in a trial setting would be helpful to enable jurors to assess more precisely the significance of the one-in-a-thousand statistic.

I.

In accordance with general usage, we described the force of the non-statistical evidence as the "prior probability" or "prior" (i.e., prior to the statistical evidence) and of the combined evidence as the "posterior probability." We suggested that a statistician, testifying as an expert, could "suggest a range of hypothetical prior probabilities, specifying the posterior probability associated with each prior. Each juror could then pick the prior estimate that most closely matched his own view of the evidence."[5] Professor Tribe objects that the average juror would have great difficulty in making a prior estimate;[6] he says, by way of illustration, that it might be "pure chance whether a particular juror converts his mental state of partial certainty to a figure like .33, .43, or somewhere in between."[7]

But we analyzed the problem of estimating prior probabilities in our article; there we pointed out that while there would be variations in jurors' estimates of the prior, in most cases the statistical evidence would be sufficiently strong so that variations in the prior would lead to insignificant differences in the result.[8] As we demonstrated in our article, using the one-in-a-thousand statistic,[9] when the prior probability increases from .25 to .50—a range of variation much larger than that suggested by Professor Tribe—the posterior probability only increases from .997 to .999. The difference of .002 is surely not great enough to lead to different outcomes in any significant number of cases.

Of course, if the statistical evidence is very weak (e.g., the print appears in one person out of two rather than one out of every thousand), then precision in the prior becomes more important.[10] But no one would engage in a statistical analysis of a print when half the population had similar prints. The most common use of Bayesian methods arises when the identifying trace is rare—usually much more rare than a frequency of one in a thousand—and in that circumstance exact specification of the prior is unimportant.[11] What is important is whether jurors, evaluating only the non-statistical evidence, believe that the defendant is far more likely to have left the print than someone chosen at random from the population.

II.

In our article we assumed that if the defendant had in fact used the knife and left the print that was found, then that print would perfectly match a sample print of the defendant's taken at the time of trial;[12] thus we excluded for simplicity the problem of "source variations" that occurs when two prints from the same source vary in their characteristics.[13] Professor Tribe does not object to the assumption in our hypothetical that the probability of source variations was zero;[14] however, he argues that, "moved by the greater ease of applying Bayes' Theorem,"[15] we overlooked in the probability factor for source variations[16] the additional possibilities that a print would not have been left on the knife because the guilty party would have worn gloves or wiped the print off.[17] However, these possibilities were not overlooked—they were expressly excluded, for we computed our probability factors "assuming that a right hand palm print was left by the person who used the knife."[18]

Given the assumption that a print was found, the issue raised by Professor Tribe's objection is whether the finding of a print is itself significant evidence in a sufficient number of cases to make it unrealistic to exclude it in an illustration. We can imagine cases in which the fact that a print has been found is itself important evidence—e.g., the print is from a right hand palm and the defendant either lacks a right hand or is convincingly left-handed. But we excluded the probability of finding a print and "assumed that leaving of a print is not per se evidence either for or against the defendant,"[19] because in the common run of cases the finding of a trace itself (apart from the information it contains) will not be of evidentiary significance. Professor Tribe does not say why the fact that a print has been found is itself important; we see no reason why our assumptions are either unreasonable or unrealistic. In the unusual case where the appearance of a trace *is* per se evidentiary, that factor would probably have to be considered separately and not mixed with the Bayesian analysis, as Professor Tribe suggests to show how complicated matters can become.[20]

III.

Professor Tribe also argues that we overlooked the fact that identifying the print on the knife as the defendant's is not dispositive of guilt because the murderer could have framed the defendant by planting his knife at the scene of the crime.[21] However, this argument misconceives the thrust of our article. We are well aware that in any case in which identification of the defendant is sought on the basis of some evidentiary trace, two distinct issues are presented: (1) is the defendant the source of the trace? and (2) did he commit the offense? Though in some unusual cases the trace may be so intimately tied to the criminal act that linking it to the defendant would be virtually conclusive evidence of his guilt, in most cases a finding that the defendant was in fact the source of the trace would be significant evidence, but not dispositive.

The purpose of Bayesian techniques, as we propose them, is to assist the factfinder in interpreting statistical evidence to decide only the issue of whether a certain trace comes from the accused. The fingerprint expert will testify that the print on the knife is similar to the defendant's print and that such prints occur with a frequency of one in a thousand in the general population. The expert statistician will then use Bayes' theorem to help jurors evaluate that statistic so that they can act more rationally in deciding whether the print came from the defendant. Neither the fingerprint expert nor the statistician could possibly testify as to the guilt of the accused, for this would be a matter wholly outside his competence. When a fingerprint expert, a chemist, or a handwriting expert makes an identification of a trace element, with or without quantification, his testimony is not ruled inadmissible because he does not testify as to the ultimate issue of guilt; we see no reason for treating the statistician differently. When we referred to "guilt" or "prior probability of guilt" in various contexts, we did not mean to imply that the expert would direct jurors to *posterior* probabilities of guilt, as Professor Tribe chooses to interpret it.[22] The significance of the conclusion that a trace came from the defendant—*i.e.*, whether it indicates guilt, a frame-up, or mere chance—must be left to other witnesses just as it is in every case in which an identification is made without the use of Bayesian methods.

Professor Tribe draws two conclusions from our "oversight." First, he argues that since we were "blinded" by the mathematics, even the adversary process cannot be relied on to correct "the jury's natural tendency to be similarly distracted."[23] Of course, the question whether jurors will be helped, misled, or simply confused by Bayesian techniques is an important one. A sensible approach to this question would be to test the use of Bayesian methods under controlled conditions, and to compare the results with the ability of the controlled jury to handle the one-in-a-thousand statistic without the use of Bayesian methods. As we reported in our article, we in fact did this informally on a small scale and the results seemed to justify further inquiry.[24] The ability of jurors to handle Bayesian techniques might also be profitably compared with their ability to handle other types of technical evidence which are being used in trials with increasing frequency.

Second, Professor Tribe asserts that it would be impractical to take the frame-up possibility into account in the Bayesian formulas and argues that the entire enterprise is therefore defective, for he claims that trial accuracy would be enhanced only if all variables are quantified.[25] It is unnecessary to evaluate Professor Tribe's argument that we should not have any hard numbers before the jury unless everything is quantified. The whole point of our article was that jurors do in fact have one hard number before them—the one-in-a-thousand statistic. Bayesian analysis is useful because it helps them to interpret that number.[26]

Of course, one could exclude all statistics as to the frequency of evidentiary traces, and then the need for Bayesian analysis would disappear, along with a major part of current forensic science learning as to trace identifications. This would be such a retrograde step—and contrary to existing case law—that Professor Tribe frowns on the cases, but draws back from repudiating them.[27]

IV.

The analysis of Bayesian methods in *Trial by Mathematics* closes with extensive arguments that they would endanger the presumption of innocence;[28] would involve the quantification of a probability of guilt which, if not "basically immoral," is at least undesirable;[29] and would further dehumanize criminal justice.[30]

Professor Tribe argues that the presumption of innocence would be endangered because "at or near the trial's start"[31] jurors would be asked "to arrive at an explicit quantitative estimate of the likely truth [of the accusation]..."[32] by assessing a prior; forced to do so on little evidence, they might base their estimate on prejudicial factors outside the evidence in the case, such as the fact of indictment.[33] It would of course be wholly improper for the prosecutor's expert to invite jurors to estimate their prior on anything but admitted evidence. As we stated, the expert should ask jurors for their estimate of the prior based on "the other [non-statistical] evidence;"[34] there is no reason to think that jurors would be more lawless with such directions than with others. Because the jury, in estimating a prior, would confine itself to consideration of evidence admitted up to that point in the trial, the prosecutor will have every incentive to use Bayes' theorem near the end of his case, when jurors would have the most evidence on which to base their estimate.[35]

The exercise of estimating a prior may in fact diminish the kind of prejudice that concerns Professor Tribe. We speculated that "a juror forced to derive a quantitative measure of his suspicion on the basis of the evidence at trial is likely to consider that evidence more carefully and rationally, and to exclude impermissible elements such as appearance or popular prejudice."[36]

Professor Tribe further objects that the presumption of innocence would be endangered by the expert's suggestion to jurors that they estimate a prior. The presumption, he argues, requires jurors to withhold all judgments—even tentative ones—about the strengths and weaknesses of the prosecutor's case until the defendant's side has been heard.[37] It does not appear likely to us that focusing on the strengths of the prosecutor's evidence—something a juror is likely to do in any event—would interfere with the juror's ability to assess the impact of the defendant's case.[38] Nor does this suspension of judgment seem necessary to uphold the other policies Professor Tribe cites as protected by the presumption of innocence: to protect the defendant from "onerous restraints" before being found guilty; to prevent interference with community acceptance of his acquittal should that be the outcome of the trial; and to deny the existence of prosecutorial omniscience.[39]

Professor Tribe's objection that jurors would have to quantify their opinions as to guilt does not seem pertinent, since Bayesian techniques will relate to the likelihood that the trace came from the defendant, not to whether he was in fact guilty. But even if a quantitative measure of the prior probability of identity would be an "upper bound" for the strength of the jurors suspicion of guilt, as Professor Tribe suggests,[40] what is wrong with that? The system is not infallible; it makes mistakes. Jurors convict when they have doubts. Why not recognize things as they are?

Professor Tribe agrees that "such compelled candor about its operation might have great value [for the system]."[41] Yet he says that quantification is unacceptable because it would reveal an acknowledged doubt and the system prohibits conviction when jurors have such doubts.[42] However, the standard "beyond a reasonable doubt" does not mean beyond any doubt. Jurors are commonly charged that reasonable doubt is not no doubt at all, but rather a doubt founded on reason and sufficient to cause a person to "hesitate to act" in a serious matter.[43] Doubts of that magnitude can be quantified, and, given the fact that jurors are allowed to convict with acknowledged doubt, there seems to be no reason why they should be denied the opportunity to use an otherwise valuable technique of weighing evidence merely because it requires them to use some quantitative measure of their uncertainty.[44]

Finally, given the narrow compass of Bayesian techniques, it seems unrealistic to argue that jurors listening to the testimony of the statistician would suddenly perceive themselves as performing no more than an automatic role and forget their humanizing function. Bayes' theorem is in fact a relatively simple tool to help explain the result of the highly complicated and technical processes which lie behind the expert's statement that the trace is similar to a source associated with the accused and that it appears with a certain frequency elsewhere. Why the Bayesian step in this process should be so deeply prejudicial to the humanity of the trial process while the large technical foundation on which it rests does not share this reproach is not apparent from the discussion in *Trial by Mathematics.*

NOTES

[1] Finkelstein & Fairley, *A Bayesian Approach to Identification Evidence*, 83 HARV. L. REV. 489 (1970) [hereinafter cited as Finkelstein & Fairley].

[2] 84 HARV. L. REV. 1329 (1971) [hereinafter cited as Tribe].

[3] Finkelstein & Fairley 496.

[4] For discussion of the mathematical basis for Bayes' theorem, see *id.* at 498–500.

[5] *Id.* at 502.

[6] Tribe 1358–59.

[7] *Id.* at 1358.

[8] Finkelstein & Fairley 505.

[9] See the bottom line of our table of posterior probabilities, Table I, *id.* at 500.

[10] If the characteristics of the print found are present in the prints of one person out of two in the general population, then when the prior increases from .25 to .50, the posterior probability increases from .400 to .666. See the top line of Table I, *id.*

[11] Exact specification of the prior in such cases is in fact so unimportant that we suggested that it could be dispensed with entirely. *Id.* at 502 n.32.

In the unusual case in which identification is sought on the basis of a trace with relatively high frequency, a more precise means of estimating the prior becomes essential. The use of blood tests as affirmative evidence in paternity suits is an example of a situation in which Bayesian analysis can be used even though the trace is relatively common, because the method of estimating the prior is more precise. *See id.* at 506–09.

[12] *Id.* at 498.

[13] *See id.* at 509–11.

[14] In the case of palm prints or fingerprints, the assumption that source variations will not be significant is not at all unrealistic.

[15] Tribe 1362.

[16] This was the factor denoted $P(H \mid G)$. Finkelstein & Fairley 498.

[17] Tribe 1362.

[18] Finkelstein & Fairley 498 n.22.

[19] *Id.*

[20] Tribe 1363–64.

[21] *Id.* at 1362–63 & n.110, 1365–66.

[22] Professor Tribe discusses our hypothetical and finds it ambiguous as to whether the expert would use Bayes' theorem to direct the jurors to estimate the probability of defendant's guilt or the probability that the print came from the defendant. *See id.* at 1363 n.110. After observing that we use the phrase "prior probability of guilt," he concludes that the first interpretation was intended. *Id.*

Assuming that our hypothetical was ambiguous, what valid purpose is served by deliberately choosing the interpretation which makes the Bayesian approach unacceptable? Our analysis of People v. Risley, 214 N.Y. 75, 108 N.E. 200 (1915), which immediately followed the hypothetical, makes it clear that in the real world only one approach is even plausible. In that analysis we applied Bayes' theorem to determine the probability that a forgery was typed on the defendant's typewriter, and concluded with the observation that Bayesian analysis could demonstrate "a very high probability that defendant's machine was used." Finkelstein & Fairley 501. Nothing was said about using Bayesian techniques to prove defendant's guilt, and it is clear on the facts that a statistician would have no competence to testify on that question.

We used the phrase "prior probability of guilt" anticipating that the expert might ask jurors to estimate the prior in terms of guilt rather than identity because this might be a more natural formulation in which to evaluate the non-statistical evidence in the case. There should be little objection to this, since if the trace seems to be related to the crime, a juror's estimate of the prior probability of guilt would not generally be larger than that of the prior probability of identity; it might well be smaller if, in the opinion of the jurors, the defendant was more likely to have been the source of the trace than to have committed the crime.

[23] Tribe 1363.

[24] Finkelstein & Fairley 502–03 n.33. It should be noted that in giving this test we explicitly asked the respondents to assume that if the print was the defendant's, then he was guilty of the crime. We omitted to make this explicit in our article and this may have been the source of some confusion.

[25] Tribe 1365.

[26] Professor Tribe implies that jurors would have greater difficulty in remembering that "impressive" Bayesian results are subject to such "fuzzy imponderables" as the frame-up possibility than in understanding the one-in-a-thousand frequency statistic. *Id.* This is, of course, an empirical question, but our experience does not support Professor Tribe's view. The subjects in our informal test seemed to be well aware that identifying a trace as coming from the defendant did not necessarily mean that he was guilty. They did, however, have difficulty in appraising the combined evidentiary significance of the one-in-a-thousand statistic and the other, non-statistical evidence.

In addition, Professor Howard Raiffa conducted an informal test with lawyers and statistics students which was similar in conception to our test. He also found that both groups were unable to assess intuitively the probability of an event from the statistical evidence. *See* H. RAIFFA, DECISION ANALYSIS: INTRODUCTORY LECTURES ON CHOICES UNDER UNCERTAINTY 20–21 (1968). The difficulty that even well-educated persons experience in drawing inferences from statistical data suggests that Bayesian methods could profitably be used by judges and other decision makers.

[27] *See* Tribe 1377 n.155.

[28] *Id.* at 1368–72.

[29] *Id.* at 1372–75.

[30] *Id.* at 1375–77.

[31] *Id.* at 1368.
[32] *Id.*

[33] *Id.* at 1369.

[34] Finkelstein & Fairley 502.

[35] Estimation of the prior after the presentation of all the evidence in the case raises the question of the interdependence of the statistical and nonstatistical evidence—*i.e.*, the problem that the jurors may take the statistical evidence into account in estimating the prior, and thus double-count that evidence. *See* Tribe 1366–68. Professor Tribe argues that the jury will be unable to make use of Bayes' theorem because the two kinds of evidence will be "hopelessly enmeshed" in the jurors' minds, *id.* at 1367, and because proper use of the method "would become completely opaque to all but the trained mathematician." *Id.* at 1368.

Whether the use of Bayes' theorem after all the evidence has been presented will in fact present serious problems of interdependence is, like the problem of possible confusion over the meaning of the Bayesian conclusion, *see* note 26 *supra*, an empirical question. As to the second point, however, proper use of Bayes' theorem is no more "opaque" than numerous other technical inputs into the trial process.

[36] Finkelstein & Fairley 517.

[37] Tribe 1370.

[38] Nor does use of Bayesian methods necessarily violate Professor Tribe's requirement of a suspension or judgment until the end of the trial. A prior probability is itself a "suspension of judgment" in a sense, representing as it does a recognition that the event in question may or may not be true; it merely has the additional feature of quoting tentative odds on the likelihood of that event.

[39] *See* Tribe 1370.

[40] *See id.* at 1372 n.138; pp. 1817–18 *infra*.

[41] Tribe 1373.

[42] *Id.* at 1374.

[43] Holland v. United States, 348 U.S. 121, 140 (1954).

[44] It would seem that the mere admissibility of the one-in-a-thousand statistic implies the willingness of the present judicial system to accept a quantified doubt as to the defendant's guilt. Hence, the quantification of doubt is already consistent with the respect that the present system shows for the defendant's rights, and the expressive functions of the reasonable doubt standard should continue to operate despite a different form of presentation.

A FURTHER CRITIQUE OF MATHEMATICAL PROOF

LAURENCE H. TRIBE

In a recent article in this *Review*,[1] I undertook to assess the usefulness, limitations, and possible dangers of employing mathematical methods in the legal process, both in the conduct of individual trials, and in the design of procedures for the trial system as a whole. Michael Finkelstein and William Fairley, addressing themselves exclusively to that part of my discussion of the use of mathematical methods in the conduct of trials which criticized their earlier work,[2] reply to several of my criticisms by suggesting that their intentions were far more modest than the methods of mathematical proof I examined.[3] Indeed, if the technique they advocated were as carefully confined as they had evidently intended, some of the problems I discussed would not arise.

Yet their good intentions do not diminish the force of my criticisms. I realized, in writing my article, that by investigating irrational as well as rational uses of theoretically sound methods, I would open myself to the "charge that . . . I have confused the avoidable costs of using a tool badly with the inherent costs of using it well."[4] As I went on to say, however, "the costs of abusing a technique must be reckoned among the costs of using it at all to the extent that the latter creates risks of the former."[5]

To illustrate the ease with which the techniques proposed by Finkelstein and Fairley could be misused, I turned to the computations that they performed in their hypothetical case and argued that those computations overlooked several critical variables.[6] In the hypothetical, a palm print similar to the defendant's was found on the knife that was used to kill his girlfriend, with whom he had quarreled violently the night before. Finkelstein and Fairley proposed the use of Bayes' Theorem to inform the jury of

Reprinted with permission from *Harvard Law Review*, Vol. 84, No. 8 (June 1971), pp. 1810–1820. Copyright © 1971 by The Harvard Law Review Association.

the precise incriminating significance of the finding that similar prints appear in no more than one person in a thousand. According to their proposal, each juror would first estimate the "prior probability of guilt"[7] based on the non-mathematical evidence as to the defendant's relationship with the deceased and their previous violent quarrels; a mathematical expert would then instruct the jury as to how much the one-in-a thousand finding increased that prior probability.[8]

I.

One of my major objections to this procedure was the ease with which its significance could be mistaken. All the mathematician could realistically help the jury conclude by applying Bayes' Theorem, I argued, was the likelihood that the print on the knife belonged to the defendant—not the likelihood that the defendant, rather than someone interested in framing him, had used the knife in the murder.[9] Yet this distinction, it seemed to me, could all too readily be blurred by the greater facility of quantifying the former probability than the latter.[10]

Indeed, the original article by Finkelstein and Fairley demonstrates the ease with which this distinction can be lost: they at least appeared to confuse the distinction between identifying the print and identifying the killer. For example, they urged that Bayesian techniques be employed to quantify "the probability that defendant *used the knife*,"[11] not simply the probability that the print was his; they mistakenly argued that "defendant is a thousand times more likely to have *committed the crime* than someone selected at random from the population";[12] and they concluded that "jurors may be surprised at the strength of the *inference of guilt* flowing from the combination of their prior suspicions and the statistical evidence."[13]

It now appears that Finkelstein and Fairley do regard the distinction between identification of the print and identification of the killer as important.[14] They disavow any intention to direct Bayes' Theorem to the ultimate probability that the defendant used the knife to kill his girlfriend; the only purpose of Bayesian techniques, as they now clarify their proposal, "is to assist the factfinder in interpreting statistical evidence to decide . . . whether a certain trace comes from the accused."[15] But the fact remains that they originally neglected to define precisely the events under consideration, failed to make clear what possibilities were excluded by assumption, and slipped into statements that overlooked precisely those risks—such as the risk of frame-up[16]—which resist ready quantification.[17] And, by doing so, they demonstrate the temptation to focus on readily quantifiable factors to the exclusion of what I have described as "soft variables,"[18] a temptation to which less sophisticated users of Bayesian analysis would be even more susceptible.

II.

Even if this temptation could be successfully resisted, however, and even if Bayesian techniques could as readily be confined to their proper compass as Finkelstein and Fairley would wish, what would the use of such techniques at trial accomplish? Their use was proposed as a means of "integrating the mathematical evidence [such as the one-in-a-thousand finding] with the non-mathematical ... so that the jury would not be confronted with an impressive number that it could not intelligently combine with the rest of the evidence, and to which it would therefore be tempted to assign disproportionate weight."[19] But the use Finkelstein and Fairley would make of Bayes' Theorem confronts the jury with a number even more impressive and yet no more conclusive. Instead of learning that prints like the defendant's appear in only one case out of a thousand, the juror learns, for example, that there is a 99.7 percent probability that the print was the defendant's.[20] Assuming he does not confuse this with a 99.7 percent probability of the defendant's guilt,[21] he is still left with the task of offsetting this number against "such fuzzy imponderables as the risk of frame-up."[22] There is simply no reason to suppose that a juror informed of the 99.7 percent conclusion will be better able to place it in perspective than would a juror informed only of the one-in-a-thousand finding. And, because the Bayesian conclusion is aimed closer to the ultimate issue of the defendant's guilt, there is at least some reason to fear precisely the opposite.[23]

III.

In addition to defending the accuracy of the technique they proposed, Finkelstein and Fairley consider my arguments that Bayesian methods would undermine the presumption of innocence, erode the values served by the reasonable doubt standard, and exacerbate the dehumanization of justice.[24]

In asserting that use of Bayesian methods in criminal trials would undermine the presumption of innocence, I advanced two quite different propositions. I argued first that the Finkelstein-Fairley proposal would create a substantial risk that the jury, invited at any given point during the trial to assess the probability of guilt in light of the evidence admitted up to that point, would make an initial assessment based in part on evidence not yet admitted, and perhaps never to be admitted at all. Such an assessment, if based on facts inadmissible at trial, "would undercut the many weighty policies that render some categories of evidence legally inadmissible";[25] or, if based instead on evidence to be admitted later in the trial, would entail counting that evidence twice, thus giving it more weight than it deserves.[26]

That it would be "wholly improper ... to invite jurors to estimate their prior on anything but admitted evidence,"[27] as Finkelstein and Fairley argue, is, of course, true—but the point is that directing jurors to estimate a prior probability on *part* of the admitted evidence might well be *treated* as such an invitation. Perhaps "there is no reason to think that jurors would be *more* lawless with such directions than with others,"[28] but there is every reason to think they would be no *less* so. Unlike the situation at the trial's end, when a juror might at least find it plausible to believe that all of the evidence was before him, a juror asked to estimate a prior probability of guilt in mid-trial *knows* that there is far more in the case, and that more was known to the charging authorities, than he is being asked to weigh. Told to estimate the likelihood of the defendant's guilt based only upon several evidentiary fragments—such as the fact of violent quarrels with the deceased in the palm-print hypothetical—a juror would be hard-pressed to put this knowledge out of his mind.[29]

If, as Finkelstein and Fairley suggest,[30] the jury might not be asked to estimate a prior probability until near the end of the prosecutor's case, then the risk that the jury will reflect in its assessment facts not introduced at trial is obviously reduced. But the risk that it will count the statistical evidence twice is correspondingly increased, for the jury, having heard that evidence already, will find it impossible wholly to ignore it in estimating the prior probability.[31]

However, the core of my concern for the presumption of innocence lay elsewhere. I explained that, even if the problems discussed above were not present, merely "directing the jury . . . to assess the probability of the accused's guilt at some point before he has presented his case"[32] must inevitably conflict with a basic function of the presumption of innocence: to express respect for the accused "by the trier's willingness to listen to all . . . [he] has to say before reaching any judgment, even a tentative one, as to his probable guilt."[33]

Finkelstein and Fairley reply by asserting the jurors are already likely to focus on "the strengths of the prosecutor's evidence"[34] before considering the defense. But it obviously does not follow from this assertion that jurors currently *estimate probable guilt* before hearing the defense, something the Finkelstein-Fairley technique would undeniably require them to do.[35] "Jurors cannot at the same time estimate probable guilt and suspend judgment until they have heard all the defendant has to say."[36] Insofar as this suspension of judgment is critical to fulfill the expressive function of the presumption of innocence as an affirmation of respect for the accused, one can only conclude that the proposed use of mathematics at trial would "interfere with . . . the complex symbolic functions of trial procedure and its associated rhetoric,"[37] symbolic functions that Finkelstein and Fairley fail to examine.

IV.

I argued next that adopting the Finkelstein-Fairley procedure would erode the values that lie behind the reasonable doubt standard by requiring society to embrace a calculated policy that juries should convict even though "conscious of the magnitude of their doubts . . . [and despite] acknowledged and quantified uncertainty."[38]

To this, Finkelstein and Fairley offer two replies. They answer first that my objection "does not seem pertinent, since Bayesian techniques will relate to the likelihood that the trace came from the defendant, not to whether he was in fact guilty";[39] because opinions as to guilt will remain unquantified, juries will not be asked to convict in the face of numerically measured doubt. Yet, as I explained in my article, even if Bayesian methods are used to quantify something less than guilt, the number they yield "sets an upper bound on the probability of guilt,"[40] making all of my objections follow a fortiori. For example, if the figure of 99.7 percent represents only the probability that the print was the defendant's, leaving a margin of doubt of .3 percent on the issue of the print's identification, it seems clear that there will be an even *larger* margin of doubt on the ultimate issue of the defendant's guilt.

But Finkelstein and Fairley go further. Even if Bayesian analysis would provide an upper bound for the probability of the defendant's guilt, they argue, it makes no difference. "The system is not infallible; it makes mistakes"—so "[w]hy not recognize things as they are?"[41]

The major problem with this argument is that it begs the question of how "things . . . are" in fact.[42] As I argued at some length in my article, "the system does *not* in fact authorize the imposition of criminal punishment when the trier recognizes a quantifiable doubt as to the defendant's guilt. Instead, the system . . . insists upon as close an approximation to certainty as seems humanly attainable in the circumstances"[43]—not the unattainable goal of certainty "beyond any doubt,"[44] to be sure, but the closest approximation thereto that human knowledge will permit.[45] As I explained, the undeniable fact that

> some mistaken verdicts are inevitably returned even by jurors who regard themselves as 'certain' [in this sense] is . . . irrelevant; such unavoidable errors are in no sense *intended*, and the fact that they must occur if trials are to be conducted at all need not undermine the effort, through the symbols of trial procedure, to express society's fundamental commitment to the protection of the defendant's rights as a person . . . [46]

by "declining to put those rights in *deliberate* jeopardy."[47] It is precisely this expressive effort that would be undermined by abandoning the insistence that *any* "doubt founded on reason,"[48] of "whatever magnitude, must be resolved in favor of the accused,"[49] and replacing it with the formulation of an "'acceptable' risk of error to which the trier is willing deliberately to subject the defendant."[50]

V.

Finally, Finkelstein and Fairley, supported in part by an informal survey they conducted, observed in their article that "jurors [using their method] may be surprised at the strength of the inference of guilt flowing from [its application] . . . ."[51] I suggested in response that techniques of proof which are so far removed from the untutored intuition "threaten to make the legal system seem even more alien and inhuman than it already does to distressingly many,"[52] and concluded that "[t]he need now is to enhance community comprehension of the trial process, not to exacerbate an already serious problem by shrouding the process in mathematical obscurity."[53]

Finkelstein and Fairley reply by characterizing my fears as "unrealistic"[54] and comparing their proposal to technical evidence generally. Yet this ignores the fact that such evidence "typically represents no more than an input into the trial process, whereas the proposed use of Bayesian methods changes the character of the trial process itself."[55] And, in any event, to say, as Finkelstein and Fairley do, that "other types of technical evidence . . . are being used in trials with increasing frequency"[56] and to note the technological complexity underlying the expert's subjective assessment of the rarity of a trace[57] is only to underscore the need to examine critically any proposed extension of the plunge into the obscure.

NOTES

[1] Tribe, *Trial by Mathematics: Precision and Ritual in the Legal Process*, 84 Harv. L. Rev. 1329 (1971) [hereinafter cited as Tribe].

[2] Finkelstein & Fairley, *A Bayesian Approach to Identification Evidence*, 83 Harv. L. Rev. 489 (1970) [hereinafter cited as Finkelstein & Fairley].

[3] *See* p. 1801 *supra*.

[4] Tribe 1331.

[5] *Id.*

[6] *Id.* at 1358–68.

[7] Finkelstein & Fairley 500.

[8] In my article I objected that "the lay trier will surely find it difficult at best, and sometimes impossible, to attach to $P(X)$ [the prior probability] a number that correctly represents his real prior assessment." Tribe 1358. Finkelstein and Fairley reply that "in most cases the statistical evidence would be sufficiently strong so that variations in the prior would lead to insignificant differences in the result." P. 1802 *supra*; see Finkelstein & Fairley 505. To establish this proposition, they point to the bottom line of Table I of their article, *id.* at 500, and observe that "when the prior probability increases from .25 to .50 . . . the posterior probability only increases from .997 to .999." P. 1803 *supra*.

However, the bottom line of Table I refers only to cases in which there is a .001 probability of finding a print like the defendant's on the knife assuming that he did not use the knife to kill—something that will be true, given the possibility of frame-up, only if a similar print appears in substantially less than one case out of every thousand. If, instead, one looks to the middle line of their Table I, Finkelstein & Fairley 500, which refers to cases in which there is a .1 probability of finding a print like the defendant's on the knife assuming that he did not use it to kill, one discovers that when the prior probability increases from .25 to .50, the posterior probability increases from .769 to .999, a very substantial difference indeed.

Finkelstein and Fairley now suggest that their technique should not be employed unless "the identifying trace is rare—usually much more rare than a frequency of one in a thousand . . . ." *See* p. 1803 *supra*. Their original article, however, suggested that the technique would yield "significant posterior probabilities" even for "relatively high frequencies such as one in a hundred," Finkelstein & Fairley 500; stressed the utility of "evidentiary traces . . . which occur quite frequently," *id.* at 501; and illustrated the use of their technique for frequencies of .5, .25, .1, .01, and .001, *id.* at 500. To be sure, limiting the original proposal to frequencies even lower than .001 would greatly diminish the significance of the objection discussed in this footnote—but it would similarly diminish the significance of the proposal itself. It leads one to wonder how the expanding set of rather imprecise limitations on the applicability of Bayesian techniques could be acceptably defined and successfully enforced. *See also* p. 1812 & note 13 *infra*; note 16 *infra*; p. 1816 *infra*.

[9] Tribe 1362–65.

[10] *Id.*

[11] Finkelstein & Fairley 498 (emphasis added).

[12] *Id.* at 497 (emphasis added).

[13] *Id.* at 517 (emphasis added). *See also id.* at 502 ("measuring probability of guilt").
Indeed, Finkelstein and Fairley explicitly used the terminology "prior probability of guilt." *Id.* at 500. They now suggest that use of this phrase was not meant to "direct jurors to *posterior* probabilities of guilt." *See* p. 1805 *supra*. Yet it is obvious that if G were defined in terms of guilt for purposes of the prior probability, after application of Bayes' Theorem it would still necessarily be defined in terms of guilt in the resulting posterior probability.
They also suggest that even if G is defined to mean only that the print is the defendant's, it is proper to ask the jury to estimate P(G), the prior probability of the print's identity, by formulating their estimate in terms of guilt. This, they claim, would be a more natural way to ask the jury to evaluate the non-statistical evidence and yet, since prior probability of guilt is typically a conservative estimate of prior probability of identity, "should [meet]...little objection." P. 1805 n.22 *supra*. To be sure, it would not ordinarily be prejudicial to the defendant to employ a prior estimate of guilt as a conservative estimate of the probability that the print was his. *See* note 40 *infra*. But this proposal does nothing to reduce the risk that the jury will misunderstand the meaning of the posterior probability obtained through Bayesian techniques; indeed, asking the jury to estimate the defendant's guilt would seem to increase substantially the danger that the jury may confuse the distinction between identity and guilt at the trial's end. Additionally, asking the jury to estimate the prior probability of the print's identity in terms of guilt is still subject to all of my objections that this procedure would undermine the presumption of innocence and erode the purposes of the reasonable doubt standard. *See* pp. 1815–19 *infra*.

[14] *See* pp. 1804–05 *supra*.

[15] P. 1805 *supra*.

[16] Another such risk is represented by the possibility "that a man about to commit murder with a knife might well choose to wear gloves, or that one who has committed murder might wipe off such prints as he happened to leave behind." Tribe 1362. Finkelstein and Fairley explain that they did not overlook the glove-wearing and erasure possibilities; rather, they "expressly excluded" such possibilities, *see* p. 1804 *supra*, by "assuming that a right hand palm print was left by the person who used the knife." Finkelstein & Fairley 498 n.22. But no such assumption was included in the original definitions of G as "the event that defendant used the knife," of H as "the event that a palm print similar to defendant's is found," or of P(H|G) as "the probability of finding the print assuming there is identity," Finkelstein & Fairley 498. If that assumption had been included, the difficulty of quantifying the probabilities of glove-wearing or erasure would have complicated the initial estimation of "the probability that defendant used the knife, P(G)," *id.* at 500, no less than it otherwise complicates the computation of P(H|G). *See* Tribe 1362–64.
Moreover, the glove-wearing and erasure possibilities are *not* in fact excluded by "assuming that a right hand palm print was left by the person who used the knife," unless one *also* assumes that the person who once used it and left his print on it must necessarily be the person who ultimately used the knife to kill—*i.e.*, unless one assumes that "used the knife" means "used the knife to kill." This is an assumption consistent with the original willingness of Finkelstein and Fairley to disregard the possibility of frame-up—presumably by a gloved person or by one who wiped off his own print—but hardly consistent with their present insistence that this possibility not be overlooked.
Finally, if G were to be consistently defined, not as the event that the defendant used the knife, but rather as the event that the defendant's print was found on the knife, then the probabilities of glove-wearing or erasure, as well as the probability of frame-up, would not enter into the Bayesian computation of a posterior probability of G. But they would have to be reflected instead in any assessment, given the posterior probability of G, of the probability that the defendant used the knife to kill, thus leaving the basic problem unsolved.
The "finding of a print is itself significant evidence," p. 1804 *supra*, to use the Finkelstein-Fairley terminology, precisely because a substantial number of guilty men would have taken care not to leave one on the murder weapon. To assume the contrary without further information is indeed both "un-reasonable" and "unrealistic." *Id.*

[17] That these oversights were made seems undeniable in light of the quotations in' the text, p. 1812 *supra*.
Contrary to the suggestion of Finkelstein and Fairley, p. 1805 n.22 *supra*, I did not find it

"ambiguous . . . whether the expert would use Bayes' theorem to direct the jurors to estimate the probability of defendant's guilt or the probability that the print came from the defendant." Although I considered the latter possibility, I concluded that it would require another step "to determine the probability of guilt from the knowledge of the probability that the print was the defendant's, a step that Finkelstein and Fairley clearly did not intend." Tribe 1363 n.110.

[18] Tribe 1361.

[19] *Id.* at 1365.

[20] This would be the result if the juror estimated the prior probability as 25%. *See* Finkelstein & Fairley 500; Tribe 1357. If the juror estimated the prior probability as 75%, he would be informed that there was a 99.96% probability that the print was the defendant's. *See* Finkelstein & Fairley 500.

[21] This confusion can entail not only ignoring the risk of frame-up and similar possibilities, but also overlooking such issues as intent. *See* Tribe 1365–66.

[22] *Id.* at 1365.

[23] I have not urged, as Finkelstein and Fairley assert, *see* p. 1806 *supra*, that no "hard numbers" should be introduced at trial "unless everything is quantified," *id.* On the contrary, I recognized in my article that, subject to careful instructions, there may indeed be occasions on which the jury should be informed of the underlying statistical evidence. *See* Tribe 1355, 1377 n.155. I argued, however, that trial accuracy might well be reduced rather than enhanced if mathematical analysis were applied to this statistical evidence to obtain a quantitative value for *one* of the variables in the case, such as the probability that the print belonged to the defendant, while *other* crucial variables necessarily remained unquantified. *Id.* at 1365.

I do not, of course, exclude the possibility that testing Bayesian methods under controlled conditions, *see* p. 1806 *supra*, might shed helpful light on the question whether trial accuracy can be increased by the use of Bayesian analysis. But I would stress that such testing must explore the impact on *the accuracy of trial outcomes* of using Bayesian analysis to quantify only one of many relevant variables, and not merely the impact of Bayesian analysis on *the accuracy with which that one variable can itself be quantified*; the survey conducted by Finkelstein and Fairley, *see* Finkelstein & Fairley 502–03 n.33, investigated only the latter.

[24] *See* pp. 1807–09 *supra*.

[25] Tribe 1369.

[26] *Id.*

[27] P. 1807 *supra*.

[28] *Id.* (emphasis added).

[29] *Cf.* Bruton v. United States, 391 U.S. 123 (1968) (conviction reversed because of risk that jury, even with instructions to disregard as to this petitioner evidence introduced against his codefendant, would be unable to exclude such evidence from its consideration of petitioner's guilt); Jackson v. Denno, 378 U.S. 368 (1964) (rejecting procedure in which jury rules on voluntariness of confession because the jury, in ruling on voluntariness, will often be unable to exclude from its consideration other evidence of guilt which tends to confirm the confession; or, alternatively, if it finds the confession involuntary and hence inadmissible, the jury will often be unable to ignore knowledge of its contents when ruling on guilt).

[30] *See* p. 1807 *supra*.

[31] That such mental gymnastics will almost certainly be beyond a jury's capacity has now been widely recognized. *See, e.g.*, note 29 *supra*. Nor does the quite separate problem of interdependence that is posed *whenever* Bayes' Theorem is used seem to raise any significant empirical question, contrary to what Finkelstein and Fairley suggest. *See* pp. 1807–08 n.35 *supra*. As I explained at greater length in my article, even if the prior could be estimated without any consideration of the statistical evidence, the proposed application of Bayes' Theorem—at any point in the trial—would entail a distorted outcome whenever some or all of the evidence that underlay the prior is conditionally dependent upon the statistical evidence, a circumstance whose presence or absence cannot be feasibly determined in any given case. *See* Tribe 1367–68. The resulting distortion, it should be emphasized, undermines the accuracy of the proposed technique in all cases, civil and criminal alike.

[32] Tribe 1370.

[33] *Id.*

[34] P. 1808 *supra*.

[35] *See* note 13 *supra*. Even if the jury were asked to estimate only the prior probability that the print was the defendant's, the same objection would obtain, for the jury would be forced to prejudge, before

hearing the defendant's side of the case, an important issue in the trial—perhaps the very issue that he will choose to contest.

[36] Tribe 1371. To describe the assessment of a prior probability of guilt as itself a "suspension of judgment," p. 1808 n.38 *supra*, seems to me mere semantic confusion. To be sure, such a probability assessment acknowledges that "the event in question may or may not be true," *id.*, but the same can be said of any probability assessment, including the final probability of guilt assessed at the trial's end.

[37] Tribe 1371.

[38] *Id.* at 1375 (emphasis omitted).

[39] P. 1808 *supra*.

[40] Tribe 1372 n.138. It is, of course, theoretically possible that the defendant is guilty even though he is not the source of the trace in question. But the likelihood of the converse—that he is not guilty although the trace is his—would typically be so much greater that it seems reasonable to assume that the probability of guilt will be lower than the probability that the defendant is the source of the trace. Finkelstein and Fairley apparently agree, for they seek to use the prior probability of guilt as a conservative estimate of the prior probability of trace identity. *See* p. 1805 n.22 *supra*.

[41] P. 1809 *supra*.

[42] It also fails to respond to my argument that an undue willingness to sacrifice others and an excessive fear of unjust conviction might flow from "the explicit quantification of jury doubts in criminal trials— whether or not it would be *factually accurate* to describe the trial system as imposing criminal sanctions in the face of quantitatively measured uncertainty in particular cases." Tribe 1373 n.140.

[43] *Id.* at 1374.

[44] *See* p. 1809 *supra*.

[45] To argue that the present system of criminal justice has already embraced the principle of convicting in the face of quantified doubt by its acceptance of such statistical evidence as the one-in-a-thousand figure, *see* p. 1809 n.44 *supra*, is to ignore, first, that the admissibility of such statistical evidence itself remains a highly controverted matter, *see* Tribe 1343–44; and second, that the introduction of a frequency statistic no more implies the existence of a quantified doubt at the end of trial than does the introduction of any other item of evidence which by itself is less than conclusive—a juror can of course feel subjectively certain of the defendant's guilt after all the evidence has been placed before him even if each individual item is not itself decisive.

[46] Tribe 1374 (footnote omitted).

[47] *Id.* (emphasis added).

[48] *See* p. 1809 *supra*.

[49] Tribe 1374.

[50] *Id.*

[51] Finkelstein & Fairley 517.

[52] Tribe 1376.

[53] *Id.* Both the survey conducted by Finkelstein and Fairley, and the informal test conducted by Professor Raiffa, *see id.* at 1375 n.148, pp. 1806–07 n.26 *supra*, underscore my conclusion that Bayesian methods can readily yield results that defy common intuition. These findings obviously support the power of such methods as tools of rational inquiry, *see id.*, but they simultaneously undermine the appropriateness of such techniques of proof in a system that ought to be as comprehensible as possible "to the larger community that the processes of adjudication must ultimately serve." Tribe 1376.

[54] *See* p. 1809 *supra*.

[55] Tribe 1375.

[56] P. 1806 *supra*.

[57] *See* p. 1809 *supra*.